FAR FROM HOME

Basic Reading and Word Study

William P. Pickett

NEWBURY HOUSE PUBLISHERS, INC.

A Division of Harper & Row

Library of Congress Cataloging-in-Publication Data

Pickett, William P., 1931-
   Far from home.

    1. English language—Text-books for foreign
speakers. 2. Readers—1950-   3. Vocabulary.
I. Title.
PE1128.P48 1986   428.6′4   86-12583
ISBN 0-88377-319-8

Cover design by Maureen Terrill
Interior design by Carson Design
Illustrations by Marsha Lacey
Border art by Kathie Kelleher

NEWBURY HOUSE PUBLISHERS, INC.
A Division of Harper & Row

Language Science
Language Teaching
Language Learning

CAMBRIDGE, MASSACHUSETTS

Printed in the U.S.A.   First printing: August 1986
63 24701   2 4 6 8 10 9 7 5 3

TABLE OF CONTENTS

Unit Four
Newcomers from Colombia

Unit Five
Newcomers from Italy

Unit Six
New Jobs for Women

INTRODUCTION

Rationale

When students begin to read, one of their biggest problems is their limited vocabulary. They know so few words that their reading becomes more like deciphering than reading. On the other hand, the best way to acquire a large vocabulary is to read. *Far From Home* is a book that addresses this dilemma. It is a reader that emphasizes word study. It is a word study text that begins every lesson with a reading selection. It helps students acquire a basic vocabulary that will enable them to read more easily, and it does this through reading as well as other exercises.

Content and Purpose

Each lesson begins with a story containing the eight key words studied in the lesson. After the reading, there are comprehension questions about each paragraph. Students should read the story to understand and enjoy it. If they do not understand it well after reading it once, they should read it again. The reading is placed first in the lesson because, as much as possible, students should learn to arrive at the meaning of new words through their context.

The next section is a mini-dictionary. It lists the first four words used in the story and gives a phonetic pronunciation and a brief definition of the words. The words are defined as clearly and as briefly as possible. While the definitions have their value, the emphasis is not on them but on the exercises that follow them. The mini-dictionary should not only help the students to learn the words of the lesson but should gradually lead them to the point where they have the confidence and ability to use an all-English dictionary.

A sentence-completion exercise comes after the mini-dictionary. There are three sets of sentences to be completed. Each set contains the four key words defined in the mini-dictionary. The students should check their answers with the help of their teacher, classmates, or the answer key. Once this is done, the students have a group of model sentences to complement the mini-dictionary. While many dictionaries provide model sentences, *Far From Home* involves the students in constructing the model sentences.

The mini-dictionary and sentence-completion exercises clarify, reinforce, and, at times, may correct the meaning the students have gotten from the context of the story. The context of the story alone cannot give students a full grasp of the word and may even mislead them. That is why the key words are presented in several sentences and in another story.

The next two sections contain the mini-dictionary and sentence-completion exercises for the remaining four key words of the lesson.

At this point in the lesson, all eight key words are tested and reinforced in a sentence-completion exercise. Then the same words are used in a paragraph-completion exercise—a modified cloze procedure. This exercise is the culmination of the first part of the lesson. The rest of the lesson is more advanced.

The next section presents the more common words that are derived from the key words or, in some cases, the word from which the key word is derived. There are no definitions in this section, but model sentences are given.

A discussion section follows. While this section is more difficult than the preceding sections, it leads the students to a more personal and independent use of the key words.

A word-building section in which a common prefix or suffix is studied completes each lesson. As a rule, the prefix or suffix is taken from one of the words in the lesson. Learning to recognize and understand prefixes and suffixes will enable students to understand the meaning of a large number of new words.

There are three lessons in a unit. At the end of each unit, there are review exercises using the twenty-four key words of the unit. In addition to these exercises specifically devoted to review, many of the words taught in earlier lessons are recycled in the stories and exercises of later lessons.

Level

Far From Home presumes that its users have studied the most basic structures of English and know the most common words. It presumes that the students know words like *wait, close, stop, chair,* and *beautiful.* It teaches words like *share, trust, waste, struggle, touch, mild, neighbor, instead of,* and *however.* It is a book for advanced beginners or low intermediates.

Word Selection

To a large extent, the stories themselves dictated the words to be studied, but a conscious effort was made to select high frequency words and idioms. The words chosen were checked for frequency with the help of the following books: *The Teacher's Word Book of 30,000 Words* by Thorndike and Lorge: *A General Service List of English Words* by Michael West: *The American Heritage Word Frequency Book* by Carroll, Davies, and Richman: *3,000 Instant Words* by Sakiey and Fry.

With a few exceptions all of the key words studied in *Far From Home* are listed among the 3,000 most commonly occurring words in English according to the Thorndike-Lorge or the Sakiey-Fry lists. Idioms are not covered in the lists consulted, but this book has only a few idioms and they are clearly ones with a very high frequency, e.g., *have to, used to, at least*.

Classroom Use and Self-Study

Far From Home is a text that can be used in the classroom or that students can study on their own. The book aims to provide highly useful material and understands that teachers and students will use the material in the way that suits them best.

An answer key is provided at the end of the book.

PRONUNCIATION KEY

To show the pronunciation of a word, most English dictionaries use symbols that are as close as possible to English spelling. The mini-dictionary section of *Far From Home* uses these same symbols. The symbols are listed below together with example words that have the sound the symbols represent.

The best way to learn to pronounce words is to listen to the pronunciation of native speakers and to imitate them. The mini-dictionary section of *Far From Home* provides pronunciation symbols because students may not always have the help of native speakers. Many students find these symbols very helpful. However, students who are not helped by them need not use them.

Vowel Sounds

a	at, bad	short *a*
ā	āge, lāte	long *a*
â(r)	câre, bâre	
ä	äre, fäther	
e	egg, bed	short *e*
ē	ēven, wē	long *e*
i	it, sick	short *i*
ī	īce, līfe	long *i*
o	on, hot	short *o*
ō	ōpen, gō	long *o*
ô ·	ôff, dôg	
oi	voice, noise	
ou	out, house	
oo	book, good	
o͞o	to͞o, fo͞od	
u	up, bus	short *u*
ū*	ūse, mūsic	long *u*
û(r)	tûrn, hûrt	
ə**		schwa

*yo͞o is also a symbol for long *u*

**ə is a special symbol that indicates a reduced vowel sound. English frequently reduces vowels that are not stressed. A reduced vowel sound is called a *schwa*.

*a*bout (ə-bout′)	t*o*day (tə-dā′)
el*e*phant (el′ə-fənt)	ind*u*stry (in′dəs-trē)
pos*i*tive (poz′ə-tiv)	

Consonant Sounds

b	box, cab	p	pay, stop
ch	child, watch	r	run, dear
d	day, sad	s	sit, this
f	five, self	sh	shut, brush
g	give, bag	t	ten, but
h	hat	th	thin, teeth
j	job	*th*	the, clothe
k	kiss, week	v	vote, have
l	let, bill	w	want, grow
m	man, room	y	yes
n	not, sun	z	zone, buzz
ng	sing	zh	vision, garage

To My Son Edward

FAR FROM HOME

Unit One
A Young Woman

One

Far From Home

    Tomiko is an accountant and she works for a large company in Boston. She's the youngest of three children. Her parents live in southern California **far** from Boston. This is Tomiko's first job and she calls her parents every Sunday. Tomiko's parents think she's **too** young to live alone, but she laughs at that idea. She's twenty-three and finished college last year. She tells them that she's happy and everything will be fine.

    Tomiko **has to** be at work by eight o'clock. She goes to work by bus because she doesn't like to drive in the Boston traffic and it's too far to walk to work. After Tomiko leaves her apartment, she **hurries** to the corner to get the bus. If she **misses** her bus, she has to wait twenty minutes for the next one and she gets to work late.

    Tomiko is a good worker. She's serious about her job and never **wastes** time. At twelve o'clock she eats a **quick** lunch. She's back at her desk by twelve-twenty. She stops work at four o'clock. She's tired by that time and is happy to go home and relax. She gets home **around** five o'clock, changes her clothes and watches TV, or listens to music.

I

Answer these questions about the story.

PARAGRAPH 1

1. Where do Tomiko's parents live?
2. Is this Tomiko's first job?
3. How often does she phone her parents?
4. Her parents don't want her to live alone. Why not?

PARAGRAPH 2

5. How does Tomiko go to work?
6. Why doesn't she walk to work?
7. What happens if she misses her bus?

PARAGRAPH 3

8. Does Tomiko work hard?
9. What time does she finish work?
10. What does she do when she gets home?

II

MINI-DICTIONARY—PART ONE

1. **far** (fär) *adverb*: at or to a great distance
   adjective: distant
2. **too** (to͞o) *adverb*: more than is good or necessary*
3. **have to** (hav to͞o or haf′tə) **has to** (haz to͞o or
   has′tə) *idiom*: be necessary; must
4. **hur·ry** (hûr′ē) *verb*: to move fast
   noun: the act of moving fast

*Another meaning of *too* is *also*: I'm going to the park, too.

III

Complete the sentences with these words.

hurry (*verb*)　　　　**too**　　　　**far** (*adverb*)　　　　**has to**

1. My brother lives a thousand miles from here. That's _____.

2. If we don't _____, we'll be late.

3

3. Jim _____ clean his room. It's dirty.

4. I'm not going to buy those shoes. They cost _____ much.

      far (*adjective*)   **have to**   **hurry** (*noun*)   **too**

5. I _____ phone my wife.

6. Ray can't do the math problems. They're _____ hard for him.

7. Carmen is swimming to the _____ side of the river.

8. The police came in a _____ .

      has to   **far**   **too**   **hurry**

9. Do we have _____ to go?

10. Paula _____ take the baby to the doctor.

11. Dan works slowly. He doesn't like to _____ .

12. This shirt is _____ small. I need a bigger one.

IV

MINI-DICTIONARY—PART TWO

---

    5. **miss** (mis) *verb*: to not hit, catch, or meet; to not be present
        noun: the act of not hitting, catching, or meeting; absence
    6. **waste** (wāst) *verb*: to use poorly
        noun: poor use of something
    7. **quick** (kwik) *adjective*: fast
    8. **a·round** (ə-round′) *preposition*: about; near in number or time*

    *Around has other meanings. Another meaning, for example, is on all sides of: They put a fence around their house and yard.

V

Complete the sentences with these words.

waste (*verb*)   **miss** (*verb*)   **around**   **quick**

1. There were _____ forty people at the party.

2. The problem is serious. We must take _____ action.

3. I don't like to _____ food. I eat everything on my plate.

4. Bill is late. He's going to _____ his train.

around   **waste** (*noun*)   **quick**   **miss** (*noun*)

5. That class is a _____ of time. We don't learn anything in it.

6. It's _____ five miles from Jane's house to the ocean.

7. I didn't go to work last Thursday or Friday. Another _____ and I'll be in trouble.

8. Do we have time for a _____ drink?

quick   **around**   **missed**   **wasting**

9. No one is using those lights. Turn them off. We're _____ energy.

10. I'm going to take a _____ shower.

11. Monique _____ class last week. She was sick.

12. The book is long. It has _____ four hundred pages.

5

VI

Complete the sentences with these words.

around	far	quick	miss
hurrying	too	have to	wastes

1. My hair is very long. I _____ get a haircut.

2. Francia is _____ thirty-five years old.

3. I don't want to _____ the dance, but I'm working to-night. I can't go.

4. How _____ is it from here to Washington, D.C.?

5. Grace _____ money. She buys books she never reads.

6. It's _____ cold to go swimming.

7. Ted is _____ to get to the post office. It closes in ten minutes.

8. There was a _____ change in the weather.

VII

Complete the story with these words.

has to	waste	too	around
missed	far	quick	hurry

A Bad Toothache

Barbara eats _____ much candy and has many prob-lems with her teeth. She _____ work today because she has a bad toothache. She's going to the dentist this afternoon.

It's _____ twelve-forty now and Barbara is eating a _____ lunch. She _____ be at the dentist's office by one o'clock. It's not _____ to the dentist's office, but she'll have to _____ to get there on time. She doesn't have a minute to _____ .

6

VIII
Word Families

1. **waste** — *verb* or *noun*
   wasteful — *adjective*: It's *wasteful* to leave lights on when no one is using them.
2. **quick** — *adjective*
   quickly — *adverb*: The secretary typed the letter *quickly*.

IX
Sharing Information

Discuss these questions and topics in pairs or small groups.

1. Name something that you **have to** do today or tomorrow.
2. Give some examples of how people **waste** time, food, money, or energy.
3. Some visitors from other countries think that people who live in the United States are always **hurrying**. What do you think?
4. **Around** what time do you eat supper?
5. Do you like to work **quickly** or do you like to take your time when you do something?
6. Complete one of the following sentences.

   I _____ **too** much.

   I _____ **too** much _____.
7. How **far** is it from where you live to where you go to school, or to where you work?
8. Give an example of something you **missed** (school, a party, a dance) and tell why.

X
Building Words with ly

The ending *ly* is added to many adjectives to form an adverb. For example, *clear* + *ly* = *clearly*, *quick* + *ly* = *quickly*.

An adjective is a word that goes with a noun and tells us something about it: *It's a clear day*. An adverb is a word that goes with a verb or an adjective: *John writes clearly*.

When *ly* is added to an adjective, it usually means *in a certain manner*. For example, *clearly* means *in a clear manner*, *quickly* means *in a quick manner*.

Adjective	*Adverb*
clear	clearly
easy	easily
free	freely
glad	gladly
happy	happily
nice	nicely
poor	poorly
quick	quickly
safe	safely
soft	softly
strong	strongly
usual	usually
warm	warmly

Complete the sentences with these words.

warmly   **usually**   **quickly**   **nicely**

1. We need your help. Come _____!

2. Dress _____ . It's cold outside.

3. The children are playing _____ .

4. I _____ sleep late on Saturday.

poorly   **safely**   **easily**   **happily**

5. Drive carefully in this snow. I want you to get home _____ .

6. Frank and Lisa are _____ married.

7. We can't use the car for a long trip. It runs _____ .

8. It's not far to the store. We can _____ walk there.

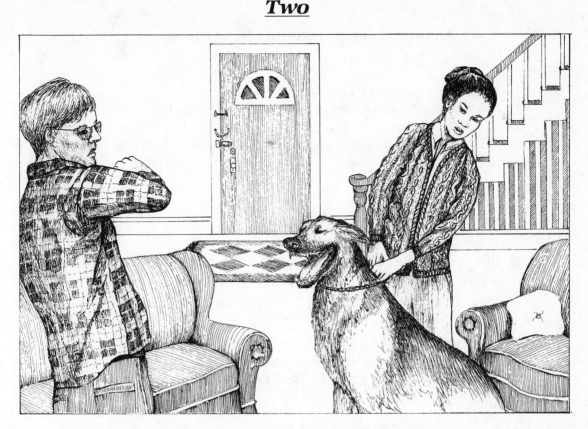

Two

Three Locks and a Dog

Tomiko likes Boston. There are many places to go and **a lot of** things to do, but it's not easy to live alone in a big city far from home. Tomiko never tells her parents, but sometimes she gets a little homesick* and sometimes she feels **afraid** at night. Tomiko has three locks on her apartment door and she **owns** a large dog.

The dog's name is King. He's good company and he **protects** Tomiko. He also protects Tomiko's apartment when she's at work. King is friendly if he knows you. **However**, he barks† at people he doesn't know. Most people are afraid of King when they hear him bark and see how big he is.

Tomiko doesn't have many friends in Boston, but she does have a boyfriend named Ted. He works in the same company as Tomiko and he's also an accountant. He likes her **a lot**, but there's one problem. He's afraid of dogs. The other night he came to visit Tomiko. She said to him, "Don't be afraid of King. He won't **bite**." However, Ted doesn't **trust** King. He's too big and barks too much to trust. Ted's afraid that King **may** bite him someday.

To be homesick means to feel sad (or "sick") because you are away from home.
†*A bark* is the sound a dog makes when it "talks". *To bark* is to make this sound.

I

Answer these questions about the story.

PARAGRAPH 1

1. Why does Tomiko like Boston?
2. Does she tell her parents about all her problems?
3. When does she feel afraid?
4. It is difficult to get into Tomiko's apartment when she's not there. Why?

PARAGRAPH 2

5. Who does King protect? What does he protect?
6. Who does King bark at?
7. How do people feel when they hear King bark and see how big he is?

PARAGRAPH 3

8. Does Tomiko have a lot of friends in Boston?
9. Where does her boyfriend work?
10. Why is Ted afraid to go to Tomiko's apartment?

II

MINI-DICTIONARY—PART ONE

---

1. **a lot (of)** (ə lot (əv) or ə-lot´(ə)) *idiom*: a large quantity or number
2. **a·fraid** (of) (ə-frād´) *adjective*: feel fear; nervous
3. **own** (ōn) *verb*: to have; to possess
   adjective: belonging to oneself
4. **pro·tect** (prə-tekt´) *verb*: to defend

III

Complete the sentences with these words.

afraid   **protect**   **a lot**   **own** (*verb*)

1. Barbara studies _____ and she does well in school.

2. Pete is _____ of his boss.

3. Martha and Raphael _____ a beautiful house.

4. It's natural for parents to _____ their children.

a lot of   **own** (*adjective*)   **protect**   **afraid**

5. Ann has her _____ business.

6. Marcel drinks _____ beer when the weather is hot.

7. When Joyce comes home alone late at night, she's _____ .

8. Put on these gloves. They'll _____ your hands.

owns   **afraid**   **a lot of**   **protect**

9. The little boy is _____ of the dark.

10. Dan locks the doors at night to _____ his family and himself.

11. Luisa is rich. She has _____ money in the bank.

12. Pablo lives in the country and he _____ a big farm.

IV
MINI-DICTIONARY—PART TWO

5. **how·ev·er** (hou-ev′ər) *conjunction*: but*
6. **bite** (bīt) *verb*: to put one's teeth into
    noun: the act or result of biting
7. **trust** (trust) *verb*: to feel that a person is honest and wants to help
    noun: a feeling that a person is honest and wants to help
8. **may** (mā) *verb*: to be possible; to not be certain†

*But and *however* are close in meaning. *But* is used more often than *however*, especially in conversation. *However* is more formal than *but*.
†*May* is also used to ask for something we want: *May I use your phone, please?*

V

Complete the sentences with these words.

trusts (*verb*)   **may**   **however**   **biting** (*verb*)

1. We _____ go to California this summer.

2. Ed is _____ an apple.

3. Everyone _____ Ann because she's honest and friendly.

4. Juanita loves Kevin. _____, she doesn't want to marry him.

however   **bite** (*noun*)   **may**   **trust** (*noun*)

5. There is little _____ between Ruth and her mother.

6. The sky is clear now. _____, it's going to rain tomorrow.

7. We _____ go to the movies tonight. We're not sure yet.

8. Ted took a _____ of the cake, but he didn't like it.

may   **trust**   **bites**   **however**

9. Sam is a good person and he likes to help people. I _____ him.

10. When the baby gets angry, he _____.

11. Nicole drives very fast. _____, she's never had an accident.

12. Our refrigerator is getting old. We _____ need a new one soon.

VI

Complete the sentences with these words.

bite	however	trust	protect
may	afraid	own	a lot of

1. Mary is a very good friend of mine. I can _____ her.

2. Paul is _____ of flying in an airplane.

3. Don't touch the animals. Some of them _____ .

4. There are _____ pretty trees in the park.

5. It _____ snow tonight.

6. The job of the police is to _____ people.

7. Habib has an old car. _____, it runs better than many new ones.

8. My daughter is seventeen and she wants her _____ phone.

VII

Complete the story with these words.

bites	protects	however	may
afraid	a lot	trusts	owns

A Barking Dog

They say that a barking dog doesn't bite. You _____ believe that, but I don't because I know a dog who barks _____ and he also _____ . No one _____ the dog.

_____, the man who _____ the dog is happy that people are _____ of his dog. The man is rich and the dog _____ him and his home.

VIII

Word Families

1. **protect** — *verb*
   protection — *noun*: Does the President need more *protection*?
2. **own** — *verb*
   owner — *noun*: Where is the *owner* of this car? It has to be moved.

IX

Sharing Information

Discuss these questions and topics in pairs or small groups.

1. Name something that you don't **own**, but that you would like to own.
2. A dog can help **protect** us and our homes. What are some other things people use to protect themselves and their homes?
3. Complete the following sentences.

   I eat **a lot of** _____ .

   I drink **a lot of** _____ .
4. Name an animal, person, or thing that you are **afraid of**.
5. Some dogs **bite**. What other animals will bite people?
6. Complete the following sentence.
   There are some nice things about living in the United States.

   However, _____ .
7. Name a person who isn't a member of your family and who you **trust** very much. Why do you trust this person?
8. Name something that you **may** do today or tomorrow.

X

Building Words with er and or

The ending *er*, (and sometimes *or*), is added to many verbs to form a noun. For example, *teach + er = teacher*; *act + or = actor*; *wash + er = washer*.

When *er* (or *or*) is added to a verb, it means a person or thing that does something. For example, *a teacher* is *a person who teaches*; *an actor* is *a person who acts*; *a washer* is *a machine that washes*.

14

Verb	Noun
act	actor
dance	dancer
direct	director
drive	driver
dry	dryer
freeze	freezer
own	owner
paint	painter
play	player
sing	singer
teach	teacher
wash	washer
write	writer

Complete these sentences.

1. A person who sings is a _____ .

2. A person who writes is a _____ .

3. A person who drives is a _____ .

4. A person who owns something is an _____ .

5. A machine that dries clothing is a _____ .

6. The part of a refrigerator that freezes food is a _____ .

7. A person who directs an activity is a _____ .

8. A person who dances is a _____ .

9. A person who plays football is a football _____ .

10. A person who paints is a _____ .

Three

Fish for Supper

Tomiko is short and a little heavy. She's **only** five feet two inches tall and she **weighs** one hundred and thirty pounds. That's not bad, but in the United States it seems that everyone is on a diet or thinking about it. If you go to any bookstore, you'll see ten to fifteen diet books. Tomiko thinks she'll feel and look better if she weighs less.

Yesterday morning Tomiko started her diet. She wants to **lose** ten pounds, but she isn't in a hurry. She knows that most people who lose **weight** too quickly gain it back. Her friend, Rose, went on a diet and lost fifteen pounds in a month. Three months later, Rose weighed more than when she started her diet. Tomiko is **trying** to lose a pound or two a week, but it's hard. The problem is that she loves ice cream and chocolate candy and she can't have any on her diet.

Tomiko has been very good today. She had orange juice, cereal, and a cup of black coffee for breakfast. For lunch, she had a lettuce and tomato salad and some soup. It's **almost** six o'clock now and

Tomiko's **starving**. She's having fish for supper. **Although** she doesn't **enjoy** fish, she eats a lot of it because she knows it will help her lose weight.

I

Answer these questions about the story.

PARAGRAPH 1

1. How tall is Tomiko?
2. How much does she weigh?
3. Why does she want to weigh less?

PARAGRAPH 2

4. When did Tomiko start her diet?
5. How much weight does she want to lose?
6. Does she want to lose weight fast?
7. What does Tomiko like that she can't eat on her diet?

PARAGRAPH 3

8. What did Tomiko have for breakfast?
9. Does she like fish?
10. Why does she eat a lot of fish?

II

MINI-DICTIONARY—PART ONE

1. **on·ly** (ōn'lē) *adverb*: and no more
   adjective: and no other person; and no other thing
2. A. **weigh** (wā) *verb*: to be a number of pounds
   B. **weight** (wāt) *noun*: the number of pounds a person or thing is
3. **lose** (lōōz) *verb*: A. to have something and then not be able to find it B. to have less of something
   The past of lose is lost.
4. **try** (trī) *verb*: to make an effort
   noun: an effort

III

Complete the sentences with these words.

lose   **weigh**   **only** (*adverb*)   **trying** (*verb*)   **weight**

1. The small bags of potatoes _____ five pounds.

2. Carlos is _____ to learn English quickly.

3. I don't know where my ring is. I hope I didn't _____ it.

4. What is the baby's _____ ?

5. The radio is _____ twenty dollars.

try (*noun*)   **lost**   **only** (*adjective*)   **weigh**

6. Leslie _____ her keys and can't find them.

7. How much do you _____ ?

8. _____ Don knows where the money is.

9. Joan didn't catch the ball, but she made a nice _____ .

only   **trying**   **weigh**   **losing**

10. Most new cars are smaller and _____ less than the old ones.

11. We go to the beach _____ in the summer.

12. Jeff is _____ his hair.

13. Brenda isn't working, but she's _____ to find a job.

IV
MINI-DICTIONARY — PART TWO

5. **al·most** (ôl′mōst or ôl-mōst′) *adverb*: a little less than; be close to
6. **starve** (stärv) *verb*: A. to be very hungry B. to die because one has no food
7. **al·though** (ôl-thō′) *conjunction*: in contrast to the fact that
8. **en·joy** (in-joi′) *verb*: to like; to get happiness from

V
Complete the sentences with these words.

although	**starving**	**almost**	**enjoy**

1. _____ your dinner!

2. _____ Carmen didn't study, she passed the exam.

3. It's _____ a mile to the supermarket.

4. You didn't eat breakfast. You must be _____ .

enjoy	**although**	**starve**	**almost**

5. I _____ cut myself with that knife.

6. Tim can't stop smoking _____ he knows he should.

7. In the winter some animals _____ because they can't find food.

8. We _____ listening to music.

almost	**starving**	**enjoys**	**although**

9. Juan _____ playing cards with his friends.

10. Are the children _____ ready for school?

11. _____ Ray's car is new, he's having problems with it.

12. Let's eat. I'm _____ .

19

VI

Complete the sentences with these words.

weighs	**almost**	**lose**	**only**
enjoy	**although**	**starving**	**tries**

1. I'm not taking an umbrella. It has _____ stopped raining.

2. Harry isn't a good basketball player, but he _____ hard.

3. _____ yourself at the party!

4. What are you looking for? Did you _____ something?

5. _____ I slept well last night, I feel tired.

6. The turkey _____ fifteen pounds.

7. We're _____ , but we don't have time to eat now.

8. You can easily walk to the bank. It's _____ three blocks from here.

VII

Complete the story with these words.

lose	**enjoys**	**only**	**although**
trying	**almost**	**weighs**	**starving**

A Thin Man

It's _____ time for lunch, and Raphael and I are _____ . _____ Raphael eats a lot and _____ big meals, he's thin. He _____ one hundred and ten pounds.

The last thing Raphael wants to do is to _____ weight. He's _____ to gain fifteen pounds, but he's been able to gain _____ a pound or two.

20

VIII
Word Families

1. **lose** — *verb*
   loss — *noun*: Jessica is unhappy about the *loss* of her watch.
   lost — *adjective*: Everyone is looking for the *lost* child.
2. **starve** — *verb*
   starvation — *noun*: In most countries everybody can get food and *starvation* is not a problem.
3. **although** — *conjunction*
   though — *conjunction*: *Though* Pete ate a good lunch, he's hungry.

   Though has the same meaning as *although* and is used in the same way.
4. **enjoy** — *verb*
   enjoyment — *noun*: Linda finds *enjoyment* in playing tennis.
   enjoyable — *adjective*: We had an *enjoyable* trip.

IX
Sharing Information

Discuss these questions and topics in pairs or small groups.

1. When a family has **only** one child, we say the child is an only child. Are you an only child, or are there other children in your family?
2. Do you want to lose **weight**, gain weight, or stay the way you are?
3. Did you ever **lose** anything that was very valuable, for example, a ring or a watch? If so, did you find it again?
4. Think about your activities, and complete the following sentence.

   I'm **trying** to _____ .
5. Talk about something that **almost** happened to you, for example, an accident. Or talk about something that you **almost** did.
6. **Starve** can mean *be very hungry*, but it can also mean *to die because there is nothing to eat*. Are there parts of the world today where people sometimes starve? If so, where?
7. Name some activities that you **enjoy**.
8. Complete the following sentence.

   Although I don't like to _____ ,
   I have to.

X
Building Words with ment

The ending *ment* is added to some verbs to form a noun. For example, *pay + ment = payment*; *command + ment = commandment*.

When *ment* is added to a verb, it usually means *the result of* or *the act of*. For example, *a payment* is *the act or result of paying*; *a commandment* is *the result of giving a command*.

Verb	Noun
advance	advancement
announce	announcement
appoint	appointment
arrange	arrangement
command	commandment
employ	employment
enjoy	enjoyment
govern	government
judge	judgement
move	movement
pay	payment
place	placement
state	statement

Complete the sentences with these words.

statement   **enjoyment**   **payment**   **placement**

1. I have one more _____ to make on my new car.

2. The exam helps in the _____ of students into the right classes.

3. The little girl is getting a lot of _____ from riding her new bicycle.

4. You made a _____ about me that I don't like.

advancements   governments   arrangements   announcements

5. The president is going to make some important _____
   on TV tonight.

6. People are living longer today because of _____ in the
   field of medicine.

7. The _____ for the trip are complete.

8. The United States and France have strong central _____ .

UNIT I
Word Review

I
In Other Words

Next to each sentence, write the word which has the same meaning or almost the same meaning as the part of the sentence in *italics*.

starving	hurries	a lot of	missed
have to	almost	only	enjoys

1. _____ The southern part of the United States doesn't usually get *much* snow.

2. _____ It's been a long trip, but we're *close to* home now.

3. _____ Tamiko *wasn't at* the meeting. He didn't feel well.

4. _____ Sylvia *likes* her science and history classes.

5. _____ I have a friend who never *moves fast*.

6. _____ *No one but* Sam has a key to the office.

7. _____ We *must* finish the job today.

8. _____ Is there a restaurant near here? I'm *very hungry*.

II
Complete the sentences with these words.

quickly	far	may	however
trying	owns	around	waste

1. I _____ need eyeglasses.

2. Barbara _____ a small boat and uses it a lot in the summer.

3. Many people _____ water because it costs so little.

4. Lisa is _____ to do better in school.

24

5. Mark and Terry did the dishes _____ and went to an early movie.

6. A new electric typewriter costs _____ two hundred dollars.

7. Is it _____ from here to your parents' house?

8. Nora is eighty-nine. _____ , she's very active.

III

Complete the story with these words.

afraid	lose	weighs	trust
protect	bite	too	although

Lions

Lions are the largest members of the cat family. An adult lion _____ four hundred pounds. _____ the lion is the king of the animal world, it spends most of the day sleeping and resting.

Lions live in groups and they attack, _____ , and kill other kinds of animals. For this reason, no other animals _____ lions.

India and certain countries in Africa have laws to _____ lions because people have killed _____ many of them. These countries are _____ that without these laws they will _____ all of their lions, and there will be none in the future.

25

Unit Two
A Young Couple

Four

Sharing the Housework

Frank and Sue are married and they have two young children. Frank is a taxi driver. When Frank and Sue got married, he thought she would stay home when they had children. He would make the money to pay the bills and she would be busy at home. But that's not the way it is. Food and clothing and their new house cost more money than he makes. Sue has to work too. She's a cashier at a department store. Since **both** of them are working, Frank and Sue **share** the housework.

Frank never cooked in his life. The first night he tried, he **burned** the rice and the chicken didn't taste right. Frank and Sue **still** laugh about his first dinner. He'll never be a great cook, but Frank is **improving** fast. He likes to cook spaghetti and meatballs, and they taste very good. Learning to cook was difficult for Frank, but now he thinks it's **fun**.

When Frank cooks, Sue washes the dishes and he **wipes** them. Although Frank likes to cook, he **hates** to do dishes. He wants to buy a dishwasher. Sue also thinks that's a good idea, but they don't have any extra money for a dishwasher. When they finish the dishes and the children are in bed, Frank and Sue read, watch TV, or talk. It's the only time during the day when they have the chance to enjoy a little peace and quiet.

I

Answer these questions about the story.

PARAGRAPH 1

1. What is Frank's job?
2. When Frank got married, did he want Sue to work outside their home?
3. Why does Sue have to work?
4. What is her job?

PARAGRAPH 2

5. What happened the first night that Frank cooked?
6. What does he like to cook?
7. Was it easy for him to learn to cook?

PARAGRAPH 3

8. Does Frank like to wash the dishes?
9. What does he want to buy?
10. Why doesn't he buy what he wants?

II

MINI-DICTIONARY—PART 1

---

1. **both** (bōth) *adjective: pronoun:* the one and the other; the two
2. **share** (shâr) *verb:* to do or use with others; to divide
   noun: the part a person does or receives
3. **burn** (bûrn) *verb:* A. to be on fire; to destroy by fire
   B. to hurt by fire or heat
   noun: injury caused by fire or heat
4. **still** (stil) *adverb:* A. before now and at this time too
   B. before then and at that time too

III

Complete the sentences with these words.

both   **sharing** (*verb*)   **burning** (*verb*)   **still**

1. The building is _____ ! Call the fire department!

2. _____ teams played well.

3. It's eleven P.M. and Paul is _____ studying.

4. Roberta bought a box of candy and she's _____ it with her friends.

still   **both**   **share** (*noun*)   **burn** (*verb*)

5. The plate is hot. If you touch it, you'll _____ your fingers.

6. When I left the office, the boss was _____ working.

7. George is lazy; he doesn't do his _____ of the work.

8. Ray and Alice are friends and _____ of them are lawyers.

burn (*noun*)   **still**   **both**   **share**

9. Is it _____ snowing?

10. Janet was in a fire; she has a _____ on her arm.

11. It's not easy to teach children to _____ their toys.

12. _____ dresses are pretty.

IV
MINI-DICTIONARY — PART 2

5. **im·prove** (im-proov') *verb*: to do or become better
6. **fun** (fun) *noun*: pleasure; a good time
7. **wipe** (wi̅ p) *verb*: to move a cloth over something to clean or dry it
8. **hate** (ha̅t) *verb*: to dislike strongly
   noun: a strong dislike

V
Complete the sentences with these words.

improving	fun	wiping	hates (*verb*)

1. Cathy is _____ the baby's hands.

2. Ed likes to talk on the phone, but he _____ to write letters.

3. We had _____ on our trip.

4. Chen makes many errors, but his English is _____ .

fun	improves	hate (*noun*)	wiped

5. The waiter _____ the table.

6. It's _____ to dance.

7. The world needs more love and less _____ .

8. The weather isn't very good; I hope it _____ .

hates	fun	wipe	improving

9. _____ your feet before you go into the house. They're dirty.

10. I have a bad cold, but it's _____ .

11. Have _____ at the picnic!

12. Our daughter _____ to clean her room.

VI

Complete the sentences with the following words.

fun	improving	hate	wiping
both	still	burn	share

1. I _____ to get up in the morning.

2. Our friend, Paula, had a baby yesterday. We _____ her joy.

3. Puerto Rico and Cuba are islands in the Caribbean. _____ islands have a tropical climate.

4. The party was a lot of _____ .

5. Does your son _____ want to be a policeman?

6. The wood is dry. It will _____ fast.

7. Sam is _____ his eyeglasses with his handkerchief.

8. We're very happy that the economy is _____ .

VII

Complete the story with the following words.

wiped	still	improving	share
hates	burn	fun	both

Too Much Sun

Sharon and Helen are single and they _____ an apartment. Yesterday they _____ went to the beach and they had _____ . After Sharon went for a swim, she _____ her face and arms with a towel and lay in the sun. She got a bad _____ and it _____ hurts today.

Helen thinks Sharon should see a doctor, but Sharon _____ to go to doctors. Sharon says she's _____ and will be fine in a day or two.

VIII
Word Families

1. **improve** — *verb*
   improvement — *noun*: The building isn't modern, but it has many *improvements* in it.
2. **fun** — *noun*
   funny — *adjective*: Everyone laughed at the *funny* story.
3. **hate** — *verb* or *noun*
   hatred — *noun*: It's difficult for Dan not to feel *hatred* for the man who killed his son.

IX
Sharing Information

Discuss the following questions and topics in pairs or small groups.

1. Complete the following sentence about the United States and Canada.

   Both countries _____ .
2. Give an example of something that you **share** or **shared** with others.
3. Did you ever **burn** yourself? How? Was the burn bad? What did you do to make it better?
4. Where did you live last year? Do you **still** live in the same place?
5. You are studying English. Is your English **improving**? What are you doing to improve your English?
6. All cars and trucks have **wipers**. Where are the wipers and what do they do?
7. Name some things that you **hate** to do.
8. Name some things that are **fun** to do.

X
Building Words with y

Y is added to some nouns to form an adjective, for example, *dirt + y = dirty, rain + y = rainy*.

When *y* is added to a noun to form an adjective, it usually means *full of* or *a lot of*. *Dirty* means *a lot of or full of dirt*; *rainy* means *a lot of rain*.

Note: *fun* changes its meaning when it adds *y*. *Fun* means *a good time*. *Funny* means *causing laughter or a smile*.

Noun	Adjective
dirt	dirty
fun	funny
health	healthy
ice	icy
juice	juicy
luck	lucky
noise	noisy
rain	rainy
rock	rocky
salt	salty
sun	sunny
thirst	thirsty
wind	windy

Complete the sentences with these words.

dirty　　　　**thirsty**　　　　**lucky**　　　　**sunny**

1. I want some soda; I'm _____ .

2. There's not a cloud in the sky. It's going to be a _____ day.

3. These clothes are _____ . I have to wash them.

4. Our team was _____ to win the game.

salty　　　　**noisy**　　　　**juicy**　　　　**icy**

5. The oranges are very _____ .

6. I don't like the taste of this food. It's too _____ .

7. Be careful! The streets and sidewalks are _____ .

8. The party was _____ .

Five

Rushing the Baby to the Hospital

Frank and Sue have a son and a daughter. Their son is six years old and he's in the first grade. He is learning to read and he enjoys school. His name is Frank also. Their daughter is two years old and her name is Sarah. She is beginning to talk. She's also a very active baby who likes to **explore** and touch everything. Frank and Sue are **proud** of their children.

Frank and Sue are careful and do not put medicine or cleaning materials where Sarah can get them. They keep medicine in a bathroom cabinet away from Sarah. They keep cleaning materials in a cabinet over the kitchen sink. However, last Saturday Sue left a bottle of bleach* under the kitchen sink. That was a big **mistake**. The baby was playing in the kitchen and **swallowed** some of the bleach. Bleach is a **poison** and can kill a baby.

Frank and Sue didn't waste a second. They **rushed** Sarah to the hospital. The hospital is about a mile from their house. They got there in three minutes. The doctor talked to Sue; he had to know what the baby swallowed. He examined Sarah and gave her some medicine. They kept her in the hospital for five hours and watched her. **Fortunately** she swallowed only a little **bit** of bleach and she was okay.

Bleach is a liquid or powder used to make clothes brighter.

I

Answer these questions about the story.

PARAGRAPH 1

   1. How old is Frank and Sue's son? How old is their daughter?
   2. Does their son like school?
   3. How do Frank and Sue feel about their children?

PARAGRAPH 2

   4. Where do Frank and Sue keep medicine?
   5. What mistake did Sue make last Saturday?
   6. What did Sarah do with the bleach?
   7. Why is it very bad to drink bleach?

PARAGRAPH 3

   8. Where did Frank and Sue take Sarah?
   9. How far is it from their house to the hospital?
  10. Did Sarah swallow much bleach?

II

MINI-DICTIONARY—PART ONE

---

   1. **ex·plore** (ək-splôr′) *verb*: A. to go through and carefully examine an area, especially one not known B. to carefully examine any idea or thing
   2. **proud** (of) (proud) *adjective*: A. very satisfied with what one does or has B. having a high opinion of oneself
   3. **mis·take** (mi-stāk′) *noun*: error
      verb: to think one thing or person is another
   4. **swal·low** (swol′ō) *verb*: to move food or drink from the mouth down the throat
      noun: the act of swallowing; the amount swallowed

III

Complete the sentences with these words.

proud   **explored**   **mistakes** (*noun*)   **swallow** (*verb*)

1. Columbus _____ the Caribbean and many of its islands.

2. Margarita is _____ of her new car.

3. These pills are large; it's difficult to _____ them.

4. No one is perfect. We all make _____ .

mistake (*verb*)   **proud**   **swallow** (*noun*)   **exploring**

5. I took one _____ of that beer and I didn't like it.

6. We frequently _____ Tom for his twin brother.

7. Doctors are _____ new ways of treating cancer.
8. Some people don't like John because they think he's too

_____ .

swallow   **mistake**   **explore**   **proud**

9. The company is going to _____ the area for oil.

10. This typewriter doesn't work well. It was a _____ to buy it.

11. Joseph is _____ of his wife.

12. I have a sore throat. It hurts to _____ .

MINI-DICTIONARY—PART TWO

5. **poi·son** (poi′zən) *noun*: a substance that can kill
   verb: to kill or hurt with poison
6. **rush** (rush) *verb*: to move fast; to hurry
   noun: the act of moving fast
7. **for·tu·nate·ly** (fôr′chə-nit-lē) *adverb*: by good luck;
   luckily
8. **bit** (bit) *noun*: a small amount

V

Complete the sentences with these words.

poison (*noun*) **rushing** (*verb*) **fortunately** **bit**

1. The fire engines are _____ to the fire.

2. I think I'll have a little _____ of wine before supper.

3. Someone put _____ into the cat's food and killed him.

4. We went to the park for a picnic. _____ the weather was nice.

bit **poisoning** (*verb*) **fortunately** **rush** (*noun*)

5. Brenda lost the key to her car. _____ she had another one.

6. Mike didn't do a _____ of work today.

7. Abdul is in a _____. He can't wait for us.

8. The smoke from the factories is _____ our air.

fortunately **bit** **rushes** **poison**

9. Debbie _____ home from work every afternoon.

10. The ice cream tastes very good. Can I have a _____ more?

11. Leo was in an auto accident. _____ he wasn't hurt.

12. The leaves of some plants contain _____.

VI

Complete the sentences with the following words.

swallowed	**rushing**	**mistake**	**explored**
poisoning	**fortunately**	**proud**	**bit**

1. Jane lets her children do anything they want. That's a big

   _____ .

2. The test was very difficult. _____ I studied for it.

3. There are parts of Australia that no one has _____ .

4. My leg hurts a _____ , but it'll be all right.

5. Barbara is _____ to get to the bank before it closes.

6. We're _____ of our country.

7. Nick didn't like the taste of the medicine. He _____ it
   quickly.

8. The pollution in our rivers is _____ many fish.

VII

Complete the story with the following words.

mistake	**rushed**	**proud**	**fortunately**
bit	**poison**	**swallowed**	**explore**

Mice in the House

Paul has a beautiful dog named Wolf and a nice house in the country.
Paul and Wolf like to go for long walks and to _____ the
woods near his house. Paul is _____ of his dog and house,
but there's one problem with the house. When the weather gets cold, mice
from the fields get into it.

Yesterday Paul bought some powder to _____ the mice. He put the powder in a dish next to the refrigerator and that was a _____. Wolf thought the powder was food and he _____ some of it. _____ Paul had put only a _____ of powder in the dish.

When Wolf got sick, Paul knew it was because of the powder, and he _____ the dog to an animal doctor. The doctor was able to save Wolf.

VIII
Word Families

1. **proud** (of) — *adjective*
   pride — *noun*: We take *pride* in our work.
   proudly — *adverb*: George is a soldier and he wears his uniform *proudly*.
2. **explore** — *verb*
   explorer — *noun*: Spain sent many *explorers* to North and South America.
   exploration — *noun*: The United States is the leader in the *exploration* of space.
3. **mistake** — *noun*
   mistaken — *adjective*: If you think Ray will help us, you're *mistaken*.
4. **poison** — *noun* or *verb*
   poisonous — *adjective*: Some snakes are *poisonous*.
5. **fortunately** — *adverb*
   fortune — *noun*: No one knows what *fortune* will bring.
   fortunate — *adjective*: Elena never gets sick. She's *fortunate*.

IX
Sharing Information

Discuss the following questions and topics in pairs or small groups.

1. Complete the following sentence.

   I'm **proud** of _____.

2. What are some of the good things that have come from the **exploration** of space by the United States and the Soviet Union?
3. Everyone makes **mistakes**. Think of a mistake that you made, or that another person made, and talk about it.
4. It's not easy to **swallow** food when you have a sore throat. What do people usually eat when their throats hurt?
5. Bleach is a **poison**. Name some other things that are **poisonous** and that are often in a home.
6. Eight o'clock in the morning and five o'clock at night are called "**rush hours**." Why do we call these times "rush hours"?
7. Complete the following sentence.

   I'm **fortunate** that _____ .
8. Sometimes we use **a bit** followed by an adjective, for example, *I'm a bit thirsty*. Which of the sentences below describe how you feel now?
   a. I'm very tired.   b. I'm *a bit* tired.   c. I'm not tired.
   a. I'm very hungry.   b. I'm *a bit* hungry.   c. I'm not hungry.

X
Building Words with un

Un is placed before many adjectives, adverbs, and verbs to form a new word.

When *un* is placed before an adjective or adverb, it means *not* or *the opposite of*, for example, *un + happy = unhappy*, which means *not happy*; *un + fortunately = unfortunately*, which means *the opposite of fortunately.*

When *un* is placed before a verb, it indicates an action which is the opposite of that verb. For example, *un + dress = undress*; *un + lock = unlock*; *un + cover = uncover*; *un + do = undo. Undress, unlock, uncover,* and *undo* are the opposite of *dress, lock, cover,* and *do.*

Adjectives, Adverbs, Verbs	New word
able	unable
afraid	unafraid
cover	uncover
do	undo
dress	undress
explored	unexplored
fortunate	unfortunate
fortunately	unfortunately
happy	unhappy
important	unimportant
kind	unkind
lock	unlock
married	unmarried
necessary	unnecessary
protected	unprotected
safe	unsafe
true	untrue

Complete the sentences with these words.

unsafe   unmarried   unfortunately   unable

1. We wanted to play tennis today. _____ it's raining.

2. The bridge is_____ . They have to fix it.

3. Jean was _____ to get the book she wanted.

4. Jeff is twenty-five, rich, and handsome; and he's still _____ .

unafraid   unnecessary   undressed   unkind

5. My visit to the doctor was _____ . There was nothing wrong with me.

6. The man looked very angry, but we were _____ .

7. I don't like Mark. Sometimes he's _____ to me.

8. Ron got _____ and went to bed.

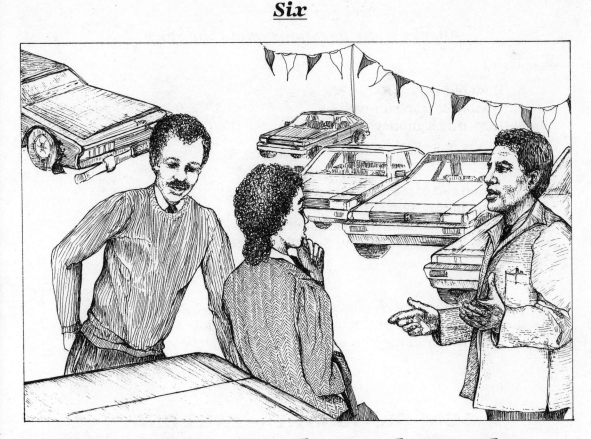

Six

Chevrolets, Fords, and Hondas

Frank and Sue have to buy a new car. Their car is eleven years old and they're having a lot of problems with it. They're going to sell it for two hundred and fifty dollars. **Of course**, a new car will cost a lot of money. All cars are **expensive**. Frank and Sue are looking for one that isn't too expensive. But it has to be a car that will run well and that they can trust.

Frank and Sue's **neighbor**, Mr. Wallace, bought a new Cadillac last month. It's a beautiful car and Mr. Wallace loves it, but it was very expensive. Mr. Wallace is a lawyer and he's rich. He can **afford** a Cadillac, but Frank and Sue can't. They're looking at Chevrolets, Fords, and Hondas. This takes a lot of time, but they plan to keep their new car for ten years. They know it would be a mistake to **choose** one quickly.

Yesterday they looked at a Honda Accord and it's **just** what they want. It looks nice, it doesn't use a lot of gas, and everyone says that it's a great car. They plan to buy it. They're going to the bank today to get a car **loan**. It should be easy for them to get the loan since both of them are working. They have saved some money to buy a car, but they also have to **borrow** five thousand dollars.

43

I

Answer these questions about the story.

PARAGRAPH 1

    1. How old is Frank and Sue's car?
    2. Does their car run well?
    3. How much money do they want for their old car?

PARAGRAPH 2

    4. When did Mr. Wallace buy his Cadillac?
    5. Is he happy with his new car?
    6. Why can he afford a Cadillac?
    7. How long do Frank and Sue plan to keep their new car?

PARAGRAPH 3

    8. Does a Honda Accord use much gas?
    9. Why are Frank and Sue going to the bank?
  10. How much money do they have to borrow?

II

MINI-DICTIONARY — PART ONE

---

    1. **of course** (əv kôrs or ə-kôrs′) *idiom*: certainly; clearly; naturally
    2. **ex·pen·sive** (ek-spen′siv) *adjective*: costing a lot
    3. **neighbor** (nā′bər) *noun*: a person who lives near another
    4. **afford** (ə-fôrd′) *verb*: to be able to pay for

III

Complete the sentences with these words.

of course　　　**expensive**　　　**afford**　　　**neighbors**

1. We're not rich, but we can _____ a new TV set.

2. Juanita lives across the street from me. We're _____ .

3. Hilton hotels are very nice and very _____ .

44

4. Florida is a great state to visit. _____ it's very hot in the summer.

| afford | of course | neighbor | expensive |

5. These shoes are _____ , but I like them and I'm going to buy them.

6. _____ we're hungry. We didn't eat lunch yet.

7. It's a beautiful apartment, but we can't _____ the rent.

8. Tim often helps those who live near him. He's a good _____ .

| expensive | afford | of course | neighbors |

9. Ray and Karen want to go to Hawaii, but they can't _____ it.

10. When I was in the hospital, many of my _____ came to see me.

11. _____ they love their children.

12. Gold is _____ .

IV

MINI-DICTIONARY—PART TWO

5. **choose** (chōōz) *verb*: to take one thing from several others; to pick; to select
6. **just** (just) *adverb*: exactly*
7. **loan** (lōn) *noun*: money that a person is given and must pay back; anything that a person is given and must return
   verb: to give money which must be paid back; to give anything which must be returned
8. **bor·row** (bôr′ō or bôr′ō) *verb*: to obtain money which must be paid back; to obtain or take anything which must be returned

*The adverb *just* has other meanings, for example, (a) *recently*: *We just got home.* (b) *only*: *I was just trying to help you.*

45

V

Complete the sentences with these words.

choose　　　　**just**　　　　**loan** (*noun*)　　　　**borrow**

1. The money I got from Jack wasn't a gift; it was a _____ .

2. Debbie looks _____ like her mother.

3. Can I _____ twenty dollars from you? I'll pay it back tomorrow.

4. The company is going to _____ a new president.

borrowed　　　　**choose**　　　　**just**　　　　**loaned** (*verb*)

5. The bank _____ us three thousand dollars.

6. Roger did _____ what we told him to do.

7. Dan _____ his friend's car to drive to the airport.

8. We should _____ our friends carefully.

loan　　　　**just**　　　　**borrowing**　　　　**choose**

9. I'm _____ Gloria's typewriter, but I have to return it tonight.

10. Your son is _____ the same age as mine.
11. Ana wants to go to college in September, but she doesn't know

which one to _____ .

12. I'll _____ the book to you, but I need it back.

VI

Complete the sentences with the following words or phrases.

loan　　　　　　**of course**　　　　**just**　　　　**borrow**
neighbors　　　**expensive**　　　**choose**　　　**afford**

1. Sally is studying to be a doctor. _____ it's not easy and she has to study a lot.

46

2. Phil and Helen are rich and they often eat in _____ restaurants.

3. The company can't _____ to hire more workers.

4. Ed feels _____ the way I do about the situation.

5. We need a _____ to start our business.

6. Alice is buying a coat, but it's hard for her to _____ between two very pretty coats.

7. I don't have a pen. Can I _____ yours for a minute?

8. Ralph lives in an apartment near my house. We're _____ .

VII

Complete the story with the following words or phrases.

choose	**loan**	**neighbors**	**borrow**
expensive	**afford**	**just**	**of course**

Buying a Computer

Mr. Gonzalez and Mr. Fisher live on the same street. They're _____ and they also own a small business. They want to buy a computer for their business. _____ most business computers are _____ and there are so many different kinds of computers that it won't be easy to _____ one.

Yesterday they visited a company that sells computers, and they were able to find one that is _____ right for their business. However, the only way they can _____ to buy the computer they want is to _____ the money for it. They're going to ask a bank for a _____ .

VIII
Word Families

1. **expensive** — *adjective*
   expense — *noun*: Food is a big *expense* for everybody.
2. **choose** — *verb*
   choice — *noun*: We must pay taxes. We have no *choice*.
3. **neighbor** — *noun*
   neighborhood — *noun*: It's a pretty *neighborhood* with tall trees and modern homes.
   neighboring — *adjective*: They may move their store to a *neighboring* city.
4. **afford** — *verb*
   affordable — *adjective*: We want to buy a house but it's hard to find one that is *affordable*.

IX
Sharing Information

Discuss the following questions and topics in pairs or small groups.

1. Big cars and good jewelry are **expensive**, but we can live without them. Name some things that are necessary and that are also expensive.
2. If you had to **choose** between being very rich or very smart, what **choice** would you make? Why?
3. Think of your **neighbors**. Talk a little about a neighbor you like. Why do you like the person?
4. Complete the following sentence.

   Of course, I like _____ , but _____ .
5. Name something that you want to do or want to buy, but that you can't **afford**.
6. Look at your watch or a clock and complete the following sentence.

   It's **just** _____ .
7. Did you ever **loan** money to a friend or relative? Did you get the money back?
8. Did you ever **borrow** money to buy or do something? Why did you borrow the money? How much time were you given to pay back the money you borrowed?

X
Building Words with able

Able is added to some words, usually verbs, and sometimes nouns, to form an adjective.

When *able* is added to a verb, it generally means *able to be* or *likely to*. For example, *wash + able = washable* which means *able to be washed, change + able = changeable* which means *likely to change.*

The suffix *able* added to a noun generally means *having* or *giving*, for example, *value + able = valuable* which means *having value, comfort + able = comfortable* which means *giving comfort.*

Verbs, Nouns	*Adjective*
accept	acceptable
afford	affordable
change	changeable
comfort	comfortable
control	controllable
enjoy	enjoyable
like	likable
pay	payable
return	returnable
understand	understandable
use	usable
value	valuable
wash	washable
work	workable

Complete the sentences with these words.

enjoyable   returnable   acceptable   changeable.

1. Delia is very _____ . You never know what she's going to do.

2. Everyone liked the movie. It was _____ .

3. I thought your plan was good, but the boss said it wasn't _____ .

4. These soda bottles are _____ for five cents each.

washable   movable   understandable   controllable

5. The desk is big and heavy, but I think it's _____ with two people.

6. There was a fire in the building. Fortunately, it was _____ and the fire fighters put it out.

7. The pants are _____, but you shouldn't put them in hot water.

8. Ken's pay is low and he works long hours. His desire for a new job is

_____ .

UNIT II
Word Review

I
In Other Words

Next to each sentence, write the word which has the same meaning or almost the same meaning as the part of the sentence in *italics*.

bit	**fortunate**	**exploring**	**hates**
just	**burning**	**improving**	**both**

1. _____ The job pays well and I was *lucky* to get it.

2. _____ My dog *doesn't like* to take a bath.

3. _____ Robert's car is *on fire*!

4. _____ Alice put a *small amount* of milk and sugar in her tea.

5. _____ Ted plays tennis well and he's *getting better*.

6. _____ The baby weighs *exactly* twenty-one pounds.

7. _____ Janet and her sister are happy it's snowing. *The two* of them like to ski.

8. _____ The company is *looking carefully at* ways to cut expenses.

II
Complete the sentences with the following words.

choose	**neighbors**	**swallow**	**share**
rushing	**proud**	**wiped**	**poisonous**

1. Steve is late. He's _____ to get to school before class starts.

2. My bike got wet, but I _____ it off.

3. There are so many good things on this menu that I don't know what

   to _____ .

4. Helen is _____ of her beautiful garden.

5. Married people _____ their lives.

6. Joyce lives around the corner from me. We're _____ .

7. Many cleaning fluids and powders are _____ .

8. The soup was so hot that I couldn't _____ it.

III

Complete the story with the following words or phrases.

loan	fun	of course	still
mistake	expensive	borrow	afford

A Boat

Karl and Anna are married and live in the city. In the summer they rent a home on a large lake. They both enjoy leaving the city to go swimming in the lake. Now Karl wants to buy a boat, but Anna says that boats are too _____ and they can't _____ one.

Karl wants to _____ the money for the boat. Anna knows they can get a _____ from the bank, but she _____ doesn't like the idea. She thinks it would be a _____ to pay so much for something they don't need. Karl says, " _____ we don't need a boat, but my business is doing well and it would be a lot of _____ to have one."

Unit Three
Two Young Men

Seven

Working and Swimming

Pete and Tom are brothers. Pete's eighteen and he's finishing high school in June. Because he likes school and books, he **spends** a lot of time reading and studying. He's only an **average** student, but he plans to go to college in September. Tom's sixteen and he doesn't like to study or read. He **prefers** to play basketball and baseball or watch TV. He's good at all sports.

In the summer Pete works at a gas station. He likes the work and he wants to make some money to help pay for his expenses at college. Tom works at Burger King. It's not great work, but it's hard for a high school student to get a summer job and Tom's happy to be working. On Saturday and Sunday, Pete and Tom often go swimming in a **pool** near their home. Tom's a very good swimmer; Pete isn't very good but he isn't bad. He's an average swimmer.

The pool is big and you have to pay to get in, but Pete and Tom have a lot of fun there. Tom likes to **dive** and swim in the **deep** end of the pool. Pete prefers to go in the **shallow** end. He can't dive well. Pete and Tom swim or sit on the **edge** of the pool until they get tired and then they go home. It's a nice way to spend a summer afternoon.

I

Answer these questions about the story.

PARAGRAPH 1

1. How old is Pete? How old is Tom?
2. Does Pete like to study?
3. What does Pete plan to do in September?
4. Does Tom prefer to read or to play sports?

PARAGRAPH 2

5. Where does Pete work in the summer? Where does Tom work?
6. Is it easy for a high school student to get a summer job?
7. What do Tom and Pete often do on Saturday and Sunday?

PARAGRAPH 3

8. Who can dive better, Pete or Tom?
9. Where do Pete and Tom sit when they're not swimming?
10. Does Pete like to go in the deep end of the pool or the shallow end?

II

MINI-DICTIONARY — PART ONE

1. **spend** (spend) *verb*: A. to use money to buy something B. to use time
   The past of *spend* is *spent*.
2. **av·er·age** (av′rij) *adjective*: ordinary
   noun: the result of adding a group of numbers and dividing by how many numbers are in the group
   verb: do on an average; get as an average quantity
3. **pre·fer** (pri-fûr′) *verb*: to like better
4. **pool** (pool) *noun*: A. small area of still water
   B. small area of water made for swimming

III

Complete the sentences with these words.

prefer   **pools**   **spends**   **average** (*adjective*)

1. The rain was heavy. There are _____ of water on the field.

2. Lisa is an _____ cook.

3. I sometimes drink tea, but I _____ coffee.

4. Clarisse _____ a lot of money on her clothes.

spending   **average** (*noun*)   **prefers**   **pool**

5. I want to go to the movies, but my wife _____ to stay home and watch TV.

6. Ben is _____ the evening at Richard's.

7. Does the motel have a _____?

8. The _____ of four, five, and nine is six.

averaged (*verb*)   **spent**   **pool**   **prefer**

9. Joyce _____ sixty dollars at the supermarket.

10. We _____ fifty miles an hour on our trip.

11. Do you _____ to go by train or bus?

12. There's a _____ of water on the kitchen floor.

5. **dive** (dīv) *verb*: to jump into water, usually head first
   noun: a jump into water, usually head first
6. **deep** (dēp) *adjective*: going far down
   adverb: far into
7. **shal·low** (shal′ō) *adjective*: not far from top to bottom; not deep
8. **edge** (ej) *noun*: the area where an object ends

V

Complete the sentences with these words.

shallow   **diving** (*verb*)   **edge**   **deep** (*adjective*)

1. The middle of the lake is very _____.

2. We can drive through this water. It's _____.

3. Roy is sitting on the _____ of the bed, putting on his shoes.

4. Nancy is _____ into the ocean.

edge   **deep** (*adverb*)   **dive** (*noun*)   **shallow**

5. Ed made a beautiful _____ into the water.

6. You're driving too close to the _____ of the road.

7. The German army moved _____ into Russia.

8. The baby can go into the water. It's very _____.

dive   **shallow**   **deep**   **edge**

9. The knife is very sharp. That's a _____ cut.

10. The books fell off the _____ of the desk.

11. Sam is afraid to _____ into the river.

12. The water is too _____ for swimming.

VI

Complete the sentences with these words.

average	spent	shallow	edge
pool	prefer	diving	deep

1. The box is _____. We can't put much in it.

2. I _____ summer to winter.

3. Kevin isn't a great baseball player, but he isn't bad. He's _____.

4. Doris is _____ into the lake from a boat.

5. Be very careful! There's a _____ hole in the ground.

6. I _____ too much money this month.

7. Let's go to the _____ today. It's a great day to swim.

8. Watch the little boy! He's near the _____ of the stairs.

VII

Complete the story with these words.

edge	deep	spend	prefer
shallow	dive	average	pool

Swimming in the River

Ruth and her brother Mike like to swim. Sometimes they go to a state

park where there is a _____ , but they _____

to swim in a river that's not far from their house. They _____

into the water from the _____ of the river and swim until

it's time to go home. When the weather is very hot, they _____

hours swimming in the cool water.

58

Although the river is _____ where they go swimming,
they aren't afraid. Ruth is an excellent swimmer and Mike is also above
_____ . Parts of the river are very safe and _____,
but they don't like to swim there.

VIII

Word Families

1. **dive** — *verb*
   diver — *noun*: The *divers* are going to the bottom of the sea to look for the lost ship.
2. **deep** — *adjective*
   deeply — *adverb*: I'm *deeply* grateful for your help.
3. **prefer** — *verb*
   preference — *noun*: We have vanilla and strawberry ice cream. What's your *preference*?
   preferable — *adjective*: If you have the money, buying a house is *preferable* to renting an apartment.

IX

Sharing Information

Discuss these questions and topics in pairs or small groups.

1. Do you like to swim? Do you think it's more fun to swim in a **pool** or in the ocean?
2. Are you tall or short, or are you **average** height?
3. Some people find politics very interesting; others do not. Do you have a **deep** interest in politics?
4. In cities that have large rivers or that are on the ocean, there are times when the police have to use **divers**. In what kind of situation would the police have to use divers?

5. Complete this sentence. I like _____,

   but I **prefer** _____.
6. Some people don't like to stand near the **edge** of a high roof or a bridge. They're afraid of standing near the edge of high places. Are you?
7. When you swim, do you stay in **shallow** water? Or do you like to swim in deep water?
8. Do you **spend** a lot of time watching TV? Reading? Talking on the phone?

59

X

Building Words with **ful**

Ful is added to some nouns to form an adjective. For example, *power + ful = powerful, beauty + ful = beautiful, help + ful = helpful.*

The suffix *ful* usually means *having a lot of* or *giving. Powerful* means *having a lot of power, beautiful* means *having a lot of beauty, helpful* means *giving help.*

Sometimes *ful* is added to a noun to form another noun. For example, *spoon + ful = spoonful, arm + ful = armful.* In these cases, *ful* means *the amount that will make the thing full. Spoonful* means *the amount that will make a spoon full, armful* means *the amount that will make an arm full.*

Noun	*Adjective*
beauty	beautiful
care	careful
color	colorful
fear	fearful
help	helpful
hope	hopeful
joy	joyful
peace	peaceful
power	powerful
rest	restful
thought	thoughtful
use	useful
waste	wasteful
youth	youthful

	Noun
arm	armful
spoon	spoonful

Complete the sentences with these words.

fearful   peaceful   useful   wasteful

1. The book helped me a lot. It was very_____.

2. Thinking about war and nuclear bombs makes me _____.

3. It's _____ to cook more food than you can eat or save.

4. Life is more _____ in the country than in big, noisy cities.

careful   hopeful   youthful   colorful

5. I'm not sure I'll get the job, but I'm _____ about it.

6. It's fall and the leaves on the trees are very _____.

7. Lillian never drives fast. She's a _____ driver.

8. Greg is forty-five years old, but he still has a _____ look.

Eight

Hunting

Pete and Tom hate to see the summer end. The pool closes and they have to go back to school. However, they like one thing about the fall. They love to **hunt**. On Saturdays in the fall they get up early and they spend the day hunting. Their father has a small truck. They borrow his truck and ride to the woods around ten miles from their house. The woods are beautiful in the fall, especially when the leaves change color.

Last Saturday Pete and Tom were walking in the woods with their rifles when they saw a deer drinking from a **stream**. The deer was almost too beautiful to **shoot**. They moved closer to it. They **hesitated** for a minute. Should they shoot the deer or let it go? Then Tom **aimed** his rifle at the deer and shot it. Tom's aim is very good; he didn't miss.

This was the first deer they ever shot. They were happy and sad at the same time. They went over to the deer. It was a **huge** animal. They tried to **lift** it, but it was too big. They had to **drag** it on the ground to their truck. The truck wasn't far and some **hunters** helped them lift the deer into the truck. They put their rifles next to the deer and drove home.

I

Answer these questions about the story.

PARAGRAPH 1
1. Why do Pete and Tom hate to see the summer end?
2. What do they like to do in the fall?
3. Whose truck do they borrow to go hunting?

PARAGRAPH 2
4. What did Pete and Tom carry with them in the woods?
5. What was the deer doing when Pete and Tom saw it?
6. Did Tom shoot the deer immediately?

PARAGRAPH 3
7. How did Pete and Tom feel after they shot the deer?
8. Why couldn't they lift the deer?
9. How did they get the deer to the truck?
10. Who helped them lift the deer into the truck?

II

MINI-DICTIONARY—PART ONE

---

1. a. **hunt** (hunt) *verb*: A. to look for animals or birds to kill or capture B. to look carefully for anything
   noun: A. the act of hunting animals or birds B. the act of looking carefully for anything
   b. **hunter** (hun′ tər) *noun*: a person who hunts
2. **stream** (strēm) *noun*: A. a body of water that flows, especially a small one B. anything that flows continuously
   verb: flow continuously
3. **shoot** (sho͞ot) *verb*: to hit with a bullet from a gun
   The past of *shoot* is *shot*.
4. **hes·i·tate** (hez′ə-tāt) *verb*: A. to stop briefly before or during an action B. to be slow or unwilling to act or decide

---

III

Complete the sentences with these words.

hunt (*verb*)   **shoot**   **stream** (*noun*)   **hesitated**   **hunters**

1. The man who robbed the bank had a gun, but he didn't _____ anyone.

2. You need a license to _____ .

3. Jennifer _____ before she opened the door.

4. The fox is running away from the _____ and the dogs.

5. We sat on the side of the _____ and put our feet into the water.

    hesitate   **shot**   **stream** (*noun*)   **hunting** (*verb*)

6. Peggy is _____ for a job.

7. If you need help, don't _____ to ask me.

8. It was five P.M. and a _____ of people were leaving the train station.

9. Lee Harvey Oswald _____ President Kennedy on November 22, 1963.

    streaming (*verb*)   **hesitated**   **hunt** (*noun*)   **shoot**

10. The _____ begins at nine o'clock.

11. Nick _____ before he answered my question.

12. Take my watch and my wallet, but don't _____ me.

13. Water was _____ from the broken pipe.

IV

MINI-DICTIONARY—PART TWO

---

5. **aim** (ām) *verb*: A. to point a gun or other thing at a person or object B. to try to do something
   noun: A. the act of pointing a gun or other thing at a person or object B. what one wishes to do; a plan
6. **huge** (hyo͞oj) *adjective*: very large
7. **lift** (lift) *verb*: to raise something to a higher position
   noun: the act of lifting
8. **drag** (drag) *verb*: to pull along on a surface

V

Complete the sentences with these words.

lift (*verb*) **aiming** (*verb*) **dragging** **huge**

1. The baby is _____ her doll behind her.

2. I want to move this desk. Can you help me to _____ it?

3. The lake is _____ . It's thirty miles long and ten miles wide.

4. Why is the police officer _____ his gun at that man?

lift (*noun*) **dragging** **huge** **aiming** (*verb*)

5. We need two strong people to give this sofa a _____ .

6. There are many _____ buildings in Chicago.

7. Beverly is _____ a big box out of the closet.

8. Our company is always _____ to make more money.

dragged **huge** **aims** (*noun*) **lift**

9. A _____ truck stopped in front of our house.

10. The bed is heavy. It's going to be hard to _____ .

65

11. Ray and Eileen _____ the boat out of the river.

12. What were the _____ of the president's trip?

VI

Complete the sentences with these words.

huge	**dragging**	**aimed**	**hesitated**
hunting	**stream**	**lift**	**shoot**

1. Judy _____ to buy the dress because it was expensive.

2. The children are putting toy boats into the _____ .

3. The horse is old and sick. They may have to _____ it.

4. The Amazon River is _____ . It's the largest river in the world.

5. Harry and Ken are _____ in the woods.

6. I _____ my flashlight at the car to help me see.

7. Please _____ your feet. I want to vacuum in front of the chair.

8. Don is _____ a large bag of leaves across the yard.

VII

Complete the story with these words.

dragged	**huge**	**hunt**	**shot**
aim	**hesitate**	**lift**	**stream**

A Hungry Bear

Phil, Susan, and their two children were camping near a _____

in a national forest. No one is allowed to _____ in the forest,

but Phil had his rifle with him.

Their youngest child was playing outside their tent when a _____

bear came looking for food. Phil got his rifle, and when he saw the bear running toward their child and tent, he didn't _____ a

moment. He _____ and killed the bear. Fortunately, Phil has

a good _____ .

The bear was too heavy to _____ , so they _____

it away from the tent and left it under a tree.

VIII
Word Families

1. **hunt** — *verb* or *noun*
   hunting — *noun*: *Hunting* and fishing are popular sports.
2. **shoot** — *verb*
   shot — *noun*: Someone tried to kill Paul, but the *shot* missed.
3. **hesitate** — *verb*
   hesitant — *adjective*: We were *hesitant* to go swimming because
   the water was cold.
   hesitantly — *adverb*: Joe was *hesitantly* telling his father about his
   automobile accident.
   hesitation — *noun*: Eva acted without *hesitation*.

IX
Sharing Information

Discuss these questions and topics in pairs or small groups.

1. Do you or does anyone in your family like to **hunt**?
2. The word **stream** usually refers to water, but it can also refer to other
   things, for example, **a stream of people** or **a stream of questions**.
   What do we mean by **a stream of people**? By **a stream of
   questions**?
3. Did you ever **shoot** a gun? Have you ever shot an animal? Do you
   think that it's okay to shoot animals, or do you think that it's wrong?
4. Complete sentence a or b.

   a. I **hesitate** to _____ .

   b. I **hesitated** before _____ .
5. Name an **aim** that you have, that is, something that you're trying or
   planning to do.

6. There are always problems in the world. Some of the problems are small. Others are **huge**. Name a huge problem that the world has today.
7. Sometimes parents **drag** a child away from something. Give an example of this.
8. Name a few things that are difficult to **lift**. Name a few things that are easy to lift.

X
Building Words with less

Less is added to some nouns to form an adjective. For example, *power + less = powerless, fear + less = fearless.*

The suffix *less* usually means *without* or *having no. Powerless* means *without power* or *having no power, fearless* means *without fear* or *having no fear.*

Noun	Adjective
aim	aimless
care	careless
end	endless
fear	fearless
help	helpless
home	homeless
hope	hopeless
need	needless
power	powerless
sleep	sleepless
sugar	sugarless
use	useless
weight	weightless

Complete the sentences with these words.

careless	sugarless	sleepless	fearless

1. You should buy _____ gum. It's better for your teeth.

2. I made some _____ mistakes on my math exam.

3. Dan will make a good soldier. He's _____ .

4. John is very tired. He had a _____ night.

68

useless   **homeless**   **endless**   **weightless**

5. People and things are _____ in outer space.

6. This clock is _____ . It won't run.

7. The movie was too long. It seemed _____ .

8. Does the city have a place where _____ people can stay at night?

Nine

A Bitter Argument

Tom and Pete live in New York State and in New York you have to go to school until you're sixteen. Then you're free to continue or to **quit**. Tom's just sixteen and he wants to quit school. He likes his science class, but he feels all of his other classes are a waste of time. They're **dull** and he's not learning much in them. The teachers say he doesn't study. He says he doesn't want to study. He wants to get a job and **earn** some money. Why does everyone have to go to school and study?

Tom's mother thinks it's **foolish** for him to quit school. She thinks it would be a big mistake. She tells him that all of the other boys and girls in the neighborhood plan to finish high school. His brother is going to college. Tom will need **at least** a high school education to get a good job. Why doesn't he finish high school and then look for a job? Tom tells his mother that he doesn't care what his brother and the other kids are doing. He wants to go to work now.

Last night, Tom and his mother had a big **argument** about his plan to quit school. She **shouted** at him and he shouted back at her.

They **argued** for more than an hour. She said he would be a **fool** to quit school. He said he didn't want to hear any more about school and what his friends were doing. It was a **bitter** argument. Will Tom listen to his mother or will he quit school?

I

Answer these questions about the story.

PARAGRAPH 1
1. How old do you have to be before you can quit school in New York State?
2. What class does Tom like?
3. How does he feel about his other classes?
4. What do the teachers say about Tom?

PARAGRAPH 2
5. Does Tom's mother think it's okay for him to quit school?
6. What does she tell him?
7. What does he tell her?

PARAGRAPH 3
8. What did Tom and his mother argue about last night?
9. How long did they argue?
10. Was it a friendly argument?

II

MINI-DICTIONARY—PART ONE

1. **quit** (kwit) *verb*: to stop doing something
2. **dull** (dul) *adjective*: A. not interesting   B. not sharp
3. **earn** (ûrn) *verb*: A. to receive money for doing work   B. to deserve something because of one's actions or qualities
4. a. **fool·ish** (foo′lish) *adjective*: stupid; not wise
   b. **fool** (fool) *noun*: a stupid person

III

Complete the sentences with these words.

earns	**dull**	**fool**	**foolish**	**quit**

1. Donna was _____ to marry Ken. He's lazy and drinks too much.

2. We went home before the end of the game. It was _____.

3. It's difficult to _____ smoking.

4. Lucy has a good job. She _____ forty-five thousand dollars a year.

5. Philippe is a _____. He never thinks before he acts.

quits	**foolish**	**earn**	**dull**

6. Our teacher gives good marks only to those who _____ them.

7. We were _____ to buy that new car. It gives us a lot of trouble.

8. Audrey never _____ trying. She'll do well in life.

9. These knives are _____. They won't cut the steak.

dull	**quit**	**earn**	**foolish**

10. Nora wants her husband to _____ drinking.

11. Most doctors _____ a lot of money.

12. It's _____ for those children to play in the street.

13. I stopped reading the book because it was _____.

IV
MINI-DICTIONARY—PART TWO

5. **at least** (at lēst) *idiom*: A. a minimum B. in any case
6. a. **ar·gue** (är´gyo͞o) *verb*: to disagree in words; to fight with words
   b. **ar·gu·ment** (är´gyə-mənt) *noun*: disagreement in words; fight with words
7. **shout** (shout) *verb*: to speak in a very loud voice
   noun: a loud cry
8. **bit·ter** (bit´ər) *adjective*: A. sharp, unpleasant taste
   B. filled with strong, unpleasant feelings

V
Complete the sentences with these words.

bitter   argue   shouting (*verb*)   **arguments   at least**

1. Stop _____! The children are sleeping.

2. I don't like grapefruit juice. It has a _____ taste.

3. Ed and Frank are good friends, but they have many _____.

4. Jerry is _____ six feet tall.

5. Nancy and Bob _____ a lot about politics. She's a Democrat and he's a Republican.

shout (*noun*)   **at least   bitter   argue**

6. I don't agree with what you're saying, but I'm not going to

_____.

7. Our new boss is strict. But, _____, she listens to people.

8. During World War II, the United States and Japan were _____ enemies.

9. We heard a _____ in the hall and went to see what was happening.

73

argue	bitter	at least	shout

10. This coffee tastes _____.

11. You don't have to _____. I can hear you.

12. In the army, you do what you're told and you don't _____.

13. A new refrigerator will cost _____ three hundred dollars.

VI

Complete the sentences with these words or phrases.

argue	dull	quit	foolish
bitter	earn	shouted	at least

1. How much money did you _____ last year?

2. I phoned you _____ three times, but no one answered.

3. Dan _____ the baseball team.

4. Mr. and Mrs. Lopez _____ about the way he drives. She thinks he drives too fast.

5. The lemonade is _____. Put some sugar in it.

6. When our team won the game, we _____ for joy.

7. The movie was so _____ that I went to sleep during it.

8. You're _____ to carry a lot of money in your wallet.

VII

Complete the story with these words or phrases.

earn	foolish	shout	at least
dull	bitter	argument	quit

Working in a Factory

Ray works in a factory and his job is very _____. The

factory is also dirty and the machines make a lot of noise. If Ray wants to talk to another worker, he must _____ .

Ray's pay is low and he wants to _____ more money. Last month, Ray and his boss had a long _____ about his salary. The boss promised to pay him more, but now the boss says it's impossible. Ray is _____ about this.

He thinks it would be _____ to keep working in the factory. Tomorrow, he's going to _____ his job and look for a new one. He wants to make _____ two dollars more an hour in his new job.

VIII

Word Families

1. **earn** — *verb*
    earnings — *noun*: The government taxes our *earnings*.
2. **foolish** — *adjective*
    fool — *verb*: a. I wasn't serious, I was *fooling*. b. It's hard to *fool* Mary. She's very smart.
    foolishly — *adverb*: Someone stole the package that we *foolishly* left in our car.
    foolishness — *noun*: Lisa hasn't been feeling well, but she won't go to a doctor. That's *foolishness*.
3. **bitter** — *adjective*
    bitterly — *adverb*: Terry cried *bitterly* when her husband died.
    bitterness — *noun*: There was much *bitterness* in the black community after the shooting of Martin Luther King, Jr.

IX

Sharing Information

Discuss these questions and topics in pairs or small groups.

1. Name some of the reasons why people **quit** their jobs.
2. Some classes are **dull** and some are interesting. What makes a class dull? What makes a class interesting?

3. In the area where you live, what do you think the average teacher **earns** in a year? The average secretary? The average doctor?
4. Complete the following sentences.

   a. A new car costs **at least** _____ dollars.

   b. I'm **at least** _____ tall.
5. Name something that people do that you think is **foolish**.
6. Most people **argue** at times. Can you tell us something you argue about and who you argue with?
7. Parents often **shout** at children. Why? Do you think it usually helps?
8. Some food, for example, a lemon, tastes **bitter**. But we also speak of bitter feelings. Name something that can cause a person to feel bitter.

X

Building Words with ness

The suffix *ness* is added to some adjectives to form a noun. For example, *dark + ness = darkness, kind + ness = kindness.*

The suffix *ness* means *the condition of being* or *the quality of being. Darkness* means *the condition of being dark, kindness* means *the quality of being kind.*

Adjective	*Noun*
bitter	bitterness
careless	carelessness
dark	darkness
foolish	foolishness
friendly	friendliness
good	goodness
great	greatness
happy	happiness
kind	kindness
serious	seriousness
sick	sickness
soft	softness
weak	weakness

Complete the sentences with these words.

happiness   **seriousness**   **weakness**   **darkness**

1. Scott often eats too much. It's a _____ of his.

2. Everyone is looking for _____ .

3. We couldn't see the house because of the _____ .

4. Does the president understand the _____ of the problem?

kindness   **sickness**   **carelessness**   **softness**

5. I like the warmth and _____ of the blanket.

6. Cancer is a _____ that we all fear.

7. It's easy to ask Elise for help because of her _____ .

8. The fire was started by the _____ of a smoker.

UNIT III
Word Review

I
In Other Words

In front of each sentence, write the word which has the same or almost the same meaning as the part of the sentence in *italics*.

aiming	**average**	**shallow**	**foolish**
earn	**at least**	**dull**	**quit**

1. _____ If we go by car, the trip will take *a minimum of* eight hours.

2. _____ The desk looks nice, but the drawers are *not deep.*

3. _____ On Friday, we *stop* work at four o'clock.

4. _____ Don is *planning* to start his own business soon.

5. _____ The show was *not interesting.*

6. _____ I was *stupid* to listen to Steve.

7. _____ Frank Sinatra isn't an *ordinary* singer. He's a superstar.

8. _____ Carpenters and plumbers *make* good money.

II
Complete the sentences with these words.

hesitant	**shouted**	**pool**	**shot**
drag	**bitter**	**dive**	**argue**

1. My sister and I often _____ about sports.

2. The police officer _____ the man in the leg.

3. Ken and Nancy are buying a _____ for their backyard.

78

4. A tree fell across the road and it took three people to _____ it away.

5. The cold war between the United States and the Soviet Union has been

long and _____ .

6. I was _____ to ask for a ride from someone I didn't know.

7. It takes a lot of practice to learn to swim and _____ well.

8. When Ralph saw that he was locked in the room, he _____ for help.

III

Complete the story with these words.

lift	**prefers**	**huge**	**spends**
stream	**hunting**	**deep**	**edge**

A Fisherman

Howard and his cousin Neil often go _____ ,

but Neil _____ to fish. Neil _____ a lot

of time fishing in a _____ that is a few miles from

his house. He sits at the _____ of the water and

waits for the fish to bite.

Neil also enjoys fishing in the ocean where the water, of

course, is _____ and the fish are larger. One day

when he was fishing in the ocean, Neil caught a _____

fish. It was so heavy that he needed help to _____

it out of the water. Neil was very proud of his big catch.

Unit Four
Newcomers from Colombia

Ten

A Struggle

Luis is from Medellín, Colombia. He came to the United States nine years **ago** and he lives in Philadelphia. He's married and has three children. Luis loves Colombia, but he wasn't able to get a good job there. That's why he came to the United States. But life in the United States has been a **struggle** for Luis. The first year was especially difficult. He didn't have any friends in Philadelphia and he **wasn't used to** the cold weather. It's never cold and it never snows in Medellín. During his second day in Philadelphia, there was a big **storm**. Twenty inches of snow fell and he couldn't go anywhere for three days.

When Luis came to the United States, he was only twenty and he didn't have many **skills**. He got a job as a **baker**. He never **baked** before, but he learned to bake by watching and working with another baker. Luis didn't know any English, but the other baker was from Argentina. They spoke Spanish. Luis worked long hours baking bread, pies, and cake. He also went to school two nights a week and learned English.

Luis worked at the **bakery** for five years, and then he started his own bakery. His business is doing very well. It's especially busy all day Saturday and Sunday morning. Today Luis has a nice car and speaks English **quite** well. He works hard and **accomplishes** a lot.

I

Answer these questions about the story.

PARAGRAPH 1

1. How long ago did Luis come to the United States?
2. Why did Luis come to the United States?
3. Has life in the United States been easy for Luis?
4. What happened the second day that he was in Philadelphia?

PARAGRAPH 2

5. How did Luis learn to bake?
6. How much English did Luis know when he came to the United States?
7. When did he go to school and why?

PARAGRAPH 3

8. What did Luis do after working at the bakery for five years?
9. When is his bakery especially busy?
10. Is Luis a hard worker?

II

MINI-DICTIONARY — PART ONE

1. **a·go** (ə-gō′) *adjective*: in the past
   Ago is placed after the noun it goes with, for example, *a minute ago.*
2. **strug·gle** (strug′əl) *noun*: hard work to get something; a fight
   verb: to work hard to get or do something
3. **be used to** (bē yo͞os to͞o or bē yo͞os′tə) *idiom*: be familiar with
4. **storm** (stôrm) *noun*: heavy rain or snow, often with strong wind

III

Complete the sentences with these words.

struggle (*noun*)   **storm**   **is used to**   **ago**

1. A _____ is coming. We may get a lot of snow.

2. Nancy moved to California six months _____ .

3. Learning English well was a _____ for Mario.

4. Paula _____ helping sick people; she's a nurse.

ago   **are used to**   **storm**   **struggling** (*verb*)

5. I ate lunch an hour _____ .

6. If this _____ continues, we're staying home tonight.

7. Dan is _____ to support his family.

8. We _____ working long hours; we often work twelve hours a day.

storm   **ago**   **struggle**   **is used to**

9. Ana is a bus driver. She _____ driving in bad weather.

10. Our new sofa came three days _____ .

11. Politics is a _____ for power.

12. I hope this _____ stops soon. I have to go shopping.

IV

MINI-DICTIONARY — PART TWO

5. **skill** (skil) *noun*: ability to do something; ability to do something well
6. a. **bake** (bāk) *verb*: to cook in an oven
   b. **baker** (bā′kər) *noun*: a person who bakes
   c. **bakery** (bāk′ə-rē or bāk′rē *noun*: a store that sells cake, pies, bread, cookies, etc.

7. **quite** (kwīt) *adverb*: to some degree; very
8. **ac·com·plish** (ə-kom′plish) *verb*: to do something; to do something well; to complete

V

Complete the sentences with these words.

baker   accomplish   skill   bakery   quite   baking

1. This room is _____ warm. I'm going to open the window.

2. Phil is a _____ . He's taking the bread out of the ovens.

3. George is _____ cookies for the party.

4. Typing is an important _____ for a secretary.

5. We'll have to work hard to _____ what we want.

6. I'm going to the _____ to buy a birthday cake.

skills   baking   accomplish   quite

7. Jennifer is _____ fish for supper.

8. Reading and writing are basic _____ .

9. Joan is _____ tall.

10. Pete talks a lot, but he doesn't _____ much.

quite   accomplished   bake   skill

11. Don is very good at fixing cars. This _____ helped him get a job at the service station.

12. Tania is _____ intelligent. She'll do well in school.

13. We _____ very little at the meeting.

14. How long will it take to _____ the potatoes?

VI

Complete the sentences with these words.

struggling	**skill**	**storm**	**accomplish**
quite	**is used to**	**baking**	**ago**

1. Gloria is _____ a cherry pie. It smells good.

2. Close the windows before you leave. We may get a _____ .

3. That stereo was _____ expensive.

4. Linda was in a bad accident. The doctors are _____ to save her life.

5. You won't _____ anything by talking to the boss. She won't change.

6. Judy travels a lot. She _____ flying.

7. Pamela and Ed visited us a week _____ .

8. A doctor needs a lot of _____ .

VII

Complete the story with these words.

skill	**storm**	**accomplish**	**baked**
quite	**are used to**	**struggle**	**ago**

Vin and Marge

Vin and Marge got married five years _____ yesterday.

They wanted to eat out, but there was a bad _____ yesterday

and they had to stay home. Vin cooked dinner and Marge _____

a cake. The dinner and the cake tasted _____ good.

Both Vin and Marge work full time and they have two young children.

Working and taking care of two small children is often a _____ .

It takes a lot of time and _____ , but they _____

it by now.

During the week, Vin and Marge have little free time so they shop,

clean the house, and visit their friends and relatives on weekends. They

_____ a lot in two days.

VIII
Word Families

1. **storm** — *noun*
   stormy — *adjective*: Look at those clouds! It's going to be a *stormy* day.
2. **skill** — *noun*
   skilled — *adjective*: Leo is a *skilled* mechanic.
   skillful — *adjective*: Janet is a *skillful* lawyer.
3. **accomplish** — *verb*
   accomplishment — *noun*: Winning the baseball championship was a great *accomplishment* for our team.

IX
Sharing Information

Discuss these questions and topics in pairs or small groups.

1. How long **ago** did you start studying English?
2. People do things differently in different countries. **Are** you **used to** the way people do things in the United States? Are you used to the weather in the United States?
3. Do you think that life is a **struggle** for everyone?
4. There are many types of **storms**, for example, snowstorms, thunderstorms, and hurricanes. Describe a bad storm that you were in, or that you read about.
5. A **skill** is an ability to do something. Cooking, driving, and sewing are skills. Name a skill that you have or wish to have.
6. In the past, people **baked** more than they do today. Why?
7. Use the word **quite** in a sentence that describes you or someone you know well, for example, "I'm quite thin."
8. Name something that you have **accomplished**, or something that you are trying to accomplish.

X

Building Words with ion

The suffix *ion* (*tion, ition, ation, sion*) is added to some verbs to form a noun. For example, *protect* + *ion* = *protection*, *add* + *ition* = *addition*.

The suffix *ion* usually means *the act of* or *the result of*. For example, *protection* means *the act of protecting* or *the result of protecting*, *addition* means *the act of adding* or *the result of adding*.

Verb	Noun
act	action
add	addition
discuss	discussion
educate	education
examine	examination
explore	exploration
hesitate	hesitation
move	motion
prepare	preparation
pronounce	pronunciation
protect	protection
separate	separation
starve	starvation

Complete the sentences with these words.

education   protection   motion   discussion

1. The store owner asked the police for better _____ .

2. Our group had an interesting _____ about marriage.

3. The _____ of the ship made me sick.

4. A good _____ will help you get a job.

examination   action   pronunciation   hesitation

5. Your _____ of English is much better now.

6. Our history _____ was long and difficult, but I think I did well.

7. It was very cold this morning, but my car started without _____ .

8. I don't think we should just talk about the problem. We must take

Eleven

_____ .

A Dream

    Luis and his wife Gloria live in a very nice apartment, but it isn't big **enough** for their family. It has only two bedrooms and they need three. They have two sons and a daughter and they want their daughter to have her own room. Their **dream** is to buy a house. They have looked at many houses that are for sale. The problem is that they don't have **enough** money for most of them. They're **searching** for a house that doesn't cost a lot and, of course, that's not easy to find.

    Yesterday they looked at four houses. One of them was an old house with **cracks** in the walls. The owners didn't take good care of it. Now they have to move to Ohio and they're in a hurry to sell. The house needs painting and many **repairs**, but it has one **advantage**. It doesn't cost too much.

    Last night Luis and Gloria talked about the house for two hours. They know that they won't find anything that costs less. **Therefore** they're going to buy it and **repair** it. The house will **require** a lot of work, but it's in a nice neighborhood and it'll look beautiful when they're finished with it. Luis and Gloria are good at painting, and some of their friends will help them with the repairs.

I

Answer these questions about the story.

PARAGRAPH 1

    1. What's the problem with Luis and Gloria's apartment?
    2. How many children do they have?
    3. What is their dream?
    4. Why can't they buy most of the houses they look at?

PARAGRAPH 2

    5. Why are the owners of the house in a hurry to sell?
    6. What does the house need?
    7. What advantage does the house have?

PARAGRAPH 3

    8. Do Luis and Gloria think they can find a house that costs less?
    9. What kind of neighborhood is the house in?
   10. Who is going to help Luis and Gloria with the repairs?

II

MINI-DICTIONARY — PART ONE

---

1. **e·nough** (i-nuf′) *adjective*: as much or as many as needed
adverb: to the amount or degree needed
When *enough* is used as an adverb, it is placed after the adjective or verb it goes with.
2. **dream** (drēm) *noun*: A. images the mind sees in sleep B. something one wants, but that is difficult or impossible to get
verb: to have a dream
The past of *dream* is *dreamt* or *dreamed*.
3. **search** (sûrch) *verb*: to look for or through something carefully
noun: the act of looking for or through something carefully
4. **crack** (krak) *noun*: a small break or separation in a wall, cup, etc.
verb: to cause a small separation in a cup, dish, etc.

III

Complete the sentences with these words.

searching (*verb*)   **enough** (*adjective*)   **crack** (*noun*)   **dream** (*noun*)

1. There's a _____ in the mirror.

2. Nick is _____ for his keys in his room.

3. Two nights ago I had a _____ and in it I won a million dollars in the lottery.

4. Do we have _____ time to stop and visit our friends?

dream (*noun*)   **search** (*noun*)   **enough** (*adverb*)   **cracked** (*verb*)

5. Many people went to Alaska in _____ of gold.

6. The water was so hot that it _____ the dish.

7. Nancy's _____ is to become a doctor.

8. Is your car big _____ for five people?

enough   **dreamt**   **crack**   **searching**

9. Grace is _____ for a job.

10. That's _____ spaghetti. I can't eat any more.

11. The workers are checking the _____ in the bridge.

12. I _____ about you last night.

IV

MINI-DICTIONARY — PART TWO

5. **re·pair** (ri-pâr′) *verb*: to put in good condition again; to fix
   noun: the act of putting in good condition again.
   Repair is often used in the plural.
6. **ad·van·tage** (ad-van′tij) *noun*: anything that helps a person or thing do or be better

7. **there·fore** (*thâr'fôr*) *adverb*: for that reason; that is why

8. **re·quire** (ri-kwī r') *verb*: A. to need B. to say something is necessary; to order

---

V

Complete the sentences with these words.

repair (*verb*)   **advantage**   **therefore**   **require**

1. Dogs are nice pets, but they _____ a lot of care.

2. A good eduction is a big _____ in life.

3. Tomorrow is a holiday. _____ we don't have to go to work.

4. They're going to _____ the road in the spring. It's in poor condition.

advantage   **repairs** (*noun*)   **requires**   **therefore**

5. I have to take my car to the service station for _____ .

6. Ken has the _____ of being a friend of the boss.

7. My wife's birthday is next week. _____ I'm buying her a gift.

8. That restaurant _____ men to wear jackets.

therefore   **requires**   **repair**   **advantage**

9. The elevator isn't working. I hope they _____ it soon.

10. The baby _____ ten or eleven hours of sleep a night.

11. The _____ of leaving early is that traffic will be light.

12. I don't feel well. _____ I'm not going to school.

VI

Complete the sentences with these words.

crack	dream	enough	therefore
require	search	repair	advantage

1. Joe is rich. _____ he can buy anything he wants.

2. Some companies _____ for oil in the ocean.

3. There is a big _____ in the sidewalk.

4. Take your watch to a jewelry store. They'll _____ it.

5. You don't have _____ experience for this job.

6. Small cars have the _____ of using less gas.

7. Parents and teachers _____ patience.

8. Paul's _____ is to be a great football player.

VII

Complete the story with these words.

therefore	enough	searching	advantages
repair	dream	require	cracks

The Old School Bus

Jack is a mechanic who works for a school system. One night he had

a _____ about the old school bus. The bus was missing and

everyone was _____ for it.

The next day Jack checked the bus. The motor didn't sound right, and

some of the seats and windows had _____ in them. Jack

feels the bus isn't safe _____ for the children. It's possible

to _____ the bus, but it will _____ a lot of

93

work and the bus will still be old. _____ Jack wants the school to buy a new one.

There are many _____ to getting a new bus. It will be bigger, cleaner, and safer. This morning Jack is going to talk to the school principal about buying a new one.

VIII
Word Families

1. **advantage** — *noun*
    advantageous — *adjective*: Our army was in an *advantageous* position when the enemy attacked.
    take advantage of — *idiom*: We should *take advantage of* this nice weather and go for a walk.
2. **require** — *verb*
    requirement — *noun*: A college education is a *requirement* for some jobs.

IX
Sharing Information

Discuss these questions and topics in pairs or small groups.

1. Do you have **enough** space in the apartment or house in which you live?
2. We all have **dreams** or hopes for the future. Name a dream or hope that you have.
3. Complete the sentence that begins with **therefore**. "Don feels very

    sick. Therefore, he _____ ."
4. When people lose something that is valuable, they **search** for it. Name something that you lost and searched for. Where did you search? Did you find it?
5. Sometimes we see **cracks** in windows. What can cause cracks in a window?
6. Are you good at making small **repairs** in your house or apartment?
7. Many people leave their family, friends, and country to live in the United States. They must have a good reason for doing something that is so difficult. What are some of the **advantages** of living in the United States?
8. Name four things that your body **requires**.

X

Building Words with dis

The prefix *dis* is placed before some nouns, verbs, and adjectives to form a new word. For example, *dis + honest = dishonest, dis + appear = disappear.*

The prefix *dis* means *not* or *the opposite of.* For example, *honest* means *not honest, disappear* means *the opposite of appear.*

Original Word	New word
advantage	disadvantage
appear	disappear
continue	discontinue
courage	discourage
honest	dishonest
like	dislike
obey	disobey
order	disorder
please	displease
repair	disrepair
respect	disrespect
satisfied	dissatisfied
trust	distrust

Complete the sentences with these words.

disrespect   dishonest   discontinue   disappeared

1. If we don't pay our phone bill soon, they'll _____ our service.

2. Sally doesn't like her teacher, but she never shows any _____.

3. My wallet _____. I can't find it anywhere.

4. We don't trust George. We think he's _____.

disadvantages   disrepair   disobeys   dissatisfied

5. The building is old and in _____.

6. There are many _____ to being poor.

7. I'm going to go to another dentist. I'm _____ with the one I have.

8. Dan gets into a lot of trouble at home because he _____ his parents.

95

Twelve

A Visit

Last Friday night Luis and Gloria went to visit some friends from Colombia. They're from the city of Medellín and they went to school with Gloria. Luis had worked hard all day and he was **weary**. He wanted to stay home and sleep, but Gloria had told their friends they were coming. Therefore he couldn't stay home. Luis was happy when his friends offered him some coffee at their place. He drank two cups of black coffee, but he could **hardly** keep his eyes open.

While Luis and Gloria were in the living room with their friends, Luis **fell asleep**. Gloria was sitting next to him on the sofa. She **pinched** his arm, but it didn't help. She pinched him again. This time he **woke up**. Luis drank another cup of coffee and opened a window for some air. He was fine for a **while** and then he fell asleep again and began to snore.* When Luis snores, he makes a lot of noise.

Gloria felt **ashamed**. She was ashamed of Luis' snoring and she was angry at him. This was the first time they were visiting their friends since they came to the United States three months ago. However, the snoring didn't **disturb** their friends. They smiled and told Gloria to let him sleep. They knew how hard he works.

Snore means to make noise through one's nose and mouth while sleeping.

I

Answer these questions about the story.

PARAGRAPH 1

1. Where did Luis and Gloria go last Friday?
2. Why did Luis want to stay home?
3. What did he drink at his friends' house?

PARAGRAPH 2

4. Where was Luis when he fell asleep?
5. What did Gloria do when she saw that he was sleeping?
6. After Luis woke up, what did he do to keep from going to sleep again?
7. What did Luis do when he fell asleep the second time?

PARAGRAPH 3

8. How did Gloria feel about Luis' snoring?
9. When had their friends come to the United States?
10. Did Luis' snoring disturb their friends?

II

MINI-DICTIONARY — PART ONE

1. **wea·ry** (wir'ē) *adjective*: very tired
2. **hard·ly** (härd'lē) *adverb*: only a little, with difficulty
3. **while** (wīl or hwīl) *conjunction*: during the time that
   noun: a period of time, especially a short period of time
4. **fall a·sleep** (fôl ə-slēp') *idiom*: begin to sleep
   The past of *fall* is *fell*.

III
Complete the sentences with these words.

while (*conjunction*)   **weary**   **fall asleep**   **hardly**

1. I watch the ten o'clock news every night, but sometimes I _____ during it.

2. The basketball team has been practicing for three hours and the players are _____.

3. Speak louder, please. We can _____ hear you.

4. I read a magazine _____ I was waiting for the dentist.

hardly   **fell asleep**   **while** (*noun*)   **weary**

5. Supper will be ready in a little _____.

6. It's _____ raining. I'm not going to wear a raincoat.

7. By the end of the day, we were _____.

8. Ralph went to bed and _____ immediately. He was very tired.

weary   **while**   **hardly**   **fall asleep**

9. Barbara drank a cup of coffee before the meeting so she wouldn't _____.

10. _____ Ray was watching the game, someone took his bicycle.

11. The battle lasted for three days and the soldiers were _____.

12. My neighbor wanted to borrow my car, but I didn't let him. I _____ know him.

98

IV

MINI-DICTIONARY — PART TWO

5. **pinch** (pinch) *verb*: to press hard between the thumb and another finger
   noun: the act of pinching
6. **wake up** (wāk up) *verb*: A. to stop sleeping B. to cause a person to stop sleeping
   The past of *wake up* is *woke up*.
7. **shame** (shām) *noun*: an unpleasant feeling that comes from doing something wrong or foolish
   a·shamed (ə-shāmd´) *adjective*: feeling shame
8. **dis·turb** (dis-tûrb´) *verb*: to take away a person's peace or quiet

V

Complete the sentences with these words.

ashamed   **pinch** (*verb*)   **wake up**   **disturbing**

1. The baby likes to _____ his mother's neck and face.

2. Al is _____ of getting drunk at the party.

3. Please turn down the music. I'm trying to study and it's _____ me.

4. _____ ! It's late!

woke up   **ashamed**   **disturb**   **pinch** (*noun*)

5. That _____ hurt. Stop it!

6. Doug is writing an important letter. Don't _____ him.

7. The alarm clock _____ Ralph and Sue.

8. You should be _____ of stealing that radio from the store.

pinched	disturb	ashamed	woke up

9. Kathy felt _____ when she forgot her father's birthday.

10. Will it _____ you if I smoke?

11. Tim _____ at six o'clock.

12. Dan didn't like it when I _____ his side.

VI

Complete the sentences with these words.

while (*conjunction*)	pinched	wake up	hardly	
fell asleep	weary	while (*noun*)	disturb	ashamed

1. The little boy _____ his brother's ear.

2. Don't _____ the dog while he's eating.

3. Steve worked twelve hours today and he's _____.

4. You should be _____ of talking that way to your mother.

5. _____ Ted was washing his car, he was thinking about his girlfriend.

6. Linda hurt her leg. She can _____ walk.

7. The movie wasn't interesting; I _____ in the middle of it.

8. What time did you _____ this morning?

9. You drive. I want to rest a _____.

VII

Complete the story with these words.

disturbs	**pinch**	**weary**	**falls asleep**
hardly	**while**	**wakes up**	**ashamed**

A Dull Teacher

Dora works during the day and goes to college at night. Her English teacher is dull; he never changes his tone of voice. At the beginning of class Dora is fine, but after a _____ she feels tired and sometimes she _____ . The teacher doesn't say anything, but her sleeping really _____ him.

Dora isn't _____ of going to sleep in class, but she is afraid of getting a poor mark, so she has asked a friend who sits behind her to _____ her when she goes to sleep. This _____ Dora, but she's still so _____ that she can _____ stay awake.

VIII

Word Families

1. **weary** — *adjective*
   weariness — *noun*: If you get more rest, your *weariness* will go away.
2. **fall asleep** — *idiom*
   asleep — *adjective*: The children are in bed, but they aren't *asleep*. I can hear them talking.
3. **wake up** — *verb*
   awake — *adjective*: It's one o'clock in the morning, but Phil is still *awake*.
4. **disturb** — *verb*
   disturbance — *noun*: There was a *disturbance* at the dance and we had to call the police.

IX

Sharing Information

Discuss the following questions and topics in pairs or small groups.

1. Long physical or mental activity can make a person feel **weary**. Is there anything you do for a long time which makes you feel weary?
2. A **while** usually means a short period of time, but it can also mean a long period of time. Name something that you haven't done, or a person you haven't seen, in a long while.
3. Think of something that you can do only with great difficulty, or that you can do only a little bit. Then complete this sentence. I can

   hardly _____.
4. Do you ever **fall asleep** in class, or when visiting friends, or when watching TV? Is it easy for you to fall asleep at night?
5. Sometimes people give a child a little **pinch** on the cheek to express their love or affection for the child. Do you think children like this?
6. What time do you usually **wake up** in the morning? Who or what wakes you up?
7. Being corrected in public will usually make a person feel **ashamed**. Give an example of another situation that will usually make a person feel ashamed.
8. Give an example of something that **disturbs** you, something that another person does and that you don't like.

X

Building Words with ance *or* ence

The suffix *ance* or *ence* is added to some adjectives and verbs to form a noun. For example, *accept + ance = acceptance*, *clear + ance = clearance*. Words that already end in *ant* or *ent* drop the final *t* and add only *ce*. For example, *intelligent* drops its final *t* and adds *ce* to form *intelligence*.

When *ance* or *ence* is added to a verb, it means *the act of* or *the result of*, for example, *acceptance* means *the act of accepting* or *the result of accepting*.

When *ance* or *ence* is added to an adjective, it means *the quality of being*, for example, *intelligence* means *the quality of being intelligent*.

Adjective or Verb	Noun
accept	acceptance
appear	appearance
assist	assistance
clear	clearance
different	difference
disturb	disturbance
enter	entrance
excellent	excellence
important	importance
independent	independence
intelligent	intelligence
obedient	obedience
silent	silence

Complete the sentences with these words.

intelligence   acceptance   independence   importance

1. The United States celebrates its _____ on July 4th.

2. We need a lawyer with a lot of skill and _____ .

3. Everyone knows the _____ of good health.

4. Glenda is waiting for a letter of _____ from the college she wants to attend.

obedience   clearance   assistance   difference

5. There's a big _____ between the weather in New York and in Florida.

6. They're having a _____ sale at the furniture store.

7. I want to thank you for your _____ at the party.

8. In the army, _____ is very important. You must follow orders.

UNIT IV
Word Review

I
In Other Words

In front of each sentence, write the word which has the same or almost the same meaning as the part of the sentence in italics.

baking	**storm**	**required**	**weary**
accomplish	**while**	**searching**	**therefore**

1. _____ Tony has two jobs. When he finishes his second job, he's *very tired.*

2. _____ We're going to get a *lot of wind and rain* tonight.

3. _____ Betty is *looking* for the money she lost.

4. _____ John and I didn't *do* much today.

5. _____ The bank *needed* more information before they gave me a loan.

6. _____ It was cloudy and cool on Saturday. *That's why* we didn't go to the beach.

7. _____ Ed is *cooking* the beans in the oven.

8. _____ It takes a little *time* for the car to warm up.

II
Complete the sentences with these words.

skill	**disturbs**	**wake up**	**crack**
fell asleep	**advantage**	**ashamed**	**pinched**

1. The children have to _____ soon, or they'll be late for school.

2. Both Greg and Don are very good carpenters, but Don has more experience and _____ than Greg.

3. I _____ myself to keep from laughing at the man.

104

4. Marilyn speaks French well; that will give her a great _____ when she visits Paris.

5. Jane should be _____ of lying to her parents.

6. There is a _____ in the lamp that fell on the floor.

7. It _____ Jenny when they have noisy parties in the apartment above her.

8. Henry _____ while driving. His car went off the road. But, fortunately, it didn't hit anything.

III
Complete the story with these words.

repairing	**while**	**enough**	**dream**	**ago**
quite	**hardly**	**struggle**	**was used to**	

A Hard Worker

Andrew was born thirty years _____ in eastern Poland. He was the oldest of three children and his father was a coal miner. His father worked hard but was paid very little. The family was _____ poor.

Andrew's _____ was to go to the United States. He could _____ speak English, but he was very good at _____ cars and he _____ hard work.

Andrew was very happy when he got his visa and left for the United States. However, finding a job in the United States was a _____. The biggest problem was that he didn't know _____ English. He worked in a factory _____ looking for a job as an auto mechanic. After a few months, he got a job at a service station and he's doing very well now.

Unit Five
Newcomers from Italy

Thirteen

A Soccer Fan

Mario lives in Chicago and he comes from Italy. He's married and has one child. Mario is a soccer* **fan** and player. When he came to the United States five years ago, he didn't know that soccer was a popular sport here. He was **amazed** when he learned that there were many soccer teams in the United States.

One Sunday afternoon, he was taking a walk and he **discovered** two teams playing soccer in a park near his house. He watched the game. When it was over, he talked to some of the players. They were from many countries. One of the teams needed another player and Mario **joined** the team. Now he's one of their best players. His son Sal is also learning how to play soccer. He's only six years old, but he can kick the ball well. His ability to play soccer amazes people. He can't wait until he's old enough to play on a team at his school.

Last week Mario and his wife Connie were visiting her cousins, who live in New Jersey, and they all went to see a soccer game. There was a large **crowd** at the game. The stadium was almost full. Mario and Connie **cheered** when their team played well. It was an

exciting game. Their team **scored** with only one minute left to play and won the game by a **score** of three to two.

*Soccer is a game in which one team tries to move the ball into the goal behind the other team. This game is called *futbol* in many countries.

I

Answer these questions about the story.

PARAGRAPH 1

1. Where does Mario come from?
2. How many children does he have?
3. What sport does he like?
4. Did he know that many people in the United States play soccer?

PARAGRAPH 2

5. What did Mario discover on his walk?
6. Is he a good soccer player?
7. Why doesn't Mario's son Sal play soccer for his school team?

PARAGRAPH 3

8. Were there many fans at the soccer game Mario and Connie went to see?
9. What did Mario and Connie do when their team played well?
10. What was the final score of the game?

II

MINI-DICTIONARY — PART ONE

1. **fan** (fan) *noun*: someone who has great interest in a sport or a famous person*
2. **a·maze** (ə-māz′) *verb*: to surprise very much
3. **dis·cov·er** (dis-kuv′ər) *verb*: to find or come to know something not known before
4. **join** (join) *verb*: A. to become a member of a group
   B. to unite; to come together

*A fan is also *an instrument to make air move so it will feel cool. In the summer, we put a fan in our living room.*

III

Complete the sentences with these words.

     amazes   **join**   **fan**   **discover**

1. Ann is going to _____ the army next week.

2. Columbus wanted to _____ a shorter way to go to India.

3. The little girl _____ me. She speaks so well and so clearly.

4. My daughter is a tennis _____ .

     fan   **amazed**   **discovered**   **joined**

5. The dancers _____ their hands.

6. The astronauts were _____ at what they saw when they landed on the moon.

7. Many people went to California after explorers _____ gold there.

8. My sister is a big _____ of Bruce Springsteen, the famous singer.

     discovered   **fan**   **join**   **amazed**

9. Come in and _____ the party.

10. I was angry when I _____ that someone took my money.

11. Dick is a basketball _____ . He goes to all the games he can.

12. Sue _____ her teacher by getting a hundred on the test.

IV

MINI-DICTIONARY — PART TWO

---

5. **crowd** (kroud) *noun*: many people in one place
6. **cheer** (chēr) *verb*: to shout and clap in support of a team or person
   noun: shouting and clapping for a team or person
7. **ex·cit·ing** (ik-sī ′tǐng) *adjective*: causing strong feelings
8. **score** (skôr) *verb*: make one or more points in a game
   noun: A. the number of points each team has in a game B. the number of points a person receives on a test

---

V

Complete the sentences with these words.

exciting   **crowd**   **scores** (*verb*)   **cheering** (*verb*)

1. Ken is the best basketball player on the team. He _____ at least fifteen points a game.

2. The book was so _____ that I couldn't stop reading it.

3. The president is going by in his car and everyone is _____ .

4. The _____ is waiting for the theater to open.

   score (*noun*)   **exciting**   **cheer** (*noun*)   **crowd**

5. *The Godfather* was a very _____ movie. Everyone liked it.

6. The _____ of the baseball game was five to three.

7. The police are trying to control the _____ , but they are having trouble.

8. A _____ went up from the fans when Muhammad Ali climbed into the boxing ring.

crowd	cheered	exciting	score

9. My trip to Africa was _____.

10. Toshio got a high _____ on his test.

11. We _____ when our team won the game.

12. It was a rainy day, so the _____ at the parade was small.

VI

Complete the sentences with these words.

score	discover	cheered	crowd
exciting	join	amazed	fan

1. The people _____ the soldiers when they returned from the war.

2. Al decided to _____ our club.

3. The story was very _____ . Everyone was listening carefully to it.

4. Dan is a baseball _____ . He doesn't play much, but he goes to many games.

5. We're trying to _____ a good restaurant for the party.

6. Lisa's knowledge of history _____ us.

7. Who won the game and what was the _____?

8. A large _____ was waiting to hear the Beatles sing.

VII

Complete the story with these words.

cheered	**scored**	**fan**	**exciting**
discovered	**joined**	**crowd**	**amazed**

A Good Football Player

Doug goes to George Washington High School. He's a football*

_____ and he watches many of the games on TV. He likes

to play too, and he _____ the high school team at the

beginning of September. The coach and the team soon _____

that Doug is very fast and now he plays every game.

On Saturday, Doug's team played an important game against Lincoln

High School. There was a big _____ at the game and the

fans _____ when the teams ran onto the field. Both teams

thought that the game would be _____ and very close, but

Doug's team _____ everyone when they won easily. Doug

_____ twelve points for his team.

*Football is a popular American game. American football is very different from soccer which is called
  futbol in other countries.

VIII

Word Families

1. **amaze** — *verb*
     amazing — *adjective*: Computers work with *amazing* speed.
     amazement — *noun*: You can imagine our *amazement* when the
             man got up and started dancing.
2. **cheer** — *verb* and *noun*
     cheerful — *adjective*: Ed is a *cheerful* person. He's always happy.
     cheerfully — *adverb*: It's spring and the birds are singing *cheer-
             fully*.
     cheerfulness — *noun*: The *cheerfulness* of the nurses helps the
             patients.

113

3. **crowd** — *noun*

    crowded — *adjective*: The store is *crowded* because of the big sale.

4. **discover** — *verb*

    discovery — *noun*: The *discovery* of oil helped the economy of Mexico.

5. **exciting** — *adjective*

    excite — *verb*: The wedding of the prince *excited* our interest.

    excited — *adjective*: The children get *excited* when they play.

    excitement — *noun*: It's a quiet town with very little *excitement*.

6. **join** — *verb*

    joint — *adjective*: My wife and I have a *joint* checking account.

IX

Sharing Information

Discuss these questions and topics in pairs or small groups.

1. Are you a sports **fan**? If so, what sport or sports do you like?
2. When we travel to a new country, we are frequently **amazed** by some of the things or activities we see because these things or activities are different from what we have or do in our first country. Did anything in a new country amaze you when you first saw it?
3. **Discover** often means *to find new information about a thing or person we already know*, for example, "Ed *discovered* that his friend was rich." Talk about something you discovered about a person or a thing you already knew.
4. Did you ever **join** a team or club? If so, what team or club did you join?
5. It is safe to be in some **crowds**, for example, a crowd watching a game or a parade. However, other crowds are dangerous. Give an example of a dangerous crowd.
6. Football and basketball teams in the United States often have cheerleaders, young women or men who lead **cheers** at their games to create excitement. Have you ever seen cheerleaders? If so, where? Do teams in your country have cheerleaders?
7. Can you talk about something that you saw or did recently, or something that happened to you that was **exciting**?
8. In different sports, there are different names for the points a player or team **scores**, for example, players score *goals* in soccer. In what sport do players score *runs*? In what sport do players score *touchdowns*?

X
Building Words with re

The prefix *re* is placed before some verbs to form a new verb. For example, *re* + *write* = *rewrite*, *re* + *visit* = *revisit*.

The prefix *re* means *again*. *Rewrite* means *to write again*, *revisit* means *to visit again*.

Verb	New verb
build	rebuild
consider	reconsider
discover	rediscover
do	redo
enter	reenter
join	rejoin
marry	remarry
name	rename
open	reopen
produce	reproduce
read	reread
visit	revisit
write	rewrite

Complete the sentences with these words.

rewrite   reopen   rename   remarry

1. The store is closed, but it'll _____ in the morning.

2. Gloria's husband died two years ago and she's going to _____ soon.

3. They decided to _____ the airport in honor of President Kennedy.

4. There are many errors in my letter. I'm going to _____ it.

rebuild   reread   revisit   rejoin

5. We weren't able to spend much time at the museum. We're going

   to _____ it tomorrow.

6. The fire completely destroyed the school, but they're going to

   _____ it.

7. Why don't you _____ the club? Everyone wants you to come back?

8. If you don't understand the story, you should _____ it.

Fourteen

An Accident

Connie loves to drive. She's a **cautious** driver and never drives too fast. However, she had an accident while she was driving home from the soccer game with Mario and her cousins. Everyone was talking about the game. Connie stopped at a red light. **Suddenly** a tan Buick **crashed** into the back of their car. The driver of the Buick had been drinking. He was driving sixty miles an hour when he **attempted** to stop, but it was too late.

Connie got out of her car and asked for the man's license and registration, and gave him her license and registration at the same time. While Connie was talking to the driver of the Buick, one of her cousins called the police. The police were there in two minutes. They asked how the accident happened and they quickly discovered that the other driver had been drinking. He could hardly walk or talk. The accident was clearly his **fault**. The police wrote a report of the accident and took the other driver away in the police car. He was too drunk to drive.

Fortunately, no one was hurt in the accident and no one can **blame** Connie for it. The other man's insurance company will have to pay for the **damage** to Connie and Mario's car. The back of their car was badly **damaged**. It will cost at least a thousand dollars to repair it. The damage to the Buick was **slight** since it was bigger and heavier than Connie's car.

I

Answer these questions about the story.

PARAGRAPH 1

1. Is Connie a careful driver?
2. What happened on the way home from the soccer game?
3. What type of car hit Connie's car?
4. How fast was the other driver going?

PARAGRAPH 2

5. What did Connie ask for from the other driver?
6. What did Connie's cousin do while she was talking to the other driver?
7. What did the police discover about the other driver?

PARAGRAPH 3

8. Was anyone hurt in the accident?
9. Who is going to pay for the damage to Connie and Mario's car?
10. Was the Buick badly damaged?

II

MINI-DICTIONARY — PART TWO

1. **cau·tious** (kô′shəs) *adjective*: very careful
2. **sud·den·ly** (sud′ən-lē) *adverb*: happening quickly
3. **crash** (krash) *verb*: to hit with great force, especially in an accident
   noun: a violent accident in a car, plane, or train
4. **at·tempt** (ə-tempt′) *verb*: to try; to make an effort
   noun: the act of trying

III

Complete the sentences with these words.

cautious   **crashed** (*verb*)   **attempting** (*verb*)   **suddenly**

1. The truck stopped _____ and we almost hit it.

2. Joan is a _____ person. She always thinks before she acts.

3. Sonia is _____ to sell her old car for six hundred dollars.

4. The bus _____ into a street light.

attempt (*noun*)   **cautious**   **suddenly**   **crash** (*noun*)

5. Larry felt sick _____ and had to leave the room.

6. Pete wasn't able to run the mile in four minutes, but he made a

   good _____ .

7. Five people were killed in the train _____ .

8. My doctor was very _____ . He checked everything.

suddenly   **attempted**   **crashed**   **cautious**

9. They _____ to complete the highway by June 1, but it was impossible.

10. Police officers have to act quickly, but they also have to be _____ .

11. _____ the lights in our house went out.

12. The baseball player _____ into the fence as he tried to catch the ball.

IV

MINI-DICTIONARY — PART TWO

5. **fault** (fôlt) *noun*: A. responsibility for something bad
   B. defect in a person or thing
6. **blame** (blām) *verb*: to hold someone responsible for something bad

noun: responsibility for something bad (*blame* is frequently used in the expression *be to blame*)
7. **dam·age** (dam'ij) *verb*: to make something less valuable; to harm
   noun: loss of value; harm
8. **slight** (slīt) *adjective*: small; not serious

V

Complete the sentences with these words.

blame (*verb*)   **fault**   **slight**   **damage** (*verb*)

1. Andy has a _____ cold. He'll be fine in a day or two.

2. The heavy wind and rain may _____ the trees.

3. It's my own _____ that I did poorly on the exam. I didn't study.

4. The food at the restaurant didn't taste good; I _____ the cook.

slight   **blame** (*noun*)   **damage** (*noun*)   **faults**

5. Paul is to _____ for the accident. He went through a red light.

6. Kim speaks English well, but she has a _____ accent.

7. Jane is a wonderful person, but she has her _____. No one is perfect.

8. The war did a lot of _____ to our country.

fault   **damaged**   **slight**   **blame**

9. We have to make some _____ changes in our plans.

10. Ralph was late for work, but it wasn't his _____. He had trouble with his car.

11. I _____ myself for everything you have suffered recently.

12. The fire _____ the whole building.

VI

Complete the sentences with these words.

fault	suddenly	cautious	attempted
damaging	blaming	slight	crashed

1. The plane lost power and _____ into the side of the mountain.

2. Pete was going to stay home, but he _____ decided to come with us.

3. I think the waiter made a _____ error in our bill.

4. Tim's lazy. It's his own _____ that he doesn't have a job.

5. Nancy is a _____ lawyer. She tries not to make any mistakes.

6. Why are they _____ me? I didn't do anything wrong.

7. The new store is _____ our business. It sells the same things we do.

8. Two men _____ to escape from jail.

VII

Complete the story with these words.

cautious	crashed	slight	damaged
attempted	blame	suddenly	fault

A Car Hits a Bus

It was raining when the bus left the station and the streets were wet.

The bus was going down a busy street when a car _____

to pass it. _____ the driver lost control of his car and

_____ into the side of the bus. The accident was not the bus

driver's _____ . The driver of the car was to _____ .

He should have been more _____ .

Fortunately all the people on the bus were okay. However, the car was

badly _____ and the driver had a _____

cut on his face.

VIII
Word Families

1. **cautious** — *adjective*
   caution — *noun*: They removed the bomb from the building with
         great *caution*.
   cautiously — *adverb*: Dan spends his money *cautiously*.
2. **suddenly** — *adverb*
   sudden — *adjective*: A *sudden* storm hit the west coast.
3. **fault** — *noun*
   faulty — *adjective*: *Faulty* wiring caused the fire.
4. **blame** — *verb and noun*
   blameless — *adjective*: The police made a mistake when they ar-
         rested Joe. He was *blameless*.
5. **slight** — *adjective*
   slightly — *adverb*: It's *slightly* warmer today.

IX
Sharing Information

Discuss these questions and topics in pairs or small groups.

1. In general, do you think that you are a **cautious** person? If you drive,
   are you a cautious driver?
2. Talk about something that you did **suddenly**, or something that happened to you suddenly.
3. Many people don't like to fly because they're afraid of plane **crashes**.
   When you get on a plane, do you worry about a crash? A little? A lot?
   Not at all?
4. Complete one of the following sentences.

   a. I **attempted** to _____ , but it wasn't possible.

   b. I **attempted** to _____ , and I was able to do it.
5. Were you ever in an automobile accident? If so, describe the accident
   and decide whose **fault** it was.

6. When something bad happens to us, we **blame** another person, or ourselves, or we may blame no one. Give an example of something bad that happened to you, and tell us if you blame another person, or yourself, or no one.

7. Fires, storms, accidents, and wars cause **damage**. Describe the damage done by a situation that you were in, or that you read about.

8. Everyone has problems. Some of our problems are big; some are **slight**. Give an example of a slight problem that you have, or that a friend of yours has.

X

Building Words with ous

The suffix *ous* is added to some nouns and verbs to form an adjective. For example, *fame + ous = famous, space + ous = spacious, religion + ous = religious.*

The suffix *ous* usually means *having, having a lot of,* or *having to do with. Famous* means *having fame, spacious* means *having a lot of space, religious* means *having to do with religion.*

Noun or Verb	*Adjective*
advantage	advantageous
caution	cautious
continue	continuous
fame	famous
joy	joyous
mountain	mountainous
mystery	mysterious
nerve	nervous
number	numerous
poison	poisonous
religion	religious
space	spacious
study	studious

Complete the sentences with these words.

numerous   **poisonous**   **joyous**   **studious**

1. Weddings are _____ occasions that bring two lives together.

2. I know Dallas very well. I have made _____ trips there.

123

3. Toshio is always in the library with his nose in a book.

   He's _____.

4. Be careful! I think that snake is _____!

   nervous   mysterious   famous   spacious

5. That's _____. My book was here a minute ago and now I don't see it.

6. Mike gets _____ about going to the doctor, so he never goes.

7. What a _____ room this is! You can put a lot in it.

8. Everyone knows about Babe Ruth. He was a _____ baseball player.

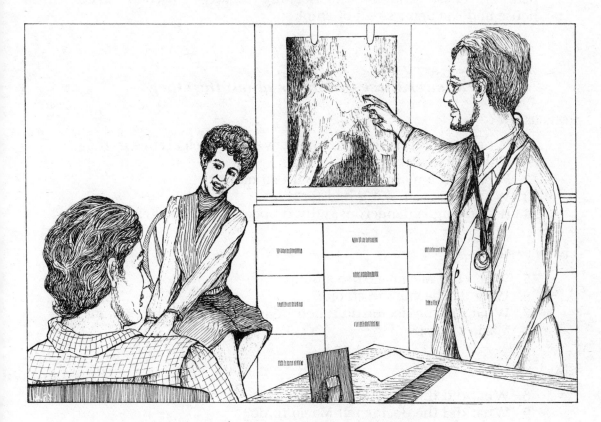

Fifteen

Two Packs a Day

Smoking is a bad habit and everyone knows it. There is a **warning** on the side of every pack of cigarettes and on all cigarette ads in the United States. It says that smoking is **dangerous** to your health. The **main** problem, of course, is that smoking can cause cancer of the lungs, but it's also bad for your heart. Although it's foolish to smoke, many people still do it. They enjoy it and find it difficult to quit.

Mario **used to** smoke two packs of cigarettes a day. He started to smoke when he was in high school. It made him feel like an adult. A month ago, he had a **pain** in his chest. The pain wasn't too bad. He thought it would go away, but it didn't. He told Connie about the pain and they both began to **worry**. Mario called the doctor. The doctor sent him to the hospital **right away** for a chest x-ray.

The doctor received the x-ray report from the hospital and examined Mario. He was fine, but the doctor **warned** him to stop smoking. Mario and Connie were very happy about the report. They were afraid that they were going to get bad news. Mario

125

stopped smoking. Now he chews gum **instead**. He feels much better. He doesn't cough in the morning the way he used to and his house and car don't smell of smoke.

I

Answer these questions about the story.

PARAGRAPH 1

1. What warning is written on every pack of cigarettes in the United States?
2. What is the main problem with smoking?
3. What else is smoking bad for?
4. If smoking is dangerous, why do people still smoke?

PARAGRAPH 2

5. When did Mario start to smoke?
6. Why did he start to smoke?
7. What did the doctor do when he learned about the pain in Mario's chest?

PARAGRAPH 3

8. What did the x-ray and the doctor's exam show?
9. What did the doctor tell Mario to do?
10. What does he do instead of smoking?

II

MINI-DICTIONARY — PART ONE

1. a. **warn** (wôrn) *verb*: to say something is not safe or may cause a problem
   b. **warn·ing** (wôr'ning) *noun*: the act of saying that something is not safe or may cause a problem
2. **dan·ger·ous** (dan'jər-əs) *adjective*: not safe; able or likely to do damage
3. **main** (mān) *adjective*: first in importance or size
4. **used to** (yo͞os to͞o or yo͞os'tə) *idiom*: to have done or been something regularly in the past

III

Complete the sentences with these words.

used to   **warn**   **main**   **dangerous**   **warning**

1. It's _____ to drive so fast. Please slow down!

2. _____ the children not to play in the street.

3. Hisako _____ live in Japan. Now she lives in San Francisco.

4. We heard on the radio that there is a storm _____ in effect. We're staying home.

5. What is the _____ idea of the chapter?

main   **used to**   **dangerous**   **warned**

6. Texas _____ be part of Mexico.

7. The waiter _____ me that the plate was very hot.

8. In the United States, most people eat their _____ meal at night.

9. Ellen's job is _____ . She's a firefighter.

warned   **main**   **used to**   **dangerous**

10. I _____ play the piano.

11. The teacher _____ us that the test would be hard.

12. The road is _____ . It has many curves.

13. The clothing department is on the _____ floor.

IV

MINI-DICTIONARY — PART TWO

5. **pain** (pān) *noun*: very unpleasant feeling; suffering
6. **wor·ry** (wûr'ē) *verb*: A. to think and be anxious
   B. to cause to think and be anxious
   noun: feeling of anxiety; what causes a person to feel anxious
7. **right a·way** (rīt ə-wā') *adverb*: immediately; now
8. **in·stead** (in-sted') *adverb*: in place of

V

Complete the sentences with these words.

right away   **pain**   **instead**   **worrying** (*verb*)

1. We wanted to go swimming, but it was too cold. So, we went for a

   walk _____ .

2. The ambulance came _____ . We didn't have to wait long.

3. Carmen is always _____ about losing her job. The store where she works may close.

4. The _____ in my arm is bad. I'm going to see a doctor.

   instead   **right away**   **worry** (*verb*)   **pain**

5. Paul is a very busy person, but he answered my letter _____ .

6. I don't like potatoes. Can I have rice _____ ?

7. Take two aspirins and the _____ will go away.

8. These big bills _____ me.

worries (*noun*)   instead   pain   right away

9. I have a _____ in my back.

10. The movie is going to start _____ .

11. When we play tennis, we forget our _____ .
12. Jim and Ann were going to play cards, but they watched TV

_____ .

VI

Complete the sentences with these words.

warned	main	right away	dangerous
worry	instead	used to	pain

1. Do you need help _____ or can I help you later?

2. The _____ in my knee is so bad that I can't walk.

3. Don't _____ about Gloria. She can take care of
   herself.

4. It _____ cost three cents to mail a letter, but now it
   costs much more.

5. The city has three libraries. The _____ library is in
   the center of the city.

6. That dog is _____ . He bites.
7. The president of the company couldn't go to the meeting; she sent the

   vice-president _____ .

8. Barbara _____ her sister not to walk in the park late
   at night.

VII

Complete the story with these words.

main	instead	warned	pain
used to	worry	right away	dangerous

A Young Boxer

Tony Lanza _____ be a boxer. He was one of the best young boxers in the state, but his parents didn't want him to box. They _____ him to quit before he got hurt. He knew that boxing was _____ , but he told his parents not to _____ . He was strong and healthy.

One night, Tony was fighting against a bigger and faster boxer. It was the _____ fight of the evening and an important fight for both boxers. Late in the fight, Tony got a bad cut over his eye. The cut was deep and the _____ was terrible. Tony couldn't see out of his eye. They stopped the fight _____ .

Tony had planned to go to a victory party after the fight, but they had to take him to the hospital _____ . The doctors saved Tony's eye, but he's not going to box any more.

VIII

Word Families

1. **dangerous** — *adjective*
   danger — *noun*: If you put your money in the bank, there is very little *danger* of losing it.
   dangerously — *adverb*: That car came *dangerously* close to us.
2. **main** — *adjective*
   mainly — *adverb*: I like all kinds of music, but I *mainly* listen to jazz.

3. **pain** — *noun*

      painful — *adjective*: Joy's sunburn is very *painful*.
      painless — *adjective*: The tests I had in the hospital were *painless*.
                  I was fortunate.

4. **instead** — *adverb*

      instead of — *preposition*: It was very hot, so I drank soda *instead of* coffee.

IX

Sharing Information

Discuss these questions and topics in pairs or small groups.

1. Some sports are **dangerous**. Others are not. Name three sports that are dangerous and three that aren't.
2. What is your favorite drink? If you can't get your favorite drink, or want a change, what do you drink **instead**?
3. Name some reasons why you are studying English. What is your **main** reason for studying English?
4. When we think of **pain**, we usually think of physical pain, but pain can also be mental or emotional. Name some things that cause mental or emotional pain.
5. When it's time for you to get up in the morning, do you get up **right away** or do you stay in bed a while?

6. Complete the following sentence. I **used to** _____ , but I don't now.
7. Every pack of cigarettes and all cigarette ads **warn** people not to smoke. Why is it that so many people continue to smoke and do not pay attention to the **warning**?

8. Complete the following sentence. Sometimes I **worry** about _____ .

X

Building Words with ing

    The suffix *ing* is added to some verbs to form a noun. For example, *run + ing = running, read + ing = reading, swim + ing = swimming*.

    The suffix *ing* usually means *the action of*. For example, *running* means *the action of running*, *reading* means *the action of reading*, *swimming* means *the action of swimming*.

Verb	Noun
begin	beginning
farm	farming
feel	feeling
hear	hearing
hunt	hunting
meet	meeting
read	reading
run	running
suffer	suffering
swim	swimming
understand	understanding
warn	warning
write	writing

Complete the sentences with these words.

hearing   farming   beginning   understanding

1. Pete moved from the country to the city. He didn't like _____.

2. Joan has a clear _____ of the problem and she has a plan to solve it.

3. You'll have to speak louder. My _____ is poor.

4. The _____ of the play is very interesting.

reading   meeting   feeling   swimming

5. I have a _____ that it's going to rain.

6. _____ is the most important skill children learn when they start school.

7. _____ is good exercise and fun.

8. We talked about our plans for three hours. It was a long _____.

132

UNIT V
Word Review

I

In Other Words

In front of each sentence, write the word which has the same or almost the same meaning as the part of the sentence in *italics*.

slight	cheered	attempting	main
crowd	suddenly	amazed	cautious

1. _____ When I buy things that cost a lot, I'm *very careful*.

2. _____ The baby is *trying* to walk, but her legs aren't strong enough yet.

3. _____ A *large number* of people came to buy tickets for the concert.

4. _____ Joyce does many things in the office, but her *most important* job is typing.

5. _____ There's a *small* crack in this dish.

6. _____ We were *very surprised* that Greg spoke French so well.

7. _____ Everyone *shouted and clapped* when Michael Jackson began to sing.

8. _____ The door opened *quickly*.

II

Complete the sentences with these words.

fault	score	worry	damage
fans	blame	exciting	warned

1. My son is doing poorly in school. I think the teacher is to _____ for this problem.

2. Shirley _____ me not to trust Jerry. I'm sorry I didn't listen to her.

133

3. We lost the game, but the _____ was close.

4. Do you think the cold weather will _____ the tomato plants?

5. The children had a very _____ day at the zoo.

6. I have a headache and it's my own _____. I drank too much wine at the party.

7. Andy enjoys life. He doesn't _____ about anything.

8. Many _____ stayed home from the game because of the rain.

III

Complete the story with these words.

dangerous	used to	crashed	pain
right away	discovered	instead	join

Skiing

Skiing is a _____ sport, and no one knows this better

than Don. He _____ ski a lot, but last winter he had a

bad accident. He was skiing down the side of a mountain, and he

_____ into a tree. Don was in a lot of _____,

and they took him to a hospital _____.

In the hospital, they _____ that Don had broken both

of his legs. Don isn't going to do any skiing this winter. He plans to swim

_____. He's going to _____ a local club

where he can go swimming every day.

Unit Six
New Jobs for Women

Sixteen

A Police Officer

When Nancy finished high school, she didn't want to go to college. **So** she went to work for a bank. She worked as a bank teller for three years. The job was interesting for a while. Everything was new and she learned a lot. However, Nancy always wanted to be a police officer. She was too young to be one when she graduated from high school, so she waited until she was twenty-one. Then she made an **appointment** to talk to a police officer at the police department.

Nancy was a little nervous when she talked to the officer, but he said she should **apply** for the job. He warned her that the job was difficult and that she would have to take both written and physical exams. She applied and took the exams. She did very well on them. Six weeks later, she received an appointment to the police department. She was **eager** to begin her new work, but for three months she had to go to school to learn to be a police officer. School was **rather** difficult, but Nancy completed the courses without much trouble.

Nancy's parents didn't like the idea of her becoming a police officer. They said that the job was too dangerous. They **suggested** that she become a computer programmer. She **replied** that she was **aware** of the dangers and that she didn't want to be a computer programmer. She wanted to be a police officer because the job would be exciting and important.

I

Answer these questions about the story.

PARAGRAPH 1

1. Did Nancy want to go to college?
2. Where did she work for three years?
3. Why was her job interesting for a while?
4. Why couldn't Nancy become a police officer when she graduated from high school?

PARAGRAPH 2

5. What warning did the police officer give Nancy?
6. How did she do on her exams?
7. Where did she have to go for three months before she started work?

PARAGRAPH 3

8. Why didn't Nancy's parents want her to be a police officer?
9. What did they suggest that she be?
10. Why did she want to become a police officer?

II

MINI-DICTIONARY — PART ONE

1. **so** (sō) *adverb*: that is why; for that reason; therefore*
2. **ap·point·ment** (ə-point′mənt) *noun*: A. an agreement to meet at a definite time and place B. the placing of a person in a job
3. **ap·ply** (ə-plī′) *verb*: to ask for something formally, usually in writing
4. **ea·ger** (for) (to) (ē′gər) *adjective*: having a strong desire

*So has other meanings. It can also mean *very*. I'm so tired I can hardly keep my eyes open.*

III

Complete the sentences with these words.

apply   **so**   **eager**   **appointment**

1. Peggy is a good student. She's always _____ to learn.

2. Dan is sixty-five. He's going to _____ for Medicare, a program that helps older people pay their medical bills.

3. What time is your _____ with the doctor?

4. We're going away for three weeks, _____ we won't see you for a while.

appointment   **apply**   **so**   **eager**

5. Ed wants to _____ to become a member of our club.

6. Ray has been in the hospital for a week. He's _____ to go home.

7. Rita just received an _____ to teach history in high school.

8. We were hungry, _____ we stopped to eat.

eager   **appointment**   **applying**   **so**

9. Carmen is calling the beauty parlor for an _____.

10. The boss likes Stan because he's an _____ worker.

11. The elevator isn't working, _____ we have to use the stairs.

12. Kim is _____ for a visa to visit the United States.

IV

MINI- DICTIONARY — PART TWO

5. **rath·er** (rath′ər) *adverb*: to some degree; quite
6. **sug·gest** (sə-jest′ or səg-jest′) *verb*: to say that it is a good idea to do or consider something

7. **re·ply** (ri-plī) *verb*: to answer; to give an answer
   noun: an answer
8. **a·ware** (of) (ə-wâr´) *adjective*: having knowledge of

V

Complete the sentences with these words.

reply (*verb*)   **aware**   **rather**   **suggest**

1. I _____ that you see a lawyer.

2. We have to _____ to her letter soon.

3. It's a big house, but the kitchen is _____ small.

4. Are you _____ that Joe and Tony are good friends?

suggest   **rather**   **aware**   **reply (*noun*)**

5. Judy wasn't _____ that her son used drugs.

6. It's raining _____ hard.
7. I invited Betty and Tom to the wedding and I'm now waiting for

   their _____ .

8. We don't know where to eat. Can you _____ a good
   restaurant near here?

aware   **reply**   **suggested**   **rather**

9. I don't think the president will _____ to that question.

10. The book was _____ interesting.

11. Are you _____ that their house costs two hundred
    thousand dollars?

12. The doctor _____ that I get more rest.

VI

Complete the sentences with these words.

suggest	aware	so	rather
appointment	reply	eager	applying

1. Although Phil isn't the best student in the class, he's _____ smart.

2. I'm _____ for a credit card.

3. Mrs. Brown is a very busy person. You have to have an _____ to see her.

4. Both teams are _____ to win.

5. The suit was very expensive, _____ I didn't buy it.

6. Sam asked the bank for a loan, but he hasn't received a _____ yet.

7. We weren't _____ that Alan had a drinking problem.

8. What do you _____ that I do?

VII

Complete the story with these words.

applied	so	eager	rather
suggested	replies	appointment	aware

Math and Marks

Eric is in his last year in high school. He did _____ poorly on his first math test and worse on his second one. _____ his math teacher phoned his parents and made an _____ to see them. They talked about Eric for an hour. The teacher said that he could do better, but that he wasn't studying enough. He _____ that Eric spend an hour every night studying math. Eric is studying more now and his work is improving.

Eric is _____ to go to college, but his marks are below

average. He's _____ that it won't be easy to get into a good

college. He _____ to four colleges and hopes that one will

take him. He's waiting to receive their _____.

VIII
Word Families

1. **appointment** — *noun*
   appoint — *verb*: The company is going to *appoint* a new president soon.
2. **apply** — *verb*
   application — *noun*: I filled out a job *application* and gave it to the secretary.
   applicant — *noun*: The school has more *applicants* than it can accept, and so a lot of people are rejected every year.
3. **eager** — *adjective*
   eagerly — *adverb*: It has been a cold winter and we're *eagerly* waiting for spring.
   eagerness — *noun*: Everyone can see Joan's *eagerness* to help the patients. She's a good nurse.
4. **suggest** — *verb*
   suggestion — *noun*: I don't know where to go on my vacation. Do you have any *suggestions*?
5. **aware** — *adjective*
   awareness — *noun*: Dan's *awareness* of the problem will help us solve it.

IX
Sharing Information

Discuss these questions and topics in pairs or small groups.

1. Complete the following sentence. I wanted to learn English, **so** I

_____.

2. People must often make an **appointment** to see a doctor or dentist. Is that easy to do? How do you make the appointment? How long do you usually have to wait to get an appointment with a doctor or a dentist?

3. When we **apply** for a job, we have to fill out an application. What are some questions that you have to answer on job applications?

4. Complete the following sentence. I'm **eager** _____

_____.

5. **Rather** means *to some degree*; *very* means *to a high degree*. Is sentence a or b more true?
   a. John D. Rockefeller was *rather* rich.
   b. John D. Rockefeller was *very* rich.

6. Ann is going to buy a car. She has three thousand dollars in the bank. She can buy a used car for three thousand dollars, or get a loan and buy a new car. Which would you **suggest**?

7. Most people don't like to write letters. When you get a letter that requires a **reply**, do you usually reply quickly or do you wait until you have to reply?

8. Complete the following question and then ask your teacher or another student to answer it.

   Are you **aware** that _____?

X

Building Words with in

The prefix *in* is placed before some adjectives and nouns to form a new word. For example, *in + correct = incorrect, in + dependent = independent.*

The prefix *in* means *not.* For example, incorrect means *not correct, independent* means *not dependent.*

Adjective or Noun	*New word*
active	inactive
complete	incomplete
correct	incorrect
dependent	independent
direct	indirect
expensive	inexpensive
experience	inexperience
formal	informal
frequent	infrequent
human	inhuman
secure	insecure
sufficient	insufficient
visible	invisible

Complete the sentences with these words.

incomplete   inexpensive   independent   inexperience

1. Mary Lou does whatever she wants. She's an _____ person.

2. Joyce didn't finish the report. It's still _____ .

3. Because of my _____ , the company didn't give me the job. I had never done that type of work before.

4. I don't have a lot of money, so I'm going to buy an _____ watch.

insufficient   informal   incorrect   insecure

5. It's an _____ party. You don't need a tie or jacket.
6. The little girl cries every time her mother leaves her. She's

   _____ .

7. We need more food for the picnic. What we have is _____ .

8. The teacher said my answer was _____ , but I still think it's right.

Seventeen

Help! Help!

It was a warm spring day and Paula was sitting on a bench in the park. She was enjoying the **mild** weather and watching the children play baseball. There wasn't a cloud in the sky. A tall, thin man **approached** her. Paula is very friendly. She trusts everyone. She looked up and smiled. The man didn't smile, but he asked her what time it was. When Paula looked at her watch, the man took her handbag. He was a **thief**.

The thief had a gun and **threatened** to shoot if Paula called for help. When he ran away, Paula waited a few seconds. Then she shouted: "Help! Help! That man is **stealing** my handbag!" Another man heard her and **chased** the thief, but the thief was too fast. There was a phone not far from the bench where Paula was sitting. She called the police.

Nancy, the new police officer, received the call for help, but by the time she **reached** the park, the thief was gone. Nancy talked to Paula. The man who stole her handbag was wearing a blue jacket and gray pants. He had brown hair. Paula was sure she would **recognize** him if she saw him again. Paula and Nancy rode

144

around the neighborhood looking for the thief. After about an hour, Paula suddenly saw a man in a blue jacket coming out of a bar. It was the thief. Nancy took him to the police station. He's in jail now.

I

Answer these questions about the story.

PARAGRAPH 1
1. Where was Paula sitting?
2. Was the weather nice?
3. What question did the man ask Paula?
4. What did the man do when Paula looked at her watch?

PARAGRAPH 2
5. What did the thief threaten to do if Paula called for help?
6. Did she chase the thief?
7. Why was it easy to call the police?

PARAGRAPH 3
8. What was the thief wearing?
9. Where did Paula see the thief?
10. Where did Nancy take the thief?

II

MINI-DICTIONARY — PART ONE

1. **mild** (mild) *adjective*: gentle; not strong or bitter; not serious
2. **ap·proach** (ə-prōch′) *verb*: to come near
   noun: A. the act of coming near B. the way leading to a city, bridge, etc.
3. **thief** (thēf) *noun*: a person who takes things that belong to another
4. **threat·en** (thret′ən) *verb*: to cause fear by saying you will punish or hurt in some way

III

Complete the sentences with these words.

approaching (*verb*)   **thief**   **mild**   **threatening**

1. A _____ broke into our apartment. Our stereo and TV are missing.

2. Tony is always _____ to leave home.

3. The plane is _____ the airport.

4. Florida has hot summers and _____ winters.

thief   **mild**   **threatened**   **approaches** (*noun*)

5. I may lose my job. The manager _____ to fire me.

6. The _____ entered the house through the window. The doors were locked.

7. The soldiers are guarding all _____ to the city.

8. This cheese is _____ .

mild   **threatened**   **approaching**   **thief**

9. Gloria's teacher _____ to send her to the principal because she talks all the time and doesn't do any work.

10. Jane has a _____ case of the flu. It's nothing to worry about.

11. I didn't take your money. I'm not a _____ .

12. It's the beginning of March and spring is quickly _____ .

IV

MINI-DICTIONARY — PART TWO

---

    5. **steal** (stēl) *verb*: to take what belongs to another.
       The past of *steal* is *stole*.
    6. **chase** (chās) *verb*: to run after to catch
       noun: the act of chasing

7. **reach** (rēch) *verb*: A. to arrive at; to come to B. to extend one's arm and hand to touch or get something
   noun: the distance a person can reach
8. **rec·og·nize** (rek′əg-nīz) *verb*: to know a person or thing from past knowledge

---

V

Complete the sentences with these words.

reach (*verb*)   **steal**   **recognized**   **chasing** (*verb*)

1. The dog is _____ the cat.

2. It took us three hours to _____ the top of the mountain.

3. Roger lost so much weight that I hardly _____ him.

4. Don't leave your check in your desk. Someone may _____ it.

stole   **reach** (*verb*)   **chase** (*noun*)   **recognized**

5. The police were able to catch the man after a long _____ .

6. It was very dark; fortunately I _____ my friend's voice.

7. Can you get the flour for me? I can't _____ that high.

8. They broke into the office last night and _____ two typewriters.

recognized   **chase**   **reach** (*noun*)   **steals**

9. Don't put that medicine within _____ of the children.

10. Paul had not seen Virginia for twenty years but he _____ her immediately.

11. I left my bicycle in the yard. I hope no one _____ it.

12. The ball went over Mike's head and he had to _____ it.

VI

Complete the sentences with these words.

chase	**stealing**	**mild**	**approaching**
recognize	**thieves**	**threatening**	**reach**

1. We want to _____ the motel before eight o'clock.

2. I have to use _____ soap. My skin is sensitive.

3. The little boy likes his parents to _____ him. It's fun to run away from them.

4. Stand back! The train is _____ .

5. The owner is _____ to increase our rent.

6. _____ like to work where no one can see them.

7. We have made so many changes. You won't _____ the apartment.

8. The judge sent the man to jail for _____ my wallet and ring.

VII

Complete the story with these words.

recognize	**chases**	**mild**	**approaching**
threaten	**thieves**	**reach**	**steal**

Two Thieves

Alex and Sam don't like to see the police. They _____

money and cars. They're professional _____ , but they

haven't taken anything for a while. Alex had a _____ heart

attack six weeks ago and he's been resting. Now he's ready to go back

to work.

Alex and Sam are _____ the First National Bank. When they get to the entrance of the bank, they put on masks to cover their faces. They don't want anyone to _____ them.

They _____ into their pockets and pull out their guns. They walk up to two bank tellers and make them fill two bags with cash. They _____ to hurt them if they call for help. Alex and Sam take the money and run out of the bank. A bank guard _____ them, but they jump into their car and drive away before the guard can stop them.

VIII
Word Families

1. **mild** — *adjective*
   mildly — *adverb*: We were *mildly* interested in Tom's story.
2. **approach** — *verb* and *noun*
   approachable — *adjective*: Everyone likes the new supervisor. She's very *approachable*.
3. **threaten** — *verb*
   threat — *noun*: The letter contained a *threat* to bomb the building.
4. **recognize** — *verb*
   recognition — *noun*: Doris works very hard for the company. She should get more *recognition* and money.

IX
Sharing Information

Discuss these questions and topics in pairs or small groups.

1. Onions, pepper, and garlic make food hot and spicy. Do you like food that is hot and spicy, or do you like food that is **mild**?
2. It is easy to talk to or **approach** some people; other people are difficult to approach. What makes a person easy to approach? What makes a person difficult to approach?
3. Parents sometimes **threaten** their children. Why do they do this? Give an example of a threat parents may make.

4. Did anyone ever **steal** anything from you? What? Did you get it back?
5. In some countries, **thieves** are punished severely. What punishment do you think is appropriate for thieves?
6. Many movies and TV shows have car **chases**. These chases are often exciting and some are funny. What type of movies and TV shows often have chases?
7. What are some things that parents lock up or put in a place where children can't **reach** them?
8. Is it easy for friends who have not seen you for many years to **recognize** you? Or have you changed so much that it's difficult for old friends to recognize you?

X
Building Words with en

The suffix *en* is added to some adjectives and nouns to form a verb. For example, *fright + en = frighten, sweet + en = sweeten, threat + en = threaten.*

The suffix *en* means *to cause, to cause to be* or *to make. Frighten* means *to cause fright, sweeten* means *to cause to be sweet, threaten* means *to make a threat.*

Adjective or Noun	*Verb*
dark	darken
deep	deepen
fright	frighten
hard	harden
less	lessen
sad	sadden
short	shorten
sick	sicken
soft	soften
sweet	sweeten
threat	threaten
weak	weaken
wide	widen

150

Complete the sentences with these words.

saddened   strengthen   softening   widen

1. Exercise and good food will _____ your body.

2. The road is narrow, but there are plans to _____ it.

3. The death of our friend _____ us.

4. The field was hard and dry, but the rain is _____ it.

shorten   harden   sweeten   frightened

5. What is put in diet soda to _____ it?

6. The loud noise _____ the dog and it ran away.

7. If you put ice cream in the freezer, it'll _____ it quickly.

8. The play is too long. The director should _____ it.

151

Eighteen

A Lot of Courage

Nancy was the first woman police officer in her city. Many people **wondered** if she would be a good police officer. They asked themselves a lot of questions. Was she strong enough? Was she old enough? Would the other police officers accept her? It was great to have policewomen on TV shows, but would they be **tough** enough to do the job in the real world? Nancy was aware of what people were saying and thinking, but it didn't disturb her. She knew she could do the job.

At first, Nancy's **partner** didn't like the idea of working with a woman, but he doesn't feel that way now. He works with Nancy most of the time and he sees that she has a lot of **courage**. She isn't afraid of danger. She's willing to take **risks**, but she doesn't take foolish ones. Her partner knows that she's a better police officer than most men.

Nancy also works well with the other police officers. She's a **pleasant** person and she smiles and laughs easily. However, she knows how to be tough and sometimes her job requires this. She's a **successful** police officer because she knows when to be kind and when to be tough. She loves her job and she never misses work. People don't wonder about Nancy any more. They know that she's a very good police officer and they're proud of her **success**.

I

Answer these questions about the story.

PARAGRAPH 1

1. Were people sure that Nancy would be a good police officer?
2. What were some of the questions that people asked themselves about her?
3. Did people's comments and thinking disturb her?

PARAGRAPH 2

4. In the beginning, did Nancy's partner like to work with her?
5. Why did her partner's feelings about her change?
6. Does Nancy take risks at work?

PARAGRAPH 3

7. Why is it easy to like Nancy?
8. Do police officers have to be tough sometimes?
9. Why is Nancy a successful police officer?
10. Does she often miss work?

II

MINI-DICTIONARY — PART ONE

1. **won·der** (wun′dər) *verb*: to be uncertain and want to know
   noun: a feeling of surprise and respect because something is very special
2. **tough** (tuf) *adjective*: A. strong and able to do what is difficult B. difficult to do
3. **at first** (at fûrst) *idiom*: in the beginning
4. **part·ner** (pärt′nər) *noun*: a person who works, lives, or shares an activity with another

III

Complete the sentences with these words.

tough   **partners**   **wonder** (*verb*)   **at first**

1. Betty and Gloria own a furniture store. They're _____.

2. School was difficult _____, but now it's easy.

3. Boxers and football players have to be _____.

4. I _____ what happened to my old friend Sam.

at first   **wonder** (*noun*)   **partner**   **tough**

5. It's not easy to choose a good marriage _____.

6. _____ the book was dull, but then it got interesting.

7. That was a _____ exam. I'm glad I studied for it.
8. The river is so large and beautiful that people look at it with

_____.

wondered   **at first**   **tough**   **partner**

9. The water feels fine now, but it was cold _____.

10. We _____ how much the bike cost.

11. Mr. Suzuki is a nice person, but he can be _____.

12. The dance is going to begin. Does everyone have a _____?

IV

MINI-DICTIONARY — PART TWO

5. **cour·age** (kûr′ij) *noun*: ability to do what is difficult and dangerous or painful
6. **risk** (risk) *noun*: danger; possibility of loss
   verb: to place in danger
7. **pleas·ant** (plez′ənt) *adjective*: nice; friendly; enjoyable
8. a. **suc·cess** (sək-ses′) *noun*: the accomplishing of what one wanted; anything that goes well
   b. **successful** (sək-ses′fəl) *adjective*: resulting in the accomplishment of what one wanted

V

Complete the sentences with these words.

pleasant   successful   risk (*noun*)   success   courage

1. The party was a _____. Everyone had a good time.

2. I put my money in the bank because there's very little _____ in that.

3. Ernie works hard. That's why he's a _____ businessman.

4. It was a _____ day. The sun was shining and it wasn't too hot.

5. You need _____ to be a good soldier.

   success   pleasant   courage   risk (*verb*)

6. Fire fighters _____ their lives to save people.
7. My friend had a serious operation. Fortunately, the operation was a

   _____ .

8. It takes _____ to quit smoking.

9. I hope you have a _____ vacation.

risks	courage	pleasant	success

10. We went for a walk around the lake. It was a _____ walk.

11. A good driver doesn't take unnecessary _____ .

12. The record was a huge _____ . It sold a million copies.

13. Ben showed _____ when he was in the hospital.

VI

Complete the sentences with these words.

pleasant	risk	tough	success
at first	wondered	partners	courage

1. I don't have the _____ to ski down that mountain.

2. Peggy's tired. She had a _____ day at work.

3. Harry and I didn't accomplish much, but our meeting was quite

_____ .

4. We tried to get Therese to come with us, but we didn't have any

_____ .

5. Fred and Tony are tennis _____ .

6. I didn't like Ronald _____ , but we became good friends.

7. Barbara _____ why her husband was so late.

8. Swimming in a pool isn't very dangerous, but there's some _____ .

VII

Complete the story with these words.

courage	success	pleasant	tough
risk	partners	at first	wondered

Their Own Store

Alice and her friend Lucy worked at a stationery store. They liked their work and their boss. He was a _____ man and easy to work for, but he didn't pay them much. One day Alice and Lucy talked about opening their own store. They _____ if they should try it. They realized they might make a lot of money, but they might also lose a lot. It would be a big _____ .

Lucy wasn't excited about the idea _____ , but she changed her mind. Alice and Lucy went to their boss to tell him they were going to quit and open their own store. Telling him this took _____ and he wasn't happy, but he wished them well.

Alice and Lucy became business _____ and they soon discovered that it's _____ to start your own business. You have to borrow money, buy many things, fix the store, advertise, keep records, and work long hours. They're going to open their store next week. Everyone hopes their store will be a _____ , but no one is sure.

VIII

Word Families

1. **wonder** — *verb* and *noun*
    wonderful — *adjective*: That meal was great. You're a *wonderful* cook.
2. **partner** — *noun*
    partnership — *noun*: George and Ralph are lawyers. They're forming a *partnership* to work together.
3. **courage** — *noun*
    courageous — *adjective*: George Washington was a *courageous* leader.
    encourage — *verb*: Banks *encourage* everyone to save money.
    encouragement — *noun*: The team is losing badly. The players need *encouragement*.
    discourage — *verb*: High prices *discourage* people from buying houses.
    discouragement — *noun*: Jennifer has not been feeling well. That's the reason for her *discouragement*.
4. **risk** — *noun* and *verb*
    risky — *adjective*: The roads are covered with ice. It's too *risky* to drive.
5. **pleasant** — *adjective*
    pleasantly — *adverb*: We were *pleasantly* surprised by your visit.
    unpleasant — *adjective*: Don and I had a big fight. It was very *unpleasant*.
6. **success** — *noun*
    succeed — *verb*: If at first you don't *succeed*, try again.
    unsuccessful — *adjective*: We tried to sell our car, but we were *unsuccessful*.

IX

Sharing Information

Discuss these questions and topics in pairs or small groups.

1. Complete the following sentence. I **wonder** _____.
2. Name something that you did that was **tough** to do, or something that you are doing now that is tough.

3. Complete the following sentences. I started to learn English _____

    ago. **At first** _____.

4. Married couples are **partners**. Marriage is a **partnership**. Love is the most important thing in this partnership, but it isn't the only important thing. How important is having common interests in a marriage? How important is money?
5. Some say that **courage** is not being afraid of danger and difficulty. Others say that courage is doing what is dangerous and difficult although we're afraid. What do you think?
6. No one can live without taking **risks**. Name some ordinary risks that people take.
7. One of the meanings of **pleasant** is enjoyable or giving pleasure. Name some activities that you find pleasant.
8. What are some things or qualities that help a person be a **success** in life?

X

Building Adjectives with ing

The *ing form* (present participle) of many verbs is used as an adjective. For example, *excite + ing = exciting, understand + ing = understanding*.

The adjective suffix *ing* adds no special meaning to the verb but makes it usable as an adjective. *Exciting* is the adjective form of the verb *excite*; *understanding* is the adjective form of the verb *understand*.

Verb	*Adjective*
amaze	amazing
come	coming
die	dying
excite	exciting
follow	following
interest	interesting
last	lasting
love	loving
miss	missing
open	opening
will	willing
win	winning
understand	understanding

Complete the sentences with these words.

missing   **following**   **exciting**   **willing**

1. That was a very _____ TV program. I liked it a lot.

2. They've looked everywhere for the _____ child, but they can't find her.

3. We want _____ workers, not people who don't want to be here.

4. You have an hour to answer the _____ questions.

dying   **understanding**   **winning**   **opening**

5. The _____ chapter of the book is the best.

6. They're going to cut down the _____ trees to plant new ones.

7. What are the _____ numbers in the contest? The prize is $500.

8. Ralph always has time to listen to his children. He's a very _____ father.

UNIT VI
Word Review

I
In Other Words

In front of each sentence, write the word which has the same or almost the same meaning as the part of the sentence in *italics*.

tough	**reply**	**rather**	**approaching**
stole	**risk**	**chase**	**pleasant**

1. _____ Ray won't swim in the pool alone. He thinks there's too much *danger*.

2. _____ We're *getting close to* the bridge.

3. _____ Mrs. Lopez works full time and has three young children. That's *difficult*.

4. _____ Throw the stick. The dog will *run to get* it and bring it back.

5. _____ Someone *took* Joan's watch.

6. _____ Are we going to eat soon? I'm *quite* hungry.

7. _____ It's a *nice* evening. Let's go out.

8. _____ Tim wrote to his parents to ask for money. He hopes they'll *answer* soon.

II
Complete the sentences with these words.

applying	**thieves**	**recognize**	**partner**
threatened	**appointment**	**mild**	**suggested**

1. Mr. Martini is a good lawyer, but you have to wait three weeks for an

   _____ to see him.

2. Jane _____ that we go to the beach tomorrow. What do you think?

161

3. The police officer _____ to give me a ticket for driving too fast. Fortunately, he only gave me a warning.

4. Betty doesn't run the gift shop alone. She has a _____.

5. Car _____ can easily get into a locked car. They don't need keys.

6. This drink tastes good. It's very _____.

7. I'm _____ for a loan. I hope I get it.

8. Do you _____ the woman in the red dress?

III

Complete the story with these words.

aware	**so**	**reach**	**wondered**
success	**at first**	**courage**	**eager**

Christopher Columbus

Christopher Columbus is probably the world's most famous explorer. He believed the world was round and he was _____ to find a new and shorter way to _____ India. He planned to do this by sailing west from Europe. No one had ever tried this before.

_____, Columbus could not get the money he needed for the trip. He asked the King of Portugal for help, but he said no. Finally, Queen Isabella of Spain gave Columbus the money he needed. In 1492, Columbus and his men sailed from Spain in three ships, the Santa Maria, the Niña, and the Pinta. They were _____ of the problems and dangers of trying to cross the ocean in three small ships, but they were men of great _____.

Columbus and his men sailed for weeks without seeing land. They didn't have much food or water left. They began to lose hope and _____ if they would ever see land again.

However, on October 12 they saw a small island; they were very happy. They landed on the island and called it San Salvador. Their trip was a _____. They had discovered a new world, but they still thought they were close to India. _____ they called the people they met on this and other islands, Indians.

Word List

Answer Key
Unit One
One
Far From Home (pages 2–8)

III	V	VI	X
1. far	1. around	1. have to	1. quickly
2. hurry	2. quick	2. around	2. warmly
3. has to	3. waste	3. miss	3. nicely
4. too	4. miss	4. far	4. usually
		5. wastes	5. safely
5. have to	5. waste	6. too	6. happily
6. too	6. around	7. hurrying	7. poorly
7. far	7. miss	8. quick	8. easily
8. hurry	8. quick		
		VII	
9. far	9. wasting		
10. has to	10. quick	1. too	
11. hurry	11. missed	2. missed	
12. too	12. around	3. around	
		4. quick	
		5. has to	
		6. far	
		7. hurry	
		8. waste	

Two
Three Locks and a Dog (pages 9–15)

III	V	VI	X
1. a lot	1. may	1. trust	1. singer
2. afraid	2. biting	2. afraid	2. writer
3. own	3. trusts	3. bite	3. driver
4. protect	4. however	4. a lot of	4. owner
		5. may	5. dryer
5. own	5. trust	6. protect	6. freezer
6. a lot of	6. however	7. however	7. director
7. afraid	7. may	8. own	8. dancer
8. protect	8. bite		9. player
		VII	10. painter
9. afraid	9. trust		
10. protect	10. bites	1. may	
11. a lot of	11. however	2. a lot	
12. owns	12. may	3. bites	
		4. trusts	
		5. however	
		6. owns	
		7. afraid	
		8. protects	

Three
Fish for Supper (pages 16–23)

III	**V**	**VI**	**X**
1. weigh	1. enjoy	1. almost	1. payment
2. trying	2. although	2. tries	2. placement
3. lose	3. almost	3. enjoy	3. enjoyment
4. weight	4. starving	4. lose	4. statement
5. only		5. although	5. announcements
	5. almost	6. weighs	6. advancements
6. lost	6. although	7. starving	7. arrangements
7. weigh	7. starve	8. only	8. governments
8. only	8. enjoy		
9. try			
	9. enjoys	**VII**	
10. weigh	10. almost		
11. only	11. although	1. almost	
12. losing	12. starving	2. starving	
13. trying		3. although	
		4. enjoys	
		5. weighs	
		6. lose	
		7. trying	
		8. only	

Word Review (pages 24–25)

I	**II**	**III**
1. a lot of	1. may	1. weighs
2. almost	2. owns	2. although
3. missed	3. waste	3. bite
4. enjoys	4. trying	4. trust
5. hurries	5. quickly	5. protect
6. only	6. around	6. too
7. have to	7. far	7. afraid
8. starving	8. however	8. lose

Unit Two
Four
Sharing the Housework (pages 28–34)

III	V	VI	X
1. burning	1. wiping	1. hate	1. thirsty
2. both	2. hates	2. share	2. sunny
3. still	3. fun	3. both	3. dirty
4. sharing	4. improving	4. fun	4. lucky
		5. still	5. juicy
5. burn	5. wiped	6. burn	6. salty
6. still	6. fun	7. wiping	7. icy
7. share	7. hate	8. improving	8. noisy
8. both	8. improves		

VI I

III	V
9. still	9. wipe
10. burn	10. improving
11. share	11. fun
12. both	12. hates

VII

1. share
2. both
3. fun
4. wiped
5. burn
6. still
7. hates
8. improving

Five
Rushing the Baby to the Hospital (pages 35–42)

III	V	VI	X
1. explored	1. rushing	1. mistake	1. unfortunately
2. proud	2. bit	2. fortunately	2. unsafe
3. swallow	3. poison	3. explored	3. unable
4. mistakes	4. fortunately	4. bit	4. unmarried
		5. rushing	5. unnecessary
5. swallow	5. fortunately	6. proud	6. unafraid
6. mistake	6. bit	7. swallowed	7. unkind
7. exploring	7. rush	8. poisoning	8. undressed
8. proud	8. poisoning		

III	V
9. explore	9. rushes
10. mistake	10. bit
11. proud	11. fortunately
12. swallow	12. poison

VII

1. explore
2. proud
3. poison
4. mistake
5. swallowed
6. fortunately
7. bit
8. rushed

Six
Chevrolets, Fords, and Hondas (pages 43–50)

III	V	VI	X
1. afford	1. loan	1. of course	1. changeable
2. neighbors	2. just	2. expensive	2. enjoyable
3. expensive	3. borrow	3. afford	3. acceptable
4. of course	4. choose	4. just	4. returnable
		5. loan	5. movable
5. expensive	5. loaned	6. choose	6. controllable
6. of course	6. just	7. borrow	7. washable
7. afford	7. borrowed	8. neighbors	8. understandable
8. neighbor	8. choose		
		VII	
9. afford	9. borrowing		
10. neighbors	10. just	1. neighbors	
11. of course	11. choose	2. of course	
12. expensive	12. loan	3. expensive	
		4. choose	
		5. just	
		6. afford	
		7. borrow	
		8. loan	

Word Review (pages 51–52)

I	II	III
1. fortunate	1. rushing	1. expensive
2. hates	2. wiped	2. afford
3. burning	3. choose	3. borrow
4. bit	4. proud	4. loan
5. improving	5. share.	5. still
6. just	6. neighbors	6. mistake
7. both	7. poison	7. of course
8. exploring	8. swallow	8. fun

Unit Three
Seven
Working and Swimming (54–61)

III	V	VI	X
1. pools	1. deep	1. shallow	1. useful
2. average	2. shallow	2. prefer	2. fearful
3. prefer	3. edge	3. average	3. wasteful
4. spends	4. diving	4. diving	4. peaceful
		5. deep	5. hopeful
5. prefers	5. dive	6. spent	6. colorful
6. spending	6. edge	7. pool	7. careful
7. pool	7. deep	8. edge	8. youthful
8. average	8. shallow		

VII

III	V
9. spent	9. deep
10. averaged	10. edge
11. prefer	11. dive
12. pool	12. shallow

VII

1. pool
2. prefer
3. dive
4. edge
5. spend
6. deep
7. average
8. shallow

Eight
Hunting (pages 62–69)

III	V	VI	X
1. shoot	1. dragging	1. hesitated	1. sugarless
2. hunt	2. lift	2. stream	2. careless
3. hesitated	3. huge	3. shoot	3. fearless
4. hunters	4. aiming	4. huge	4. sleepless
5. stream		5. hunting	5. weightless
	5. lift	6. aimed	6. useless
6. hunting	6. huge	7. lift	7. endless
7. hesitate	7. dragging	8. dragging	8. homeless
8. stream	8. aiming		
9. shot		**VII**	
	9. huge		
10. hunt	10. lift	1. stream	
11. hesitated	11. dragged	2. hunt	
12. shoot	12. aims	3. huge	
13. streaming		4. hesitate	
		5. shot	
		6. aim	
		7. lift	
		8. dragged	

Nine
A Bitter Argument (pages 70–77)

III	V	VI	X
1. foolish	1. shouting	1. earn	1. weakness
2. dull	2. bitter	2. at least	2. happiness
3. quit	3. arguments	3. quit	3. darkness
4. earns	4. at least	4. argue	4. seriousness
5. fool	5. argue	5. bitter	5. softness
		6. shouted	6. sickness
6. earn	6. argue	7. dull	7. kindness
7. foolish	7. at least	8. foolish	8. carelessness
8. quits	8. bitter		
9. dull	9. shout	**VII**	
10. quit	10. bitter	1. dull	
11. earn	11. shout	2. shout	
12. dull	12. argue	3. earn	
13. foolish	13. at least	4. argument	
		5. bitter	
		6. foolish	
		7. quit	
		8. at least	

Word Review (pages 78–79)

I	II	III
1. at least	1. argue	1. hunting
2. shallow	2. shot	2. prefers
3. quit	3. pool	3. spends
4. aiming	4. drag	4. stream
5. dull	5. bitter	5. edge
6. foolish	6. hesitant	6. deep
7. average	7. dive	7. huge
8. earn	8. shouted	8. lift

Unit Four
Ten
A Struggle (pages 82–88)

III	V	VI	X
1. storm	1. quite	1. baking	1. protection
2. ago	2. baker	2. storm	2. discussion
3. struggle	3. baking	3. quite	3. motion
4. is used to	4. skill	4. struggling	4. education
	5. accomplish	5. accomplish	5. pronunciation
5. ago	6. bakery	6. is used to	6. examination
6. storm		7. ago	7. hesitation
7. struggling	7. baking	8. skill	8. action
8. are used to	8. skills		
	9. quite	**VII**	
9. is used to	10. accomplish		
10. ago		1. ago	
11. struggle	11. skill	2. storm	
12. storm	12. quite	3. baked	
	13. accomplished	4. quite	
	14. bake	5. struggle	
		6. skill	
		7. are used to	
		8. accomplish	

Eleven
A Dream (pages 89–95)

III	V	VI	X
1. crack	1. require	1. therefore	1. discontinue
2. searching	2. advantage	2. search	2. disrespect
3. dream	3. therefore	3. crack	3. disappeared
4. enough	4. repair	4. repair	4. dishonest
		5. enough	5. disrepair
5. search	5. repairs	6. advantage	6. disadvantages
6. cracked	6. advantage	7. require	7. dissatisfied
7. dream	7. therefore	8. dream	8. disobeys
8. enough	8. requires		
		VII	
9. searching	9. repair		
10. enough	10. requires	1. dream	
11. crack	11. advantage	2. searching	
12. dreamt	12. therefore	3. cracks	
		4. enough	
		5. repair	
		6. require	
		7. therefore	
		8. advantages	

Twelve
A Visit (pages 96–103)

III
1. fall asleep
2. weary
3. hardly
4. while

5. while
6. hardly
7. weary
8. fell asleep

9. fall asleep
10. while
11. weary
12. hardly

V
1. pinch
2. ashamed
3. disturbing
4. wake up

5. pinch
6. disturb
7. woke up
8. ashamed

9. ashamed
10. disturb
11. woke up
12. pinched

VI
1. pinched
2. disturb
3. weary
4. ashamed
5. while
6. hardly
7. fell asleep
8. wake up
9. while

VII
1. while
2. falls asleep
3. disturbs
4. ashamed
5. pinch
6. wakes up
7. weary
8. hardly

X
1. independence
2. intelligence
3. importance
4. acceptance
5. difference
6. clearance
7. assistance
8. obedience

Word Review (pages 104–105)

I
1. weary
2. storm
3. searching
4. accomplish
5. required
6. therefore
7. baking
8. while

II
1. wake up
2. skill
3. pinched
4. advantage
5. ashamed
6. cracked
7. disturbs
8. fell asleep

III
1. ago
2. quite
3. dream
4. hardly
5. repairing
6. was used to
7. struggle
8. enough
9. while

Unit Five
Thirteen
A Soccer Fan (pages 108–116)

III	V	VI	X
1. join	1. scores	1. cheered	1. reopen
2. discover	2. exciting	2. join	2. remarry
3. amazes	3. cheering	3. exciting	3. rename
4. fan	4. crowd	4. fan	4. rewrite
		5. discover	5. revisit
5. joined	5. exciting	6. amazed	6. rebuild
6. amazed	6. score	7. score	7. rejoin
7. discovered	7. crowd	8. crowd	8. reread
8. fan	8. cheer		

VII

III	V
9. join	9. exciting
10. discovered	10. score
11. fan	11. cheered
12. amazed	12. crowd

VII
1. fan
2. joined
3. discovered
4. crowd
5. cheered
6. exciting
7. amazed
8. scored

Fourteen
An Accident (pages 117–124)

III	V	VI	X
1. suddenly	1. slight	1. crashed	1. joyous
2. cautious	2. damage	2. suddenly	2. numerous
3. attempting	3. fault	3. slight	3. studious
4. crashed	4. blame	4. fault	4. poisonous
		5. cautious	5. mysterious
5. suddenly	5. blame	6. blaming	6. nervous
6. attempt	6. slight	7. damaging	7. spacious
7. crash	7. faults	8. attempted	8. famous
8. cautious	8. damage		

III	V
9. attempted	9. slight
10. cautious	10. fault
11. suddenly	11. blame
12. crashed	12. damaged

VII
1. attempted
2. suddenly
3. crashed
4. fault
5. blame
6. cautious
7. damaged
8. slight

Fifteen
Two Packs a Day (pages 125–132)

III
1. dangerous
2. warn
3. used to
4. warning
5. main

6. used to
7. warned
8. main
9. dangerous

10. used to
11. warned
12. dangerous
13. main

V
1. instead
2. right away
3. worrying
4. pain

5. right away
6. instead
7. pain
8. worry

9. pain
10. right away
11. worries
12. instead

VI
1. right away
2. pain
3. worry
4. used to
5. main
6. dangerous
7. instead
8. warned

VII
1. used to
2. warned
3. dangerous
4. worry
5. main
6. pain
7. right away
8. instead

X
1. farming
2. understanding
3. hearing
4. beginning
5. feeling
6. reading
7. swimming
8. meeting

Word Review (pages 133–134)

I
1. cautious
2. attempting
3. crowd
4. main
5. slight
6. amazed
7. cheered
8. suddenly

II
1. blame
2. warned
3. score
4. damage
5. exciting
6. fault
7. worry
8. fans

III
1. dangerous
2. used to
3. crashed
4. pain
5. right away
6. discovered
7. instead
8. join

Unit Six
Sixteen
A Police Officer (pages 136–143)

III	V	VI	X
1. eager	1. suggest	1. rather	1. independent
2. apply	2. reply	2. applying	2. incomplete
3. appointment	3. rather	3. appointment	3. inexperience
4. so	4. aware	4. eager	4. inexpensive
		5. so	5. informal
5. apply	5. aware	6. reply	6. insecure
6. eager	6. rather	7. aware	7. insufficient
7. appointment	7. reply	8. suggest	8. incorrect
8. so	8. suggest		
		VII	
9. appointment	9. reply		
10. eager	10. rather	1. rather	
11. so	11. aware	2. so	
12. applying	12. suggested	3. appointment	
		4. suggested	
		5. eager	
		6. aware	
		7. applied	
		8. replies	

Seventeen
Help! Help! (pages 144–151)

III	V	VI	X
1. thief	1. chasing	1. reach	1. strengthen
2. threatening	2. reach	2. mild	2. widen
3. approaching	3. recognized	3. chase	3. saddened
4. mild	4. steal	4. approaching	4. softening
		5. threatening	5. sweeten
5. threatened	5. chase	6. thieves	6. frightened
6. thief	6. recognized	7. recognize	7. harden
7. approaches	7. reach	8. stealing	8. shorten
8. mild	8. stole		
		VII	
9. threatened	9. reach		
10. mild	10. recognized	1. steal	
11. thief	11. steals	2. thieves	
12. approaching	12. chase	3. mild	
		4. approaching	
		5. recognize	
		6. reach	
		7. threaten	
		8. chases	

Eighteen
A Lot of Courage (pages 152–160)

III

1. partners
2. at first
3. tough
4. wonder

5. partner
6. at first
7. tough
8. wonder

9. at first
10. wondered
11. tough
12. partner

V

1. success
2. risk
3. successful
4. pleasant
5. courage

6. risk
7. success
8. courage
9. pleasant

10. pleasant
11. risks
12. success
13. courage

VI

1. courage
2. tough
3. pleasant
4. success
5. partners
6. at first
7. wondered
8. risk

VII

1. pleasant
2. wondered
3. risk
4. at first
5. courage
6. partners
7. tough
8. success

X

1. exciting
2. missing
3. willing
4. following
5. opening
6. dying
7. winning
8. understanding

Word Review (pages 161–163)

I

1. risk
2. approaching
3. tough
4. chase
5. stole
6. rather
7. pleasant
8. reply

II

1. appointment
2. suggested
3. threatened
4. partner
5. thieves
6. mild
7. applying
8. recognize

III

1. eager
2. reach
3. at first
4. aware
5. courage
6. wondered
7. success
8. so

6

The Throwing-Nets

She walked quickly away from the river, because the Embankment was wide and well-lit. There was a tangle of narrow streets between there and the Royal Arctic Institute, which was the only place Lyra was sure of being able to find, and into that dark maze she hurried now.

If only she knew London as well as she knew Oxford! Then she would have known which streets to avoid; or where she could scrounge some food; or, best of all, which doors to knock on and find shelter. In that cold night, the dark alleys all around were alive with movement and secret life, and she knew none of it.

Pantalaimon became a wildcat and scanned the dark all around with his night-piercing eyes. Every so often he'd stop, bristling, and she would turn aside from the entrance she'd been about to go down. The night was full of noises: bursts of drunken laughter, two raucous voices raised in song, the clatter and whine of some badly-oiled machine in a basement. Lyra walked delicately through it all, her senses magnified and mingled with Pantalaimon's, keeping to the shadows and the narrow alleys.

From time to time she had to cross a wider, well-lit street, where the tramcars hummed and sparked under their anbaric wires. There were rules for crossing London streets, but she took no notice, and when anyone shouted, she fled.

It was a fine thing to be free again. She knew that Pantalaimon, padding on wildcat-paws beside her, felt the same joy as she did to be in the open air, even if it was murky London air laden with fumes and soot and clangorous with noise. Some time soon they'd have to think over the meaning of what they'd heard in Mrs Coulter's flat, but not yet. And some time eventually they'd have to find a place to sleep.

At a crossroads near the corner of a big department store, whose windows shone brilliantly over the wet pavement, there was a coffee stall: a little hut on wheels with a counter under the wooden flap that swung up like an awning. Yellow light glowed inside, and the fragrance of coffee drifted out. The white-coated owner was leaning on the counter talking to the two or three customers.

It was tempting. Lyra had been walking for an hour now, and it was cold and damp. With Pantalaimon a sparrow, she went up to the counter and reached up to gain the owner's attention.

"Cup of coffee and a ham sandwich, please," she said.

"You're out late, my dear," said a gentleman in a top hat and white silk muffler.

"Yeah," she said, turning away from him to scan the busy intersection. A theatre nearby was just emptying, and crowds milled around the lighted foyer, calling for cabs, wrapping coats around their shoulders. In the other direction was the entrance of a Chthonic Railway Station, with more crowds pouring up and down the steps.

"Here you are, love," said the coffee-stall man. "Two shillings."

"Let me pay for this," said the man in the top hat.

Lyra thought, why not? I can run faster than him, and I might need all my money later. The top-hatted man dropped a coin on the counter and smiled down at her. His dæmon was a lemur. It clung to his lapel, staring round-eyed at Lyra.

She bit into her sandwich and kept her eyes on the busy street. She had no idea where she was, because she had never seen a map of London, and she didn't even know how big it was or how far she'd have to walk to find the country.

"What's your name?" said the man.

"Alice."

"That's a pretty name. Let me put a drop of this into your coffee … warm you up…"

He was unscrewing the top of a silver flask.

"I don't like that," said Lyra. "I just like coffee."

"I bet you've never had brandy like this before."

"I have. I was sick all over the place. I had a whole bottle, or nearly."

"Just as you like," said the man, tilting the flask into his own cup. "Where are you going, all alone like this?"

"Going to meet my father."

"And who's he?"

"He's a murderer."

"He's what?"

"I told you, he's a murderer. It's his profession. He's doing a job tonight. I got his clean clothes in here, 'cause he's usually all covered in blood when he's finished a job."

"Ah! You're joking."

"I en't."

The lemur uttered a soft mewing sound and clambered slowly up behind the man's head, to peer out at her. She drank her coffee stolidly and ate the last of her sandwich.

"Good night," she said. "I can see my father coming now. He looks a bit angry."

The top-hat man glanced around, and Lyra set off towards the theatre crowd. Much as she would have liked to see the Chthonic

Railway (Mrs Coulter had said it was not really intended for people of their class) she was wary of being trapped underground; better to be out in the open, where she could run, if she had to.

On and on she walked, and the streets became darker and emptier. It was drizzling, but even if there'd been no clouds the city sky was too tainted with light to show the stars. Pantalaimon thought they were going north, but who could tell?

Endless streets of little identical brick houses, with gardens only big enough for a dustbin; great gaunt factories behind wire fences, with one anbaric light glowing bleakly high up on a wall and a night-watchman snoozing by his brazier; occasionally a dismal oratory, only distinguished from a warehouse by the crucifix outside. Once she tried the door of one of these places, only to hear a groan from the bench a foot away in the darkness. She realized that the porch was full of sleeping figures, and fled.

"Where we going to sleep, Pan?" she said as they trudged down a street of closed and shuttered shops.

"A doorway somewhere."

"Don't want to be seen, though. They're all so open."

"There's a canal down there…"

He was looking down a side-road to the left. Sure enough, a patch of dark glimmer showed open water, and when they cautiously went to look, they found a canal basin where a dozen or so barges were tied up at the wharves, some high in the water, some low and laden under the gallows-like cranes. A dim light shone in one window of a wooden hut, and a thread of smoke rose from the metal chimney; otherwise the only lights were high up on the wall of the warehouse or the gantry of a crane, leaving the ground in gloom. The wharves were piled with barrels of coal-spirit, with stacks of great round logs, with rolls of cahuchuc-covered cable.

Lyra tiptoed up to the hut and peeped in at the window. An old man was laboriously reading a picture-story paper and smoking a pipe, with his spaniel-dæmon curled up asleep on the table. As she looked, the man got up and brought a blackened kettle from the iron stove and poured some hot water into a cracked mug before settling back with his paper.

"Should we ask him to let us in, Pan?" she whispered, but he was distracted; he was a bat, an owl, a wildcat again; she looked all round, catching his panic, and then saw them at the same time as he did: two men running at her, one from each side, the nearer holding a throwing-net.

Pantalaimon uttered a harsh scream and launched himself as a leopard at the closer man's dæmon, a savage-looking fox, bowling her backwards so that she tangled with the man's legs. The man cursed and dodged aside, and Lyra darted past him towards the open spaces of the wharf. What she mustn't do was get boxed in a corner.

Pantalaimon, an eagle now, swooped at her and cried, "Left! Left!"

She swerved that way and saw a gap between the coal-spirit barrels and the end of a corrugated iron shed, and darted for it like a bullet.

But those throwing-nets!

She heard a hiss in the air, and past her cheek something lashed and sharply stung, and loathsome tarred strings across her face, her arms, her hands tangled and held her, and she fell, snarling and tearing and struggling in vain.

"Pan! Pan!"

But the fox-dæmon tore at the cat-Pantalaimon, and Lyra felt the pain in her own flesh, and sobbed a great cry as he fell. One man was swiftly lashing cords around her, around her limbs, her throat, body, head, bundling her over and over on the wet ground. She was helpless, exactly like a fly being trussed by a spider. Poor hurt Pan was dragging himself towards her, with the fox-dæmon worrying his back, and he had no strength left to change, even; and the other man was lying in a puddle, with an arrow through his neck –

The whole world grew still as the man tying the net saw it too.

Pantalaimon sat up and blinked, and then there was a soft thud, and the net-man fell choking and gasping right across Lyra, who cried out in horror: that was *blood* gushing out of him!

Running feet, and someone hauled the man away and bent over him; then other hands lifted Lyra, a knife snicked and pulled and the net-strings fell away one by one, and she tore them off, spitting, and hurled herself down to cuddle Pantalaimon.

Kneeling, she twisted to look up at the newcomers. Three dark men, one armed with a bow, the others with knives; and as she turned, the bowman caught his breath.

"That en't Lyra?"

A familiar voice, but she couldn't place it till he stepped forward and the nearest light fell on his face and the hawk-dæmon on his shoulder. Then she had it. A gyptian! A real Oxford gyptian!

"Tony Costa," he said. "Remember? You used to play with my little brother Billy off the boats in Jericho, afore the Gobblers got him."

"Oh, God, Pan, we're safe!" she sobbed, but then a thought rushed into her mind: it was the Costas' boat she'd hijacked that day. Suppose he remembered?

"Better come along with us," he said. "You alone?"

"Yeah. I was running away…"

"All right, don't talk now. Just keep quiet. Jaxer, move them bodies into the shadow. Kerim, look around."

Lyra stood up shakily, holding the wildcat-Pantalaimon to her breast. He was twisting to look at something, and she followed his gaze, understanding and suddenly curious too: what had happened to the dead men's dæmons? They were fading, that was the answer; fading and drifting away like atoms of smoke, for all that they tried to cling to their men. Pantalaimon hid his eyes, and Lyra hurried blindly after Tony Costa.

"What are you doing here?" she said.

"Quiet, gal. There's enough trouble awake without stirring more. We'll talk on the boat."

He led her over a little wooden bridge into the heart of the canal basin. The other two men were padding silently after them. Tony turned along the waterfront and out on to a wooden jetty, from which he stepped on board a narrow-boat and swung open the door to the cabin.

"Get in," he said. "Quick now."

Lyra did so, patting her bag (which she had never let go, even in the net) to make sure the alethiometer was still there. In the long narrow cabin, by the light of a lantern on a hook, she saw a stout powerful woman with grey hair, sitting at a table with a paper. Lyra recognized her as Billy's mother.

"Who's this?" the woman said. "That's never Lyra?"

"That's right. Ma, we got to move. We killed two men out in the basin. We thought they was Gobblers, but I reckon they were Turk traders. They'd caught Lyra. Never mind talk – we'll do that on the move."

"Come here, child," said Ma Costa.

Lyra obeyed, half happy, half apprehensive, for Ma Costa had hands like bludgeons, and now she was sure: it *was* their boat she had captured with Roger and the other colleger. But the boat-mother set her hands on either side of Lyra's face, and her dæmon, the yellow-eyed hawk, crooned a quick welcome to

Pantalaimon. Then Ma Costa folded her great arms around Lyra and pressed her to her breast.

"I dunno what you're a-doing here, but you look wore out. You can have Billy's crib, soon's I've got a hot drink in you. Set you down there, child."

It looked as if her piracy was forgiven, or at least forgotten. Lyra slid on to the cushioned bench behind a well-scrubbed pine table-top as the low rumble of the gas-engine shook the boat.

"Where we going?" Lyra asked.

Ma Costa was setting a saucepan of milk on the iron stove and riddling the grate to stir the fire up.

"Away from here. No talking now. We'll talk in the morning."

And she said no more, handing Lyra a cup of milk when it was ready, swinging herself up on deck when the boat began to move, exchanging occasional whispers with the men. Lyra sipped the milk and lifted a corner of the blind to watch the dark wharves move past. A minute or two later she was sound asleep.

She awoke in a narrow bed, with that comforting engine-rumble deep below. She sat up, banged her head, cursed, felt around, and got up more carefully. A thin grey light showed her three other bunks, each empty and neatly made, one below hers and the other two across the tiny cabin. She swung over the side to find herself in her underclothes, and saw the dress and the wolfskin coat folded at the end of her bunk together with her shopping bag. The alethiometer was still there.

She dressed quickly and went through the door at the end to find herself in the cabin with the stove, where it was warm. There was no one there. Through the windows she saw a grey swirl of fog on each side, with occasional dark shapes that might have been buildings or trees.

Before she could go out on deck, the outer door opened and

Ma Costa came down, swathed in an old tweed coat on which the damp had settled like a thousand tiny pearls.

"Sleep well?" she said, reaching for a frying pan. "Now sit down out the way and I'll make ye some breakfast. Don't stand about; there en't room."

"Where are we?" said Lyra.

"On the Grand Junction Canal. You keep out of sight, child. I don't want to see you topside. There's trouble."

She sliced a couple of rashers of bacon into the frying pan, and cracked an egg to go with them.

"What sort of trouble?"

"Nothing we can't cope with, if you stay out the way."

And she wouldn't say any more till Lyra had eaten. The boat slowed at one point, and something banged against the side, and she heard men's voices raised in anger; but then someone's joke made them laugh, and the voices drew away and the boat moved on.

Presently Tony Costa swung down into the cabin. Like his mother, he was pearled with damp, and he shook his woollen hat over the stove to make the drops jump and spit.

"What we going to tell her, Ma?"

"Ask first, tell after."

He poured some coffee into a tin cup and sat down. He was a powerful, dark-faced man, and now she could see him in daylight, Lyra saw a sad grimness in his expression.

"Right," he said. "Now you tell us what you was doing in London, Lyra. We had you down as being took by the Gobblers."

"I was living with this lady, right…"

Lyra clumsily collected her story and shook it into order as if she were settling a pack of cards ready for dealing. She told them everything, except about the alethiometer.

"And then last night at this cocktail party I found out what they were really doing. Mrs Coulter was one of the Gobblers herself, and she was going to use me to help her catch more kids. And what they do is —"

Ma Costa left the cabin and went out to the cockpit. Tony waited till the door was shut, and went on:

"We know what they do. Least, we know part of it. We know they don't come back. Them kids is taken up North, far out the way, and they do experiments on 'em. At first we reckoned they tried out different diseases and medicines, but there'd be no reason to start that all of a sudden two or three years back. Then we thought about the Tartars, maybe there's some secret deal they're making up Siberia way; because the Tartars want to move North just as much as the rest, for the coal-spirit and the fire-mines, and there's been rumours of war for even longer than the Gobblers been going. And we reckoned the Gobblers were buying off the Tartar chiefs by giving 'em kids, cause the Tartars eat 'em, don't they? They bake children and eat 'em."

"They never!" said Lyra.

"They do. There's plenty of other things to be told, and all. You ever heard of the Nälkäinens?"

Lyra said "No. Not even with Mrs Coulter. What are they?"

"That's a kind of ghost they have up there in those forests. Same size as a child, and they got no heads. They feel their way about at night and if you're a-sleeping out in the forest they get ahold of you and won't nothing make 'em let go. Nälkäinens, that's a Northern word. And the Windsuckers, they're dangerous too. They drift about in the air. You come across clumps of 'em floated together sometimes, or caught snagged on a bramble. As soon as they touch you, all the strength goes out of you. You can't see 'em except as a kind of shimmer in the air. And the Breathless Ones…"

"Who are they?"

"Warriors half-killed. Being alive is one thing, and being dead's another, but being half-killed is worse than either. They just can't die, and living is altogether beyond 'em. They wander about for ever. They're called the Breathless Ones because of what's been done to 'em."

"And what's that?" said Lyra, wide-eyed.

"The North Tartars snap open their ribs and pull out their lungs. There's an art to it. They do it without killing 'em, but their lungs can't work any more without their dæmons pumping 'em by hand, so the result is they're halfway between breath and no breath, life and death, half-killed, you see. And their dæmons got to pump and pump all day and night, or else perish with 'em. You come across a whole platoon of Breathless Ones in the forest sometimes, I've heard. And then there's the *panserbjørne* – you heard of them? That means armoured bears. They're like a kind of Polar bear, except—"

"Yes! I have heard of them! One of the men last night, he said that my uncle, Lord Asriel, he's being imprisoned in a fortress guarded by the armoured bears."

"Is he, now? And what was he doing up there?"

"Exploring. But the way the man was talking I don't think my uncle's on the same side as the Gobblers. I think they were glad he was in prison."

"Well, he won't get out if the armoured bears are guarding him. They're like mercenaries, you know what I mean by that? They sell their strength to whoever pays. They got hands like men, and they learned the trick of working iron way back, meteoric iron mostly, and they make great sheets and plates of it to cover theirselves with. They been raiding the Skraelings for centuries. They're vicious killers, absolutely pitiless. But they keep their word. If you make a bargain with a *panserbjørn*, you can rely on it."

Lyra considered these horrors with awe.

"Ma don't like to hear about the North," Tony said after a few moments, "because of what might've happened to Billy. We know they took him up North, see."

"How d'you know that?"

"We caught one of the Gobblers, and made him talk. That's how we know a little about what they're doing. Them two last night weren't Gobblers; they were too clumsy. If they'd been Gobblers we'd've took 'em alive. See, the gyptian people, we been hit worse than most by these Gobblers, and we're a-coming together to decide what to do about it. That's what we was doing in the basin last night, taking on stores, 'cause we're going to a big muster up in the Fens, what we call a Roping. And what I reckon is we're a-going to send out a rescue party, when we heard what all the other gyptians know, when we put our knowledge together. That's what I'd do, if I was John Faa."

"Who's John Faa?"

"The king of the gyptians."

"And you're really going to rescue the kids? What about Roger?"

"Who's Roger?"

"The Jordan College Kitchen boy. He was took same as Billy the day before I come away with Mrs Coulter. I bet if I was took he'd come and rescue me. If you're going to rescue Billy, I want to come too and rescue Roger."

And Uncle Asriel, she thought; but she didn't mention that.

7
John Faa

Now that Lyra had a task in mind, she felt much better. Helping Mrs Coulter had been all very well, but Pantalaimon was right: she wasn't really doing any work there, she was just a pretty pet. On the gyptian boat, there was real work to do, and Ma Costa made sure she did it. She cleaned and swept, she peeled potatoes and made tea, she greased the propellor-shaft bearings, she kept the weed-trap clear over the propellor, she washed dishes, she opened lock gates, she tied the boat up at mooring-posts, and within a couple of days she was as much at home with this new life as if she'd been born gyptian.

What she didn't notice was that the Costas were alert every second for unusual signs of interest in Lyra from the waterside people. If she hadn't realized it, she was important, and Mrs Coulter and the Oblation Board were bound to be searching everywhere for her. Indeed, Tony heard from gossip in pubs along the way that the police were making raids on houses and farms and building yards and factories without any explanation, though there was a rumour that they were searching for a missing girl. And that in itself was odd, considering all the kids that had gone missing without being looked for. Gyptians and land folk alike were getting jumpy and nervous.

And there was another reason for the Costas' interest in Lyra; but she wasn't to learn that for a few days yet.

So they took to keeping her below decks when they passed a lock-keeper's cottage or a canal basin, or anywhere there were likely to be idlers hanging about. Once they passed through a town where the police were searching all the boats that came along the waterway, and holding up the traffic in both directions. The Costas were equal to that, though. There was a secret compartment beneath Ma's bunk, where Lyra lay cramped for two hours while the police banged up and down the length of the boat unsuccessfully.

"Why didn't their dæmons find me, though?" she asked afterwards, and Ma showed her the lining of the secret space: cedarwood, which had a soporific effect on dæmons; and it was true that Pantalaimon had spent the whole time happily asleep by Lyra's head.

Slowly, with many halts and detours, the Costas' boat drew nearer the Fens, that wide and never fully mapped wilderness of huge skies and endless marshland in eastern Anglia. The furthest fringe of it mingled indistinguishably with the creeks and tidal inlets of the shallow sea, and the other side of the sea mingled indistinguishably with Holland; and parts of the Fens had been drained and dyked by Hollanders, some of whom had settled there; so the language of the Fens was thick with Dutch. But parts had never been drained or planted or settled at all, and in the wildest central regions, where eels slithered and waterbirds flocked, where eerie marsh-fires flickered and waylurkers tempted careless travellers to their doom in the swamps and bogs, the gyptian people had always found it safe to muster.

And now by a thousand winding channels and creeks and watercourses, gyptian boats were moving in towards the Byanplats, the only patch of slightly higher ground in the hundreds of square miles of marsh and bog. There was an ancient wooden meeting hall there with a huddle of permanent dwellings around it, and wharves and jetties and an Eelmarket. When a Byanroping was called, a summons or muster of gyptians, so many boats filled the waterways that you could walk for a mile in any direction over their decks; or so it was said. The gyptians ruled in the Fens. No one else dared enter, and while the gyptians kept the peace and traded fairly, the landlopers turned a blind eye to the incessant smuggling and the occasional feuds. If a gyptian body floated ashore down the coast, or got snagged in a fish-net, well – it was only a gyptian.

Lyra listened enthralled to tales of the Fen-dwellers, of the great ghost dog Black Shuck, of the marsh-fires arising from bubbles of witch-oil, and began to think of herself as gyptian even before they reached the Fens. She had soon slipped back into her Oxford voice, and now she was acquiring a gyptian one, complete with Fen-Dutch words. Ma Costa had to remind her of a few things.

"You en't gyptian, Lyra. You might pass for gyptian with practice, but there's more to us than gyptian language. There's deeps in us and strong currents. We're water people all through, and you en't, you're a fire person. What you're most like is marsh-fire, that's the place you have in the gyptian scheme; you got witch-oil in your soul. Deceptive, that's what you are, child."

Lyra was hurt.

"I en't never deceived anyone! You ask…"

There was no one to ask, of course, and Ma Costa laughed, but kindly.

"Can't you see I'm a-paying you a compliment, you gosling?" she said, and Lyra was pacified, though she didn't understand.

When they reached the Byanplats it was evening, and the sun was about to set in a splash of bloody sky. The low island and the

113

Zaal were humped blackly against the light, like the clustered buildings around; threads of smoke rose into the still air, and from the press of boats all around came the smells of frying fish, of smokeleaf, of jenniver-spirit.

They tied up close to the Zaal itself, at a mooring Tony said had been used by their family for generations. Presently Ma Costa had the frying-pan going, with a couple of fat eels hissing and sputtering and the kettle on for potato-powder. Tony and Kerim oiled their hair, put on their finest leather jackets and blue spotted neckerchiefs, loaded their fingers with silver rings, and went to greet some old friends in the neighbouring boats and drink a glass or two in the nearest bar. They came back with important news.

"We got here just in time. The Roping's this very night. And they're a-saying in the town – what d'you think of this? – they're saying that the missing child's on a gyptian boat, and she's a-going to appear tonight at the Roping!"

He laughed loudly and ruffled Lyra's hair. Ever since they'd entered the Fens he had been more and more good-tempered, as if the savage gloom his face showed outside were only a disguise. And Lyra felt an excitement growing in her breast as she ate quickly and washed the dishes before combing her hair, tucking the alethiometer into the wolfskin coat pocket, and jumping ashore with all the other families making their way up the slope to the Zaal.

She had thought Tony was joking. She soon found that he wasn't, or else that she looked less like a gyptian than she'd thought, for many people stared, and children pointed, and by the time they reached the great doors of the Zaal they were walking alone between a crowd on either side, who had fallen back to stare and give them room.

And then Lyra began to feel truly nervous. She kept close to Ma

Costa, and Pantalaimon became as big as he could and took his panther-shape to reassure her. Ma Costa trudged up the steps as if nothing in the world could possibly either stop her or make her go more quickly, and Tony and Kerim walked proudly on either side like princes.

The hall was lit by naphtha lamps, which shone brightly enough on the faces and bodies of the audience, but left the lofty rafters hidden in darkness. The people coming in had to struggle to find room on the floor, where the benches were already crowded; but families squeezed up to make space, children occupying laps and dæmons curling up underfoot or perching out of the way on the rough wooden walls.

At the front of the Zaal there was a platform with eight carved wooden chairs set out. As Lyra and the Costas found space to stand along the edge of the hall (there was nowhere left to sit), eight men appeared from the shadows at the rear of the platform and stood in front of the chairs. A ripple of excitement swept over the audience as they hushed one another and shoved themselves into spaces on the nearest bench. Finally there was silence and seven of the men on the platform sat down.

The one who remained was in his seventies, but tall and bull-necked and powerful. He wore a plain canvas jacket and a checked shirt, like many gyptian men; there was nothing to mark him out but the air of strength and authority he had. Lyra recognized it: Uncle Asriel had it, and so did the Master of Jordan. This man's dæmon was a crow, very like the Master's raven.

"That's John Faa, the lord of the western gyptians," Tony whispered.

John Faa began to speak, in a deep slow voice.

"Gyptians! Welcome to the Roping. We've come to listen and come to decide. You all know why. There are many families here

115

who've lost a child. Some have lost two. Someone is taking them. To be sure, landlopers are losing children too. We have no quarrel with landlopers over this.

"Now there's been talk about a child and a reward. Here's the truth to stop all gossip. The child's name is Lyra Belacqua, and she's being sought by the landloper police. There is a reward of one thousand sovereigns for giving her up to them. She's a landloper child, and she's in our care, and there she's going to stay. Anyone tempted by those thousand sovereigns had better find a place neither on land nor on water. We en't giving her up."

Lyra felt a blush from the roots of her hair to the soles of her feet; Pantalaimon became a brown moth to hide. Eyes all around were turning to them, and she could only look up at Ma Costa for reassurance.

But John Faa was speaking again:

"Talk all we may, we won't change owt. We must act if we want to change things. Here's another fact for you: the Gobblers, these child-thieves, are a-taking their prisoners to a town in the far North, way up in the land of dark. I don't know what they do with 'em there. Some folk say they kill 'em, other folk say different. We don't know.

"What we do know is that they do it with the help of the landloper police and the clergy. Every power on land is helping 'em. Remember that. They know what's going on and they'll help it whenever they can.

"So what I'm proposing en't easy. And I need your agreement. I'm proposing that we send a band of fighters up North to rescue them kids and bring 'em back alive. I'm proposing that we put our gold into this, and all the craft and courage we can muster. Yes, Raymond van Gerrit?"

A man in the audience had raised his hand, and John Faa sat down to let him speak.

"Beg pardon, Lord Faa. There's landloper kids as well as gyptians been taken captive. Are you saying we should rescue them as well?"

John Faa stood up to answer.

"Raymond, are you saying we should fight our way through every kind of danger to a little group of frightened children, and then say to some of them that they can come home, and to the rest that they have to stay? No, you're a better man than that. Well, do I have your approval, my friends?"

The question caught them by surprise, for there was a moment's hesitation; but then a full-throated roar filled the hall, and hands were clapped in the air, fists shaken, voices raised in excited clamour. The rafters of the Zaal shook, and from their perches up in the dark a score of sleeping birds woke up in fear and flapped their wings, and little showers of dust drifted down.

John Faa let the noise continue for a minute, and then raised his hand for silence again.

"This'll take a while to organize. I want the heads of the families to raise a tax and muster a levy. We'll meet again here in three days' time. In between now and then I'm a-going to talk with the child I mentioned before, and with Farder Coram, and form a plan to put before you when we meet. Good night to ye all."

His massive, plain, blunt presence was enough to calm them. As the audience began to move out of the great doors into the chilly evening, to go to their boats or to the crowded bars of the little settlement, Lyra said to Ma Costa:

"Who are the other men on the platform?"

"The heads of the six families, and the other man is Farder Coram."

It was easy to see who she meant by the other man, because he was the oldest one there. He walked with a stick and all the time he'd been sitting behind John Faa he'd been trembling as if with an ague.

"Come on," said Tony. "I'd best take you up to pay your respects to John Faa. You call him Lord Faa. I don't know what you'll be asked, but mind you tell the truth."

Pantalaimon was a sparrow now, and sat curiously on Lyra's shoulder, his claws deep in the wolfskin coat, as she followed Tony through the crowd up to the platform.

He lifted her up. Knowing that everyone still in the hall was staring at her, and conscious of those thousand sovereigns she was suddenly worth, she blushed and hesitated. Pantalaimon darted to her breast and became a wildcat, sitting up in her arms and hissing softly as he looked around.

Lyra felt a push, and stepped forward to John Faa. He was stern and massive and expressionless, more like a pillar of rock than a man, but he stooped and held out his hand to shake. When she put hers in, it nearly vanished.

"Welcome, Lyra," he said.

Close to, she felt his voice rumbling like the earth itself. She would have been nervous but for Pantalaimon, and the fact that John Faa's stony expression had warmed a little. He was treating her very gently.

"Thank you, Lord Faa," she said.

"Now you come in the parley room and we'll have a talk," said John Faa. "Have they been feeding you proper, the Costas?"

"Oh, yes. We had eels for supper."

"Proper Fen eels, I expect."

The parley room was a comfortable place with a big fire, sideboards laden with silver and porcelain, and a heavy table darkly polished by the years, at which twelve chairs were drawn up.

The other men from the platform had gone elsewhere, but the old shaking man was still with them. John Faa helped him to a seat at the table.

"Now you sit here on my right," John Faa said to Lyra, and

118

took the chair at the head of the table himself. Lyra found herself opposite Farder Coram. She was a little frightened by his skull-like face and his continual trembling. His dæmon was a beautiful autumn-coloured cat, massive in size, who stalked along the table with upraised tail and elegantly inspected Pantalaimon, touching noses briefly before settling on Farder Coram's lap, half-closing her eyes and purring softly.

A woman whom Lyra hadn't noticed came out of the shadows with a tray of glasses, set it down by John Faa, curtseyed and left. John Faa poured little glasses of jenniver from a stone crock for himself and Farder Coram, and wine for Lyra.

"So," John Faa said. "You run away, Lyra."

"Yes."

"And who was the lady you run away from?"

"She was called Mrs Coulter. And I thought she was nice but I found out she was one of the Gobblers. I heard someone say what the Gobblers were, they were called the General Oblation Board, and she was in charge of it, it was all her idea. And they was all working on some plan, I dunno what it was, only they was going to make me help her get kids for 'em. But they never knew…"

"They never knew what?"

"Well, first they never knew that I knew some kids what had been took. My friend Roger the Kitchen boy from Jordan College, and Billy Costa, and a girl out the Covered Market in Oxford. And another thing… My uncle, right, Lord Asriel. I heard them talking about his journeys to the North, and I don't reckon he's got anything to do with the Gobblers. Because I spied on the Master and the Scholars of Jordan, right, I hid in the Retiring Room where no one's supposed to go except them, and I heard him tell them all about his expedition up North, and the Dust he saw, and he brought back the head of

Stanislaus Grumman, what the Tartars had made a hole in. And now the Gobblers've got him locked up somewhere. The armoured bears are guarding him. And I want to rescue him."

She looked fierce and stubborn as she sat there, small against the high carved back of the chair. The two old men couldn't help smiling, but whereas Farder Coram's smile was a hesitant, rich, complicated expression that trembled across his face like sunlight chasing shadows on a windy March day, John Faa's smile was slow, warm, plain and kindly.

"You better tell us what you did hear your uncle say that evening," said John Faa. "Don't leave anything out, mind. Tell us everything."

Lyra did, more slowly than she'd told the Costas but more honestly, too. She was afraid of John Faa, and what she was most afraid of was his kindness. When she'd finished, Farder Coram spoke for the first time. His voice was rich and musical, with as many tones in it as there were colours in his dæmon's fur.

"This Dust," he said. "Did they ever call it anything else, Lyra?"

"No. Just Dust. Mrs Coulter told me what it was, elementary particles, but that's all she called it."

"And they think that by doing something to children, they can find out more about it?"

"Yes. But I don't know what. Except my uncle…. There's something I forgot to tell you. When he was showing them lantern slides, there was another one he had. It was the Roarer –"

"The what?" said John Faa.

"The Aurora," said Farder Coram. "Is that right, Lyra?"

"Yeah, that's it. And in the lights of the Roarer there was like a city. All towers and churches and domes and that. It was a bit like Oxford, that's what I thought, anyway. And Uncle Asriel, he was more interested in that, I think, but the Master and the other

Scholars were more interested in Dust, like Mrs Coulter and Lord Boreal and them."

"I see," said Farder Coram. "That's very interesting."

"Now, Lyra," said John Faa, "I'm a-going to tell you something. Farder Coram here, he's a wise man. He's a see-er. He's been a-follering all what's been going on with Dust and the Gobblers and Lord Asriel and everything else, and he's been a-follering *you*. Every time the Costas went to Oxford, or half a dozen other families come to that, they brought back a bit of news. About you, child. Did you know that?"

Lyra shook her head. She was beginning to be frightened. Pantalaimon was growling too deep for anyone to hear, but she could feel it in her fingertips down inside his fur.

"Oh, yes," said John Faa, "all your doings, they all get back to Farder Coram here."

Lyra couldn't hold it in.

"We didn't *damage* it! Honest! It was only a bit of mud! And we never got very far –"

"What are you talking about, child?" said John Faa.

Farder Coram laughed. When he did that, his shaking stopped and his face became bright and young.

But Lyra wasn't laughing. With trembling lips she said, "And even if we had found the bung, we'd never've took it out! It was just a joke. We wouldn't've sunk it, never!"

Then John Faa began to laugh too. He slapped a broad hand on the table so hard the glasses rang, and his massive shoulders shook, and he had to wipe away the tears from his eyes. Lyra had never seen such a sight, never heard such a bellow; it was like a mountain laughing.

"Oh, yes," he said when he could speak again, "we heard about that too, little girl! I don't suppose the Costas have set foot anywhere since then without being reminded of it. You better leave a guard on your boat, Tony, people say. Fierce little girls round here! Oh, that story went all over the Fens, child. But we en't going to punish you for it. No, no! Ease your mind."

He looked at Farder Coram, and the two old men laughed again, but more gently. And Lyra felt contented, and safe.

Finally John Faa shook his head and became serious again.

"I were saying, Lyra, as we knew about you from a child. From a baby. You oughter know what we know. I can't guess what they told you at Jordan College about where you came from, but they don't know the whole truth of it. Did they ever tell you who your parents were?"

Now Lyra was completely dazed.

"Yes," she said. "They said I was – they said they – they said Lord Asriel put me there because my mother and father died in an airship accident. That's what they told me."

"Ah, did they? Well now, child, I'm a-going to tell you a story, a true story. I know it's true, because a gyptian woman told me, and they all tell the truth to John Faa and Farder Coram. So this is the truth about yourself, Lyra. Your father never perished in no airship accident, because your father is Lord Asriel."

Lyra could only sit in wonder.

"Here's how it came about," John Faa went on. "When he was a young man, Lord Asriel went exploring all over the North, and came back with a great fortune. And he was a high-spirited man, quick to anger, a passionate man.

"And your mother, she was passionate too. Not so well-born as him, but a clever woman. A scholar, even, and those who saw her said she was very beautiful. She and your father, they fell in love as soon's they met.

"The trouble was, your mother was already married. She'd married a politician. He was a member of the King's party, one of his closest advisers. A rising man.

"Now when your mother found herself with child, she feared to tell her husband the child wasn't his. And when the baby was born – that's you, girl – it was clear from the look of you that you didn't favour her husband, but your true father, and she thought it best to hide you away and give out that you'd died.

"So you was took to Oxfordshire, where your father had estates, and put in the care of a gyptian woman to nurse. But someone whispered to your mother's husband what had happened, and he came a-flying down and ransacked the cottage where the gyptian woman had been, only she'd fled to the great house; and the husband followed after, in a murderous passion.

"Your father was out a-hunting, but they got word to him and he came riding back in time to find your mother's husband at the foot of the great staircase. Another moment and he'd have forced open the closet where the gyptian woman was hiding with you, but Lord Asriel challenged him, and they fought there and then, and Lord Asriel killed him.

"The gyptian woman heard and saw it all, Lyra, and that's how we know.

"The consequence was a great lawsuit. Your father en't the kind of man to deny or conceal the truth, and it left the judges with a problem. He'd killed all right, he'd shed blood, but he was defending his home and his child against an intruder. On t'other hand, the law allows any man to avenge the violation of his wife, and the dead man's lawyers argued that he were doing just that.

"The case lasted for weeks, with volumes of argument back and forth. In the end the judges punished Lord Asriel by confiscating all his property and all his land, and left him a poor man; and he had been richer than a king.

"As for your mother, she wanted nothing to do with it, nor with you. She turned her back. The gyptian nurse told me she'd often been afeared of how your mother would treat you, because she was a proud and scornful woman. So much for her.

"Then there was you. If things had fallen out different, Lyra, you might have been brought up a gyptian, because the nurse begged the court to let her have you; but we gyptians got little standing in the law. The court decided you was to be placed in a Priory, and so you were, with the Sisters of Obedience at Watlington. You won't remember.

"But Lord Asriel wouldn't stand for that. He had a hatred of priors and monks and nuns, and being a high-handed man he just rode in one day and carried you off. Not to look after himself, nor to give to the gyptians; he took you to Jordan College, and dared the law to undo it.

"Well, the law let things be. Lord Asriel went back to his explorations, and you grew up at Jordan College. The one thing he said, your father, the one condition he made, was that your mother shouldn't be let see you. If she ever tried to do that, she was to be prevented, and he was to be told, because all the anger in his nature had turned against her now. The Master promised faithfully to do that; and so time passed.

"Then come all this anxiety about Dust. And all over the country, all over the world, wise men and women too began a-worrying about it. It weren't of any account to us gyptians, until they started taking our kids. That's when we got interested. And we got connections in all sorts of places you wouldn't imagine, including Jordan College. You wouldn't know, but there's been someone a-watching over you and reporting to us ever since you been there. 'Cause we got an interest in you, and that gyptian woman who nursed you, she never stopped being anxious on your behalf."

"Who was it watching over me?" said Lyra. She felt immensely important and strange, that all her doings should be an object of concern so far away.

124

"It was a Kitchen servant. It was Bernie Johansen, the pastry cook. He's half-gyptian; you never knew that, I'll be bound."

Bernie was a kindly, solitary man, one of those rare people whose dæmon was the same sex as himself. It was Bernie she'd shouted at in her despair when Roger was taken. And Bernie had been telling the gyptians everything! She marvelled.

"So anyway," John Faa went on, "we heard about you going away from Jordan College, and how it came about at a time when Lord Asriel was imprisoned and couldn't prevent it. And we remembered what he'd said to the Master that he must never do, and we remembered that the man your mother had married, the politician Lord Asriel killed, was called Edward Coulter."

"Mrs Coulter?" said Lyra, quite stupefied. "*She* en't my mother?"

"She is. And if your father had been free she wouldn't never have dared to defy him, and you'd still be at Jordan, not knowing a thing. But what the Master was a-doing letting you go is a mystery I can't explain. He was charged with your care. All I can guess is that she had some power over him."

Lyra suddenly understood the Master's curious behaviour on the morning she'd left.

"But he didn't want to…" she said, trying to remember it exactly. "He … I had to go and see him first thing that morning, and I mustn't tell Mrs Coulter… It was like he wanted to protect me from Mrs Coulter…" She stopped, and looked at the two men carefully, and then decided to tell them the whole truth about the Retiring Room. "See, there was something else. That evening I hid in the Retiring Room, I saw the Master try to poison Lord Asriel. I saw him put some powder in the wine and I told my uncle and he knocked the decanter off the table and spilled it. So I saved his life. I could never understand why the Master would want to poison him, because he was always so

125

kind. Then on the morning I left he called me in early to his study, and I had to go secretly so no one would know, and he said…" Lyra racked her brains to try and remember exactly what it was the Master had said. No good; she shook her head. "The only thing I could understand was that he gave me something and I had to keep it secret from her, from Mrs Coulter. I suppose it's all right if I tell you…"

She felt in the pocket of the wolfskin coat and took out the velvet package. She laid it on the table, and she sensed John Faa's massive simple curiosity and Farder Coram's bright flickering intelligence both trained on it like searchlights.

When she laid the alethiometer bare, it was Farder Coram who spoke first.

"I never thought I'd ever set eyes on one of them again. That's a symbol-reader. Did he tell you anything about it, child?"

"No. Only that I'd have to work out how to read it by myself. And he called it an alethiometer."

"What's that mean?" said John Faa, turning to his companion.

"That's a Greek word. I reckon it's from *aletheia*, which means truth. It's a truth-measure. And have you worked out how to use it?" he said to her.

"No. Least, I can make the three short hands point to different pictures, but I can't do anything with the long one. It goes all over. Except sometimes, right, sometimes when I'm sort of concentrating, I can make the long needle go this way or that just by thinking it."

"What's it do, Farder Coram?" said John Faa. "And how do you read it?"

"All these pictures round the rim," said Farder Coram, holding it delicately towards John Faa's blunt strong gaze, "they're symbols, and each one stands for a whole series of things. Take the anchor, there. The first meaning of that is hope, because hope holds you fast like an anchor so you don't give way. The second meaning is steadfastness. The third meaning is snag, or prevention. The fourth meaning is the sea. And so on, down to ten, twelve, maybe a never-ending series of meanings."

"And do you know them all?"

"I know some, but to read it fully I'd need the book. I seen the book and I know where it is, but I en't got it."

"We'll come back to that," said John Faa. "Go on with how you read it."

"You got three hands you can control," Farder Coram explained, "and you use them to ask a question. By pointing to three symbols you can ask any question you can imagine, because you've got so many levels of each one. Once you got your question framed, the other needle swings round and points to more symbols that give you the answer."

"But how does it know what level you're a-thinking of when you set the question?" said John Faa.

"Ah, by itself it don't. It only works if the questioner holds the levels in their mind. You got to know all the meanings, first, and there must be a thousand or more. Then you got to be able to hold 'em in your mind without fretting at it or pushing for an answer, and just watch while the needle wanders. When it's gone round its full range you'll know what the answer is. I know how it works because I seen it done once by a wise man in Uppsala, and that's the only time I ever saw one before. Do you know how rare these are?"

"The Master told me there was only six made," Lyra said.

"Whatever the number, it en't large."

"And you kept this secret from Mrs Coulter, like the Master told you?" said John Faa.

"Yes. But her dæmon, right, he used to go in my room. And I'm sure he found it."

"I see. Well, Lyra, I don't know as we'll ever understand the full truth, but this is my guess, as good as I can make it. The Master was given a charge by Lord Asriel to look after you and keep you safe from your mother. And that was what he did, for ten years or more. Then Mrs Coulter's friends in the Church helped her set up this Oblation Board, for what purpose we don't know, and there she was, as powerful in her way as Lord Asriel was in his. Your parents, both strong in the world, both ambitious, and the Master of Jordan holding you in the balance between them.

"Now the Master's got a hundred things to look after. His first concern is his college and the scholarship there. So if he sees a threat to that, he has to move agin it. And the Church in recent times, Lyra, it's been a-getting more commanding. There's councils for this and councils for that; there's talk of reviving the Office of Inquisition, God forbid. And the Master has to tread warily between all these powers. He has to keep Jordan College on the right side of the Church, or it won't survive.

"And another concern of the Master is you, child. Bernie Johansen was always clear about that. The Master of Jordan and the other Scholars, they loved you like their own child. They'd do anything to keep you safe, not just because they'd promised to Lord Asriel that they would, but for your own sake. So if the Master gave you up to Mrs Coulter when he'd promised Lord Asriel he wouldn't, he must have thought you'd be safer with her than in Jordan College, in spite of all appearances. And when he set out to poison Lord Asriel, he must have thought that what Lord Asriel was a-doing would place all of them in danger, and maybe all of us, too; maybe all the world. I see the Master as a man having terrible choices to make; whatever he chooses will do harm; but maybe if he does the right thing, a little less harm will come about than if he chooses wrong. God preserve me from having to make that sort of choice.

"And when it come to the point where he had to let you go, he gave you the symbol-reader and bade you keep it safe. I wonder what he had in mind for you to do with it; as you couldn't read it, I'm foxed as to what he was a-thinking."

"He said Uncle Asriel presented the alethiometer to Jordan College years before," Lyra said, struggling to remember. "He was going to say something else, and then someone knocked at the door and he had to stop. What I thought was, he might have wanted me to keep it away from Lord Asriel too."

"Or even the opposite," said John Faa.

"What d'you mean, John?" said Farder Coram.

"He might have had it in mind to ask Lyra to return it to Lord Asriel, as a kind of recompense for trying to poison him. He might have thought the danger from Lord Asriel had passed. Or that Lord Asriel could read some wisdom from this instrument and hold back from his purpose. If Lord Asriel's held captive now, it might help set him free. Well, Lyra, you better take this symbol-reader and keep it safe. If you kept it safe so far I en't worried about leaving it with you. But there might come a time when we need to consult it, and I reckon we'll ask for it then."

He folded the velvet over it and slid it back across the table. Lyra wanted to ask all kinds of questions, but suddenly she felt shy of this massive man, with his little eyes so sharp and kindly among their folds and wrinkles.

One thing she had to ask, though.

"Who was the gyptian woman who nursed me?"

"Why, it was Billy Costa's mother, of course. She won't have told you, because I en't let her, but she knows what we're a-talking of here, so it's all out in the open.

"Now you best be getting back to her. You got plenty to be a-thinking of, child. When three days is gone past we'll have another Roping and discuss all there is to do. You be a good girl. Good night, Lyra."

"Good night, Lord Faa. Good night, Farder Coram," she said politely, clutching the alethiometer to her breast with one hand and scooping up Pantalaimon with the other.

Both old men smiled kindly at her. Outside the door of the parley room Ma Costa was waiting and, as if nothing had happened since Lyra was born, the boat-mother gathered her into her great arms and kissed her before bearing her off to bed.

8

Frustration

Lyra had to adjust to her new sense of her own story, and that couldn't be done in a day. To see Lord Asriel as her father was one thing, but to accept Mrs Coulter as her mother was nowhere near so easy. A couple of months ago she would have rejoiced, of course, and she knew that too, and felt confused.

But, being Lyra, she didn't fret about it for long, for there was the Fen town to explore and many gyptian children to amaze. Before the three days were up she was an expert with a punt (in her eyes, at least) and she'd gathered a gang of urchins about her with tales of her mighty father, so unjustly made captive.

"And then one evening the Turkish Ambassador was a guest at Jordan for dinner. And he was under orders from the Sultan hisself to kill my father, right, and he had a ring on his finger with a hollow stone full of poison. And when the wine come round he made as if to reach across my father's glass, and he sprinkled the poison in. It was done so quick that no one else saw him, but –"

"What sort of poison?" demanded a thin-faced girl.

"Poison out of a special Turkish serpent," Lyra invented, "what they catch by playing a pipe to lure out and then they throw it a sponge soaked in honey and the serpent bites it and can't get his fangs free, and they catch it and milk the venom out of it. Anyway, my father seen what the Turk done, and he says Gentlemen, I want to propose a toast of friendship between Jordan College and the College of Izmir, which was the college the Turkish Ambassador belonged to. And to show our willingness to be friends, he says, we'll swap glasses and drink each other's wine.

"And the Ambassador was in a fix then, 'cause he couldn't refuse to drink without giving deadly insult, and he couldn't drink it because he knew it was poisoned. He went pale and he fainted right away at the table. And when he come round they was all still sitting there, waiting and looking at him. And then he had to either drink the poison or own up."

"So what did he do?"

"He drunk it. It took him five whole minutes to die, and he was in torment all the time."

"Did you see it happen?"

"No, 'cause girls en't allowed at the High Table. But I seen his body afterwards when they laid him out. His skin was all withered like an old apple, and his eyes were starting from his head. In fact they had to push 'em back in the sockets…"

And so on.

Meanwhile, around the edges of the Fen country, the police were knocking at doors, searching attics and outhouses, inspecting papers and interrogating everyone who claimed to have seen a blonde little girl; and in Oxford the search was even fiercer. Jordan College was scoured from the dustiest boxroom to the darkest cellar, and so were Gabriel and St Michael's, till the heads of all the colleges issued a joint protest asserting their ancient rights. The only notion Lyra had of the search for her was the incessant drone of the gas engines of airships crisscrossing the skies. They weren't visible, because the clouds were low and by statute airships had to keep a certain height above Fen country, but who knew what cunning spy-devices they might carry? Best to keep under cover when she heard them, or wear the oilskin sou'wester over her bright distinctive hair.

And she questioned Ma Costa about every detail of the story of her birth. She wove the details into a mental tapestry even clearer and sharper than the stories she made up, and lived over and over again the flight from the cottage, the concealment in the closet, the harsh-voiced challenge, the clash of swords –

"Swords? Great God, girl, you dreaming?" Ma Costa said. "Mr Coulter had a gun, and Lord Asriel knocked it out his hand and struck him down with one blow. Then there was two shots. I wonder you don't remember; you ought to, little as you were. The first shot was Edward Coulter, who reached his gun and fired, and the second was Lord Asriel, who tore it out his grasp a second time and turned it on him. Shot him right between the eyes and dashed his brains out. Then he says, cool as paint, 'Come out, Mrs Costa, and bring the baby,' because you were setting up such a howl, you and that dæmon both; and he took you up and dandled you and sat you on his shoulders, walking up and down in high good humour with the dead man at his feet, and called for wine and bade me swab the floor."

By the end of the fourth repetition of the story Lyra was perfectly convinced she did remember it, and even volunteered details of the colour of Mr Coulter's coat and the cloaks and furs hanging in the closet. Ma Costa laughed.

And whenever she was alone, Lyra took out the alethiometer and pored over it like a lover with a picture of the beloved. So each image had several meanings, did it? Why shouldn't she work them out? Wasn't she Lord Asriel's daughter?

Remembering what Farder Coram had said, she tried to focus

her mind on three symbols taken at random, and clicked the hands round to point at them. She found that if she held the alethiometer just so in her palms and gazed at it in a particular lazy way, as she thought of it, the long needle would begin to move more purposefully. Instead of its wayward divagations around the dial it swung smoothly from one picture to another. Sometimes it would pause at three, sometimes two, sometimes five or more, and although she understood nothing of it, she gained a deep calm enjoyment from it, unlike anything she'd known. Pantalaimon would crouch over the dial, sometimes as a cat, sometimes as a mouse, swinging his head round after the needle; and once or twice the two of them shared a glimpse of meaning that felt as if a shaft of sunlight had struck through clouds to light up a majestic line of great hills in the distance – something far beyond, and never suspected. And Lyra thrilled at those times with the same deep thrill she'd felt all her life on hearing the word North.

So the three days passed, with much coming and going between the multitude of boats and the Zaal. And then came the evening of the second Roping. The hall was more crowded than before, if that was possible. Lyra and the Costas got there in time to sit at the front, and as soon as the flickering lights showed that the place was crammed, John Faa and Farder Coram came out on the platform and sat behind the table. John Faa didn't have to make a sign for silence; he just put his great hands flat on the table and looked at the people below, and the hubbub died.

"Well," he said, "you done what I asked. And better than I hoped. I'm a-going to call on the heads of the six families now to come up here and give over their gold and recount their promises. Nicholas Rokeby, you come first."

A stout black-bearded man climbed on to the platform and laid a heavy leather bag on the table.

"That's our gold," he said. "And we offer thirty-eight men."

"Thank you, Nicholas," said John Faa. Farder Coram was making a note. The first man stood at the back of the platform as John Faa called for the next, and the next; and each came up, laid a bag on the table and announced the number of men he could muster. The Costas were part of the Stefanski family, and naturally Tony had been one of the first to volunteer. Lyra noticed his hawk-dæmon shifting from foot to foot and spreading her wings as the Stefanski money and the promise of twenty-three men were laid before John Faa.

When the six family heads had all come up, Farder Coram showed his piece of paper to John Faa, who stood up to address the audience again.

"Friends, that's a muster of one hundred and seventy men. I thank you proudly. As for the gold, I make no doubt from the weight of it that you've all dug deep in your coffers, and my warm thanks go out for that as well.

"What we're a-going to do next is this. We're a-going to charter a ship and sail North, and find them kids and set 'em free. From what we know, there might be some fighting to do. It won't be the first time, nor it won't be the last, but we never had to fight yet with people who kidnap children, and we shall have to be uncommon cunning. But we en't going to come back without our kids. Yes, Dirk Vries?"

A man stood up and said, "Lord Faa, do you know why they captured them kids?"

"We heard it's a theological matter. They're making an experiment, but what nature it is we don't know. To tell you all the truth, we don't even know whether any harm is a-coming to 'em. But whatever it is, good or bad, they got no right to reach out by night and pluck little children out the hearts of their families. Yes, Raymond van Gerrit?"

The man who'd spoken at the first meeting stood up and said,

135

"That child, Lord Faa, the one you spoke of as being sought, the one as is sitting in the front row now. I heard as all the folk living around the edge of the Fens is having their houses turned upside down on her account. I heard there's a move in Parliament this very day to rescind our ancient privileges on account of this child. Yes, friends," he said, over the babble of shocked whispers, "they're a-going to pass a law doing away with our right to free movement in and out the Fens. Now, Lord Faa, what we want to know is this: who is this child on account of which we might come to such a pass? She en't a gyptian child, not as I heard. How comes it that a landloper child can put us all in danger?"

Lyra looked up at John Faa's massive frame. Her heart was thumping so much she could hardly hear the first words of his reply.

"Now spell it out, Raymond, don't be shy," he said. "You want us to give this child up to them she's a-fleeing from, is that right?"

The man stood obstinately frowning, but said nothing.

"Well, perhaps you would, and perhaps you wouldn't," John Faa continued. "But if any man or woman needs a reason for doing good, ponder on this. That little girl is the daughter of Lord Asriel, no less. For them as has forgotten, it were Lord Asriel who interceded with the Turk for the life of Sam Broekman. It were Lord Asriel who allowed gyptian boats free passage on the canals through his property. It were Lord Asriel who defeated the Watercourse Bill in Parliament, to our great and lasting benefit. And it were Lord Asriel who fought day and night in the floods of '53, and plunged headlong in the water twice to pull out young Ruud and Nellie Koopman. You forgotten that? Shame, shame on you, shame.

"And now that same Lord Asriel is held in the farthest coldest darkest regions of the wild, captive, in the fortress of Svalbard.

Do I need to tell you the kind of creatures a-guarding him there? And this is his little daughter in our care, and Raymond van Gerrit would hand her over to the authorities for a bit of peace and quiet. Is that right, Raymond? Stand up and answer, man."

But Raymond van Gerrit had sunk to his seat, and nothing would make him stand. A low hiss of disapproval sounded through the great hall, and Lyra felt the shame he must be feeling, as well as a deep glow of pride in her brave father.

John Faa turned away, and looked at the other men on the platform.

"Nicholas Rokeby, I'm a-putting you in charge of finding a vessel, and commanding her once we sail. Adam Stefanski, I want you to take charge of the arms and munitions, and command the fighting. Roger van Poppel, you look to all the other stores, from food to cold-weather clothing. Simon Hartmann, you be treasurer, and account to us all for a proper apportionment of our gold. Benjamin de Ruyter, I want you to take charge of spying. There's a great deal we ought to find out, and I'm a-giving you the charge of that, and you'll report to Farder Coram. Michael Canzona, you're going to be responsible for co-ordinating the first four leaders' work, and you'll report to me, and if I die, you're my second in command and you'll take over.

"Now I've made my dispositions according to custom, and if any man or woman seeks to disagree, they may do so freely."

After a moment a woman stood up.

"Lord Faa, en't you a-taking any women on this expedition to look after them kids once you found 'em?"

"No, Nell. We shall have little space as it is. Any kids we free will be better off in our care than where they've been."

"But supposing you find out that you can't rescue 'em without some women in disguise as guards or nurses or whatever?"

"Well, I hadn't thought of that," John Faa admitted. "We'll consider that most carefully when we retire into the parley room, you have my promise."

She sat down and a man stood up.

"Lord Faa, I heard you say that Lord Asriel is in captivity. Is it part of your plan to rescue him? Because if it is, and if he's in the power of them bears as I think you said, that's going to need more than a hundred and seventy men. And good friend as Lord Asriel is to us, I don't know as there's any call on us to go as far as that."

"Adriaan Braks, you're not wrong. What I had it in my mind to do was to keep our eyes and ears open and see what knowledge we can glean while we're in the North. It may be that we can do something to help him, and it may not, but you can trust me not to use what you've provided, man and gold, for any purpose outside the stated one of finding our children and bringing 'em home."

Another woman stood up.

"Lord Faa, we don't know what them Gobblers might've been doing to our children. We all heard rumours and stories of fearful things. We hear about children with no heads, or about children cut in half and sewn together, or about things too awful to mention. I'm truly sorry to distress anyone, but we all heard this kind of thing, and I want to get it out in the open. Now in case you find anything of that awful kind, Lord Faa, I hope you're a-going to take powerful revenge. I hope you en't going to let thoughts of mercy and gentleness hold your hand back from striking and striking hard, and delivering a mighty blow to the heart of that infernal wickedness. And I'm sure I speak for any mother as has lost a child to the Gobblers."

There was a loud murmur of agreement as she sat down. Heads were nodding all over the Zaal.

John Faa waited for silence, and said:

"Nothing will hold my hand, Margaret, save only judgement. If I stay my hand in the North, it will only be to strike the harder in the South. To strike a day too soon is as bad as striking a hundred miles off. To be sure, there's a warm passion behind what you say. But if you give in to that passion, friends, you're a-doing what I always warned you agin: you're a-placing the satisfaction of your own feelings above the work you have to do. Our work here is first rescue, then punishment. It en't gratification for upset feelings. Our feelings don't matter. If we rescue the kids but we can't punish the Gobblers, we've done the main task. But if we aim to punish the Gobblers first and by doing so lose the chance of rescuing the kids, we've failed.

"But be assured of this, Margaret. When the time comes to punish, we shall strike such a blow as'll make their hearts faint and fearful. We shall strike the strength out of 'em. We shall leave them ruined and waste, broken and shattered, torn in a thousand pieces and scattered to the four winds. My own hammer is thirsty for blood, friends. She en't tasted blood since I slew the Tartar champion on the steppes of Kazakhstan; she's been a-hanging in my boat and dreaming; but she can smell blood in the wind from the North. She spoke to me last night and told me of her thirst, and I said soon, gal, soon. Margaret, you can worry about a hundred things, but don't you worry that John Faa's heart is too soft to strike a blow when the time comes. And the time will come under judgement. Not under passion.

"Is there anyone else who wants to speak? Speak if you will."

But no one did, and presently John Faa reached for the closing bell and rang it hard and loud, swinging it high and shaking the peals out of it so that they filled the hall and rang the rafters.

John Faa and the other men left the platform for the parley room. Lyra was a little disappointed. Didn't they want her there too? But Tony laughed.

"They got plans to make," he said. "You done your part, Lyra. Now it's for John Faa and the council."

"But I en't done nothing yet!" Lyra protested, as she followed the others reluctantly out of the Hall and down the cobbled road towards the jetty. "All I done was run away from Mrs Coulter! That's just a beginning. I want to go North!"

"Tell you what," said Tony, "I'll bring you back a walrus tooth, that's what I'll do."

Lyra scowled. For his part, Pantalaimon occupied himself by making monkey-faces at Tony's dæmon, who closed her tawny eyes in disdain. Lyra drifted to the jetty and hung about with her new companions, dangling lanterns on strings over the black water to attract the goggle-eyed fishes who swam slowly up to be lunged at with sharp sticks and missed.

But her mind was on John Faa and the parley room, and before long she slipped away up the cobbles again to the Zaal. There was a light in the parley room window. It was too high to look through, but she could hear a low rumble of voices inside.

So she walked up to the door and knocked on it firmly five times. The voices stopped, a chair scraped across the floor, and the door opened, spilling warm naphtha light out on the damp step.

"Yes?" said the man who'd opened it.

Beyond him Lyra could see the other men around the table, with bags of gold stacked neatly, and papers and pens, and glasses and a crock of jenniver.

"I want to come North," Lyra said so they could all hear it. "I want to come and help rescue the kids. That's what I set out to do when I run away from Mrs Coulter. And before that, even, I meant to rescue my friend Roger the Kitchen boy from Jordan who was took. I want to come and help. I can do navigation and I can take anbaromagnetic readings off the Aurora, and I know what parts of a bear you can eat, and all kinds of useful things. You'd be sorry if you got up there and then found you needed me and found you'd left me behind. And like that woman said, you might need women to play a part – well, you might need kids too. You don't know. So you oughter take me, Lord Faa, excuse me for interrupting your talk."

She was inside the room now, and all the men and their dæmons were watching her, some with amusement and some with irritation, but she had eyes only for John Faa. Pantalaimon sat up in her arms, his wildcat eyes blazing green.

John Faa said, "Lyra, there en't no question of taking you into danger, so don't delude yourself, child. Stay here and help Ma Costa and keep safe. That's what you got to do."

"But I'm learning how to read the alethiometer, too. It's coming clearer every day! You're bound to need that – bound to!"

He shook his head.

"No," he said. "I know your heart was set on going North, but it's my belief not even Mrs Coulter was going to take you. If you want to see the North you'll have to wait till all this trouble's over. Now off you go."

Pantalaimon hissed quietly, but John Faa's dæmon took off from the back of his chair and flew at them with black wings, not threateningly, but like a reminder of good manners; and Lyra turned on her heel as the crow glided over her head and wheeled back to John Faa. The door shut behind her with a decisive click.

"We *will* go," she said to Pantalaimon. "Let 'em try to stop us. We *will*!"

9

The Spies

Over the next few days, Lyra concocted a dozen plans and dismissed them impatiently; for they all boiled down to stowing away, and how could you stow away on a narrow boat? To be sure, the real voyage would involve a proper ship, and she knew enough stories to expect all kinds of hiding-places on a full-sized vessel: the lifeboats, the hold, the bilges, whatever they were; but she'd have to get to the ship first, and leaving the Fens meant travelling the gyptian way.

And even if she got to the coast on her own, she might stow away on the wrong ship. It would be a fine thing to hide in a lifeboat and wake up on the way to High Brazil.

Meanwhile, all around her the tantalizing work of assembling the expedition was going on day and night. She hung around Adam Stefanski, watching as he made his choice of the volunteers for the fighting force. She pestered Roger van Poppel with suggestions about the stores they needed to take: had he remembered snow-goggles? Did he know the best place to get Arctic maps?

The man she most wanted to help was Benjamin de Ruyter, the spy. But he had slipped away in the early hours of the morning after the second Roping, and naturally no one could say where he'd gone or when he'd return. So in default, Lyra attached herself to Farder Coram.

"I think it'd be best if I helped you, Farder Coram," she said, "because I probably know more about the Gobblers than anyone else, being as I was nearly one of them. Probably you'll need me to help you understand Mr de Ruyter's messages."

He took pity on the fierce, desperate little girl and didn't send her away. Instead he talked to her, and listened to her memories of Oxford and of Mrs Coulter, and watched as she read the alethiometer.

"Where's that book with all the symbols in?" she asked him one day.

"In Heidelberg," he said.

"And is there just the one?"

"There may be others, but that's the one I've seen."

"I bet there's one in Bodley's Library in Oxford," she said.

She could hardly take her eyes off Farder Coram's dæmon, who was the most beautiful dæmon she'd ever seen. When Pantalaimon was a cat he was lean and ragged and harsh, but Sophonax, for that was her name, was golden-eyed and elegant beyond measure, fully twice as large as a real cat and richly furred. When the sunlight touched her, it lit up more shades of tawny-brown-leaf-hazel-corn-gold-autumn-mahogany than Lyra could name. She longed to touch that fur, to rub her cheeks against it, but of course she never did; for it was the grossest breach of etiquette imaginable to touch another person's dæmon. Dæmons might touch each other, of course, or fight; but the prohibition against human-dæmon contact went so deep that even in battle no warrior would touch an enemy's dæmon. It was utterly forbidden. Lyra couldn't remember having to be told that: she just knew it, as instinctively as she felt that nausea was bad and comfort good. So although she admired the fur of Sophonax and even speculated on what it might feel like, she never made the slightest move to touch her, and never would.

Sophonax was as sleek and healthy and beautiful as Farder Coram was ravaged and weak. He might have been ill, or he might have suffered a crippling blow, but the result was that he could not walk without leaning on two sticks, and he trembled constantly like an aspen leaf. His mind was sharp and clear and powerful, though, and soon Lyra came to love him for his knowledge and for the firm way he directed her.

"What's that hourglass mean, Farder Coram?" she asked, over the alethiometer, one sunny morning in his boat. "It keeps coming back to that."

"There's often a clue there if you look more close. What's that little old thing on top of it?"

She screwed up her eyes and peered.

"That's a skull!"

"So what d'you think that might mean?"

"Death… Is that death?"

"That's right. So in the hourglass range of meanings you get death. In fact after time, which is the first one, death is the second one."

"D'you know what I noticed, Farder Coram? The needle stops there on the second go round! On the first round it kind of twitches, and on the second it stops. Is that saying it's the second meaning, then?"

"Probably. What are you asking it, Lyra?"

"I'm a-thinking…" She stopped, surprised to find that she'd actually been asking a question without realizing it. "I just put three pictures together because … I was thinking about Mr de Ruyter, see… And I put together the serpent and the crucible and the beehive, to ask how he's a-getting on with his spying, and –"

"Why them three symbols?"

"Because I thought the serpent was cunning, like a spy ought to be, and the crucible could mean like knowledge, what you kind of distil, and the beehive was hard work, like bees are always working hard; so out of the hard work and the cunning comes the knowledge, see, and that's the spy's job; and I pointed to them and I thought the question in my mind, and the needle stopped at death... D'you think that could be really working, Farder Coram?"

"It's working all right, Lyra. What we don't know is whether we're reading it right. That's a subtle art. I wonder if –"

Before he could finish his sentence, there was an urgent knock at the door, and a young gyptian man came in.

"Beg pardon, Farder Coram, there's Jacob Huismans just come back, and he's sore wounded."

"He was with Benjamin de Ruyter," said Farder Coram. "What's happened?"

"He won't speak," said the young man. "You better come, Farder Coram, cause he won't last long, he's a-bleeding inside."

Farder Coram and Lyra exchanged a look of alarm and wonderment, but only for a second, and then Farder Coram was hobbling out on his sticks as fast as he could manage, with his dæmon padding ahead of him. Lyra came too, hopping with impatience.

The young man led them to a boat tied up at the sugar-beet jetty, where a woman in a red flannel apron held open the door for them. Seeing her suspicious glance at Lyra, Farder Coram said, "It's important the girl hears what Jacob's got to say, mistress."

So the woman let them in and stood back, with her squirrel-dæmon perched silent on the wooden clock. On a bunk under a patchwork coverlet lay a man whose white face was damp with sweat and whose eyes were glazed.

"I've sent for the physician, Farder Coram," said the woman shakily. "Please don't agitate him. He's in an agony of pain. He come in off Peter Hawker's boat just a few minutes ago."

"Where's Peter now?"

"He's a-tying up. It was him said I had to send for you."

"Quite right. Now, Jacob, can ye hear me?"

Jacob's eyes rolled to look at Farder Coram sitting on the opposite bunk, a foot or two away.

"Hello, Farder Coram," he murmured.

Lyra looked at his dæmon. She was a ferret, and she lay very still beside his head, curled up but not asleep, for her eyes were open and glazed like his.

"What happened?" said Farder Coram.

"Benjamin's dead," came the answer. "He's dead, and Gerard's captured."

His voice was hoarse and his breath was shallow. When he stopped speaking his dæmon uncurled painfully and licked his cheek, and taking strength from that he went on:

"We was breaking into the Ministry of Theology, because Benjamin had heard from one of the Gobblers we caught that the headquarters was there, that's where all the orders was coming from…"

He stopped again.

"You captured some Gobblers?" said Farder Coram.

Jacob nodded, and cast his eyes at his dæmon. It was unusual for dæmons to speak to other humans than their own, but it happened sometimes, and she spoke now.

"We caught three Gobblers in Clerkenwell and made them tell us who they were working for and where the orders came from and so on. They didn't know where the kids were being taken, except it was North to Lapland…"

146

She had to stop and pant briefly, her little chest fluttering, before she could go on.

"And so them Gobblers told us about the Ministry of Theology and Lord Boreal. Benjamin said him and Gerard Hook should break into the Ministry and Frans Broekman and Tom Mendham should go and find out about Lord Boreal."

"Did they do that?"

"We don't know. They never came back. Farder Coram, it were like everything we did, they knew about before we did it, and for all we know Frans and Tom were swallowed alive as soon as they got near Lord Boreal."

"Come back to Benjamin," said Farder Coram, hearing Jacob's breathing getting harsher and seeing his eyes close in pain.

Jacob's dæmon gave a little mew of anxiety and love, and the woman took a step or two closer, her hands to her mouth; but she didn't speak, and the dæmon went on faintly:

"Benjamin and Gerard and us went to the Ministry at White Hall and found a little side door, it not being fiercely guarded, and we stayed on watch outside while they unfastened the lock and went in. They hadn't been in but a minute when we heard a cry of fear, and Benjamin's dæmon came a-flying out and beckoned to us for help and flew in again, and we took our knife and ran in after her; only the place was dark, and full of wild forms and sounds that were confusing in their frightful movements; and we cast about, but there was a commotion above, and a fearful cry, and Benjamin and his dæmon fell from a high staircase above us, his dæmon a-tugging and a-fluttering to hold him up, but all in vain, for they crashed on the stone floor and both perished in a moment.

"And we couldn't see anything of Gerard, but there was a howl from above in his voice and we were too terrified and stunned to move, and then an arrow shot down at our shoulder and pierced deep down within…"

The dæmon's voice was fainter, and a groan came from the wounded man. Farder Coram leaned forward and gently pulled back the counterpane, and there protruding from his shoulder was the feathered end of an arrow in a mass of clotted blood. The shaft and the head were so deep in the poor man's chest that only six inches or so remained above the skin. Lyra felt faint.

There was the sound of feet and voices outside on the jetty.

Farder Coram sat up and said, "Here's the physician, Jacob. We'll leave you now. We'll have a longer talk when you're feeling better."

He clasped the woman's shoulder on the way out. Lyra stuck close to him on the jetty, because there was a crowd gathering already, whispering and pointing. Farder Coram gave orders for Peter Hawker to go at once to John Faa, and then said:

"Lyra, as soon as we know whether Jacob's going to live or die, we must have another talk about that alethiometer. You go and occupy yourself elsewhere, child; we'll send for you."

Lyra wandered away on her own, and went to the reedy bank to sit and throw mud into the water. She knew one thing: she was not pleased or proud to be able to read the alethiometer – she was afraid. Whatever power was making that needle swing and stop, it knew things like an intelligent being.

"I reckon it's a spirit," Lyra said, and for a moment she was tempted to throw the little thing into the middle of the fen.

"I'd see a spirit if there was one in there," said Pantalaimon. "Like that old ghost in Godstow. I saw that when you didn't."

"There's more than one kind of spirit," said Lyra reprovingly. "You can't see all of 'em. Anyway, what about those old dead Scholars without their heads? I saw them, remember."

"That was only a night-ghast."

"It was not. They were proper spirits all right, and you know it. But whatever spirit's moving this blooming needle en't that sort of spirit."

"It might not be a spirit," said Pantalaimon stubbornly.

"Well what else could it be?"

"It might be… It might be elementary particles."

She scoffed.

"It could be!" he insisted. "You remember that photo-mill they got at Gabriel? Well then."

At Gabriel College there was a very holy object kept on the high altar of the Oratory, covered (now Lyra thought about it) with a black velvet cloth, like the one around the alethiometer. She had seen it when she accompanied the Librarian of Jordan to a service there. At the height of the invocation the Intercessor lifted the cloth to reveal in the dimness a glass dome inside which there was something too distant to see, until he pulled a string attached to a shutter above, letting a ray of sunlight through to strike the dome exactly. Then it became clear: a little thing like a weathervane, with four sails black on one side and white on the other, that began to whirl around as the light struck it. It illustrated a moral lesson, the Intercessor explained, for the black of ignorance fled from the light, whereas the wisdom of white rushed to embrace it. Lyra took his word for that, but the little whirling vanes were delightful whatever they meant, and all done by the power of photons, said the Librarian as they walked home to Jordan.

So perhaps Pantalaimon was right. If elementary particles could push a photo-mill around, no doubt they could make light work of a needle; but it still troubled her.

"Lyra! Lyra!"

It was Tony Costa, waving to her from the jetty.

"Come over here," he called. "You got to go and see John Faa at the Zaal. Run, gal, it's urgent."

She found John Faa with Farder Coram and the other leaders, looking troubled.

John Faa spoke:

"Lyra, child, Farder Coram has told me about your reading of that instrument. And I'm sorry to say that poor Jacob has just died. I think we're going to have to take you with us after all, against my inclinations. I'm troubled in my mind about it, but there don't seem to be any alternative. As soon as Jacob's buried according to custom we'll take our way. You understand me, Lyra: you're a-coming too, but it en't an occasion for joy or jubilation. There's trouble and danger ahead for all on us.

"I'm a-putting you under Farder Coram's wing. Don't you be a trouble or a hazard to him, or you'll be a-feeling the force of my wrath. Now cut along and explain to Ma Costa, and hold yourself in readiness to leave."

The next two weeks passed more busily than any time of Lyra's life so far. Busily, but not quickly, for there were tedious stretches of waiting, of hiding in damp crabbed closets, of watching a dismal rain-soaked autumn landscape roll past the window, of hiding again, of sleeping near the gas-fumes of the engine and waking with a sick headache, and worst of all, of never once being allowed out into the air to run along the bank or clamber over the deck or haul at the lock gates or catch a mooring-rope thrown from the lockside.

Because of course she had to remain hidden. Tony Costa told her of the gossip in the waterside pubs: that there was a hunt the length of the kingdom for a little fair-haired girl, with a big reward for her discovery and severe punishment for anyone concealing her. There were strange rumours, too: people said she was the only child to have escaped from the Gobblers, and she had terrible secrets in her possession. Another rumour said she wasn't a human child at all but a pair of spirits in the form of child and dæmon, sent to this world by the infernal powers in order to work great ruin; and yet another rumour said it was no child but a fully grown human, shrunk by magic and in the pay of the Tartars, come to spy on good English people and prepare the way for a Tartar invasion.

Lyra heard these tales at first with glee and later with despondency. All those people hating and fearing her! And she longed to be out of this narrow boxy cabin. She longed to be North already, in the wide snows under the blazing Aurora. And sometimes she longed to be back at Jordan College, scrambling over the roofs with Roger with the Steward's Bell tolling half an hour to dinner time and the clatter and sizzle and shouting of the Kitchen... Then she wished passionately that nothing had changed, nothing would ever change, that she could be Lyra of Jordan College for ever and ever.

The one thing that drew her out of her boredom and irritation was the alethiometer. She read it every day, sometimes with Farder Coram and sometimes on her own, and she found that she could sink more and more readily into the calm state in which the symbol-meanings clarified themselves, and those great mountain-ranges touched by sunlight emerged into vision.

She struggled to explain to Farder Coram what it felt like.

"It's almost like talking to someone, only you can't quite hear them, and you feel kind of stupid because they're cleverer than you, only they don't get cross or anything... And they know such a lot, Farder Coram! As if they knew everything, almost! Mrs Coulter was clever, she knew ever such a lot, but this is a different kind of knowing... It's like understanding, I suppose..."

He would ask specific questions, and she would search for answers.

"What's Mrs Coulter doing now?" he'd say, and her hands would move at once, and he'd say, "Tell me what you're doing."

"Well, the Madonna is Mrs Coulter, and I think my *mother* when I put the hand there; and the ant is *busy* – that's easy, that's the top meaning; and the hourglass has got *time* in its meanings, and partway down there's *now*, and I just fix my mind on it."

"And how do you know where these meanings are?"

"I kind of see 'em. Or feel 'em rather, like climbing down a ladder at night, you put your foot down and there's another rung. Well, I put my mind down and there's another meaning, and I kind of sense what it is. Then I put 'em all together. There's a trick in it like focusing your eyes."

"Do that then, and see what it says."

Lyra did. The long needle began to swing at once, and stopped, moved on, stopped again in a precise series of sweeps and pauses. It was a sensation of such grace and power that Lyra, sharing it, felt like a young bird learning to fly. Farder Coram, watching from across the table, noted the places where the needle stopped, and watched the little girl holding her hair back from her face and biting her lower lip just a little, her eyes following the needle at first but then, when its path was settled, looking elsewhere on the dial. Not randomly, though. Farder Coram was a chess player, and he knew how chess players looked at a game in play. An expert player seemed to see lines of force and influence on the board, and looked along the important lines and ignored the weak ones; and Lyra's eyes moved the same way, according to some similar magnetic field that she could see and he couldn't.

The needle stopped at the thunderbolt, the infant, the serpent, the elephant, and at a creature Lyra couldn't find a name for: a sort of lizard with big eyes and a tail curled around the twig it stood on. It repeated the sequence time after time, while Lyra watched.

"What's that lizard mean?" said Farder Coram, breaking into her concentration.

"It don't make sense… I can see what it says, but I must be misreading it. The thunderbolt I think is anger, and the child … I think it's me … I was getting a meaning for that lizard thing, but you talked to me, Farder Coram, and I lost it. See, it's just floating any old where."

"Yes, I see that. I'm sorry, Lyra. You tired now? D'you want to stop?"

"No, I don't," she said, but her cheeks were flushed and her eyes bright. She had all the signs of fretful over-excitement, and it was made worse by her long confinement in this stuffy cabin.

He looked out of the window. It was nearly dark, and they were travelling along the last stretch of inland water before reaching the coast. Wide brown scummed expanses of an estuary extended under a dreary sky to a distant group of coal-spirit tanks, rusty and cobwebbed with pipework, beside a refinery where a thick smear of smoke ascended reluctantly to join the clouds.

"Where are we?" said Lyra. "Can I go outside just for a bit, Farder Coram?"

"This is Colby water," he said. "The estuary of the river Cole. When we reach the town we'll tie up by the Smokemarket and go on foot to the docks. We'll be there in an hour or two…"

But it was getting dark, and in the wide desolation of the creek nothing was moving but their own boat and a distant coal-barge labouring towards the refinery; and Lyra was so flushed and tired, and she'd been inside for so long; so Farder Coram went on:

"Well, I don't suppose it'll matter just for a few minutes in the open air. I wouldn't call it fresh; ten't fresh except when it's blowing off the sea; but you can sit out on top and look around till we get closer in."

Lyra leapt up, and Pantalaimon became a seagull at once, eager to stretch his wings in the open. It was cold outside and, although she was well wrapped up, Lyra was soon shivering. Pantalaimon, on the other hand, leapt into the air with a loud caw of delight, and wheeled and skimmed and darted now ahead of the boat, now behind the stern. Lyra exulted in it, feeling with him as he flew, and urging him mentally to provoke the old tillerman's cormorant-dæmon into a race. But she ignored him and settled down sleepily on the handle of the tiller near her man.

There was no life out on this bitter brown expanse, and only the steady chug of the engine and the subdued splashing of the water under the bows broke the wide silence. Heavy clouds hung low without offering rain; the air beneath was grimy with smoke. Only Pantalaimon's flashing elegance had anything in it of life and joy.

As he soared up out of a dive with wide wings white against the grey, something black hurtled at him and struck. He fell sideways in a flutter of shock and pain, and Lyra cried out, feeling it sharply. Another little black thing joined the first; they moved not like birds but like flying beetles, heavy and direct, and with a droning sound.

As Pantalaimon fell, trying to twist away and make for the boat and Lyra's desperate arms, the black things kept driving into him, droning, buzzing, and murderous. Lyra was nearly mad with Pantalaimon's fear and her own, but then something swept past her and upward.

It was the tillerman's dæmon, and clumsy and heavy as she looked, her flight was powerful and swift. Her head snapped this way and that – there was a flutter of black wings, a shiver of white

– and a little black thing fell to the tarred roof of the cabin at Lyra's feet just as Pantalaimon landed on her outstretched hand.

Before she could comfort him, he changed into his wildcat-shape and sprang down on the creature, batting it back from the edge of the roof, where it was crawling swiftly to escape. Pantalaimon held it firmly down with a needle-filled paw and looked up at the darkening sky, where the black wing-flaps of the cormorant were circling higher as she cast around for the other.

Then the cormorant glided swiftly back and croaked something to the tillerman, who said, "It's gone. Don't let that other one escape. Here –" and he flung the dregs out of the tin mug he'd been drinking from, and tossed it to Lyra.

She clapped it over the creature at once. It buzzed and snarled like a little machine.

"Hold it still," said Farder Coram from behind her, and then he was kneeling to slip a piece of card under the mug.

"What is it, Farder Coram?" she said shakily.

"Let's go below and have a look. Take it careful, Lyra. Hold that tight."

She looked at the tillerman's dæmon as she passed, intending to thank her, but her old eyes were closed. She thanked the tillerman instead.

"You oughter stayed below," was all he said.

She took the mug into the cabin, where Farder Coram had found a beer glass. He held the tin mug upside down over it and then slipped the card out from between them, so that the creature fell into the glass. He held it up so they could see the angry little thing clearly.

It was about as long as Lyra's thumb, and dark green, not black. Its wing cases were erect, like a ladybird's about to fly, and the wings inside were beating so furiously that they were only a blur. Its six clawed legs were scrabbling on the smooth glass.

"What is it?" she said.

Pantalaimon, a wildcat still, crouched on the table six inches away, his green eyes following it round and round inside the glass.

"If you was to crack it open," said Farder Coram, "you'd find no living thing in there. No animal nor insect, at any rate. I seen one of these things afore, and I never thought I'd see one again this far north. Afric things. There's a clockwork running in there, and pinned to the spring of it, there's a bad spirit with a spell through its heart."

"But who sent it?"

"You don't even need to read the symbols, Lyra; you can guess as easy as I can."

"Mrs Coulter?"

"Course. She en't only explored up North; there's strange things aplenty in the southern wild. It was Morocco where I saw one of these last. Deadly dangerous; while the spirit's in it, it won't never stop, and when you let the spirit free it's so monstrous angry it'll kill the first thing it gets at."

"But what was it after?"

"Spying. I was a cursed fool to let you up above. And I should have let you think your way through the symbols without interrupting."

"I see it now!" said Lyra, suddenly excited. "It means air, that lizard thing! I saw that, but I couldn't see why, so I tried to work it out and I lost it."

"Ah," said Farder Coram, "then I see it too. It en't a lizard, that's why; it's a chameleon. And it stands for air because they don't eat nor drink, they just live on air."

"And the elephant —"

"Africa," he said, and, "Aha."

They looked at each other. With every revelation of the

alethiometer's power, they became more awed by it.

"It was telling us about these things all the time," said Lyra. "We oughter listened. But what can we do about this'un, Farder Coram? Can we kill it or something?"

"I don't know as we can do anything. We shall just have to keep him shut up tight in a box and never let him out. What worries me more is the other one, as got away. He'll be a-flying back to Mrs Coulter now, with the news that he's seen you. Damn me, Lyra, but I'm a fool."

He rattled about in a cupboard and found a smoke-leaf tin about three inches in diameter. It had been used for holding screws, but he tipped those out and wiped the inside with a rag before inverting the glass over it with the card still in place over the mouth.

After a tricky moment when one of the creature's legs escaped and thrust the tin away with surprising strength, they had it captured and the lid screwed down tight.

"As soon's we get about the ship I'll run some solder round the edge to make sure of it," Farder Coram said.

"But don't clockwork run down?"

"Ordinary clockwork, yes. But like I said, this'un's kept tight wound by the spirit pinned to the end. The more he struggles, the tighter it's wound, and the stronger the force is. Now let's put this feller out the way…"

He wrapped the tin in a flannel cloth to stifle the incessant buzzing and droning, and stowed it away under his bunk.

It was dark now, and Lyra watched through the window as the lights of Colby came closer. The heavy air was thickening into mist, and by the time they tied up at the wharves alongside the Smokemarket everything in sight was softened and blurred. The darkness shaded into pearly silver-grey veils laid over the warehouses and the cranes, the wooden market-stalls and the granite many-chimneyed building the market was named after, where day and night fish hung kippering in the fragrant oakwood smoke. The chimneys were contributing their thickness to the clammy air, and the pleasant reek of smoked herring and mackerel and haddock seemed to breathe out of the very cobbles.

Lyra, wrapped up in an oilskin and with a large hood hiding her revealing hair, walked along between Farder Coram and the tillerman. All three dæmons were alert, scouting around corners ahead, watching behind, listening for the slightest footfall.

But they were the only figures to be seen. The citizens of Colby were all indoors, probably sipping jenniver beside roaring stoves. They saw no one until they reached the dock, and the first man they saw there was was Tony Costa, guarding the gates.

"Thank God you got here," he said quietly, letting them through. "We just heard as Jack Verhoeven's bin shot and his boat sunk, and no one'd heard where you was. John Faa's on board already and jumping to go."

The vessel looked immense to Lyra: a wheelhouse and funnel amidships, a high fo'c'sle and a stout derrick over a canvas-covered hatch; yellow light agleam in the portholes and the bridge, and white light at the masthead; and three or four men on deck, working urgently at things she couldn't see.

She hurried up the wooden gangway ahead of Farder Coram, and looked around with excitement. Pantalaimon became a monkey and clambered up the derrick at once, but she called him down again; Farder Coram wanted them indoors, or below, as you called it on board ship.

Down some stairs, or a companionway, there was a small saloon where John Faa was talking quietly with Nicholas Rokeby, the gyptian in charge of the vessel. John Faa did nothing hastily. Lyra was waiting for him to greet her, but he finished his remarks about the tide and pilotage before turning to the incomers.

"Good evening, friends," he said. "Poor Jack Verhoeven's dead, perhaps you've heard. And his boys captured."

"We have bad news too," said Farder Coram, and told of their encounter with the flying spirits.

John Faa shook his great head, but didn't reproach them.

"Where is the creature now?" he said.

Farder Coram took out the leaf-tin and laid it on the table. Such a furious buzzing came from it that the tin itself moved slowly over the wood.

"I've heard of them clockwork devils, but never seen one," John Faa said. "There en't no way of taming it and turning it back, I do know that much. Nor is it any use weighing it down with lead and dropping it in the ocean, because one day it'd rust through and out the devil would come and make for the child wherever she was. No, we'll have to keep it by, and exercise our vigilance."

Lyra being the only female on board (for John Faa had decided against taking women, after much thought), she had a cabin to herself. Not a grand cabin, to be sure; in fact little more than a closet with a bunk and a scuttle, which was the proper name for porthole. She stowed her few things in the drawer below the bunk and ran up excitedly to lean over the rail and watch England vanish behind, only to find that most of England had vanished in the mist before she got there.

But the rush of water below, the movement in the air, the ship's lights glowing bravely in the dark, the rumble of the engine, the smells of salt and fish and coal-spirit, were exciting enough by themselves. It wasn't long before another sensation joined them, as the vessel began to roll in the German Ocean swell. When someone called Lyra down for a bite of supper, she found she was less hungry than she'd thought, and presently she decided it would be a good idea to lie down, for Pantalaimon's sake, because the poor creature was feeling sadly ill at ease.

And so began her journey to the North.

Part Two

Bolvangar

10

The Consul and the Bear

John Faa and the other leaders had decided that they would make for Trollesund, the main port of Lapland. The witches had a consulate in the town, and John Faa knew that without their help, or at least their friendly neutrality, it would be impossible to rescue the captive children.

He explained his idea to Lyra and Farder Coram next day, when Lyra's seasickness had abated slightly. The sun was shining brightly and the green waves were dashing against the bows, bearing white streams of foam as they curved away. Out on the deck, with the breeze blowing and the whole sea a-sparkle with light and movement, she felt little sickness at all; and now that Pantalaimon had discovered the delights of being a seagull and then a stormy petrel and skimming the wave-tops, Lyra was too absorbed by his glee to wallow in landlubberly misery.

John Faa, Farder Coram, and two or three others sat in the stern of the ship, with the sun full on them, talking about what to do next.

"Now Farder Coram knows these Lapland witches," John Faa said. "And if I en't mistaken there's an obligation there."

"That's right, John," said Farder Coram. "It were forty years back, but that's nothing to a witch. Some of 'em live to many times that."

"What happened to bring this obligation about, Farder Coram?" said Adam Stefanski, the man in charge of the fighting troop.

"I saved a witch's life," Farder Coram explained. "She fell out of the air, being pursued by a great red bird like to nothing I'd seen before. She fell injured in the marsh and I set out to find her. She was like to drowning, and I got her on board and shot that bird down, and it fell into a bog, to my regret, for it was as big as a bittern, and flame-red."

"Ah," the other men murmured, captured by Farder Coram's story.

"Now when I got her in the boat," he went on, "I had the most grim shock I'd ever known, because that young woman had no dæmon."

It was as if he'd said, "She had no head." The very thought was repugnant. The men shuddered, their dæmons bristled or shook themselves or cawed harshly, and the men soothed them. Pantalaimon crept into Lyra's breast, their hearts beating together.

"At least," Farder Coram said, "that's what it seemed. Being as she'd fell out of the air, I more than suspected she was a witch. She looked exactly like a young woman, thinner than some and prettier than most, but not seeing that dæmon gave me a hideous turn."

"En't they got dæmons then, the witches?" said the other man, Michael Canzona.

"Their dæmons is invisible, I expect," said Adam Stefanski. "He was there all the time, and Farder Coram never saw him."

"No, you're wrong, Adam," said Farder Coram. "He weren't there at all. The witches have the power to separate theirselves from their dæmons a mighty sight further'n what we can. If need be they can send their dæmons far abroad on the wind or the clouds, or down below the ocean. And this witch I found, she hadn't been resting above an hour when her dæmon came a-flying back, because he'd felt her fear and her injury, of course. And it's my belief, though she never admitted to this, that the great red bird I shot was another witch's dæmon, in pursuit. Lord! That made me shiver, when I thought of that. I'd have stayed my hand; I'd have taken any measures on sea or land; but there it was. Anyway, there was no doubt I'd saved her life, and she gave me a token of it, and said I was to call on her help if ever it was needed. And once she sent me help when the Skraelings shot me with a poison arrow. We had other connections, too... I haven't seen her for many years, but she'll remember."

"And does she live at Trollesund, this witch?"

"No, no. They live in forests and on the tundra, not in a seaport among men and women. Their business is with the wild. But they keep a consul there, and I shall get word to her, make no doubt about that."

Lyra was keen to know more about the witches, but the men had turned their talk to the matter of fuel and stores, and presently she grew impatient to see the rest of the ship. She wandered along the deck towards the bows, and soon made the acquaintance of an Able-Seaman by flicking at him the pips she'd saved from the apple she'd eaten at breakfast. He was a stout and placid man, and when he'd sworn at her and been sworn at in return, they became great friends. He was called Jerry. Under his guidance she found out that having something to do prevented you from feeling seasick, and that even a job like scrubbing a deck could be satisfying, if it was done in a seamanlike way. She was very taken with this notion, and later on she folded the blankets on her bunk in a seamanlike way, and put her possessions in the closet in a seamanlike way, and used "stow" instead of "tidy" for the process of doing so.

After two days at sea, Lyra decided that this was the life for her. She had the run of the ship, from the engine room to the bridge, and she was soon on first-name terms with all the crew. Captain Rokeby let her signal to a Hollands frigate by pulling the handle of the steam-whistle; the cook suffered her help in mixing plum-duff; and only a stern word from John Faa prevented her from climbing the foremast to inspect the horizon from the crow's nest.

All the time they were steaming north, and it grew colder daily. The ship's stores were searched for oilskins that could be cut down for her, and Jerry showed her how to sew, an art she learned willingly from him, though she had scorned it at Jordan and avoided instruction from Mrs Lonsdale. Together they made a waterproof bag for the alethiometer that she could wear around her waist, in case she fell in the sea, she said. With it safely in place she clung to the rail in her oilskins and sou'wester as the stinging spray broke over the bows and surged along the deck. She still felt seasick occasionally, especially when the wind got up and the ship plunged heavily over the crests of the grey-green waves, and then it was Pantalaimon's job to distract her from it by skimming the waves as a stormy petrel, because she could feel his boundless glee in the dash of wind and water, and forget her nausea. From time to time he even tried being a fish, and once joined a school of dolphins, to their surprise and pleasure. Lyra stood shivering in the fo'c'sle and laughed with delight as her beloved Pantalaimon, sleek and powerful, leapt from the water with half a dozen other swift grey shapes. It was pleasure, but not simple pleasure, for there was pain and fear in it too. Suppose he loved being a dolphin more than he loved her?

Her friend the Able-Seaman was nearby, and he paused as he adjusted the canvas cover of the forward hatch to look out at the little girl's dæmon skimming and leaping with the dolphins. His own dæmon, a seagull, had her head tucked under her wing on the capstan. He knew what Lyra was feeling.

"I remember when I first went to sea, my Belisaria hadn't settled on one form, I was that young, and she loved being a porpoise. I was afraid she'd settle like that. There was one old sailorman on my first vessel who could never go ashore at all, because his dæmon had settled as a dolphin, and he could never leave the water. He was a wonderful sailor; best navigator you ever knew; could have made a fortune at the fishing; but he wasn't happy like it. He was never quite happy till he died and he could be buried at sea."

"Why do dæmons have to settle?" Lyra said. "I want Pantalaimon to be able to change for ever. So does he."

"Ah, they always have settled, and they always will. That's part of growing up. There'll come a time when you'll be tired of his changing about, and you'll want a settled kind of form for him."

"I never will!"

"Oh, you will. You'll want to grow up like all the other girls. Anyway, there's compensations for a settled form."

"What are they?"

"Knowing what kind of person you are. Take old Belisaria. She's a seagull, and that means I'm a kind of seagull too. I'm not grand and splendid nor beautiful, but I'm a tough old thing and I can survive anywhere and always find a bit of food and company. That's worth knowing, that is. And when your dæmon settles, you'll know the sort of person you are."

"But suppose your dæmon settles in a shape you don't like?"

"Well, then, you're discontented, en't you? There's plenty of folk as'd like to have a lion as a dæmon and they end up with a poodle. And till they learn to be satisfied with what they are, they're going to be fretful about it. Waste of feeling, that is."

But it didn't seem to Lyra that she would ever grow up.

One morning there was a different smell in the air, and the ship was moving oddly, with a brisker rocking from side to side instead of the plunging and soaring. Lyra was on deck a minute after she woke up, gazing greedily at the land: such a strange sight, after all that water, for though they had only been at sea a few days, Lyra felt as if they'd been on the ocean for months. Directly ahead of the ship a mountain rose, green-flanked and snow-capped, and a little town and harbour lay below it: wooden houses with steep roofs, an oratory spire, cranes in the harbour, and clouds of gulls wheeling and crying. The smell was of fish, but mixed with it came land-smells too: pine-resin and earth and something animal and musky, and something else that was cold and blank and wild: it might have been snow. It was the smell of the North.

Seals frisked around the ship, showing their clown-faces above the water before sinking back without a splash. The wind that lifted spray off the white-capped waves was monstrously cold, and searched out every gap in Lyra's wolfskin, and her hands were soon aching and her face numb. Pantalaimon, in his ermine-shape, warmed her neck for her, but it was too cold to stay outside for long without work to do, even to watch the seals, and Lyra went below to eat her breakfast porridge and look through the porthole in the saloon.

Inside the harbour the water was calm, and as they moved past the massive breakwater Lyra began to feel unsteady from the lack of motion. She and Pantalaimon avidly watched as the ship inched ponderously towards the quayside. During the next hour the sound of the engine died away to a quiet background rumble, voices shouted orders or queries, ropes were thrown, gangways lowered, hatches opened.

"Come on, Lyra," said Farder Coram. "Is everything packed?"

Lyra's possessions, such as they were, had been packed ever since she'd woken up and seen the land. All she had to do was run to the cabin and pick up the shopping bag, and she was ready.

The first thing she and Farder Coram did ashore was to visit the house of the Witch-Consul. It didn't take long to find it; the little town was clustered around the harbour, with the oratory and the Governor's house the only buildings of any size. The Witch-Consul lived in a green-painted wooden house within sight of the sea, and when they rang the bell it jangled loudly in the quiet street.

A servant showed them into a little parlour and brought them coffee. Presently the Consul himself came in to greet them. He was a fat man with a florid face and a sober black suit, whose name was Martin Lanselius. His dæmon was a little serpent, the same intense and brilliant green as his eyes, which were the only witch-like thing about him; though Lyra was not sure what she had been expecting a witch to look like.

"How can I help you, Farder Coram?" he said.

"In two ways, Dr Lanselius. First, I'm anxious to get in touch with a witch-lady I met some years ago, in the Fen country of Eastern Anglia. Her name is Serafina Pekkala."

Dr Lanselius made a note with a silver pencil.

"How long ago was your meeting with her?" he said.

"Must be forty years. But I think she would remember."

"And what is the second way in which you seek my help?"

"I'm representing a number of gyptian families who've lost children. We've got reason to believe there's an organization capturing these children, ours and others, and bringing them to the North for some unknown purpose. I'd like to know whether you or your people have heard of anything like this a-going on."

Dr Lanselius sipped his coffee blandly.

"It's not impossible that notice of some such activity might have come our way," he said. "You realize, the relations between my people and the Northlanders are perfectly cordial. It would be difficult for me to justify disturbing them."

Farder Coram nodded as if he understood very well.

"To be sure," he said. "And it wouldn't be necessary for me to ask you if I could get the information any other way. That was why I asked about the witch-lady first."

Now Dr Lanselius nodded as if *he* understood. Lyra watched this game with puzzlement and respect. There were all kinds of things going on beneath it, and she saw that the Witch-Consul was coming to a decision.

"Very well," he said. "Of course, that's true, and you'll realize that your name is not unknown to us, Farder Coram. Serafina Pekkala is queen of a witch-clan in the region of Lake Enara. As for your other question, it is of course understood that this information is not reaching you through me."

"Quite so."

"Well, in this very town there is a branch of an organization called the Northern Progress Exploration Company, which pretends to be searching for minerals, but which is really controlled by something called the General Oblation Board of London. This organization, I happen to know, imports children. This is not generally known in the town; the Norroway government is not officially aware of it. The children don't remain here long. They are taken some distance inland."

"Do you know where, Dr Lanselius?"

"No. I would tell you if I did."

"And do you know what happens to them there?"

For the first time, Dr Lanselius glanced at Lyra. She looked stolidly back. The little green serpent-dæmon raised her head from the Consul's collar and whispered tongue-flickeringly in his ear.

The Consul said, "I have heard the phrase *the Maystadt Process* in connection with this matter. I think they use that in order to avoid calling what they do by its proper name. I have also heard the word *intercision*, but what it refers to I could not say."

"And are there any children in the town at the moment?" said Farder Coram.

He was stroking his dæmon's fur as she sat alert in his lap. Lyra noticed that she had stopped purring.

"No, I think not," said Dr Lanselius. "A group of about twelve arrived a week ago and moved out the day before yesterday."

"Ah! As recent as that? Then that gives us a bit of hope. How did they travel, Dr Lanselius?"

"By sledge."

"And you have no idea where they went?"

"Very little. It is not a subject we are interested in."

"Quite so. Now, you've answered all my questions very fairly, sir, and here's just one more. If you were me, what question would you ask of the Consul of the Witches?"

For the first time Dr Lanselius smiled.

"I would ask where I could obtain the services of an armoured bear," he said.

Lyra sat up, and felt Pantalaimon's heart leap in her hands.

"I understood the armoured bears to be in the service of the Oblation Board," said Farder Coram in surprise. "I mean, the Northern Progress Company, or whatever they're calling themselves."

"There is at least one who is not. You will find him at the sledge depot at the end of Langlokur Street. He earns a living there at the moment, but such is his temper and the fear he engenders in the dogs, his employment might not last for long."

"Is he a renegade, then?"

"It seems so. His name is Iorek Byrnison. You asked what I would ask, and I told you. Now here is what I would do: I would seize the chance to employ an armoured bear, even if it were far more remote than this."

Lyra could hardly sit still. Farder Coram, however, knew the etiquette for meetings such as this, and took another spiced honey-cake from the plate. While he ate it, Dr Lanselius turned to Lyra.

"I understand that you are in possession of an alethiometer," he said, to her great surprise; for how could he have known that?

"Yes," she said, and then, prompted by a nip from Pantalaimon, added, "Would you like to look at it?"

"I should like that very much."

She fished inelegantly in the oilskin pouch and handed him the velvet package. He unfolded it and held it up with great care, gazing at the face like a scholar gazing at a rare manuscript.

"How exquisite!" he said. "I have seen one other example, but it was not so fine as this. And do you possess the books of readings?"

"No," Lyra began, but before she could say any more, Farder Coram was speaking.

"No, the great pity is that although Lyra owns the alethiometer itself, there's no means of reading it whatsoever," he said. "It's just as much of a mystery as the pools of ink the Hindus use for reading the future. And the nearest book of readings I know of is in the Abbey of St Johann at Heidelberg."

Lyra could see why he was saying this: he didn't want Dr Lanselius to know of Lyra's power. But she could also see something Farder Coram couldn't, which was the agitation of Dr Lanselius's dæmon, and she knew at once that it was no good to pretend.

So she said, "Actually I *can* read it," speaking half to Dr

Lanselius and half to Farder Coram, and it was the Consul who responded.

"That is wise of you," he said. "Where did you obtain this one?"

"The Master of Jordan College in Oxford gave it to me," she said. "Dr Lanselius, do you know who made them?"

"They are said to originate in the city of Prague," said the Consul. "The scholar who invented the first alethiometer was apparently trying to discover a way of measuring the influences of the planets, according to the ideas of astrology. He intended to make a device that would respond to the idea of Mars or Venus as a compass responds to the idea of North. In that he failed, but the mechanism he invented was clearly responding to something, even if no one knew what it was."

"And where did they get the symbols from?"

"Oh, this was in the seventeenth century. Symbols and emblems were everywhere. Buildings and pictures were designed to be read like books. Everything stood for something else; if you had the right dictionary you could read Nature itself. It was hardly surprising to find philosophers using the symbolism of their time to interpret knowledge that came from a mysterious source. But, you know, they haven't been used seriously for two centuries or so."

He handed the instrument back to Lyra, and added:

"May I ask a question? Without the books of symbols, how do you read it?"

"I just make my mind go clear and then it's sort of like looking down into water. You got to let your eyes find the right level, because that's the only one that's in focus. Something like that," she said.

"I wonder if I might ask to see you do it?" he said.

Lyra looked at Farder Coram, wanting to say yes but waiting

for his approval. The old man nodded.

"What shall I ask?" said Lyra.

"What are the intentions of the Tartars with regard to Kamchatka?"

That wasn't hard. Lyra turned the hands to the camel, which meant Asia, which meant Tartars; to the cornucopia, for Kamchatka, where there were gold mines; and to the ant, which meant activity, which meant purpose and intention. Then she sat still, letting her mind hold the three levels of meaning together in focus, and relaxed for the answer, which came almost at once. The long needle trembled on the dolphin, the helmet, the baby and the anchor, dancing between them and on to the crucible in a complicated pattern that Lyra's eyes followed without hesitation, but which was incomprehensible to the two men.

When it had completed the movements several times Lyra looked up. She blinked once or twice as if she were coming out of a trance.

"They're going to pretend to attack it, but they're not really going to, because it's too far away and they'd be too stretched out," she said.

"Would you tell me how you read that?"

"The dolphin, one of its deep-down meanings is playing, sort of like being playful," she explained. "I know it's that one because it stopped that number of times and it just got clear at that level but nowhere else. And the helmet means war, and both together they mean pretend to go to war but not be serious. And the baby means – it means difficult – it'd be too hard for them to attack it, and the anchor says why, because they'd be stretched out as tight as an anchor rope. I just see it all like that, you see."

Dr Lanselius nodded.

"Remarkable," he said. "I am very grateful. I shall not forget that."

Then he looked strangely at Farder Coram, and back at Lyra.

"Could I ask you for one more demonstration?" he said. "In the yard behind this house, you will find several sprays of cloud-pine hanging on the wall. One of them has been used by Serafina Pekkala, and the others have not. Could you tell which is hers?"

"Yeah!" said Lyra, always ready to show off, and she took the alethiometer and hurried out. She was eager to see cloud-pine, because the witches used it for flying, and she'd never seen any before.

While she was gone, the Consul said, "Do you realize who this child is?"

"She's the daughter of Lord Asriel," said Farder Coram. "And her mother is Mrs Coulter, of the Oblation Board."

"And apart from that?"

The old gyptian had to shake his head. "No," he said, "I don't know any more. But she's a strange innocent creature, and I wouldn't have her harmed for the world. How she comes to read that instrument I couldn't guess, but I believe her when she talks of it. Why, Dr Lanselius? What do you know about her?"

"The witches have talked about this child for centuries past," said the Consul. "Because they live so close to the place where the veil between the worlds is thin, they hear immortal whispers from time to time, in the voices of those beings who pass between the worlds. And they have spoken of a child such as this, who has a great destiny that can only be fulfilled elsewhere – not in this world, but far beyond. Without this child, we shall all die. So the witches say. But she must fulfil this destiny in ignorance of what she is doing, because only in her ignorance can we be saved. Do you understand that, Farder Coram?"

"No," said Farder Coram, "I'm unable to say that I do."

"What it means is that she must be free to make mistakes. We must hope that she does not, but we can't guide her. I am glad to have seen this child before I die."

"But how did you recognize her as being that particular child? And what did you mean about the beings who pass between the worlds? I'm at a loss to understand you, Dr Lanselius, for all that I judge you're an honest man…"

But before the Consul could answer, the door opened and Lyra came in triumphantly bearing a small spray of pine.

"This is the one!" she said. "I tested 'em all, and this is it, I'm sure."

The Consul looked at it closely, and then nodded.

"Correct," he said. "Well, Lyra, that is remarkable. You are lucky to have an instrument like that, and I wish you well with it. I would like to give you something to take away with you…"

He took the spray and broke off a twig for her.

"Did she fly with this?" Lyra said, awed.

"Yes, she did. I can't give you all of it, because I need it to contact her, but this will be enough. Look after it."

"Yes, I will," she said. "Thank you."

And she tucked it into her purse beside the alethiometer. Farder Coram touched the spray of pine as if for luck, and on his face was an expression Lyra had never seen before: almost a longing. The Consul showed them to the door, where he shook hands with Farder Coram, and shook Lyra's hand too.

"I hope you find success," he said, and stood on his doorstep in the piercing cold to watch them up the little street.

"He knew the answer about the Tartars before I did," Lyra told Farder Coram. "The alethiometer told me, but I never said. It was the crucible."

"I expect he was testing you, child. But you done right to be polite, being as we can't be sure what he knows already. And that was a useful tip about the bear. I don't know how we would a heard otherwise."

176

They found their way to the depot, which was a couple of concrete warehouses in a scrubby area of waste ground where thin weeds grew between grey rocks and pools of icy mud. A surly man in an office told them that they could find the bear off duty at six, but they'd have to be quick, because he usually went straight to the yard behind Einarsson's Bar, where they gave him drink.

Then Farder Coram took Lyra to the best outfitter's in town and bought her some proper cold-weather clothing. They bought a parka made of reindeer skin, because reindeer hair is hollow and insulates well; and the hood was lined with wolverine fur, because that sheds the ice that forms when you breathe. They bought underclothing and boot liners of reindeer calf skin, and silk gloves to go inside big fur mittens. The boots and mittens were made of skin from the reindeer's forelegs, because that is extra tough, and the boots were soled with the skin of the bearded seal, which is as tough as walrus-hide, but lighter. Finally they bought a waterproof cape that enveloped her completely, made of semi-transparent seal intestine.

With all that on, and a silk muffler around her neck and a woollen cap over her ears and the big hood pulled forward, she was uncomfortably warm; but they were going to much colder regions than this.

John Faa had been supervising the unloading of the ship, and was keen to hear about the Witch-Consul's words, and even keener to learn of the bear.

"We'll go to him this very evening," he said. "Have you ever spoken to such a creature, Farder Coram?"

"Yes, I have; and fought one, too, though not by myself, thank God. We must be ready to treat with him, John. He'll ask a lot, I've no doubt, and be surly and difficult to manage; but we must have him."

"Oh, we must. And what of your witch?"

"Well, she's a long way off, and a clan-queen now," said Farder Coram. "I did hope it might be possible for a message to reach her, but it would take too long to wait for a reply."

"Ah, well. Now let me tell you what *I've* found, old friend."

For John Faa had been fidgeting with impatience to tell them something. He had met a prospector on the quayside, a New Dane by the name of Lee Scoresby, from the country of Texas, and this man had a balloon, of all things. The expedition he'd been hoping to join had failed for lack of funds even before it had left Amsterdam, so he was stranded.

"Think what we might do with the help of an aëronaut, Farder Coram!" said John Faa, rubbing his great hands together. "I've engaged him to sign up with us. Seems to me we struck lucky a-coming here."

"Luckier still if we had a clear idea of where we were going," said Farder Coram, but nothing could damp John Faa's pleasure in being on campaign once more.

After darkness had fallen, and when the stores and equipment had all been safely unloaded and stood in waiting on the quay, Farder Coram and Lyra walked along the waterfront and looked for Einarsson's Bar. They found it easily enough: a crude concrete shed with a red neon sign flashing irregularly over the door and the sound of loud voices through the condensation-frosted windows.

A pitted alley beside it led to a sheet-metal gate into a rear yard, where a lean-to shed stood crazily over a floor of frozen mud. Dim light through the rear window of the bar showed a vast pale form crouching upright and gnawing at a haunch of meat which it held in both hands. Lyra had an impression of blood-stained muzzle and face, small malevolent black eyes, and an immensity of dirty matted yellowish fur. As it gnawed, hideous growling, crunching, sucking noises came from it.

Farder Coram stood by the gate and called:

"Iorek Byrnison!"

The bear stopped eating. As far as they could tell, he was looking at them directly, but it was impossible to read any expression on his face.

"Iorek Byrnison," said Farder Coram again. "May I speak to you?"

Lyra's heart was thumping hard, because something in the bear's presence made her feel close to coldness, danger, brutal power, but a power controlled by intelligence; and not a human intelligence, nothing like a human, because of course bears had no dæmons. This strange hulking presence gnawing its meat was like nothing she had ever imagined, and she felt a profound admiration and pity for the lonely creature.

He dropped the reindeer leg in the dirt and slumped on all fours to the gate. Then he reared up massively, ten feet or more high, as if to show how mighty he was, to remind them how useless the gate would be as a barrier, and he spoke to them from that height.

"Well? Who are you?"

His voice was so deep it seemed to shake the earth. The rank smell that came from his body was almost overpowering.

"I'm Farder Coram, from the gyptian people of Eastern Anglia. And this little girl is Lyra Belacqua."

"What do you want?"

"We want to offer you employment, Iorek Byrnison."

"I am employed."

The bear dropped on all fours again. It was very hard to detect any expressive tones in his voice, whether of irony or anger, because it was so deep and so flat.

"What do you do at the sledge depot?" Farder Coram asked.

"I mend broken machinery and articles of iron. I lift heavy objects."

"What kind of work is that for a *panserbjørn*?"

"Paid work."

Behind the bear, the door of the bar opened a little way and a man put down a large earthenware jar before looking up to peer at them.

"Who's that?"

"Strangers," said the bear.

The bartender looked as if he was going to ask something more, but the bear lurched towards him suddenly and the man shut the door in alarm. The bear hooked a claw through the handle of the jar and lifted it to his mouth. Lyra could smell the tang of the raw spirits that splashed out.

After swallowing several times, the bear put the jar down and turned back to gnaw his haunch of meat, heedless of Farder Coram and Lyra, it seemed; but then he spoke again.

"What work are you offering?"

"Fighting, in all probability," said Farder Coram. "We're moving North until we find a place where they've taken some children captive. When we find it, we'll have to fight to get the children free; and then we'll bring them back."

"And what will you pay?"

"I don't know what to offer you, Iorek Byrnison. If gold is desirable to you, we have gold."

"No good."

"What do they pay you at the sledge depot?"

"My keep here in meat and spirits."

Silence from the bear; and then he dropped the ragged bone and lifted the jar to his muzzle again, drinking the powerful spirits like water.

"Forgive me for asking, Iorek Byrnison," said Farder Coram,

"but you could live a free proud life on the ice hunting seals and walruses, or you could go to war and win great prizes. What ties you to Trollesund and Einarsson's Bar?"

Lyra felt her skin shiver all over. She would have thought a question like that, which was almost an insult, would enrage the great creature beyond reason, and she wondered at Farder Coram's courage in asking it. Iorek Byrnison put down his jar and came close to the gate to peer at the old man's face. Farder Coram didn't flinch.

"I know the people you are seeking, the child-cutters," the bear said. "They left town the day before yesterday to go North with more children. No one will tell you about them; they pretend not to see, because the child-cutters bring money and business. Now I don't like the child-cutters, so I shall answer you politely. I stay here and drink spirits because the men here took my armour away, and without that, I can hunt seals but I can't go to war; and I am an armoured bear: war is the sea I swim in and the air I breathe. The men of this town gave me spirits and let me drink till I was asleep, and then they took my armour away from me. If I knew where they keep it, I would tear down the town to get it back. If you want my service, the price is this: get me back my armour. Do that, and I shall serve you in your campaign, either until I am dead or until you have a victory. The price is my armour. I want it back, and then I shall never need spirits again."

11

Armour

W hen they returned to the ship, Farder Coram and John Faa and the other leaders spent a long time in conference in the saloon, and Lyra went to her cabin to consult the alethiometer. Within five minutes she knew exactly where the bear's armour was, and why it would be difficult to get it back.

She wondered whether to go to the saloon and tell John Faa and the others, but decided that they'd ask her if they wanted to know. Perhaps they knew already.

She lay on her bunk thinking of that savage mighty bear, and the careless way he drank his fiery spirit, and the loneliness of him in his dirty lean-to. How different it was to be human, with one's dæmon always there to talk to! In the silence of the still ship, without the continual creak of metal and timber or the rumble of the engine or the rush of water along the side, Lyra gradually fell asleep, with Pantalaimon on her pillow sleeping too.

She was dreaming of her great imprisoned father when suddenly, for no reason at all, she woke up. She had no idea what time it was. There was a faint light in the cabin that she took for moonlight, and it showed her new cold-weather furs that lay stiffly in the corner of the cabin. No sooner did she see them than she longed to try them on again.

When they were on she had to go out on deck, and a minute later she opened the door at the top of the companionway and stepped out.

At once she saw that something strange was happening in the sky. She thought it was clouds, moving and trembling under a nervous agitation, but Pantalaimon whispered:

"The Aurora!"

Her wonder was so strong that she had to clutch the rail to keep from falling.

The sight filled the northern sky; the immensity of it was scarcely conceivable. As if from Heaven itself, great curtains of delicate light hung and trembled. Pale green and rose-pink, and as transparent as the most fragile fabric, and at the bottom edge a profound and fiery crimson like the fires of Hell, they swung and shimmered loosely with more grace than the most skilful dancer. Lyra thought she could even hear them: a vast distant whispering swish. In the evanescent delicacy she felt something as profound as she'd felt close to the bear. She was moved by it: it was so beautiful it was almost holy; she felt tears prick her eyes, and the tears splintered the light even further into prismatic rainbows. It wasn't long before she found herself entering the same kind of trance as when she consulted the alethiometer. Perhaps, she thought calmly, whatever moves the alethiometer's needle is making the Aurora glow too. It might even be Dust itself. She thought that without noticing that she'd thought it, and she soon forgot it, and only remembered it much later.

And as she gazed, the image of a city seemed to form itself behind the veils and streams of translucent colour: towers and domes, honey-coloured temples and colonnades, broad boulevards and sunlit parkland. Looking at it gave her a sense of vertigo, as if she were looking not up but down, and across a gulf so wide that nothing could ever pass over it. It was a whole universe away.

But something *was* moving across it, and as she tried to focus her eyes on the movement, she felt faint and dizzy, because the little thing moving wasn't part of the Aurora or of the other universe behind it. It was in the sky over the roofs of the town. When she could see it clearly, she had come fully awake and the sky-city was gone.

The flying thing came closer and circled the ship on outspread wings. Then it glided down and landed with brisk sweeps of its powerful pinions, and came to a halt on the wooden deck a few yards from Lyra.

In the Aurora's light she saw a great bird, a beautiful grey goose whose head was crowned with a flash of pure white. And yet it wasn't a bird: it was a dæmon, though there was no one in sight but Lyra herself. The idea filled her with sickly fear.

The bird said:

"Where is Farder Coram?"

And suddenly Lyra realized who it must be. This was the dæmon of Serafina Pekkala, the clan-queen, Farder Coram's witch-friend.

She stammered to reply:

"I – he's – I'll go and get him…"

She turned and scampered down the companionway to the cabin Farder Coram occupied, and opened the door to speak into the darkness:

"Farder Coram! The witch's dæmon's come! He's waiting on the deck! He flew here all by hisself – I seen him coming in the sky –"

The old man said, "Ask him to wait on the after-deck, child."

The goose made his stately way to the stern of the ship, where he looked around, elegant and wild simultaneously, and a cause of fascinated terror to Lyra, who felt as though she were entertaining a ghost.

Then Farder Coram came up, wrapped in his cold-weather gear, closely followed by John Faa. Both old men bowed respectfully, and their dæmons also acknowledged the visitor.

"Greetings," said Farder Coram. "And I'm happy and proud to see you again, Kaisa. Now, would you like to come inside, or would you prefer to stay out here in the open?"

"I would rather stay outside, thank you, Farder Coram. Are you warm enough for a while?"

Witches and their dæmons felt no cold, but they were aware that other humans did.

Farder Coram assured him that they were well wrapped up, and said, "How is Serafina Pekkala?"

"She sends her greetings to you, Farder Coram, and she is well and strong. Who are these two people?"

Farder Coram introduced them both. The goose-dæmon looked hard at Lyra.

"I have heard of this child," he said. "She is talked about among witches. So you have come to make war?"

"Not war, Kaisa. We are going to free the children taken from us. And I hope the witches will help."

"Not all of them will. Some clans are working with the Dust-hunters."

"Is that what you call the Oblation Board?"

"I don't know what this Board may be. They are Dust-hunters. They came to our regions ten years ago with philosophical instruments. They paid us to allow them to set up stations in our lands, and they treated us with courtesy."

"What is this Dust?"

"It comes from the sky. Some say it has always been there,

some say it is newly falling. What is certain is that when people become aware of it, a great fear comes over them, and they'll stop at nothing to discover what it is. But it is not of any concern to witches."

"And where are they now, these Dust-hunters?"

"Four days north-east of here, at a place called Bolvangar. Our clan made no agreement with them, and because of our ancient obligation to you, Farder Coram, I have come to show you how to find these Dust-hunters."

Farder Coram smiled, and John Faa clapped his great hands together in satisfaction.

"Thank you kindly, sir," he said to the goose. "But tell us this: do you know anything more about these Dust-hunters? What do they do at this Bolvangar?"

"They have put up buildings of metal and concrete, and some underground chambers. They burn coal-spirit, which they bring in at great expense. We don't know what they do, but there is an air of hatred and fear over the place and for miles around. Witches can see these things where other humans can't. Animals keep away too. No birds fly there; lemmings and foxes have fled. Hence the name Bolvangar: the fields of evil. They don't call it that. They call it The Station. But to everyone else it is Bolvangar."

"And how are they defended?"

"They have a company of Northern Tartars armed with rifles. They are good soldiers, but they lack practice, because no one has ever attacked the settlement since it was built. Then there is a wire fence around the compound, which is filled with anbaric force. There may be other means of defence that we don't know about, because as I say they have no interest for us."

Lyra was bursting to ask a question, and the goose-dæmon knew it and looked at her as if giving permission.

"Why do the witches talk about me?" she said.

"Because of your father, and his knowledge of the other worlds," the dæmon replied.

That surprised all three of them. Lyra looked at Farder Coram, who looked back in mild wonder, and at John Faa, whose expression was troubled.

"Other worlds?" he said. "Pardon me, sir, but what worlds would those be? Do you mean the stars?"

"Indeed, no."

"Perhaps the world of spirits?" said Farder Coram.

"Nor that."

"Is it the city in the lights?" said Lyra. "It is, en't it?"

The goose turned his stately head towards her. His eyes were black, surrounded by a thin line of pure sky-blue, and their gaze was intense.

"Yes," he said. "Witches have known of the other worlds for thousands of years. You can see them sometimes in the Northern Lights. They aren't part of this universe at all; even the furthest stars are part of this universe, but the lights show us a different universe entirely. Not further away, but interpenetrating with this one. Here, on this deck, millions of other universes exist, unaware of one another…"

He raised his wings and spread them wide before folding them again.

"There," he said, "I have just brushed ten million other worlds, and they knew nothing of it. We are as close as a heartbeat, but we can never touch or see or hear these other worlds except in the Northern Lights."

"And why there?" said Farder Coram.

"Because the charged particles in the Aurora have the property of making the matter of this world thin, so that we can see through it for a brief time. Witches have always known this, but we seldom speak of it."

"My father believes in it," Lyra said. "I know because I heard him talking and showing pictures of the Aurora."

"Is this anything to do with Dust?" said John Faa.

"Who can say?" said the goose-dæmon. "All I can tell you is that the Dust-hunters are as frightened of it as if it were deadly poison. That is why they imprisoned Lord Asriel."

"But why?" Lyra said.

"They think he intends to use Dust in some way in order to make a bridge between this world and the world beyond the Aurora."

There was a lightness in Lyra's head.

She heard Farder Coram say, "And does he?"

"Yes," said the goose-dæmon. "They don't believe he can, because they think he is mad to believe in the other worlds in the first place. But it is true: that is his intention. And he is so powerful a figure that they feared he would upset their own plans, so they made a pact with the armoured bears to capture him and keep him imprisoned in the fortress of Svalbard, out of the way. Some say they helped the new bear-king to gain his throne, as part of the bargain."

Lyra said, "Do the witches want him to make this bridge? Are they on his side or against him?"

"That is a question with too complicated an answer. Firstly, the witches are not united. There are differences of opinion among us. Secondly, Lord Asriel's bridge will have a bearing on a war being waged at the present between some witches and various other forces, some in the spirit world. Possession of the bridge, if it ever existed, would give a huge advantage to whoever held it. Thirdly, Serafina Pekkala's clan – my clan – is not yet part of any alliance, though great pressure is being put on us to declare for one side or another. You see, these are questions of high politics, and not easily answered."

"What about the bears?" said Lyra. "Whose side are they on?"

"On the side of anyone who pays them. They have no interest whatever in these questions; they have no dæmons; they are unconcerned about human problems. At least, that is how bears used to be, but we have heard that their new king is intent on changing their old ways… At any rate, the Dust-hunters have paid them to imprison Lord Asriel, and they will hold him on Svalbard until the last drop of blood drains from the body of the last bear alive."

"But not all bears!" Lyra said. "There's one who en't on Svalbard at all. He's an outcast bear, and he's going to come with us."

The goose gave Lyra another of his piercing looks. This time she could feel his cold surprise.

Farder Coram shifted uncomfortably, and said, "The fact is, Lyra, I don't think he is. We heard he's serving out a term as an indentured labourer; he en't free, as we thought he might be, he's under sentence. Till he's discharged he won't be free to come, armour or no armour; and he won't never have that back, either."

"But he said they tricked him! They made him drunk and stole it away!"

"We heard a different story," said John Faa. "He's a dangerous rogue, is what we heard."

"If —" Lyra was passionate; she could hardly speak for indignation — "if the alethiometer says something, I know it's true. And I asked it, and it said that he was telling the truth, they did trick him, and they're telling lies and not him. I believe him, Lord Faa! Farder Coram — you saw him too, and you believe him, don't you?"

"I thought I did, child. I en't so certain of things as you are."

"But what are they afraid of? Do they think he's going to go round killing people as soon's he gets his armour on? He could kill dozens of 'em now!"

"He has done," said John Faa. "Well, if not dozens, then some. When they first took his armour away he went a-rampaging round looking for it. He tore open the police house and the bank and I don't know where else, and there's at least two men who died. The only reason they didn't shoot to kill him is because of his wondrous skill with metals; they wanted to use him like a labourer."

"Like a slave!" Lyra said hotly. "They hadn't got the right!"

"Be that as it may, they might have shot him for the killings he done, but they didn't. And they bound him over to labour in the town's interest until he's paid off the damage and the blood-money."

"John," said Farder Coram, "I don't know how you feel, but it's my belief they'll never let him have that armour back. The longer they keep him, the more angry he'll be when he gets it."

"But if *we* get his armour back he'll come with us and never bother 'em again," said Lyra. "I promise, Lord Faa."

"And how are we going to do that?"

"I know where it is!"

There was a silence, in which they all three became aware of the witch's dæmon and his fixed stare at Lyra. All three turned to him, and their own dæmons too, who had until then affected the extreme politeness of keeping their eyes modestly away from this singular creature, here without his body.

"You won't be surprised," said the goose, "to know that the alethiometer is one other reason the witches are interested in you, Lyra. Our consul told us about your visit this morning. I believe it was Dr Lanselius who told you about the bear."

"Yes, it was," said John Faa. "And she and Farder Coram went theirselves and talked to him. I daresay what Lyra says is true, but if we go breaking the law of these people we'll only get involved in a quarrel with them, and what we ought to be doing is pushing on towards this Bolvangar, bear or no bear."

"Ah, but you en't seen him, John," said Farder Coram. "And I do believe Lyra. We could promise on his behalf, maybe. He might make all the difference."

"What do you think, sir?" said John Faa to the witch's dæmon.

"We have few dealings with bears. Their desires are as strange to us as ours are to them. If this bear is an outcast, he might be less reliable than they are said to be. You must decide for yourselves."

"We will," said John Faa firmly. "But now, sir, can you tell us how to get to Bolvangar from here?"

The goose-dæmon began to explain. He spoke of valleys and hills, of the tree-line and the tundra, of star-sightings. Lyra listened a while, and then lay back in the deck-chair with Pantalaimon curled around her neck, and thought of the grand vision the goose-dæmon had brought with him. A bridge between two worlds... This was far more splendid than anything she could have hoped for! And only her great father could have conceived it. As soon as they had rescued the children, she would go to Svalbard with the bear and take Lord Asriel the alethiometer, and use it to help set him free; and they'd build the bridge together, and be the first across...

Sometime in the night John Faa must have carried Lyra to her bunk, because that was where she awoke. The dim sun was as high in the sky as it was going to get, only a hand's breadth above the horizon, so it must be nearly noon, she thought. Soon, when they moved further north, there would be no sun at all.

She dressed quickly and ran on deck to find nothing very much happening. All the stores had been unloaded, sledges and dog-teams had been hired and were waiting to go; everything was ready and nothing was moving. Most of the gyptians were sitting in a smoke-filled café facing the water, eating spice-cakes and drinking strong sweet coffee at the long wooden tables under the fizz and crackle of some ancient anbaric lights.

"Where's Lord Faa?" she said, sitting down with Tony Costa and his friends. "And Farder Coram? Are they getting the bear's armour for him?"

"They're a-talking to the Sysselman. That's their word for governor. You seen this bear, then, Lyra?"

"Yeah!" she said, and explained all about him. As she talked, someone else pulled a chair up and joined the group at the table.

"So you've spoken to old Iorek?" he said.

She looked at the newcomer with surprise. He was a tall, lean man with a thin black moustache and narrow blue eyes, and a perpetual expression of distant and sardonic amusement. She felt strongly about him at once, but she wasn't sure whether it was liking she felt, or dislike. His dæmon was a shabby hare as thin and tough-looking as he was.

He held out his hand and she shook it warily.

"Lee Scoresby," he said.

"The aëronaut!" she exclaimed. "Where's your balloon? Can I go up in it?"

"It's packed away right now, miss. You must be the famous Lyra. How did you get on with Iorek Byrnison?"

"You know him?"

"I fought beside him in the Tunguska campaign. Hell, I've known Iorek for years. Bears are difficult critters no matter what, but he's a problem, and no mistake. Say, are any of you gentlemen in the mood for a game of hazard?"

A pack of cards had appeared from nowhere in his hand. He riffled them with a snapping noise.

"Now I've heard of the card-power of your people," Lee

Scoresby was saying, cutting and folding the cards over and over with one hand and fishing a cigar out of his breast pocket with the other, "and I thought you wouldn't object to giving a simple Texan traveller the chance to joust with your skill and daring on the field of pasteboard combat. What do you say, gentlemen?"

Gyptians prided themselves on their ability with cards, and several of the men looked interested and pulled their chairs up. While they were agreeing with Lee Scoresby what to play and for what stakes, his dæmon flicked her ears at Pantalaimon, who understood and leapt lightly to her side as a squirrel.

She was speaking for Lyra's ears too, of course, and Lyra heard her say quietly, "Go straight to the bear and tell him direct. As soon as they know what's going on they'll move his armour somewhere else."

Lyra got up, taking her spice-cake with her, and no one noticed; Lee Scoresby was already dealing the cards, and every suspicious eye was on his hands.

In the dull light, fading through an endless afternoon, she found her way to the sledge depot. It was something she knew she had to do, but she felt uneasy about it, and afraid, too.

Outside the largest of the concrete sheds the great bear was working, and Lyra stood by the open gate to watch. Iorek Byrnison was dismantling a gas-engined tractor that had crashed; the metal covering of the engine was twisted and buckled and one runner bent upwards. The bear lifted the metal off as if it were cardboard, and turned it this way and that in his great hands, seeming to test it for some quality or other, before setting a rear paw on one corner and then bending the whole sheet in such a way that the dents sprang out and the shape was restored. Leaning it against the wall, he lifted the massive weight of the tractor with one paw and laid it on its side before bending to examine the crumpled runner.

As he did so, he caught sight of Lyra. She felt a bolt of cold fear strike at her, because he was so massive and so alien. She was gazing through the chain-link fence about forty yards from him, and she thought how he could clear the distance in a bound or two and sweep the wire aside like a cobweb, and she almost turned and ran away; but Pantalaimon said, "Stop! Let me go and talk to him."

He was a tern, and before she could answer he'd flown off the fence and down to the icy ground beyond it. There was an open gate a little way along, and Lyra could have followed him, but she hung back unwillingly. Pantalaimon looked at her, and then became a badger.

She knew what he was doing. Dæmons could move no more than a few yards from their humans, and if she stood by the fence and he remained a bird, he wouldn't get near the bear; so he was going to pull.

She felt angry and miserable. His badger-claws dug into the earth and he walked forward. It was such a strange tormenting feeling when your dæmon was pulling at the link between you; part physical pain deep in the chest, part intense sadness and love. And she knew it was the same for him. Everyone tested it when they were growing up: seeing how far they could pull apart, coming back with intense relief.

He tugged a little harder.

"Don't, Pan!"

But he didn't stop. The bear watched, motionless. The pain in Lyra's heart grew more and more unbearable, and a sob of longing rose in her throat.

"Pan –"

Then she was through the gate, scrambling over the icy mud towards him, and he turned into a wildcat and sprang up into her arms, and then they were clinging together tightly with little shaky sounds of unhappiness coming from them both.

"I thought you really *would* –"

"No –"

"I couldn't *believe* how much it hurt –"

And then she brushed the tears away angrily and sniffed hard. He nestled in her arms, and she knew she would rather die than let them be parted and face that sadness again; it would send her mad with grief and terror. If she died they'd still be together, like the Scholars in the crypt at Jordan.

Then girl and dæmon looked up at the solitary bear. He had no dæmon. He was alone, always alone. She felt such a stir of pity and gentleness for him that she almost reached out to touch his matted pelt, and only a sense of courtesy towards those cold ferocious eyes prevented her.

"Iorek Byrnison," she said.

"Well?"

"Lord Faa and Farder Coram have gone to try and get your armour for you."

He didn't move or speak. It was clear what he thought of their chances.

"I know where it is, though," she said, "and if I told you, maybe you could get it by yourself, I don't know."

"How do you know where it is?"

"I got a symbol-reader. I think I ought to tell you, Iorek Byrnison, seeing as they tricked you out of it in the first place. I don't think that's right. They shouldn't've done that. Lord Faa's going to argue with the Sysselman, but probably they won't let you have it whatever he says. So if I tell you, will you come with us and help rescue the kids from Bolvangar?"

"Yes."

"I…" She didn't mean to be nosy, but she couldn't help being curious. She said, "Why don't you just make some more armour out of this metal here, Iorek Byrnison?"

"Because it's worthless. Look," he said and, lifting the engine-cover with one paw, he extended a claw on the other hand and ripped right through it like a tin-opener. "My armour is made of sky-iron, made for me. A bear's armour is his soul, just as your dæmon is your soul. You might as well take *him* away –" indicating Pantalaimon – "and replace him with a doll full of sawdust. That is the difference. Now, where is my armour?"

"Listen, you got to promise not to take vengeance. They done wrong taking it, but you just got to put up with that."

"All right. No vengeance afterwards. But no holding back as I take it, either. If they fight, they die."

"It's hidden in the cellar of the priest's house," she told him. "He thinks there's a spirit in it, and he's been a-trying to conjure it out. But that's where it is."

He stood high up on his hind legs, and looked west, so that the last of the sun coloured his face a creamy brilliant yellow-white amid the gloom. She could feel the power of the great creature coming off him like waves of heat.

"I must work till sunset," he said. "I gave my word this morning to the master here. I still owe a few minutes' work."

"The sun's set where I am," she pointed out, because from her point of view it had vanished behind the rocky headland to the south-west.

He dropped to all fours.

"It's true," he said, with his face now in shadow like hers. "What's your name, child?"

"Lyra Belacqua."

"Then I owe you a debt, Lyra Belacqua," he said.

Then he turned and lurched away, padding so swiftly across the freezing ground that Lyra couldn't keep up, even running. She did run, though, and Pantalaimon flew up as a seagull to watch where the bear went and called down to tell her where to follow.

Iorek Byrnison bounded out of the depot and along the narrow street before turning into the main street of the town, past the courtyard of the Sysselman's residence where a flag hung in the still air and a sentry marched stiffly up and down, down the hill past the end of the street where the Witch-Consul lived. The sentry by this time had realized what was happening, and was trying to gather his wits, but Iorek Byrnison was already turning a corner near the harbour.

People stopped to watch or scuttled out of his careering way. The sentry fired two shots in the air, and set off down the hill after the bear, spoiling the effect by skidding on the icy slope and only regaining his balance after seizing the nearest railings. Lyra was not far behind. As she passed the Sysselman's house she was aware of a number of figures coming out into the courtyard to see what was going on, and thought she saw Farder Coram among them; but then she was past, hurtling down the street towards the corner where the sentry was already turning to follow the bear.

The priest's house was older than most, and made of costly bricks. Three steps led up to the front door, which was now hanging in matchwood splinters, and from inside the house came screams and the crashing and tearing of more wood. The sentry hesitated outside, his rifle at the ready; but then as passers-by began to gather and people looked out of windows from across the street, he realized that he had to act, and fired a shot into the air before running in.

A moment later, the whole house seemed to shake. Glass broke in three windows and a tile slid off the roof, and then a maidservant ran out, terrified, her clucking hen of a dæmon flapping after her.

Another shot came from inside the house, and then a

full-throated roar made the servant scream. As if fired from a cannon, the priest himself came hurtling out, with his pelican-dæmon in a wild flutter of feathers and injured pride. Lyra heard orders shouted, and turned to see a squad of armed policemen hurrying around the corner, some with pistols and some with rifles, and not far behind them came John Faa and the stout, fussy figure of the Sysselman.

A rending, splintering sound made them all look back at the house. A window at ground level, obviously opening on a cellar, was being wrenched apart with a crash of glass and a screech of tearing wood. The sentry who'd followed Iorek Byrnison into the house came running out and stood to face the cellar window, rifle at his shoulder; and then the window tore open completely, and out there climbed Iorek Byrnison, the bear in armour.

Without it he was formidable. With it, he was terrifying. It was rust-red, and crudely riveted together: great sheets and plates of dented discoloured metal that scraped and screeched as they rode over one another. The helmet was pointed like his muzzle, with slits for eyes, and it left the lower part of his jaw bare for tearing and biting.

The sentry fired several shots, and the policemen levelled their weapons too, but Iorek Byrnison merely shook the bullets off like rain-drops, and lunged forward in a screech and clang of metal before the sentry could escape, and knocked him to the ground. His dæmon, a husky dog, darted at the bear's throat, but Iorek Byrnison took no more notice of him than he would of a fly and, dragging the sentry to him with one vast paw, he bent and enclosed his head in his jaws. Lyra could see exactly what would happen next: he'd crush the man's skull like an egg, and there would follow a bloody fight, more deaths, and more delay; and they would never get free, with or without the bear.

Without even thinking she darted forward and put her hand

on the one vulnerable spot in the bear's armour, the gap that appeared between the helmet and the great plate over his shoulders when he bent his head, where she could see the yellow-white fur dimly between the rusty edges of metal. She dug her fingers in, and Pantalaimon instantly flew to the same spot and became a wildcat, crouched to defend her; but Iorek Byrnison was still, and the riflemen held their fire.

"Iorek!" she said in a fierce undertone. "Listen! You owe me a debt, right. Well now you can repay it. Do as I ask. Don't fight these men. Just turn around and walk away with me. We *want* you, Iorek, you can't stay here. Just come down the harbour with me and don't even look back. Farder Coram and Lord Faa, let them do the talking, they'll make it all right. Leave go this man and come away with me…"

The bear slowly opened his jaws. The sentry's head, bleeding and wet and ash-pale, fell to the ground as he fainted, and his dæmon set about calming and gentling him as the bear stepped away beside Lyra.

No one else moved. They watched as the bear turned away from his victim at the bidding of the little girl with the cat-dæmon, and then they shuffled aside to make room as Iorek Byrnison padded heavily through the midst of them at Lyra's side and made for the harbour.

Her mind was all on him, and she didn't see the confusion behind her, the fear and the anger that rose up safely when he was gone. She walked with him, and Pantalaimon padded ahead of them both as if to clear the way.

When they reached the harbour, Iorek Byrnison dipped his head and unfastened the helmet with a claw, letting it clang on the frozen ground. Gyptians came out of the café, having sensed that something was going on, and watched in the gleam of the anbaric lights on the ship's deck as Iorek Byrnison shrugged off the rest of his armour and left it in a heap on the quayside. Without a word to anyone he padded to the water and slipped into it without a ripple, and vanished.

"What's happened?" said Tony Costa, hearing the indignant voices from the streets above, as the townsfolk and the police made their way to the harbour.

Lyra told him, as clearly as she could.

"But where's he gone now?" he said. "He en't just left his armour on the ground? They'll have it back, as soon's they get here!"

Lyra was afraid they might, too, for around the corner came the first policemen, and then more, and then the Sysselman and the priest and twenty or thirty onlookers, with John Faa and Farder Coram trying to keep up.

But when they saw the group on the quayside they stopped, for someone else had appeared. Sitting on the bear's armour with one ankle resting on the opposite knee was the long-limbed form of Lee Scoresby, and in his hand was the longest pistol Lyra had ever seen, casually pointing at the ample stomach of the Sysselman.

"Seems to me you ain't taken very good care of my friend's armour," he said conversationally. "Why, look at the rust! And I wouldn't be surprised to find moths in it, too. Now you just stand where you are, still and easy, and don't anybody move till the bear comes back with some lubrication. Or I guess you could all go home and read the newspaper. 'S up to you."

"There he is!" said Tony, pointing to a ramp at the far end of the quay, where Iorek Byrnison was emerging from the water, dragging something dark with him. Once he was up on the quayside he shook himself, sending great sheets of water flying in all directions, till his fur was standing up thickly again. Then he bent to take the black object in his teeth once more and dragged it along to where his armour lay. It was a dead seal.

"Iorek," said the aëronaut, standing up lazily and keeping his pistol firmly fixed on the Sysselman. "Howdy."

The bear looked up and growled briefly, before ripping the seal open with one claw. Lyra watched fascinated as he laid the skin out flat and tore off strips of blubber, which he then rubbed all over his armour, packing it carefully into the places where the plates moved over one another.

"Are you with these people?" the bear said to Lee Scoresby as he worked.

"Sure. I guess we're both hired hands, Iorek."

"Where's your balloon?" said Lyra to the Texan.

"Packed away in two sledges," he said. "Here comes the boss."

John Faa and Farder Coram, together with the Sysselman, came down the quay with four armed policemen.

"Bear!" said the Sysselman, in a high, harsh voice. "For now, you are allowed to depart in the company of these people. But let me tell you that if you appear within the town limits again, you will be treated mercilessly."

Iorek Byrnison took not the slightest notice, but continued to rub the seal-blubber all over his armour; the care and attention he was paying the task reminding Lyra of her own devotion to Pantalaimon. Just as the bear had said: the armour was his soul. The Sysselman and the policemen withdrew, and slowly the other townspeople turned and drifted away, though a few remained to watch.

John Faa put his hands to his mouth and called, "Gyptians!"

They were all ready to move. They had been itching to get under way ever since they had disembarked; the sledges were packed, the dog-teams were in their traces.

John Faa said, "Time to move out, friends. We're all assembled now, and the road lies open. Mr Scoresby, you all a-loaded?"

"Ready to go, Lord Faa."

"And you, Iorek Byrnison?"

"When I am clad," said the bear.

He had finished oiling the armour. Not wanting to waste the seal-meat, he lifted the carcass in his teeth and flipped it on to the back of Lee Scoresby's larger sledge before donning the armour. It was astonishing to see how lightly he dealt with it: the sheets of metal were almost an inch thick in places, and yet he swung them round and into place as if they were silk robes. It took him less than a minute, and this time there was no harsh scream of rust.

So in less than half an hour, the expedition was on its way northwards. Under a sky peopled with millions of stars and a glaring moon, the sledges bumped and clattered over the ruts and stones until they reached clear snow at the edge of town. Then the sound changed to a quiet crunch of snow and creak of timber; and the dogs began to step out eagerly, and the motion became swift and smooth.

Lyra, wrapped up so thickly in the back of Farder Coram's sledge that only her eyes were exposed, whispered to Pantalaimon:

"Can you see Iorek?"

"He's padding along beside Lee Scoresby's sledge," the dæmon replied, looking back in his ermine-form as he clung to her wolverine-fur hood.

Ahead of them, over the mountains to the north, the pale arcs and loops of the Northern Lights began to glow and tremble. Lyra saw them through half-closed eyes, and felt a sleepy thrill of perfect happiness, to be speeding north under the Aurora. Pantalaimon struggled against her sleepiness, but it was too strong; he curled up as a mouse inside her hood. He could tell her when they woke, and it was probably a marten, or a dream, or some kind of harmless local spirit; but something was following the train of sledges, swinging lightly from branch to branch of the close-clustering pine trees, and it put him uneasily in mind of a monkey.

12

The Lost Boy

They travelled for several hours and then stopped to eat. While the men were lighting fires and melting snow for water, with Iorek Byrnison watching Lee Scoresby roast seal-meat close by, John Faa spoke to Lyra.

"Lyra, can you see that instrument to read it?" he said.

The moon itself had long set. The light from the Aurora was brighter than moonlight, but it was inconstant. However, Lyra's eyes were keen, and she fumbled inside her furs and tugged out the black velvet bag.

"Yes, I can see all right," she said. "But I know where most of the symbols are by now, anyway. What shall I ask it, Lord Faa?"

"I want to know more about how they're defending this place, Bolvangar," he said.

Without even having to think about it, she found her fingers moving the hands to point to the helmet, the griffin, and the crucible, and felt her mind settle into the right meanings like a complicated diagram in three dimensions. At once the needle began to swing round, back, round and on further, like a bee dancing its message to the hive. She watched it calmly, content not to know at first but to know that a meaning was coming, and then it began to clear. She let it dance on until it was certain.

"It's just like the witch's dæmon said, Lord Faa. There's a company of Tartars guarding the station, and they got wires all round it. They don't really expect to be attacked, that's what the symbol-reader says. But Lord Faa..."

"What, child?"

"It's a-telling me something else. In the next valley there's a village by a lake where the folk are troubled by a ghost."

John Faa shook his head impatiently, and said, "That don't matter now. There's bound to be spirits of all kinds among these forests. Tell me again about them Tartars. How many, for instance? What are they armed with?"

Lyra dutifully asked, and reported the answer:

"There's sixty men with rifles, and they got a couple of larger guns, sort of cannons. They got fire-throwers too. And ... their dæmons are all wolves, that's what it says."

That caused a stir among the older gyptians, those who'd campaigned before.

"The Sibirsk regiments have wolf-dæmons," said one.

John Faa said, "I never met fiercer. We shall have to fight like tigers. And consult the bear; he's a shrewd warrior, that one."

Lyra was impatient, and said, "But Lord Faa, this ghost – I think it's the ghost of one of the kids!"

"Well, even if it is, Lyra, I don't know what anyone could do about it. Sixty Sibirsk riflemen, and fire-throwers... Mr Scoresby, step over here if you would, for a moment."

While the aëronaut came to the sledge, Lyra slipped away and spoke to the bear.

"Iorek, have you travelled this way before?"

"Once," he said in that deep flat voice.

"There's a village near, en't there?"

"Over the ridge," he said, looking up through the sparse trees.

"Is it far?"

"For you or for me?"

"For me," she said.

"Too far. Not at all far for me."

"How long would it take you to get there, then?"

"I could be there and back three times by next moonrise."

"Because Iorek, listen: I got this symbol-reader that tells me things, you see, and it's told me that there's something important I got to do over in that village, and Lord Faa won't let me go there. He just wants to get on quick, and I know that's important too. But unless I go and find out what it is, we might not know what the Gobblers are really doing."

The bear said nothing. He was sitting up like a human, his great paws folded in his lap, his dark eyes looking into hers down the length of his muzzle. He knew she wanted something.

Pantalaimon spoke: "Can you take us there and catch up with the sledges later on?"

"I could. But I have given my word to Lord Faa to obey him, not anyone else."

"If I got his permission?" said Lyra.

"Then yes."

She turned and ran back through the snow.

"Lord Faa! If Iorek Byrnison takes me over the ridge to the village, we can find out whatever it is, and then catch the sledges up further on. He knows the route," she urged. "And I wouldn't ask, except it's like what I did before, Farder Coram, you remember, with that chameleon? I didn't understand it then, but it was true, and we found out soon after. I got the same feeling now. I can't understand properly what it's saying, only I know it's important. And Iorek Byrnison knows the way, he says he could get there and back three times by next moonrise, and I couldn't be safer than I'd be with him, could I? But he won't go without he gets Lord Faa's permission."

There was a silence. Farder Coram sighed. John Faa was frowning, and his mouth inside the fur hood was set grimly.

But before he could speak, the aëronaut put in:

"Lord Faa, if Iorek Byrnison takes the little girl, she'll be as safe as if she was here with us. All bears are true, but I've known Iorek for years, and nothing under the sky will make him break his word. Give him the charge to take care of her and he'll do it, make no mistake. As for speed, he can lope for hours without tiring."

"But why should not some men go?" said John Faa.

"Well, they'd have to walk," Lyra pointed out, "because you couldn't run a sledge over that ridge. Iorek Byrnison can go faster than any man over that sort of country, and I'm light enough so's he won't be slowed down. And I promise, Lord Faa, I promise not to be any longer than I need, and not to give anything away about us, or to get in any danger."

"You're sure you need to do this? That symbol-reader en't playing the fool with you?"

"It never does, Lord Faa, and I don't think it could."

John Faa rubbed his chin.

"Well, if all comes out right, we'll have a piece more knowledge than we do now. Iorek Byrnison," he called, "are you willing to do as this child bids?"

"I do your bidding, Lord Faa. Tell me to take the child there, and I will."

"Very well. You are to take her where she wishes to go and do as she bids. Lyra, I'm a-commanding *you* now, you understand?"

"Yes, Lord Faa."

"You go and search for whatever it is, and when you've found it, you turn right round and come back. Iorek Byrnison, we'll be a-travelling on by that time, so you'll have to catch us up."

The bear nodded his great head.

"Are there any soldiers in the village?" he said to Lyra. "Will I need my armour? We shall be swifter without it."

"No," she said. "I'm certain of that, Iorek. Thank you, Lord Faa, and I promise I'll do just as you say."

Tony Costa gave her a strip of dried seal-meat to chew, and with Pantalaimon as a mouse inside her hood, Lyra clambered on to the great bear's back, gripping his fur with her mittens and his narrow muscular back between her knees. His fur was wondrously thick, and the sense of immense power she felt was overwhelming. As if she weighed nothing at all, he turned and loped away in a long swinging run up towards the ridge and into the low trees.

It took some time before she was used to the movement, and then she felt a wild exhilaration. She was riding a bear! And the Aurora was swaying above them in golden arcs and loops, and all around was the bitter Arctic cold and the immense silence of the North.

Iorek Byrnison's paws made hardly any sound as they padded forward through the snow. The trees were thin and stunted here, for they were on the edge of the tundra, but there were brambles and snagging bushes in the path. The bear ripped through them as if they were cobwebs.

They climbed the low ridge, among outcrops of black rock, and were soon out of sight of the party behind them. Lyra wanted to talk to the bear, and if he had been human she would already have been on familiar terms with him; but he was so strange and wild and cold that she was shy, almost for the first time in her life. So as he loped along, his great legs swinging tirelessly, she sat with the movement and said nothing. Perhaps he preferred that anyway, she thought; she must seem a little prattling cub, only just past babyhood, in the eyes of an armoured bear.

She had seldom considered herself before, and found the experience interesting but uncomfortable; very like riding the bear, in fact. Iorek Byrnison was pacing swiftly, moving both legs on one side of his body at the same time, and rocking from side to side in a steady powerful rhythm. She found she couldn't just sit: she had to ride actively.

They had been travelling for an hour or more, and Lyra was stiff and sore but deeply happy, when Iorek Byrnison slowed down and stopped.

"Look up," he said.

Lyra raised her eyes and had to wipe them with the inside of her wrist, for she was so cold that tears were blurring them. When she could see clearly she gasped at the sight of the sky. The Aurora had faded to a pallid trembling glimmer, but the stars were as bright as diamonds, and across the great dark diamond-scattered vault, hundreds upon hundreds of tiny black shapes were flying out of the east and south towards the north.

"Are they birds?" she said.

"They are witches," said the bear.

"Witches! What are they doing?"

"Flying to war, maybe. I have never seen so many at one time."

"Do you know any witches, Iorek?"

"I have served some. And fought some, too. This is a sight to frighten Lord Faa. If they are flying to the aid of your enemies, you should all be afraid."

"Lord Faa wouldn't be frightened. You en't afraid, are you?"

"Not yet. When I am, I shall master the fear. But we had better tell Lord Faa about the witches, because the men might not have seen them."

He moved on more slowly, and she kept watching the sky until her eyes splintered again with tears of cold, and she saw no end to the numberless witches flying north.

Finally Iorek Byrnison stopped and said, "There is the village."

They were looking down a broken, rugged slope towards a cluster of wooden buildings beside a wide stretch of snow as flat as could be, which Lyra took to be the frozen lake. A wooden jetty showed her she was right. They were no more than five minutes from the place.

"What do you want to do?" the bear asked.

Lyra slipped off his back, and found it hard to stand. Her face was stiff with cold and her legs were shaky, but she clung to his fur and stamped until she felt stronger.

"There's a child or a ghost or something down in that village," she said, "or maybe near it, I don't know for certain. I want to go and find him and bring him back to Lord Faa and the others if I can. I thought he was a ghost, but the symbol-reader might be telling me something I can't understand."

"If he is outside," said the bear, "he had better have some shelter."

"I don't think he's dead..." said Lyra, but she was far from sure. The alethiometer had indicated something uncanny and unnatural, which was alarming; but who was she? Lord Asriel's daughter. And who was under her command? A mighty bear. How could she possibly show any fear?

"Let's just go and look," she said.

She clambered on his back again, and he set off down the broken slope, walking steadily and not pacing any more. The dogs of the village smelled or heard or sensed them coming, and began to howl frightfully; and the reindeer in their enclosure moved about nervously, their antlers clashing like dry sticks. In the still air every movement could be heard for a long way.

As they reached the first of the houses, Lyra looked to right and left, peering hard into the dimness, for the Aurora was fading and the moon still far from rising. Here and there a light flickered under a snow-thick roof, and Lyra thought she saw pale faces behind some of the window-panes, and imagined their astonishment to see a child riding a great white bear.

At the centre of the little village there was an open space next to the jetty, where boats had been drawn up, mounds under the snow. The noise of the dogs was deafening, and just as Lyra thought it must have wakened everyone, a door opened and a man came out holding a rifle. His wolverine-dæmon leapt on to the woodstack beside the door, scattering snow.

Lyra slipped down at once and stood between him and Iorek Byrnison, conscious that she had told the bear there was no need for his armour.

The man spoke in words she couldn't understand. Iorek Byrnison replied in the same language, and the man gave a little moan of fear.

"He thinks we are devils," Iorek told Lyra. "What shall I say?"

"Tell him we're not devils, but we've got friends who are. And we're looking for… Just a child. A strange child. Tell him that."

As soon as the bear had said that, the man pointed to the right, indicating some place further off, and spoke quickly.

Iorek Byrnison said, "He asks if we have come to take the child away. They are afraid of it. They have tried to drive it away, but it keeps coming back."

"Tell him we'll take it away with us, but they were very bad to treat it like that. Where is it?"

The man explained, gesticulating fearfully. Lyra was afraid he'd fire his rifle by mistake, but as soon as he'd spoken he hastened inside his house and shut the door. Lyra could see faces at every window.

"Where is the child?" she said.

"In the fish-house," the bear told her, and turned to pad down towards the jetty.

Lyra followed. She was horribly nervous. The bear was making for a narrow wooden shed, raising his head to sniff this way and that, and when he reached the door he stopped and said, "In there."

Lyra's heart was beating so fast she could hardly breathe. She raised her hand to knock at the door and then, feeling that that was ridiculous, took a deep breath to call out, but realized that she didn't know what to say. Oh, it was so dark now! She should have brought a lantern...

There was no choice, and anyway, she didn't want the bear to see her being afraid. He had spoken of mastering his fear: that was what she'd have to do. She lifted the strap of reindeer hide holding the latch in place, and tugged hard against the frost binding the door shut. It opened with a snap. She had to kick aside the snow piled against the foot of the door before she could pull it wide, and Pantalaimon was no help, running back and forth in his ermine-shape, a white shadow over the white ground, uttering little frightened sounds.

"Pan, for God's sake!" she said. "Be a bat. Go and *look* for me..."

But he wouldn't, and he wouldn't speak either. She had never seen him like this except once, when she and Roger in the crypt at Jordan had moved the dæmon-coins into the wrong skulls. He was even more frightened than she was. As for Iorek Byrnison, he was lying in the snow nearby, watching in silence.

"Come out," Lyra said as loud as she dared. "Come out!"

Not a sound came in answer. She pulled the door a little wider, and Pantalaimon leapt up into her arms, pushing and pushing at her in his cat-form, and said, "Go away! Don't stay here! Oh, Lyra, go now! Turn back!"

Trying to hold him still, she was aware of Iorek Byrnison getting to his feet, and turned to see a figure hastening down the track from the village, carrying a lantern. When he came close enough to speak, he raised the lantern and held it to show his face: an old man with a broad, lined face, and eyes nearly lost in a thousand wrinkles. His dæmon was an Arctic fox.

He spoke, and Iorek Byrnison said:

"He says that it's not the only child of that kind. He's seen others in the forest. Sometimes they die quickly, sometimes they don't die. This one is tough, he thinks. But it would be better for him if he died."

"Ask him if I can borrow his lantern," Lyra said.

The bear spoke, and the man handed it to her at once, nodding vigorously. She realized that he'd come down in order to bring it to her, and thanked him, and he nodded again and stood back, away from her and the hut and away from the bear.

Lyra thought suddenly: what if the child is Roger? And she prayed with all her force that it wouldn't be. Pantalaimon was clinging to her, an ermine again, his little claws hooked deep into her anorak.

She lifted the lantern high and took a step into the shed, and then she saw what it was that the Oblation Board was doing, and what was the nature of the sacrifice the children were having to make.

The little boy was huddled against the wood drying-rack where hung row upon row of gutted fish, all as stiff as boards. He was clutching a piece of fish to him as Lyra was clutching Pantalaimon, with both hands, hard, against her heart; but that was all he had, a piece of dried fish; because he had no dæmon at all. The Gobblers had cut it away. That was *intercision*, and this was a severed child.

13

Fencing

Her first impulse was to turn and run, or to be sick. A human being with no dæmon was like someone without a face, or with their ribs laid open and their heart torn out: something unnatural and uncanny that belonged to the world of night-ghasts, not the waking world of sense.

So Lyra clung to Pantalaimon and her head swam and her gorge rose, and cold as the night was, a sickly sweat moistened her flesh with something colder still.

"Ratter," said the boy. "You got my Ratter?"

Lyra was in no doubt what he meant.

"No," she said in a voice as frail and frightened as she felt. Then, "What's your name?"

"Tony Makarios," he said. "Where's Ratter?"

"I don't know…" she began, and swallowed hard to govern her nausea. "The Gobblers…" But she couldn't finish. She had to go out of the shed and sit down by herself in the snow, except that of course she wasn't by herself, she was never by herself, because Pantalaimon was always there. Oh, to be cut from him as this little boy had been parted from his Ratter! The worst thing in the world! She found herself sobbing, and Pantalaimon was whimpering too, and in both of them there was a passionate pity and sorrow for the half-boy.

Then she got to her feet again.

"Come on," she called in a trembling voice. "Tony, come out. We're going to take you somewhere safe."

There was a stir of movement in the fish-house, and he appeared at the door, still clutching his dried fish. He was dressed in warm enough garments, a thickly padded and quilted coal-silk anorak and fur boots, but they had a second-hand look and didn't fit well. In the wider light outside that came from the faint trails of the Aurora and the snow-covered ground he looked more lost and piteous even than he had at first, crouching in the lantern-light by the fish-racks.

The villager who'd brought the lantern had retreated a few yards, and called down to them.

Iorek Byrnison interpreted: "He says you must pay for that fish."

Lyra felt like telling the bear to kill him, but she said, "We're taking the child away for them. They can afford to give one fish to pay for that."

The bear spoke. The man muttered, but didn't argue. Lyra set his lantern down in the snow and took the half-boy's hand to guide him to the bear. He came helplessly, showing no surprise and no fear at the great white beast standing so close, and when Lyra helped him to sit on Iorek's back, all he said was:

"I dunno where my Ratter is."

"No, nor do we, Tony," she said. "But we'll… We'll punish the Gobblers. We'll do that, I promise. Iorek, is that all right if I sit up there too?"

"My armour weighs far more than children," he said.

So she scrambled up behind Tony and made him cling to the long stiff fur, and Pantalaimon sat inside her hood, warm and close and full of pity. Lyra knew that Pantalaimon's impulse was

215

to reach out and cuddle the little half-child, to lick him and gentle him and warm him as his own dæmon would have done; but the great taboo prevented that, of course.

They rode through the village and up towards the ridge, and the villagers' faces were open with horror and a kind of fearful relief at seeing that hideously mutilated creature taken away by a little girl and a great white bear.

In Lyra's heart, revulsion struggled with compassion, and compassion won. She put her arms around the skinny little form to hold him safe. The journey back to the main party was colder, and harder, and darker, but it seemed to pass more quickly for all that. Iorek Byrnison was tireless, and Lyra's riding became automatic, so that she was never in danger of falling off. The cold body in her arms was so light that in one way he was easy to manage, but he was inert; he sat stiffly without moving as the bear moved, so in another way he was difficult too.

From time to time the half-boy spoke.

"What's that you said?" asked Lyra.

"I says is she gonna know where I am?"

"Yeah, she'll know, she'll find you and we'll find her. Hold on tight now, Tony. It en't far from here…"

The bear loped onwards. Lyra had no idea how tired she was until they caught up with the gyptians. The sledges had stopped to rest the dogs, and suddenly there they all were, Farder Coram, Lord Faa, Lee Scoresby, all lunging forward to help and then falling back silent as they saw the other figure with Lyra. She was so stiff that she couldn't even loosen her arms around his body, and John Faa himself had to pull them gently open and lift her off.

"Gracious God, what is this?" he said. "Lyra, child, what have you found?"

"He's called Tony," she mumbled through frozen lips. "And

they cut his dæmon away. That's what the Gobblers do."

The men held back, fearful; but the bear spoke, to Lyra's weary amazement, chiding them.

"Shame on you! Think what this child has done! You might not have more courage, but you should be ashamed to show less."

"You're right, Iorek Byrnison," said John Faa, and turned to give orders. "Build that fire up and heat some soup for the child. For both children. Farder Coram, is your shelter rigged?"

"It is, John. Bring her over and we'll get her warm…"

"And the little boy," said someone else. "He can eat and get warm, even if…"

Lyra was trying to tell John Faa about the witches, but they were all so busy, and she was so tired. After a confusing few minutes full of lantern light, woodsmoke, figures hurrying to and fro, she felt a gentle nip on her ear from Pantalaimon's ermine-teeth, and woke to find the bear's face a few inches from hers.

"The witches," Pantalaimon whispered. "I called Iorek."

"Oh yeah," she mumbled. "Iorek, thank you for taking me there and back. I might not remember to tell Lord Faa about the witches, so you better do that instead of me."

She heard the bear agree, and then she fell asleep properly.

When she woke up, it was as close to daylight as it was ever going to get. The sky was pale in the south-east, and the air was suffused with a grey mist, through which the gyptians moved like bulky ghosts, loading sledges and harnessing dogs to the traces.

She saw it all from the shelter on Farder Coram's sledge, inside which she lay under a heap of furs. Pantalaimon was fully awake before she was, trying the shape of an Arctic fox before reverting to his favourite ermine.

Iorek Byrnison was asleep in the snow nearby, his head on his great paws; but Farder Coram was up and busy, and as soon as he saw Pantalaimon emerge, he limped across to wake Lyra properly.

She saw him coming, and sat up to speak.

"Farder Coram, I know what it was that I couldn't understand! The alethiometer kept saying *bird* and *not*, and that didn't make sense, because it meant *no dæmon* and I didn't see how it could be... What is it?"

"Lyra, I'm afraid to tell you this after what you done, but that little boy died an hour ago. He couldn't settle, he couldn't stay in one place; he kept asking after his dæmon, where she was, was she a-coming soon, and all; and he kept such a tight hold on that bare old piece of fish as if... Oh, I can't speak of it, child; but he closed his eyes finally and fell still, and that was the first time he looked peaceful, for he was like any other dead person then, with their dæmon gone in the course of nature. They've been a-trying to dig a grave for him, but the earth's bound like iron. So John Faa ordered a fire built, and they're a-going to cremate him, so as not to have him despoiled by carrion-eaters.

"Child, you did a brave thing and a good thing, and I'm proud of you. Now we know what terrible wickedness those people are capable of, we can see our duty plainer than ever. What you must do is rest and eat, because you fell asleep too soon to restore yourself last night, and you have to eat in these temperatures to stop yourself getting weak..."

He was fussing around, tucking the furs into place, tightening the tension-rope across the body of the sledge, running the traces through his hands to untangle them.

"Farder Coram, where is the little boy now? Have they burned him yet?"

"No, Lyra, he's a-lying back there."

"I want to go and see him."

He couldn't refuse her that, for she'd seen worse than a dead body, and it might calm her. So with Pantalaimon as a white hare bounding delicately at her side, she trudged along the line of sledges to where some men were piling brushwood.

The boy's body lay under a checkered blanket beside the path. She knelt and lifted the blanket in her mittened hands. One man was about to stop her, but the others shook their heads.

Pantalaimon crept close as Lyra looked down on the poor wasted face. She slipped her hand out of the mitten and touched his eyes. They were marble-cold, and Farder Coram had been right; poor little Tony Makarios was no different from any other human whose dæmon had departed in death. Oh, if they took Pantalaimon from her! She swept him up and hugged him as if she meant to press him right into her heart. And all little Tony had was his pitiful piece of fish…

Where was it?

She pulled the blanket down. It was gone.

She was on her feet in a moment, and her eyes flashed fury at the men nearby.

"Where's his fish?"

They stopped, puzzled, unsure what she meant; though some of their dæmons knew, and looked at one another. One of the men began to grin uncertainly.

"Don't you *dare* laugh! I'll tear your lungs out if you laugh at him! That's all he had to cling on to, just an old dried fish, that's all he had for a dæmon to love and be kind to! Who's took it from him? Where's it gone?"

Pantalaimon was a snarling snow leopard, just like Lord Asriel's dæmon, but she didn't see that; all she saw was right and wrong.

"Easy, Lyra," said one man. "Easy, child."

"Who's took it?" she flared again, and the gyptian took a step back from her passionate fury.

"I didn't know," said another man apologetically. "I thought it was just what he'd been eating. I took it out his hand because I thought it was more respectful. That's all, Lyra."

"Then where is it?"

The man said uneasily, "Not thinking he had a need for it, I gave it to my dogs. I do beg your pardon."

"It en't my pardon you need, it's his," she said, and turned at once to kneel again, and laid her hand on the dead child's icy cheek.

Then an idea came to her, and she fumbled inside her furs. The cold air struck through as she opened her anorak, but in a few seconds she had what she wanted, and took a gold coin from her purse before wrapping herself close again.

"I want to borrow your knife," she said to the man who'd taken the fish, and when he let her have it, she said to Pantalaimon: "What was her name?"

He understood, of course, and said, "Ratter."

She held the coin tight in her left mittened hand and, holding the knife like a pencil, scratched the lost dæmon's name deeply into the gold.

"I hope that'll do, if I provide for you like a Jordan Scholar," she whispered to the dead boy, and forced his teeth apart to slip the coin into his mouth. It was hard, but she managed it, and managed to close his jaw again.

Then she gave the man back his knife and turned in the morning twilight to go back to Farder Coram.

He gave her a mug of soup straight off the fire, and she sipped it greedily.

"What we going to do about them witches, Farder Coram?" she said. "I wonder if your witch was one of them."

"*My* witch? I wouldn't presume that far, Lyra. They might be going anywhere. There's all kinds of concerns that play on the life of witches; things invisible to us; mysterious sicknesses they fall prey to, which we'd shrug off; causes of war quite beyond our understanding; joys and sorrows bound up with the flowering of tiny plants up on the tundra… But I wish I'd seen them a-flying, Lyra. I wish I'd been able to see a sight like that. Now drink up all that soup. D'you want some more? There's some pan-bread a-cooking too. Eat up, child, because we're on our way soon."

The food revived Lyra, and presently the chill at her soul began to melt. With the others, she went to watch the little half-child laid on his funeral pyre, and bowed her head and closed her eyes for John Faa's prayers; and then the men sprinkled coal-spirit and set matches to it, and it was blazing in a moment.

Once they were sure he was safely burned, they set off to travel again. It was a ghostly journey. Snow began to fall early on, and soon the world was reduced to the grey shadows of the dogs ahead, the lurching and creaking of the sledge, the biting cold, and a swirling sea of big flakes only just darker than the sky and only just lighter than the ground.

Through it all the dogs continued to run, tails high, breath puffing steam. North and further north they ran, while the pallid noontide came and went and the twilight folded itself again around the world. They stopped to eat and drink and rest in a gap in the hills, and to get their bearings, and while John Faa talked to Lee Scoresby about the way they might best use the balloon, Lyra thought of the spy-fly; and she asked Farder Coram what had happened to the smoke-leaf tin he'd trapped it in.

"I've got it tucked away tight," he said. "It's down in the bottom of that kit-bag, but there's nothing to see; I soldered it shut on board ship, like I said I would. I don't know what we're a-going to do with it, to tell you the truth; maybe we could drop it down a fire-mine, maybe that would settle it. But you needn't worry, Lyra. While I've got it, you're safe."

The first chance she had, she plunged her arm down into the stiffly-frosted canvas of the kit-bag and brought up the little tin. She could feel the buzz it was making before she touched it.

While Farder Coram was talking to the other leaders, she took the tin to Iorek Byrnison and explained her idea. It had come to her when she remembered his slicing so easily through the metal of the engine-cover.

He listened, and then took the lid of a biscuit-tin and deftly folded it into a small flat cylinder. She marvelled at the skill of his hands: unlike most bears, he and his kin had opposable thumb-claws with which they could hold things still to work on them; and he had some innate sense of the strength and flexibility of metals which meant that he only had to lift it once or twice, flex it this way and that, and he could run a claw over it in a circle to score it for folding. He did this now, folding the sides in and in until they stood in a raised rim and then making a lid to fit it. At Lyra's bidding he made two: one the same size as the original smoke-leaf tin, and another just big enough to contain the tin itself and a quantity of hairs and bits of moss and lichen all packed down tight to smother the noise. When it was closed, it was the same size and shape as the alethiometer.

When that was done, she sat next to Iorek Byrnison as he gnawed a haunch of reindeer that was frozen as hard as wood.

"Iorek," she said, "is it hard not having a dæmon? Don't you get lonely?"

"Lonely?" he said. "I don't know. They tell me this is cold. I don't know what cold is, because I don't freeze. So I don't know what lonely means either. Bears are made to be solitary."

"What about the Svalbard bears?" she said. "There's thousands of them, en't there? That's what I heard."

He said nothing, but ripped the joint in half with a sound like a splitting log.

"Beg pardon, Iorek," she said. "I hope I en't offended you. It's just that I'm curious. See, I'm extra curious about the Svalbard bears because of my father."

"Who is your father?"

"Lord Asriel. And they got him captive on Svalbard, you see. I think the Gobblers betrayed him and paid the bears to keep him in prison."

"I don't know. I am not a Svalbard bear."

"I thought you was…"

"No. I was a Svalbard bear, but I am not now. I was sent away as a punishment because I killed another bear. So I was deprived of my rank and my wealth and my armour and sent out to live at the edge of the human world and fight when I could find employment at it, or work at brutal tasks and drown my memory in raw spirits."

"Why did you kill the other bear?"

"Anger. There are ways among bears of turning away our anger with each other, but I was out of my own control. So I killed him and I was justly punished."

"And you were wealthy and high-ranking," said Lyra, marvelling. "Just like my father, Iorek! That's just the same with him after I was born. He killed someone too and they took all his wealth away. That was long before he got made a prisoner on Svalbard, though. I don't know anything about Svalbard, except it's in the farthest North… Is it all covered in ice? Can you get there over the frozen sea?"

"Not from this coast. The sea is sometimes frozen south of it, sometimes not. You would need a boat."

"Or a balloon, maybe."

"Or a balloon, yes, but then you would need the right wind."

He gnawed the reindeer haunch, and a wild notion flew into Lyra's mind as she remembered all those witches in the night sky; but she said nothing about that. Instead she asked Iorek Byrnison about Svalbard, and listened eagerly as he told her of the slow-crawling glaciers; of the rocks and ice-floes where the bright-tusked walruses lay in groups of a hundred or more, of the seas teeming with seals, of narwhals clashing their long white tusks above the icy water; of the great grim iron-bound coast, the cliffs a thousand feet and more high, where the foul cliff-ghasts perched and swooped; of the coal-pits and the fire-mines where the bearsmiths hammered out mighty sheets of iron and riveted them into armour...

"If they took your armour away, Iorek, where did you get this set from?"

"I made it myself in Nova Zembla from sky-metal. Until I did that I was incomplete."

"So bears can make their own souls..." she said. There was a great deal in the world to know. "Who is the King of Svalbard?" she went on. "Do bears have a King?"

"He is called Iofur Raknison."

That name shook a little bell in Lyra's mind. She'd heard it before, but where? And not in a bear's voice, either, nor in a gyptian's. The voice that had spoken it was a Scholar's, precise and pedantic and lazily arrogant, very much a Jordan College voice. She tried it again in her mind. Oh, she knew it so well!

And then she had it: the Retiring Room. The Scholars listening to Lord Asriel. It was the Palmerian Professor who had said something about Iofur Raknison. He'd used the word *panserbjørne*, which Lyra didn't know, and she hadn't known that Iofur Raknison was a bear; but what was it he'd said? The King of Svalbard was vain, and he could be flattered. There was something else, if only she could remember it, but so much had happened since then...

"If your father is a prisoner of the Svalbard bears," said Iorek

Byrnison, "he will not escape. There is no wood there to make a boat. On the other hand, if he is a nobleman, he will be treated fairly. They will give him a house to live in and a servant to wait on him, and food and fuel."

"Could the bears ever be defeated, Iorek?"

"No."

"Or tricked, maybe?"

He stopped gnawing and looked at her directly. Then he said, "You will never defeat the armoured bears. You have seen my armour; now look at my weapons."

He dropped the meat and held out his paws, palm upward, for her to look at. Each black pad was covered in horny skin an inch or more thick, and each of the claws was as long as Lyra's hand at least, and as sharp as a knife. He let her run her hands over them wonderingly.

"One blow will crush a seal's skull," he said. "Or break a man's back, or tear off a limb. And I can bite. If you had not stopped me in Trollesund, I would have crushed that man's head like an egg. So much for strength; now for trickery. You cannot trick a bear. You want to see proof? Take a stick and fence with me."

Eager to try, she snapped a stick off a snow-laden bush, trimmed all the side-shoots off, and swished it from side to side like a rapier. Iorek Byrnison sat back on his haunches and waited, forepaws in his lap. When she was ready she faced him, but she didn't like to stab at him because he looked so peaceable. So she flourished it, feinting to right and left, not intending to hit him at all, and he didn't move. She did that several times, and not once did he move so much as an inch.

Finally she decided to thrust at him directly, not hard, but just to touch the stick to his stomach. Instantly his paw reached forward and flicked the stick aside.

Surprised, she tried again, with the same result. He moved far more quickly and surely than she did. She tried to hit him in earnest, wielding the stick like a fencer's foil, and not once did it land on his body. He seemed to know what she intended before she did, and when she lunged at his head, the great paw swept the stick aside harmlessly, and when she feinted, he didn't move at all.

She became exasperated, and threw herself into a furious attack, jabbing and lashing and thrusting and stabbing, and never once did she get past those paws. They moved everywhere, precisely in time to parry, precisely at the right spot to block.

Finally she was frightened, and stopped. She was sweating inside her furs, out of breath, exhausted, and the bear still sat impassive. If she had had a real sword with a murderous point, he would have been quite unharmed.

"I bet you could catch bullets," she said, and threw the stick away. "How do you *do* that?"

"By not being human," he said. "That's why you could never trick a bear. We see tricks and deceit as plain as arms and legs. We can see in a way humans have forgotten. But you know about this; you can understand the symbol-reader."

"That en't the same, is it?" she said. She was more nervous of the bear now than when she had seen his anger.

"It is the same," he said. "Adults can't read it, as I understand. As I am to human fighters, so you are to adults with the symbol-reader."

"Yes, I suppose," she said, puzzled and unwilling. "Does that mean I'll forget how to do it when I grow up?"

"Who knows? I have never seen a symbol-reader, nor anyone who could read them. Perhaps you are different from others."

He dropped to all fours again and went on gnawing his meat. Lyra had unfastened her furs, but now the cold was striking in again and she had to do them up. All in all, it was a disquieting episode. She wanted to consult the alethiometer there and then, but it was too cold, and besides, they were calling for her because it was time to move on. She took the tin boxes that Iorek Byrnison had made, put the empty one back into Farder Coram's kit-bag, and put the one with the spy-fly in it together with the alethiometer in the pouch at her waist. She was glad when they were moving again.

The leaders had agreed with Lee Scoresby that when they reached the next stopping-place, they would inflate his balloon and he would spy from the air. Naturally Lyra was eager to fly with him, and naturally it was forbidden; but she rode with him on the way there and pestered him with questions.

"Mr Scoresby, how would you fly to Svalbard?"

"You'd need a dirigible with a gas engine, something like a zeppelin, or else a good south wind. But hell, I wouldn't dare. Have you ever seen it? The bleakest barest most inhospitable godforsaken dead-end of nowhere."

"I was just wondering, if Iorek Byrnison wanted to go back…"

"He'd be killed. Iorek's in exile. As soon as he set foot there they'd tear him to pieces."

"How do you inflate your balloon, Mr Scoresby?"

"Two ways. I can make hydrogen by pouring sulphuric acid on to iron filings. You catch the gas it gives off and gradually fill the balloon like that. The other way is to find a ground-gas vent near a fire-mine. There's a lot of gas under the ground here, and rock-oil besides. I can make gas from rock-oil, if I need to, and from coal as well; it's not hard to make gas. But the quickest way is to use ground-gas. A good vent will fill the balloon in an hour."

"How many people can you carry?"

"Six, if I need to."

"Could you carry Iorek Byrnison in his armour?"

"I have done. I rescued him one time from the Tartars, when he was cut off and they were starving him out – that was in the Tunguska campaign; I flew in and took him off. Sounds easy, but hell, I had to calculate the weight of that old boy by guesswork. And then I had to bank on finding ground-gas under the ice-fort he'd made. But I could see what kind of ground it was from the air, and I reckoned we'd be safe in digging. See, to go down I have to let gas out of the balloon, and I can't get airborne again without more. Anyway, we made it, armour and all."

"Mr Scoresby, you know the Tartars make holes in people's heads?"

"Oh, sure. They've been doing that for thousands of years. In the Tunguska campaign we captured five Tartars alive, and three of them had holes in their skulls. One of them had two."

"They do it to *each other*?"

"That's right. First they cut part-way around a circle of skin on the scalp, so they can lift up a flap and expose the bone. Then they cut a little circle of bone out of the skull, very carefully so they don't penetrate the brain, and then they sew the scalp back over."

"I thought they did it to their enemies!"

"Hell, no. It's a great privilege. They do it so the gods can talk to them."

"Did you ever hear of an explorer called Stanislaus Grumman?"

"Grumman? Sure. I met one of his team when I flew over the Yenisei River two years back. He was going to live among the Tartar tribes up that way. Matter of fact, I think *he* had that hole in the skull done. It was part of an initiation ceremony, but the man who told me didn't know much about it."

"So… If he was like an honorary Tartar, they wouldn't have killed him?"

"Killed him? Is he dead then?"

"Yeah. I saw his head," Lyra said proudly. "My father found it. I saw it when he showed it to the Scholars at Jordan College in Oxford. They'd scalped it, and all."

"Who'd scalped it?"

"Well, the Tartars, that's what the Scholars thought… But maybe it wasn't."

"It might not have been Grumman's head," said Lee Scoresby. "Your father might have been misleading the Scholars."

"I suppose he might," said Lyra thoughtfully. "He was asking them for money."

"And when they saw the head, they gave him the money?"

"Yeah."

"Good trick to play. People are shocked when they see a thing like that; they don't like to look too close."

"Especially Scholars," said Lyra.

"Well, you'd know better than I would. But if that was Grumman's head, I'll bet it wasn't the Tartars who scalped him. They scalp their enemies, not their own, and he was a Tartar by adoption."

Lyra turned that over in her mind as they drove on. There were wide currents full of meaning flowing fast around her: the Gobblers and their cruelty, their fear of Dust, the city in the Aurora, her father in Svalbard, her mother… And where was she? The alethiometer, the witches flying northwards. And poor little Tony Makarios; and the clockwork spy-fly; and Iorek Byrnison's uncanny fencing…

She fell asleep. And every hour they drew closer to Bolvangar.

14
Bolvangar Lights

The fact that the Gyptians had heard or seen nothing of Mrs Coulter worried Farder Coram and John Faa more than they let Lyra know; but they weren't to know that she was worried too. Lyra feared Mrs Coulter and thought about her often. And whereas Lord Asriel was now "father", Mrs Coulter was never "mother". The reason for that was Mrs Coulter's dæmon, the golden monkey, who had filled Pantalaimon with a powerful loathing and who, Lyra felt, had pried into her secrets, particularly that of the alethiometer.

And they were bound to be chasing her; it was silly to think otherwise. The spy-fly proved that, if nothing else.

But when an enemy did strike, it wasn't Mrs Coulter. The gyptians had planned to stop and rest their dogs, repair a couple of sledges, and get all their weapons into shape for the assault on Bolvangar. John Faa hoped that Lee Scoresby might find some ground-gas to fill his smaller balloon (for he had two, apparently) and go up to spy out the land. However, the aëronaut attended to the condition of the weather as closely as a sailor, and he said there was going to be a fog; and sure enough, as soon as they stopped, a thick mist descended. Lee Scoresby knew he'd see nothing from the sky, so he had to content himself with checking his equipment, though it was all in meticulous order. Then, with no warning at all, a volley of arrows flew out of the dark.

Three gyptian men went down at once, and died so silently that no one heard a thing. Only when they slumped clumsily across the dog-traces or lay unexpectedly still did the nearest men notice what was happening, and then it was already too late, because more arrows were flying at them. Some men looked up, puzzled by the fast irregular knocking sounds that came from up and down the line as arrows hurtled into wood or frozen canvas.

The first to come to his wits was John Faa, who shouted orders from the centre of the line. Cold hands and stiff limbs moved to obey as yet more arrows flew down like rain, straight rods of rain tipped with death.

Lyra was in the open, and the arrows were passing over her head. Pantalaimon heard before she did, and became a leopard and knocked her over, making her less of a target. Brushing snow out of her eyes, she rolled over to try and see what was happening, for the semi-darkness seemed to be overflowing with confusion and noise. She heard a mighty roar, and the clang and scrape of Iorek Byrnison's armour as he leapt fully clad over the sledges and into the fog, and that was followed by screams, snarling, crunching and tearing sounds, great smashing blows, cries of terror and roars of bearish fury as he laid them waste.

But who was *them*? Lyra had seen no enemy figures yet. The gyptians were swarming to defend the sledges, but that (as even Lyra could see) made them better targets; and their rifles were not easy to fire in gloves and mittens; she had only heard four or five shots, as against the ceaseless knocking rain of arrows. And more and more men fell every minute.

Oh, John Faa! she thought in anguish. You didn't foresee this, and I didn't help you!

But she had no more than a second to think that, for there was

231

a mighty snarl from Pantalaimon, and something – another dæmon – hurtled at him and knocked him down, crushing all the breath out of Lyra herself; and then hands were hauling at her, lifting her, stifling her cry with foul-smelling mittens, tossing her through the air into another's arms, and then pushing her flat down into the snow again, so that she was dizzy and breathless and hurt all at once. Her arms were hauled behind till her shoulders cracked, and someone lashed her wrists together, and then a hood was crammed over her head to muffle her screams, for scream she did, and lustily:

"Iorek! Iorek Byrnison! Help me!"

But could he hear? She couldn't tell; she was hurled this way and that, crushed on to a hard surface which then began to lurch and bump like a sledge. The sounds that reached her were wild and confused. She might have heard Iorek Byrnison's roar, but it was a long way off, and then she was jolting over rough ground, arms twisted, mouth stifled, sobbing with rage and fear. And strange voices spoke around her.

"Pan!" she gasped.

"I'm here, ssh, I'll help you breathe. Keep still…"

His mouse-paws tugged at the hood until her mouth was freer, and she gulped at the frozen air.

"Who are they?" she whispered.

"They look like Tartars. I think they hit John Faa."

"No –"

"I saw him fall. But he should have been ready for this sort of attack. We know that."

"But we should have helped him! We should have been watching the alethiometer!"

"Hush. Pretend to be unconscious."

There was a whip cracking, and the howl of racing dogs. From the way she was being jerked and bounced about, Lyra could tell how fast they were going, and though she strained to hear the sounds of battle, all she made out was a forlorn volley of shots, muffled by the distance, and then the creak and rush and soft paw-thuds in the snow were all there was to hear.

"They'll take us to the Gobblers," she whispered.

The word *severed* came to their mind. Horrible fear filled Lyra's body, and Pantalaimon nestled close against her.

"I'll fight," he said.

"So will I. I'll *kill* them."

"So will Iorek when he finds out. He'll crush them to death."

"How far are we from Bolvangar?"

He didn't know, but they thought it was less than a day's ride. After they had been driving along for such a time that her body was in torment from cramp, the pace slackened a little, and someone roughly pulled off the hood.

She looked up at a broad Asiatic face, under a wolverine hood, lit by flickering lamplight. His black eyes showed a glint of satisfaction, especially when Pantalaimon slid out of Lyra's anorak to bare his white ermine-teeth in a hiss. The man's dæmon, a big heavy wolverine, snarled back, but Pantalaimon didn't flinch.

The man hauled Lyra up to a sitting position and propped her against the side of the sledge. She kept falling sideways because her hands were still tied behind her, and so he tied her feet together instead and released her hands.

Through the snow that was falling and the thick fog, she saw how powerful this man was, and the sledge-driver too, how balanced in the sledge, how much at home in this land in a way the gyptians weren't.

The man spoke, but of course she understood nothing. He tried a different language with the same result. Then he tried English.

"You name?"

233

Pantalaimon bristled warningly, and she knew what he meant at once. So these men didn't know who she was! They hadn't kidnapped her because of her connection with Mrs Coulter; so perhaps they weren't in the pay of the Gobblers after all.

"Lizzie Brooks," she said.

"Lissie Broogs," he said after her. "We take you nice place. Nice peoples."

"Who are you?"

"Samoyed peoples. Hunters."

"Where are you taking me?"

"Nice place. Nice peoples. You have *panserbjørn*?"

"For protection."

"No good! Ha, ha, bear no good! We got you anyway!"

He laughed loudly. Lyra controlled herself and said nothing.

"Who those peoples?" the man asked next, pointing back the way they had come.

"Traders."

"Traders... What they trade?"

"Fur, spirits," she said. "Smoke-leaf."

"They sell smoke-leaf, buy furs?"

"Yes."

He said something to his companion, who spoke back briefly. All the time the sledge was speeding onwards, and Lyra pulled herself up more comfortably to try and see where they were heading; but the snow was falling thickly, and the sky was dark, and presently she became too cold to peer out any longer, and lay down. She and Pantalaimon could feel each other's thoughts, and tried to keep calm, but the thought of John Faa dead... And what had happened to Farder Coram? And would Iorek manage to kill the other Samoyeds? And would they ever manage to track her down?

For the first time, she began to feel a little sorry for herself.

After a long time, the man shook her by the shoulder and handed her a strip of dried reindeer-meat to chew. It was rank and tough, but she was hungry, and there was nourishment in it. After chewing it she felt a little better. She slipped her hand slowly into her furs till she was sure the alethiometer was still there, and then carefully withdrew the spy-fly tin and slipped it down into her fur boot. Pantalaimon crept in as a mouse and pushed it as far down as he could, tucking it under the bottom of her reindeer-skin legging.

When that was done she closed her eyes. Fear had made her exhausted, and soon she slipped uneasily into sleep.

She woke up when the motion of the sledge changed. It was suddenly smoother, and when she opened her eyes there were passing lights dazzling above her, so bright she had to pull the hood further over her head before peering out again. She was horribly stiff and cold, but she managed to pull herself upright enough to see that the sledge was driving swiftly between a row of high poles, each carrying a glaring anbaric light. As she got her bearings, they passed through an open metal gate at the end of the avenue of lights and into a wide open space like an empty market-place or an arena for some game or sport. It was perfectly flat and smooth and white, and about a hundred yards across. Around the edge ran a high metal fence.

At the far end of this arena the sledge halted. They were outside a low building, or a range of low buildings over which the snow lay deeply. It was hard to tell, but she had the impression that tunnels connected one part of the buildings with another, tunnels humped under the snow. At one side a stout metal mast had a familiar look, though she couldn't say what it reminded her of.

Before she could take much more in, the man in the sledge cut through the cord around her ankles, and hauled her out roughly while the driver shouted at the dogs to make them still. A door opened in the building a few yards away, and an anbaric light came on overhead, swivelling to find them, like a searchlight.

Lyra's captor thrust her forward like a trophy, without letting go, and said something. The figure in the padded coal-silk anorak answered in the same language, and Lyra saw his features: he was not a Samoyed or a Tartar. He could have been a Jordan Scholar. He looked at her, and particularly at Pantalaimon.

The Samoyed spoke again, and the man from Bolvangar said to Lyra, "You speak English?"

"Yes," she said.

"Does your dæmon always take that form?"

Of all the unexpected questions! Lyra could only gape. But Pantalaimon answered it in his own fashion by becoming a falcon, and launching himself from her shoulder at the man's dæmon, a large marmot, which struck up at Pantalaimon with a swift movement and spat as he circled past on swift wings.

"I see," said the man in a tone of satisfaction, as Pantalaimon returned to Lyra's shoulder.

The Samoyed men were looking expectant, and the man from Bolvangar nodded and took off a mitten to reach into a pocket. He took out a draw-string purse and counted out a dozen heavy coins into the hunter's hand.

The two men checked the money, and then stowed it carefully, each man taking half. Without a backward glance they got in the sledge, and the driver cracked the whip and shouted to the dogs; and they sped away across the wide white arena and into the avenue of lights, gathering speed until they vanished into the dark beyond.

The man was opening the door again.

"Come in quickly," he said. "It's warm and comfortable. Don't stand out in the cold. What is your name?"

His voice was an English one, without any accent Lyra could name. He sounded like the sort of people she had met at Mrs Coulter's: smart and educated and important.

"Lizzie Brooks," she said.

"Come in, Lizzie. We'll look after you here, don't worry."

He was colder than she was, even though she'd been outside for far longer; he was impatient to be in the warm again. She decided to play slow and dim-witted and reluctant, and dragged her feet as she stepped over the high threshold into the building.

There were two doors, with a wide space between them so that not too much warm air escaped. Once they were through the inner doorway Lyra found herself sweltering in what seemed unbearable heat, and had to pull open her furs and push back her hood.

They were in a space about eight feet square, with corridors to the right and left and in front of her the sort of reception desk you might see in a hospital. Everything was brilliantly lit, with the glint of shiny white surfaces and stainless steel. There was the smell of food in the air, familiar food, bacon and coffee, and under it a faint perpetual hospital-medical smell; and coming from the walls all around was a slight humming sound, almost too low to hear, the sort of sound you had to get used to or go mad.

Pantalaimon at her ear, a goldfinch now, whispered, "Be stupid and dim. Be really slow and stupid."

Adults were looking down at her: the man who'd brought her in, another man wearing a white coat, a woman in a nurse's uniform.

"English," the first man was saying. "Traders, apparently."

"Usual hunters? Usual story?"

"Same tribe, as far as I could tell. Sister Clara, could you take little, umm, and see to her?"

237

"Certainly, Doctor. Come with me, dear," said the nurse, and Lyra obediently followed.

They went along a short corridor with doors on the right and a canteen on the left, from which came a clatter of knives and forks, and voices, and more cooking-smells. The nurse was about as old as Mrs Coulter, Lyra guessed, with a brisk, blank, sensible air; she would be able to stitch a wound or change a bandage, but never to tell a story. Her dæmon (and Lyra had a moment of strange chill when she noticed) was a little white trotting dog (and after a moment she had no idea why it had chilled her).

"What's your name, dear?" said the nurse, opening a heavy door.

"Lizzie."

"Just Lizzie?"

"Lizzie Brooks."

"And how old are you?"

"Eleven."

Lyra had been told that she was small for her age, whatever that meant. It had never affected her sense of her own importance, but she realized that she could use the fact now to make Lizzie shy and nervous and insignificant, and shrank a little as she went into the room.

She was half expecting questions about where she had come from and how she had arrived, and she was preparing answers; but it wasn't only imagination the nurse lacked, it was curiosity as well. Bolvangar might have been on the outskirts of London, and children might have been arriving all the time, for all the interest Sister Clara seemed to show. Her pert neat little dæmon trotted along at her heels just as brisk and blank as she was.

In the room they entered there was a couch and a table and two chairs and a filing cabinet, and a glass cupboard with medicines and bandages, and a wash-basin. As soon as they were inside, the nurse took Lyra's outer coat off and dropped it on the shiny floor.

"Off with the rest, dear," she said. "We'll have a quick little look to see you're nice and healthy, no frostbite or sniffles, and then we'll find some nice clean clothes. We'll pop you in the shower, too," she added, for Lyra had not changed or washed for days, and in the enveloping warmth, that was becoming more and more evident.

Pantalaimon fluttered in protest, but Lyra quelled him with a scowl. He settled on the couch as one by one all Lyra's clothes came off, to her resentment and shame; but she still had the presence of mind to conceal it and act dull-witted and compliant.

"And the money-belt, Lizzie," said the nurse, and untied it herself with strong fingers. She went to drop it on the pile with Lyra's other clothes, but stopped, feeling the edge of the alethiometer.

"What's this?" she said, and unbuttoned the oilcloth.

"Just a sort of toy," said Lyra. "It's mine."

"Yes, we won't take it away from you, dear," said Sister Clara, unfolding the black velvet. "That's pretty, isn't it, like a compass. Into the shower with you," she went on, putting the alethiometer down and whisking back a coal-silk curtain in the corner.

Lyra reluctantly slipped under the warm water and soaped herself while Pantalaimon perched on the curtain-rail. They were both conscious that he mustn't be too lively, for the dæmons of dull people were dull themselves. When she was washed and dry the nurse took her temperature and looked into her eyes and ears and throat, and then measured her height and put her on some scales before writing a note on a clipboard. Then she gave Lyra some pyjamas and a dressing-gown. They were clean, and of good quality, like Tony Makarios's anorak, but again there was a second-hand air about them. Lyra felt very uneasy.

"These en't mine," she said.

"No, dear. Your clothes need a good wash."

"Am I going to get my own ones back?"

"I expect so. Yes, of course."

"What is this place?"

"It's called the Experimental Station."

That wasn't an answer, and whereas Lyra would have pointed that out and asked for more information, she didn't think Lizzie Brooks would; so she assented dumbly in the dressing and said no more.

"I want my toy back," she said stubbornly when she was dressed.

"Take it, dear," said the nurse. "Wouldn't you rather have a nice woolly bear, though? Or a pretty doll?"

She opened a drawer where some soft toys lay like dead things. Lyra made herself stand and pretend to consider for several seconds before picking out a rag doll with big vacant eyes. She had never had a doll, but she knew what to do, and pressed it absently to her chest.

"What about my money-belt?" she said. "I like to keep my toy in there."

"Go on, then, dear," said Sister Clara, who was filling in a form on pink paper.

Lyra hitched up her unfamiliar pyjamas and tied the oilskin pouch around her waist.

"What about my coat and boots?" she said. "And my mittens and things?"

"We'll have them cleaned for you," said the nurse automatically.

Then a telephone buzzed, and while the nurse answered it, Lyra stooped quickly to recover the other tin, the one containing the spy-fly, and put it in the pouch with the alethiometer.

"Come along, Lizzie," said the nurse, putting the receiver down. "We'll go and find you something to eat. I expect you're hungry."

She followed Sister Clara to the canteen, where a dozen round white tables were covered in crumbs and the sticky rings where drinks had been carelessly put down. Dirty plates and cutlery were stacked on a steel trolley. There were no windows, so to give an illusion of light and space one wall was covered in a huge photogram showing a tropical beach, with bright blue sky and white sand and coconut palms.

The man who had brought her in was collecting a tray from a serving hatch.

"Eat up," he said.

There was no need to starve, so she ate the stew and mashed potatoes with relish. There was a bowl of tinned peaches and ice cream to follow. As she ate, the man and the nurse talked quietly at another table, and when she had finished, the nurse brought her a glass of warm milk and took the tray away.

The man came to sit down opposite. His dæmon, the marmot, was not blank and incurious as the nurse's dog had been, but sat politely on his shoulder watching and listening.

"Now, Lizzie," he said. "Have you eaten enough?"

"Yes, thank you."

"I'd like you to tell me where you come from. Can you do that?"

"London," she said.

"And what are you doing so far north?"

"With my father," she mumbled. She kept her eyes down, avoiding the gaze of the marmot, and trying to look as if she was on the verge of tears.

"With your father? I see. And what's he doing in this part of the world?"

"Trading. We come with a load of New Danish smoke-leaf and we was buying furs."

"And was your father by himself?"

"No. There was my uncles and all, and some other men," she said vaguely, not knowing what the Samoyed hunter had told him.

"Why did he bring you on a journey like this, Lizzie?"

"'Cause two years ago he brung my brother and he says he'll bring me next, only he never. So I kept asking him, and then he did."

"And how old are you?"

"Eleven."

"Good, good. Well, Lizzie, you're a lucky little girl. Those huntsmen who found you brought you to the best place you could be."

"They never found me," she said doubtfully. "There was a fight. There was lots of 'em and they had arrows..."

"Oh, I don't think so. I think you must have wandered away from your father's party and got lost. Those huntsmen found you on your own and brought you straight here. That's what happened, Lizzie."

"I saw a fight," she said. "They was shooting arrows and that... I want my dad," she said more loudly, and felt herself beginning to cry.

"Well, you're quite safe here until he comes," said the doctor.

"But I saw them shooting arrows!"

"Ah, you thought you did. That often happens in the intense cold, Lizzie. You fall asleep and have bad dreams and you can't remember what's true and what isn't. That wasn't a fight, don't worry. Your father is safe and sound and he'll be looking for you now and soon he'll come here because this is the only place for hundreds of miles, you know, and what a surprise he'll have to find you safe and sound! Now Sister Clara will take you along to the dormitory where you'll meet some other little girls and boys who got lost in the wilderness just like you. Off you go. We'll have another little talk in the morning."

Lyra stood up, clutching her doll, and Pantalaimon hopped on to her shoulder as the nurse opened the door to lead them out.

More corridors, and Lyra was tired by now, so sleepy she kept yawning and could hardly lift her feet in the woolly slippers they'd given her. Pantalaimon was drooping, and he had to change to a mouse and settle inside her dressing-gown pocket. Lyra had the impression of a row of beds, children's faces, a pillow, and then she was asleep.

Someone was shaking her. The first thing she did was to feel at her waist, and both tins were still there, still safe; so she tried to open her eyes, but oh, it was hard; she had never felt so sleepy.

"Wake up! Wake up!"

It was a whisper in more than one voice. With a huge effort, as if she were pushing a boulder up a slope, Lyra forced herself to wake up.

In the dim light from a very low-powered anbaric bulb over the doorway she saw three other girls clustered around her. It wasn't easy to see, because her eyes were slow to focus, but they seemed about her own age, and they were speaking English.

"She's awake."

"They gave her sleeping pills. Must've…"

"What's your name?"

"Lizzie," Lyra mumbled.

"Is there a load more new kids coming?" demanded one of the girls.

"Dunno. Just me."

"Where'd they get you then?"

Lyra struggled to sit up. She didn't remember taking a sleeping pill, but there might well have been something in the drink she'd had. Her head felt full of eiderdown, and there was a faint pain throbbing behind her eyes.

"Where is this place?"

"Middle of nowhere. They don't tell us."

"They usually bring more'n one kid at a time..."

"What do they do?" Lyra managed to ask, gathering her doped wits as Pantalaimon stirred into wakefulness with her.

"We dunno," said the girl who was doing most of the talking. She was a tall, red-haired girl with quick twitchy movements and a strong London accent. "They sort of measure us and do these tests and that –"

"They measure Dust," said another girl, friendly and plump and dark-haired.

"*You* don't know," said the first girl.

"They do," said the third, a subdued-looking child cuddling her rabbit-dæmon. "I heard 'em talking."

"Then they take us away one by one and that's all we know. No one comes back," said the redhead.

"There's this boy, right," said the plump girl, "he reckons –"

"Don't tell her that!" said the redhead. "Not yet."

"Is there boys here as well?" said Lyra.

"Yeah. There's lots of us. There's about thirty, I reckon."

"More'n that," said the plump girl. "More like forty."

"Except they keep taking us away," said the redhead. "They usually start off with bringing a whole bunch here, and then there's a lot of us, and one by one they all disappear."

"They're Gobblers," said the plump girl. "You know Gobblers. We was all scared of 'em till we was caught..."

Lyra was gradually coming more and more awake. The other girls' dæmons, apart from the rabbit, were close by listening at

244

the door, and no one spoke above a whisper. Lyra asked their names. The red-haired girl was Annie, the dark plump one Bella, the thin one Martha. They didn't know the names of the boys, because the two sexes were kept apart for most of the time. They weren't treated badly.

"It's all right here," said Bella, "there's not much to do, except they give us tests and make us do exercises and then they measure us and take our temperature and stuff. It's just boring really."

"Except when Mrs Coulter comes," said Annie.

Lyra had to stop herself crying out, and Pantalaimon fluttered his wings so sharply that the other girls noticed.

"He's nervous," said Lyra, soothing him. "They must've gave us some sleeping pills, like you said, 'cause we're all dozy. Who's Mrs Coulter?"

"She's the one who trapped us, most of us, anyway," said Martha. "They all talk about her, the other kids. When she comes, you know there's going to be kids disappearing."

"She likes watching the kids, when they take us away, she likes seeing what they do to us. This boy Simon, he reckons they kill us, and Mrs Coulter watches."

"They *kill* us?" said Lyra, shuddering.

"Must do. 'Cause no one comes back."

"They're always going on about dæmons too," said Bella. "Weighing them and measuring them and all…"

"They *touch* your *dæmons*?"

"No! God! They put scales there and your dæmon has to get on them and change, and they make notes and take pictures. And they put you in this cabinet and measure Dust, all the time, they never stop measuring Dust."

"What dust?" said Lyra.

"We dunno," said Annie. "Just something from space. Not

real dust. If you en't got any Dust, that's good. But everyone gets Dust in the end."

"You know what I heard Simon say?" said Bella. "He said that the Tartars make holes in their skulls to let the Dust in."

"Yeah, *he'd* know," said Annie scornfully. "I think I'll ask Mrs Coulter when she comes."

"You wouldn't dare!" said Martha admiringly.

"I would."

"When's she coming?" said Lyra.

"The day after tomorrow," said Annie.

A cold drench of terror went down Lyra's spine, and Pantalaimon crept very close. She had one day in which to find Roger and discover whatever she could about this place, and either escape or be rescued; and if all the gyptians had been killed, who would help the children stay alive in the icy wilderness?

The other girls went on talking, but Lyra and Pantalaimon nestled down deep in the bed and tried to get warm, knowing that for hundreds of miles all around her little bed there was nothing but fear.

15

The Dæmon-Cages

It wasn't Lyra's way to brood; she was a sanguine and practical child, and besides, she wasn't imaginative. No one with much imagination would have thought seriously that it was possible to come all this way and rescue her friend Roger; or, having thought it, an imaginative child would immediately have come up with several ways in which it was impossible. Being a practised liar doesn't mean you have a powerful imagination. Many good liars have no imagination at all; it's that which gives their lies such wide-eyed conviction.

So now she was in the hands of the Oblation Board, Lyra didn't fret herself into terror about what had happened to the gyptians. They were all good fighters, and even though Pantalaimon said he'd seen John Faa shot, he might have been mistaken; or if he wasn't mistaken, John Faa might not have been seriously hurt. It had been bad luck that she'd fallen into the hands of the Samoyeds, but the gyptians would be along soon to rescue her, and if they couldn't manage it, nothing would stop Iorek Byrnison from getting her out; and then they'd fly to Svalbard in Lee Scoresby's balloon and rescue Lord Asriel.

In her mind, it was as easy as that.

So next morning, when she awoke in the dormitory, she was

curious and ready to deal with whatever the day would bring. And eager to see Roger – in particular, eager to see him before he saw her.

She didn't have long to wait. The children in their different dormitories were woken at half-past seven by the nurses who looked after them. They washed and dressed and went with the others to the canteen for breakfast.

And there was Roger.

He was sitting with five other boys at a table just inside the door. The queue for the hatch went right past them, and she was able to pretend to drop a handkerchief and crouch to pick it up, bending low next to his chair, so that Pantalaimon could speak to Roger's dæmon Salcilia.

She was a chaffinch, and she fluttered so wildly that Pantalaimon had to be a cat and leap at her, pinning her down to whisper. Such brisk fights or scuffles between children's dæmons were common, luckily, and no one took much notice, but Roger went pale at once. Lyra had never seen anyone so white. He looked up at the blank haughty stare she gave him, and the colour flooded back into his cheeks as he brimmed over with hope, excitement, and joy; and only Pantalaimon, shaking Salcilia firmly, was able to keep Roger from shouting out and leaping up to greet his Jordan playmate.

Lyra looked away, acting as disdainfully as she could, and rolled her eyes at her new friends, leaving Pantalaimon to explain. The four girls collected their trays of cornflakes and toast and sat together, an instant gang, excluding everyone else in order to gossip about them.

You can't keep a large group of children in one place for long without giving them plenty to do, and in some ways Bolvangar was run like a school, with timetabled activities such as gymnastics and "art". Boys and girls were kept separate except for breaks and mealtimes, so it wasn't until mid-morning, after an hour and a half of sewing directed by one of the nurses, that Lyra had the chance to talk to Roger. But it had to look natural; that was the difficulty. All the children there were more or less at the same age, and it was the age when boys talk to boys and girls to girls, each making a conspicuous point of ignoring the opposite sex.

She found her chance in the canteen again, when the children came in for a drink and a biscuit. Lyra sent Pantalaimon, as a fly, to talk to Salcilia on the wall next to their table while she and Roger kept quietly in their separate groups. It was difficult to talk while your dæmon's attention was somewhere else, so Lyra pretended to look glum and rebellious as she sipped her milk with the other girls. Half her thoughts were with the tiny buzz of talk between the dæmons, and she wasn't really listening, but at one point she heard another girl with bright blonde hair say a name that made her sit up.

It was the name of Tony Makarios. As Lyra's attention snapped towards that, Pantalaimon had to slow down his whispered conversation with Roger's dæmon, and both children listened to what the girl was saying.

"No, I know why they took him," she said, as heads clustered close nearby. "It was because his dæmon didn't change. They thought he was older than he looked, or summing, and he weren't really a young kid. But really his dæmon never changed very often because Tony hisself never thought much about anything. I seen her change. She was called Ratter…"

"Why are they so interested in dæmons?" said Lyra.

"No one knows," said the blonde girl.

"I know," said one boy who'd been listening. "What they do is kill your dæmon and then see if you die."

"Well how come they do it over and over with different kids?" said someone. "They'd only need to do it once, wouldn't they?"

"I know what they do," said the first girl.

She had everyone's attention now. But because they didn't want to let the staff know what they were talking about, they had to adopt a strange, half-careless, indifferent manner, while listening with passionate curiosity.

"How?" said someone.

"'Cause I was with him when they came for him. We was in the linen room," she said.

She was blushing hotly. If she was expecting jeers and teasing, they didn't come. All the children were subdued, and no one even smiled.

The girl went on, "We was keeping quiet and then the nurse came in, the one with the soft voice. And she says, Come on, Tony, I know you're there, come on, we won't hurt you… And he says, What's going to happen? And she says, We just put you to sleep, and then we do a little operation, and then you wake up safe and sound. But Tony didn't believe her. He says –"

"The holes!" said someone. "They make a hole in your head like the Tartars! I *bet*!"

"Shut up! What else did the nurse say?" someone else put in.

By this time, a dozen or more children were clustered around her table, their dæmons as urgent to know as they were, all wide-eyed and tense.

The blonde girl went on, "Tony wanted to know what they was gonna do with Ratter, see. And the nurse says, Well, she's going to sleep too, just like when you do. And Tony says, You're gonna kill her, en't yer? I know you are. We all know that's what happens. And the nurse says, No, of course not. It's just a little operation. Just a little cut. It won't even hurt, but we put you to sleep to make sure."

All the room had gone quiet now. The nurse who'd been supervising had left for a moment, and the hatch to the kitchen was shut so no one could hear from there.

"What sort of cut?" said a boy, his voice quiet and frightened. "Did she say what sort of cut?"

"She just said, It's something to make you more grown up. She said everyone had to have it, that's why grown-ups' dæmons don't change like ours do. So they have a cut to make them one shape for ever, and that's how you get grown up."

"But –"

"Does that mean –"

"What, all grown-ups've had this cut?"

"What about –"

Suddenly all the voices stopped as if they themselves had been cut, and all eyes turned to the door. Sister Clara stood there, bland and mild and matter-of-fact, and beside her was a man in a white coat whom Lyra hadn't seen before.

"Bridget McGinn," he said.

The blonde girl stood up trembling. Her squirrel-dæmon clutched her breast.

"Yes, sir?" she said, her voice hardly audible.

"Finish your drink and come with Sister Clara," he said. "The rest of you run along and go to your classes."

Obediently the children stacked their mugs on the stainless-steel trolley before leaving in silence. No one looked at Bridget McGinn except Lyra, and she saw the blonde girl's face vivid with fear.

The rest of that morning was spent in exercise. There was a small gymnasium at the Station, because it was hard to exercise outside during the long Polar night, and each group of children took turns to play in there, under the supervision of a nurse. They had to form teams and throw balls around, and at first Lyra, who had never in her life played at anything like this, was at a loss what to do. But she was quick and athletic, and a natural leader, and soon found herself enjoying it. The shouts of the children, the shrieks and hoots of the dæmons, filled the little gymnasium and soon banished fearful thoughts; which of course was exactly what the exercise was intended to do.

At lunchtime, when the children were queueing once again in the canteen, Lyra felt Pantalaimon give a chirrup of recognition, and turned to find Billy Costa standing just behind her.

"Roger told me you was here," he muttered.

"Your brother's coming, and John Faa and a whole band of gyptians," she said. "They're going to take you home."

He nearly cried aloud with joy, but subdued the cry into a cough.

"And you got to call me Lizzie," Lyra said, "*never* Lyra. And you got to tell me everything you know, right."

They sat together, with Roger close by. It was easier to do this at lunchtime, when children spent more time coming and going between the tables and the hatch and the canteen was crowded. Under the clatter of knives and forks and plates Billy and Roger both told her as much as they knew. Billy had heard from a nurse that children who had had the operation were often taken to hostels further south, which might explain how Tony Makarios came to be wandering in the wild. But Roger had something even more interesting to tell her.

"I found a hiding-place," he said.

"What? Where?"

"See that picture…" He meant the big photogram of the tropical beach. "If you look in the top right corner, you see that ceiling panel?"

The ceiling consisted of large rectangular panels set in a framework of metal strips, and the corner of the panel above the picture had lifted slightly.

"I saw that," Roger said, "and I thought the others might be like it, so I lifted 'em, and they're all loose. They just lift up. Me and this boy tried it one night in our dormitory, before they took him away. There's a space up there and you can crawl inside…"

"How far can you crawl in the ceiling?"

"I dunno. We just went in a little way. We reckoned when it was time we could hide up there, but they'd probably find us."

Lyra saw it not as a hiding-place but as a highway. It was the best thing she'd heard since she'd arrived. But before they could talk any more, a doctor banged on a table with a spoon and began to speak.

"Listen, children," he said. "Listen carefully. Every so often we have to have a fire drill. It's very important that we all get dressed properly and make our way outside without any panic. So we're going to have a practice fire drill this afternoon. When the bell rings you must stop whatever you're doing and do what the nearest grown-up says. Remember where they take you. That's the place you must go to if there's a real fire."

Well, thought Lyra, there's an idea.

During the first part of the afternoon, Lyra and four other girls were tested for Dust. The doctors didn't say that was what they were doing, but it was easy to guess. They were taken one by one to a laboratory, and of course this made them all very frightened; how cruel it would be, Lyra thought, if she perished without striking a blow at them! But they were not going to do that operation just yet, it seemed.

"We want to make some measurements," the doctor explained. It was hard to tell the difference between these people: all the men looked similar in their white coats and with their clipboards and pencils, and the women resembled one another too, the uniforms and their strange bland calm manner making them all look like sisters.

"I was measured yesterday," Lyra said.

"Ah, we're making different measurements today. Stand on the metal plate – oh, slip your shoes off first. Hold your dæmon, if you like. Look forward, that's it, stare at the little green light. Good girl…"

Something flashed. The doctor made her face the other way and then to left and right, and each time something clicked and flashed.

"That's fine. Now come over to this machine and put your hand into the tube. Nothing to harm you, I promise. Straighten your fingers. That's it."

"What *are* you measuring?" she said. "Is it Dust?"

"Who told you about Dust?"

"One of the other girls, I don't know her name. She said we was all over Dust. I en't dusty, at least I don't think I am. I had a shower yesterday."

"Ah, it's a different sort of dust. You can't see it with your ordinary eyesight. It's a special dust. Now clench your fist – that's right. Good. Now if you feel around in there you'll find a sort of handle thing – got that? Take hold of that, there's a good girl. Now can you put your other hand over this way – rest it on this brass globe. Good. Fine. Now you'll feel a slight tingling, nothing to worry about, it's just a slight anbaric current…"

Pantalaimon, in his most tense and wary wildcat-form, prowled with lightning-eyed suspicion around the apparatus, continually returning to rub himself against Lyra.

She was sure by now that they weren't going to perform the operation on her yet, and sure too that her disguise as Lizzie Brooks was secure; so she risked a question.

"Why do you cut people's dæmons away?"

"What? Who's been talking to you about that?"

254

"This girl, I dunno her name. She said you cut people's dæmons away."

"Nonsense…"

He was agitated, though. She went on:

"'Cause you take people out one by one and they never come back. And some people reckon you just kill 'em, and other people say different, and this girl told me you cut –"

"It's not true at all. When we take children out, it's because it's time for them to move on to another place. They're growing up. I'm afraid your friend is alarming herself. Nothing of the sort! Don't even think about it. Who is your friend?"

"I only come here yesterday, I don't know anyone's name."

"What does she look like?"

"I forget. I think she had sort of brown hair … light brown, maybe … I dunno."

The doctor went to speak quietly to the nurse. As the two of them conferred, Lyra watched their dæmons. This nurse's was a pretty bird, just as neat and incurious as Sister Clara's dog, and the doctor's was a large heavy moth. Neither moved. They were awake, for the bird's eyes were bright and the moth's feelers waved languidly, but they weren't animated, as she would have expected them to be. Perhaps they weren't really anxious or curious at all.

Presently the doctor came back and they went on with the examination, weighing her and Pantalaimon separately, looking at her from behind a special screen, measuring her heartbeat, placing her under a little nozzle that hissed and gave off a smell like fresh air.

In the middle of one of the tests, a loud bell began to ring and kept ringing.

"The fire alarm," said the doctor, sighing. "Very well. Lizzie, follow Sister Betty."

"But all their outdoor clothes are down in the dormitory building, Doctor. She can't go outside like this. Should we go there first, do you think?"

He was annoyed at having his experiments interrupted, and snapped his fingers in irritation.

"I suppose this is just the sort of thing the practice is meant to show up," he said. "What a nuisance."

"When I came yesterday," Lyra said helpfully, "Sister Clara put my other clothes in a cupboard in that first room where she looked at me. The one next door. I could wear them."

"Good idea!" said the nurse. "Quick, then."

With a secret glee, Lyra hurried there behind the nurse and retrieved her proper furs and leggings and boots, and pulled them on quickly while the nurse dressed herself in coal-silk.

Then they hurried out. In the wide arena in front of the main group of buildings, a hundred or so people, adults and children, were milling about: some in excitement, some in irritation, many just bewildered.

"See?" one adult was saying. "It's worth doing this to find out what chaos we'd be in with a real fire."

Someone was blowing a whistle and waving their arms, but no one was taking much notice. Lyra saw Roger and beckoned. Roger tugged Billy Costa's arm and soon all three of them were together in a maelstrom of running children.

"No one'll notice if we take a look around," said Lyra. "It'll take 'em ages to count everyone, and we can say we just followed someone else and got lost."

They waited till most of the grown-ups were looking the other way, and then Lyra scooped up some snow and rammed it into a loose powdery snowball, and hurled it at random into the crowd. In a moment all the children were doing it, and the air was full of flying snow. Screams of laughter covered completely the shouts of the adults trying to regain control, and then the three children were around the corner and out of sight.

The snow was so thick that they couldn't move quickly, but it didn't seem to matter; no one was following. Lyra and the others scrambled over the curved roof of one of the tunnels, and found themselves in a strange moonscape of regular hummocks and hollows, all swathed in white under the black sky and lit by reflections from the lights around the arena.

"What we looking for?" said Billy.

"Dunno. Just looking," said Lyra, and led the way to a squat, square building a little apart from the rest, with a low-powered anbaric light at the corner.

The hubbub from behind was as loud as ever, but more distant. Clearly the children were making the most of their freedom, and Lyra hoped they'd keep it up for as long as they could. She moved around the edge of the square building, looking for a window. The roof was only seven feet or so off the ground, and unlike the other buildings, it had no roofed tunnel to connect it with the rest of the Station.

There was no window, but there was a door. A notice above it said ENTRY STRICTLY FORBIDDEN in red letters.

Lyra set her hand on it to try, but before she could turn the handle, Roger said:

"Look! A bird! Or –"

His *or* was an exclamation of doubt, because the creature swooping down from the black sky was no bird at all: it was someone Lyra had seen before.

"The witch's dæmon!"

The goose beat his great wings, raising a flurry of snow as he landed.

"Greetings, Lyra," he said. "I followed you here, though you didn't see me. I have been waiting for you to come out into the open. What is happening?"

She told him quickly.

"Where are the gyptians?" she said. "Is John Faa safe? Did they fight off the Samoyeds?"

"Most of them are safe. John Faa is wounded, though not severely. The men who took you were hunters and raiders who often prey on parties of travellers, and alone they can travel more quickly than a large party. The gyptians are still a day's journey away."

The two boys were staring in fear at the goose-dæmon and at Lyra's familiar manner with him, because of course they'd never seen a dæmon without his human before, and they knew little about witches.

Lyra said to them, "Listen, you better go and keep watch, right. Billy, you go that way, and Roger, watch out the way we just come. We en't got long."

They ran off to do as she said, and then Lyra turned back to the door.

"Why are you trying to get in there?" said the goose-dæmon.

"Because of what they do here. They cut –" she lowered her voice – "they cut people's dæmons away. Children's. And I think maybe they do it in here. At least, there's *something* here, and I was going to look. But it's locked..."

"I can open it," said the goose, and beat his wings once or twice, throwing snow up against the door; and as he did, Lyra heard something turn in the lock.

"Go in carefully," said the dæmon.

Lyra pulled opened the door against the snow and slipped inside. The goose-dæmon came with her. Pantalaimon was agitated and fearful, but he didn't want the witch's dæmon to see his fear, so he had flown to Lyra's breast and taken sanctuary inside her furs.

As soon as her eyes had adjusted to the light, Lyra saw why.

In a series of glass cases on shelves around the walls were all the dæmons of the severed children: ghost-like forms of cats, or birds, or rats, or other creatures, each bewildered and frightened and as pale as smoke.

The witch's dæmon gave a cry of anger, and Lyra clutched Pantalaimon to her and said, "Don't look! Don't look!"

"Where are the children of these dæmons?" said the goose-dæmon, shaking with rage.

Lyra explained fearfully about her encounter with little Tony Makarios, and looked over her shoulder at the poor caged dæmons, who were clustering forwards pressing their pale faces to the glass. Lyra could hear faint cries of pain and misery. In the dim light from a low-powered anbaric bulb she could see a name on a card at the front of each case, and yes, there was an empty one with *Tony Makarios* on it. There were four or five other empty ones with names on, too.

"I want to let these poor things go!" she said fiercely. "I'm going to smash the glass and let 'em out –"

And she looked around for something to do it with, but the place was bare. The goose-dæmon said, "Wait."

He was a witch's dæmon, and much older than she was, and stronger. She had to do as he said.

"We must make these people think someone forgot to lock the place and shut the cages," he explained. "If they see broken glass and footprints in the snow, how long do you think your disguise will last? And it must hold out till the gyptians come. Now do exactly as I say: take a handful of snow, and when I tell you, blow a little of it against each cage in turn."

She ran outside. Roger and Billy were still on guard, and there was still a noise of shrieking and laughter from the arena, because only a minute or so had gone by.

She grabbed a big double handful of the light powdery snow, and then came back to do as the goose-dæmon said. As she blew a little snow on each cage, the goose made a clicking sound in his throat, and the catch at the front of the cage came open.

When she had unlocked them all, she lifted the front of the first one, and the pale form of a sparrow fluttered out, but fell to the ground before she could fly. The goose tenderly bent and nudged her upright with his beak, and the sparrow became a mouse, staggering and confused. Pantalaimon leapt down to comfort her.

Lyra worked quickly, and within a few minutes every dæmon was free. Some were trying to speak, and they clustered around her feet and even tried to pluck at her leggings, though the taboo held them back. She could tell why, poor things; they missed the heavy solid warmth of their humans' bodies; just as Pantalaimon would have done, they longed to press themselves against a heartbeat.

"Now, quick," said the goose. "Lyra, you must run back and mingle with the other children. Be brave, child. The gyptians are coming as fast as they can. I must help these poor dæmons to find their people…" He came closer and said quietly, "But they'll never be one again. They're sundered for ever. This is the most wicked thing I have ever seen… Leave the footprints you've made; I'll cover them up. Hurry now…"

"Oh, please! Before you go! Witches… They do fly, don't they? I wasn't dreaming when I saw them flying the other night?"

"Yes, child; why?"

"Could they pull a balloon?"

"Undoubtedly, but –"

"Will Serafina Pekkala be coming?"

"There isn't time to explain the politics of witch-nations.

There are vast powers involved here, and Serafina Pekkala must guard the interests of her clan. But it may be that what's happening here is part of all that's happening elsewhere. Lyra, you're needed inside. Run, run!"

She ran, and Roger, who was watching wide-eyed as the pale dæmons drifted out of the building, waded towards her through the thick snow.

"They're – it's like the crypt in Jordan – they're dæmons!"

"Yes, hush. Don't tell Billy, though. Don't tell anyone yet. Come on back."

Behind them, the goose was beating his wings powerfully, throwing snow over the tracks they'd made; and near him, the lost dæmons were clustering or drifting away, crying little bleak cries of loss and longing. When the footprints were covered, the goose turned to herd the pale dæmons together. He spoke, and one by one they changed, though you could see the effort it cost them, until they were all birds; and like fledglings they followed the witch's dæmon, fluttering and falling and running through the snow after him, and finally, with great difficulty, taking off. They rose in a ragged line, pale and spectral against the deep black sky, slowly gaining height, feeble and erratic though some of them were, and though others lost their will and fluttered downwards; but the great grey goose wheeled round and nudged them back, herding them gently on until they were lost against the profound dark.

Roger was tugging at Lyra's arm.

"Quick," he said, "they're nearly ready."

They stumbled away to join Billy, who was beckoning from the corner of the main building. The children were tired now, or else the adults had regained some authority, because people were lining up raggedly by the main door, with much jostling and pushing. Lyra and the other two slipped out from the corner and mingled with them, but before they did, Lyra said:

"Pass the word around among all the kids – they got to be ready to escape. They got to know where the outdoor clothes are and be ready to get them and run out as soon as we give the signal. And they got to keep this a deadly secret, understand?"

Billy nodded, and Roger said, "What's the signal?"

"The fire bell," said Lyra. "When the time comes, I'll set it off."

They waited to be counted off. If anyone in the Oblation Board had had anything to do with a school, they would have arranged this better: because they had no regular group to go to, each child had to be ticked off against the complete list, and of course they weren't in alphabetical order; and none of the adults was used to keeping control. So there was a good deal of confusion, despite the fact that no one was running around any more.

Lyra watched and noticed. They weren't very good at this at all. They were slack in a lot of ways, these people; they grumbled about fire drills, they didn't know where the outdoor clothes should be kept, they couldn't get children to stand in line properly; and their slackness might be to her advantage.

They had almost finished when there came another distraction, though, and from Lyra's point of view, it was the worst possible.

She heard the sound as everyone else did. Heads began to turn and scan the dark sky for the zeppelin, whose gas-engine was throbbing clearly in the still air.

The one lucky thing was that it was coming from the direction opposite to the one in which the grey goose had flown. But that was the only comfort. Very soon it was visible, and a murmur of excitement went around the crowd. Its fat sleek silver form drifted over the avenue of lights, and its own lights blazed downwards from the nose and the cabin slung beneath the body.

The pilot cut the speed and began the complex business of adjusting the height. Lyra realized what the stout mast was for: of course, it was a mooring mast. As the adults ushered the children inside, with everyone staring back and pointing, the ground crew clambered up the ladders in the mast and prepared to attach the mooring cables. The engines were roaring, and snow was swirling up from the ground, and the faces of passengers showed in the cabin windows.

Lyra looked, and there was no mistake. Pantalaimon clutched at her, became a wildcat, hissed in hatred, because looking out with curiosity was the beautiful dark-haired head of Mrs Coulter, with her golden dæmon in her lap.

16

The Silver Guillotine

Lyra ducked her head at once under the shelter of her wolverine hood, and shuffled in through the double doors with the other children. Time enough later to worry about what she'd say when they came face to face: she had another problem to deal with first, and that was how to hide her furs where she could get at them without asking permission.

But luckily, there was such disorder inside, with the adults trying to hurry the children through so as to clear the way for the passengers from the zeppelin, that no one was watching very carefully. Lyra slipped out of the anorak, the leggings and the boots and bundled them up as small as she could before shoving through the crowded corridors to her dormitory.

Quickly she dragged a locker to the corner, stood on it, and pushed at the ceiling. The panel lifted, just as Roger had said, and into the space beyond she thrust the boots and leggings. As an afterthought, she took the alethiometer from her pouch and hid it in the inmost pocket of the anorak before shoving that through too.

She jumped down, pushed back the locker, and whispered to Pantalaimon, "We must just pretend to be stupid till she sees us, and then say we were kidnapped. And nothing about the gyptians or Iorek Byrnison especially."

Because Lyra now realized, if she hadn't done so before, that all the fear in her nature was drawn to Mrs Coulter as a compass needle is drawn to the Pole. All the other things she'd seen, and even the hideous cruelty of the intercision, she could cope with; she was strong enough; but the thought of that sweet face and gentle voice, the image of that golden playful monkey, was enough to melt her stomach and make her pale and nauseous.

But the gyptians were coming. Think of that. Think of Iorek Byrnison. And don't give yourself away, she said, and drifted back towards the canteen, where a lot of noise was coming from.

Children were lining up to get hot drinks, some of them still in their coal-silk anoraks. Their talk was all of the zeppelin and its passenger.

"It was *her* – with the monkey-dæmon –"

"Did she get you, too?"

"She said she'd write to my mum and dad and I bet she never…"

"She never told us about kids getting killed. She never said nothing about that."

"That monkey, he's the *worst* – he caught my Karossa and nearly killed her – I could feel all weak…"

They were as frightened as Lyra was. She found Annie and the others, and sat down.

"Listen," she said, "can you keep a secret?"

"Yeah!"

The three faces turned to her, vivid with expectation.

"There's a plan to escape," Lyra said quietly. "There's some people coming to take us away, right, and they'll be here in about a day. Maybe sooner. What we all got to do is be ready as soon as the signal goes and get our cold-weather clothes at once and run out. No waiting about. You just got to run. Only if you don't get your anoraks and boots and stuff you'll die of cold."

"What signal?" Annie demanded.

"The fire bell, like this afternoon. It's all organized. All the kids're going to know and none of the grown-ups. Especially not *her*."

Their eyes were gleaming with hope and excitement. And all through the canteen the message was being passed around. Lyra could tell that the atmosphere had changed. Outside, the children had been energetic and eager for play; then when they had seen Mrs Coulter they were bubbling with a suppressed hysterical fear; but now there was a control and purpose to their talkativeness. Lyra marvelled at the effect hope could have.

She watched through the open doorway, but carefully, ready to duck her head, because there were adult voices coming, and then Mrs Coulter herself was briefly visible, looking in and smiling at the happy children, with their hot drinks and their cake, so warm and well-fed. A little shiver ran almost instantaneously through the whole canteen, and every child was still and silent, staring at her.

Mrs Coulter smiled and passed on without a word. Little by little the talk started again.

Lyra said, "Where do they go to talk?"

"Probably the conference room," said Annie. "They took us there once," she added, meaning her and her dæmon. "There was about twenty grown-ups there and one of 'em was giving a lecture and I had to stand there and do what he told me, like seeing how far my Kyrillion could go away from me, and then he hypnotized me and did some other things… It's a big room with a lot of chairs and tables and a little platform. It's behind the front office. Hey, I bet *they're* going to pretend the fire drill went off all right. I bet they're scared of her, same as we are…"

For the rest of the day, Lyra stayed close to the other girls, watching, saying little, remaining inconspicuous. There was exercise, there was sewing, there was supper, there was playtime in the lounge: a big shabby room with board games and a few tattered books and a table-tennis table. At some point Lyra and the others became aware that there was some kind of subdued emergency going on, because the adults were hurrying to and fro or standing in anxious groups talking urgently. Lyra guessed they'd discovered the dæmons' escape, and were wondering how it had happened.

But she didn't see Mrs Coulter, which was a relief. When it was time for bed, she knew she had to let the other girls into her confidence.

"Listen," she said, "do they ever come round and see if we're asleep?"

"They just look in once," said Bella. "They just flash a lantern round, they don't really look."

"Good. 'Cause I'm going to go and look round. There's a way through the ceiling that this boy showed me…"

She explained, and before she'd even finished, Annie said, "I'll come with you!"

"No, you better not, 'cause it'll be easier if there's just one person missing. You can all say you fell asleep and you don't know where I've gone."

"But if I came with you –"

"More likely to get caught," said Lyra.

Their two dæmons were staring at each other, Pantalaimon as a wildcat, Annie's Kyrillion as a fox. They were quivering. Pantalaimon uttered the lowest, softest hiss and bared his teeth, and Kyrillion turned aside and began to groom himself unconcernedly.

"All right then," said Annie, resigned.

It was quite common for struggles between children to be

settled by their dæmons in this way, with one accepting the dominance of the other. Their humans accepted the outcome without resentment, on the whole, so Lyra knew that Annie would do as she asked.

They all contributed items of clothing to bulk out Lyra's bed and make it look as if she was still there, and swore to say they knew nothing about it. Then Lyra listened at the door to make sure no one was coming, jumped up on the locker, pushed up the panel and hauled herself through.

"Just don't say anything," she whispered down to the three faces watching.

Then she dropped the panel gently back into place and looked around.

She was crouching in a narrow metal channel supported in a framework of girders and struts. The panels of the ceilings were slightly translucent, so some light came up from below, and in the faint gleam Lyra could see this narrow space (only two feet or so in height) extending in all directions around her. It was crowded with metal ducts and pipes, and it would be easy to get lost in, but provided she kept to the metal and avoided putting any weight on the panels, and as long as she made no noise, she should be able to go from one end of the Station to the other.

"It's just like back in Jordan, Pan," she whispered, "looking in the Retiring Room."

"If you hadn't done that, none of this would have happened," he whispered back.

"Then it's up to me to undo it, isn't it?"

She got her bearings, working out approximately which direction the conference room was in, and then set off. It was a far from easy journey. She had to move on hands and knees, because the space was too low to crouch in, and every so often she had to squeeze under a big square duct or lift herself over some heating pipes. The metal channels she crawled in followed the tops of internal walls, as far as she could tell, and as long as she stayed in them she felt a comforting solidity below her; but they were very narrow, and had sharp edges, so sharp that she cut her knuckles and her knee on them, and before long she was sore all over, and cramped, and dusty.

But she knew roughly where she was, and she could see the dark bulk of her furs crammed in above the dormitory to guide her back. She could tell where a room was empty because the panels were dark, and from time to time she heard voices from below, and stopped to listen, but it was only the cooks in the kitchen, or the nurses in what Lyra, in her Jordan way, thought of as their common room. They were saying nothing interesting, so she moved on.

At last she came to the area where the conference room should be, according to her calculations; and sure enough, there was an area free of any pipework, where air-conditioning and heating ducts led down at one end, and where all the panels in a wide rectangular space were lit evenly. She placed her ear to the panel, and heard a murmur of male adult voices, so she knew she had found the right place.

She listened carefully, and then inched her way along till she was as close as she could get to the speakers. Then she lay full-length in the metal channel and leaned her head sideways to hear as well as she could.

There was the occasional clink of cutlery, or the sound of glass on glass as drink was poured, so they were having dinner as they talked. There were four voices, she thought, including Mrs Coulter's. The other three were men. They seemed to be discussing the escaped dæmons.

"But who is in charge of supervising that section?" said Mrs Coulter's gentle musical voice.

"A research student called McKay," said one of the men. "But there are automatic mechanisms to prevent this sort of thing happening –"

"They didn't work," she said.

"With respect, they did, Mrs Coulter. McKay assures us that he locked all the cages when he left the building at eleven hundred hours today. The outer door of course would not have been open in any case, because he entered and left by the inner door, as he normally did. There's a code that has to be entered in the ordinator controlling the locks, and there's a record in its memory of his doing so. Unless that's done, an alarm goes off."

"But the alarm didn't go off," she said.

"It did. Unfortunately, it rang when everyone was outside, taking part in the fire drill."

"But when you went back inside –"

"Unfortunately both alarms are on the same circuit; that's a design fault that will have to be rectified. What it meant was that when the fire bell was turned off after the practice, the laboratory alarm was turned off as well. Even then it would still have been picked up, because of the normal checks that would have taken place after every disruption of routine; but by that time, Mrs Coulter, you had arrived unexpectedly, and if you recall, you asked specifically to meet the laboratory staff there and then, in your room. Consequently, no one returned to the laboratory until some time later."

"I see," said Mrs Coulter coldly. "In that case, the dæmons must have been released during the fire drill itself. And that widens the list of suspects to include every adult in the Station. Had you considered that?"

"Had you considered that it might have been done by a child?" said someone else.

She was silent, and the second man went on:

"Every adult had a task to do, and every task would have taken their full attention, and every task was done. There is no possibility that any of the staff here could have opened the door. None. So either someone came from outside altogether with the intention of doing that, or one of the children managed to find his way there, open the door and the cages, and return to the front of the main building."

"And what are you doing to investigate?" she said. "No; on second thoughts, don't tell me. Please understand, Dr Cooper, I'm not criticizing out of malice. We have to be quite extraordinarily careful. It was an atrocious lapse to have allowed both alarms to be on the same circuit. That must be corrected at once. Possibly the Tartar officer in charge of the guard could help your investigation? I merely mention that as a possibility. Where were the Tartars during the fire drill, by the way? I suppose you have considered that?"

"Yes, we have," said the man wearily. "The guard was fully occupied on patrol, every man. They keep meticulous records."

"I'm sure you're doing your very best," she said. "Well, there we are. A great pity. But enough of that for now. Tell me about the new separator."

Lyra felt a thrill of fear. There was only one thing this could mean.

"Ah," said the doctor, relieved to find the conversation turning to another subject, "there's a real advance. With the first model we could never entirely overcome the risk of the patient dying of shock, but we've improved that no end."

"The Skraelings did it better by hand," said a man who hadn't spoken yet.

"Centuries of practice," said the other man.

"But simply *tearing* was the only option for some time," said the main speaker, "however distressing that was to the adult

271

operators. If you remember, we had to discharge quite a number for reasons of stress-related anxiety. But the first big breakthrough was the use of anaesthesia combined with the Maystadt anbaric scalpel. We were able to reduce death from operative shock to below five per cent."

"And the new instrument?" said Mrs Coulter.

Lyra was trembling. The blood was pounding in her ears, and Pantalaimon was pressing his ermine-form against her side, and whispering, "Hush, Lyra, they won't do it – we won't let them do it –"

"Yes, it was a curious discovery by Lord Asriel himself that gave us the key to the new method. He discovered that an alloy of manganese and titanium has the property of insulating body from dæmon. By the way, what is happening with Lord Asriel?"

"Perhaps you haven't heard," said Mrs Coulter. "Lord Asriel is under suspended sentence of death. One of the conditions of his exile in Svalbard was that he gave up his philosophical work entirely. Unfortunately, he managed to obtain books and materials, and he's pushed his heretical investigations to the point where it's positively dangerous to let him live. At any rate, it seems that the Consistorial Court of Discipline has begun to debate the question of the sentence of death, and the probability is that it'll be carried out. But your new instrument, Doctor. How does it work?"

"Ah – yes – sentence of death, you say? Gracious God … I'm sorry. The new instrument. We're investigating what happens when the intercision is made with the patient in a conscious state, and of course that couldn't be done with the Maystadt Process. So we've developed a kind of guillotine, I suppose you could say. The blade is made of manganese and titanium alloy, and the child is placed in a compartment – like a small cabin – of alloy mesh, with the dæmon in a similar compartment connecting with it. While there is a connection, of course, the link remains. Then the blade is brought down between them, severing the link at once. They are then separate entities."

"I should like to see it," she said. "Soon, I hope. But I'm tired now. I think I'll go to bed. I want to see all the children tomorrow. We shall find out who opened that door."

There was the sound of chairs being pushed back, polite expressions, a door closing. Then Lyra heard the others sit down again, and go on talking, but more quietly.

"What is Lord Asriel up to?"

"I think he's got an entirely different idea of the nature of Dust. That's the point. It's profoundly heretical, you see, and the Consistorial Court of Discipline can't allow any other interpretation than the authorized one. And besides, he wants to experiment –"

"To experiment? With Dust?"

"Hush! Not so loud…"

"Do you think she'll make an unfavourable report?"

"No, no. I think you dealt with her very well."

"Her *attitude* worries me…"

"Not philosophical, you mean?"

"Exactly. A *personal* interest. I don't like to use the word, but it's almost ghoulish."

"That's a bit strong."

"But do you remember the first experiments, when she was so keen to see them pulled apart –"

Lyra couldn't help it: a little cry escaped her, and at the same time she tensed and shivered, and her foot knocked against a stanchion.

"What was that?"

"In the ceiling –"

"Quick!"

The sound of chairs being thrown aside, feet running, a table pulled across the floor. Lyra tried to scramble away, but there was so little space, and before she could move more than a few yards the ceiling panel beside her was thrust up suddenly, and she was looking into the startled face of a man. She was close enough to see every hair in his moustache. He was as startled as she was, but with more freedom to move, he was able to thrust a hand into the gap and seize her arm.

"A child!"

"Don't let her go –"

Lyra sank her teeth into his large freckled hand. He cried out, but didn't let go, even when she drew blood. Pantalaimon was snarling and spitting, but it was no good, the man was much stronger than she was, and he pulled and pulled until her other hand, desperately clinging to the stanchion, had to loosen, and she half-fell through into the room.

Still she didn't utter a sound. She hooked her legs over the sharp edge of the metal above, and struggled upside down, scratching, biting, punching, spitting in passionate fury. The men were gasping and grunting with pain or exertion, but they pulled and pulled.

And suddenly all the strength went out of her.

It was as if an alien hand had reached right inside where no hand had a right to be, and wrenched at something deep and precious.

She felt faint, dizzy, sick, disgusted, limp with shock.

One of the men was *holding* Pantalaimon.

He had seized Lyra's dæmon in his human hands, and poor Pan was shaking, nearly out of his mind with horror and disgust. His wildcat shape, his fur now dull with weakness, now sparking glints of anbaric alarm… He curved towards his Lyra as she reached with both hands for him…

They fell still. They were captured.

She *felt* those hands… It wasn't *allowed*… Not *supposed* to touch… *Wrong*…

"Was she on her own?"

A man was peering into the ceiling space.

"Seems to be on her own…"

"Who is she?"

"The new child."

"The one the Samoyed hunters…"

"Yes."

"You don't suppose *she* … the dæmons…"

"Could well be. But not on her own, surely?"

"Should we tell –"

"I think that would put the seal on things, don't you?"

"I agree. Better she doesn't hear at all."

"But what can we do about this?"

"She can't go back with the other children."

"Impossible!"

"There's only one thing we *can* do, it seems to me."

"Now?"

"Have to. Can't leave it till the morning. She wants to watch."

"We could do it ourselves. No need to involve anyone else."

The man who seemed to be in charge, the man who wasn't holding either Lyra or Pantalaimon, tapped his teeth with a thumbnail. His eyes were never still; they flicked and slid and darted this way and that. Finally he nodded.

"Now. Do it now," he said. "Otherwise she'll talk. The shock will prevent that, at least. She won't remember who she is, what she saw, what she heard… Come on."

Lyra couldn't speak. She could hardly breathe. She had to let herself be carried through the Station, along white empty corridors, past rooms humming with anbaric power, past the

275

dormitories where children slept with their dæmons on the pillow beside them, sharing their dreams; and every second of the way she watched Pantalaimon, and he reached for her, and their eyes never left each other.

Then a door which opened by means of a large wheel; a hiss of air; and a brilliantly-lit chamber with dazzling white tiles and stainless steel. The fear she felt was almost a physical pain; it was a physical pain, as they pulled her and Pantalaimon over towards a large cage of pale silver mesh, above which a great pale silver blade hung poised to separate them for ever and ever.

She found a voice at last, and screamed. The sound echoed loudly off the shiny surfaces, but the heavy door had hissed shut; she could scream and scream for ever, and not a sound would escape.

But Pantalaimon, in answer, had twisted free of those hateful hands – he was a lion, an eagle; he tore at them with vicious talons, great wings beat wildly, and then he was a wolf, a bear, a polecat – darting, snarling, slashing, a succession of transformations too quick to register, and all the time leaping, flying, dodging from one spot to another as their clumsy hands flailed and snatched at the empty air.

But they had dæmons too, of course. It wasn't two against three, it was two against six. A badger, an owl and a baboon were all just as intent to pin Pantalaimon down, and Lyra was crying to them, "Why? Why are *you* doing this? Help us! You shouldn't be helping them!"

And she kicked and bit more passionately than ever, until the man holding her gasped and let go for a moment – and she was free, and Pantalaimon sprang towards her like a spark of lightning, and she clutched him to her fierce breast, and he dug his wildcat-claws into her flesh, and every stab of pain was dear to her.

"Never! Never! Never!" she cried, and backed against the wall to defend him to their death.

But they fell on her again, three big brutal men, and she was only a child, shocked and terrified; and they tore Pantalaimon away, and threw her into one side of the cage of mesh and carried him, struggling still, around to the other. There was a mesh barrier between them, but he was still part of her, they were still joined. For a second or so more, he was still her own dear soul.

Above the panting of the men, above her own sobs, above the high wild howl of her dæmon, Lyra heard a humming sound, and saw one man (bleeding from the nose) operate a bank of switches. The other two looked up, and her eyes followed theirs. The great pale silver blade was rising slowly, catching the brilliant light. The last moment in her complete life was going to be the worst by far.

"What is going on here?"

A light, musical voice: her voice. Everything stopped.

"What are you doing? And who is this child –"

She didn't complete the word *child*, because in that instant she recognized Lyra. Through tear-blurred eyes Lyra saw her totter and clutch at a bench; her face, so beautiful and composed, grew in a moment haggard and horror-struck.

"Lyra –" she whispered.

The golden monkey darted from her side in a flash, and tugged Pantalaimon out from the mesh cage as Lyra fell out herself. Pantalaimon pulled free of the monkey's solicitous paws and stumbled to Lyra's arms.

"Never, never," she breathed into his fur, and he pressed his beating heart to hers.

They clung together like survivors of a shipwreck, shivering on a desolate coast. Dimly she heard Mrs Coulter speaking to the men, but she couldn't even interpret her tone of voice. And then they were leaving that hateful room, and Mrs Coulter was half-carrying, half-supporting her along a corridor, and then there was a door, a bedroom, scent in the air, soft light.

Mrs Coulter laid her gently on the bed. Lyra's arm was so tight around Pantalaimon that she was trembling with the force of it. A tender hand stroked her head.

"My dear, dear child," said that sweet voice. "However did you come to be here?"

17

The Witches

Lyra moaned and trembled uncontrollably, just as if she had been pulled out of water so cold that her heart had nearly frozen. Pantalaimon simply lay against her bare skin, inside her clothes, loving her back to herself, but aware all the time of Mrs Coulter, busy preparing a drink of something, and most of all of the golden monkey, whose hard little fingers had run swiftly over Lyra's body when only Pantalaimon could have noticed; and who had felt, around her waist, the oilskin pouch with its contents.

"Sit up, dear, and drink this," said Mrs Coulter, and her gentle arm slipped around Lyra's back and lifted her.

Lyra clenched herself, but relaxed almost at once as Pantalaimon thought to her: We're only safe as long as we pretend. She opened her eyes and found that they'd been containing tears, and to her surprise and shame she sobbed and sobbed.

Mrs Coulter made sympathetic sounds and put the drink into the monkey's hands while she mopped Lyra's eyes with a scented handkerchief.

"Cry as much as you need to, darling," said that soft voice, and Lyra determined to stop as soon as she possibly could. She struggled to hold back the tears, she pressed her lips together,

279

she choked down the sobs that still shook her chest.

Pantalaimon played the same game: fool them, fool them. He became a mouse and crept away from Lyra's hand to sniff timidly at the drink in the monkey's clutch. It was innocuous: an infusion of camomile, nothing more. He crept back to Lyra's shoulder and whispered, "Drink it."

She sat up and took the hot cup in both hands, alternately sipping and blowing to cool it. She kept her eyes down. She must pretend harder than she'd ever done in her life.

"Lyra, darling," Mrs Coulter murmured, stroking her hair. "I thought we'd lost you for ever! What happened? Did you get lost? Did someone take you out of the flat?"

"Yeah," Lyra whispered.

"Who was it, dear?"

"A man and a woman."

"Guests at the party?"

"I think so. They said you needed something that was downstairs and I went to get it and they grabbed hold of me and took me in a car somewhere. But when they stopped I ran out quick and dodged away and they never caught me. But I didn't know where I was…"

Another sob shook her briefly, but they were weaker now, and she could pretend this one was caused by her story.

"And I just wandered about trying to find my way back, only these Gobblers caught me… And they put me in a van with some other kids and took me somewhere, a big building, I dunno where it was."

With every second that went past, with every sentence she spoke, she felt a little strength flowing back. And now that she was doing something difficult and familiar and never quite predictable, namely lying, she felt a sort of mastery again, the same sense of complexity and control that the alethiometer gave her. She had to be careful not

280

to say anything obviously impossible; she had to be vague in some places and invent plausible details in others; she had to be an artist, in short.

"How long did they keep you in this building?" said Mrs Coulter.

Lyra's journey along the canals and her time with the gyptians had taken weeks: she'd have to account for that time. She invented a voyage with the Gobblers to Trollesund, and then an escape, lavish with details from her observation of the town; and a time as maid-of-all-work at Einarsson's Bar, and then a spell working for a family of farmers inland, and then being caught by the Samoyeds and brought to Bolvangar.

"And they were going to – going to cut –"

"Hush, dear, hush. I'm going to find out what's been going on."

"But why were they going to do that? I never done anything wrong! All the kids are afraid of what happens in there, and no one knows. But it's horrible. It's worse than anything… Why are they doing that, Mrs Coulter? Why are they so cruel?"

"There, there… You're safe, my dear. They won't ever do it to you. Now I know you're here, and you're safe, you'll never be in danger again. No one's going to harm you, Lyra darling; no one's ever going to hurt you…"

"But they do it to other children! Why?"

"Ah, my love –"

"It's Dust, isn't it?"

"Did they tell you that? Did the doctors say that?"

"The kids know it. All the kids talk about it, but no one knows! And they nearly done it to me – you got to tell me! You got no right to keep it secret, not any more!"

"Lyra … Lyra, Lyra. Darling, these are big difficult ideas, Dust and so on. It's not something for children to worry about.

But the doctors do it for the children's own good, my love. Dust is something bad, something wrong, something evil and wicked. Grown-ups and their dæmons are infected with Dust so deeply that it's too late for them. They can't be helped... But a quick operation on children means they're safe from it. Dust just won't stick to them ever again. They're safe and happy and –"

Lyra thought of little Tony Makarios. She leaned forward suddenly and retched. Mrs Coulter moved back and let go.

"Are you all right, dear? Go to the bathroom –"

Lyra swallowed hard and brushed her eyes.

"You don't have to do that to us," she said. "You could just leave us. I bet Lord Asriel wouldn't let anyone do that if he knew what was going on. If he's got Dust and you've got Dust, and the Master of Jordan and every other grown-up's got Dust, it must be all right. When I get out I'm going to tell all the kids in the world about this. Anyway, if it was so good, why'd you stop them doing it to me? If it was good you should've let them do it. You should have been glad."

Mrs Coulter was shaking her head and smiling a sad wise smile.

"Darling," she said, "some of what's good has to hurt us a little, and naturally it's upsetting for others if *you're* upset... But it doesn't mean your dæmon is taken away from you. He's still there! Goodness me, a lot of the grown-ups here have had the operation. The nurses seem happy enough, don't they?"

Lyra blinked. Suddenly she understood their strange blank incuriosity, the way their little trotting dæmons seemed to be sleepwalking.

Say nothing, she thought, and shut her mouth hard.

"Darling, no one would ever dream of performing an operation on a child without testing it first. And no one in a thousand years would take a child's dæmon away altogether! All that happens is a little cut, and then everything's peaceful. For ever! You see, your dæmon's a wonderful friend and companion when you're young, but at the age we call puberty, the age you're coming to very soon, darling, dæmons bring all sort of troublesome thoughts and feelings, and that's what lets Dust in. A quick little operation before that, and you're never troubled again. And your dæmon stays with you, only … just not connected. Like a … like a wonderful pet, if you like. The best pet in the world! Wouldn't you like that?"

Oh, the wicked liar, oh, the shameless untruths she was telling! And even if Lyra hadn't known them to be lies (Tony Makarios; those caged dæmons) she would have hated it with a furious passion. Her dear soul, the darling companion of her heart, to be cut away and reduced to a little trotting *pet*? Lyra nearly blazed with hatred, and Pantalaimon in her arms became a polecat, the most ugly and vicious of all his forms, and snarled.

But they said nothing. Lyra held Pantalaimon tight and let Mrs Coulter stroke her hair.

"Drink up your camomile," said Mrs Coulter softly. "We'll have them make up a bed for you in here. There's no need to go back and share a dormitory with other girls, not now I've got my little assistant back. My favourite! The best assistant in the world. D'you know, we searched all over London for you, darling? We had the police searching every town in the land. Oh, I missed you so much! I can't tell you how happy I am to find you again…"

All the time, the golden monkey was prowling about restlessly, one minute perching on the table swinging his tail, the next clinging to Mrs Coulter and chittering softly in her ear, the next pacing the floor with tail erect. He was betraying Mrs Coulter's impatience, of course, and finally she couldn't hold it in.

"Lyra, dear," she said, "I think that the Master of Jordan gave you something before you left. Isn't that right? He gave you an alethiometer. The trouble is, it wasn't his to give. It was left in his care. It's really too valuable to be carried about – d'you know, it's one of only two or three in the world! I think the Master gave it to you in the hope that it would fall into Lord Asriel's hands. He told you not to tell me about it, didn't he?"

Lyra twisted her mouth.

"Yes, I can see. Well, never mind, darling, because you *didn't* tell me, did you? So you haven't broken any promises. But listen, dear, it really ought to be properly looked after. I'm afraid it's so rare and delicate that we can't let it be at risk any longer."

"Why shouldn't Lord Asriel have it?" Lyra said, not moving.

"Because of what he's doing. You know he's been sent away to exile, because he's got something dangerous and wicked in mind. He needs the alethiometer to finish his plan, but believe me, dear, the last thing anyone should do is let him have it. The Master of Jordan was sadly mistaken. But now that you know, it really would be better to let me have it, wouldn't it? It would save you the trouble of carrying it around, and all the worry of looking after it – and really it must have been such a puzzle, wondering what a silly old thing like that was any good for…"

Lyra wondered how she had ever, ever, ever found this woman to be so fascinating and clever.

"So if you've got it now, dear, you'd really better let me have it to look after. It's in that belt around your waist, isn't it? Yes, that was a clever thing to do, putting it away like this…"

Her hands were at Lyra's skirt, and then she was unfastening the stiff oilcloth. Lyra tensed herself. The golden monkey was crouching at the end of the bed, trembling with anticipation, little black hands to his mouth. Mrs Coulter pulled the belt away from Lyra's waist and unbuttoned the pouch. She was breathing fast. She took out the black velvet cloth and unfolded it, finding the tin box Iorek Byrnison had made.

Pantalaimon was a cat again, tensed to spring. Lyra drew her legs up away from Mrs Coulter, and swung them down to the floor so that she too could run when the time came.

"What's this?" said Mrs Coulter, as if amused. "What a funny old tin! Did you put it in here to keep it safe, dear? All this moss... You have been careful, haven't you? Another tin, inside the first one! And soldered! Who did this, dear?"

She was too intent on opening it to wait for an answer. She had a knife in her handbag with a lot of different attachments, and she pulled out a blade and dug it under the lid.

At once a furious buzzing filled the room.

Lyra and Pantalaimon held themselves still. Mrs Coulter, puzzled, curious, pulled at the lid, and the golden monkey bent close to look.

Then in a dazzling moment the black form of the spy-fly hurtled out of the tin and crashed hard into the monkey's face.

He screamed and flung himself backwards; and of course it was hurting Mrs Coulter too, and she cried out in pain and fright with the monkey, and then the little clockwork devil swarmed upwards at her, up her breast and throat towards her face.

Lyra didn't hesitate. Pantalaimon sprang for the door and she was after him at once, and she tore it open and raced away faster than she had ever run in her life.

"Fire alarm!" Pantalaimon shrieked, as he flew ahead of her.

She saw a button on the next corner, and smashed the glass with her desperate fist. She ran on, heading towards the dormitories, smashed another alarm and another, and then people began to come out into the corridor, looking up and down for the fire.

By this time she was near the kitchen, and Pantalaimon flashed a thought into her mind, and she darted in. A moment later she had turned on all the gas taps and flung a match at the nearest burner. Then she dragged a bag of flour from a shelf and hurled it at the edge of a table so it burst and filled the air with white, because she had heard that flour will explode if it's treated like that near a flame.

Then she ran out and on as fast as she could towards her own dormitory. The corridors were full now: children running this way and that, vivid with excitement, for the word *escape* had got around. The oldest were making for the store-rooms where the clothing was kept, and herding the younger ones with them. Adults were trying to control it all, and none of them knew what was happening. Shouting, pushing, crying, jostling people were everywhere.

Through it all Lyra and Pantalaimon darted like fish, making always for the dormitory, and just as they reached it, there was a dull explosion from behind that shook the building.

The other girls had fled: the room was empty. Lyra dragged the locker to the corner, jumped up, hauled the furs out of the ceiling, felt for the alethiometer. It was still there. She tugged the furs on quickly, pulling the hood forward, and then Pantalaimon, a sparrow at the door, called:

"Now!"

She ran out. By luck a group of children who'd already found some cold-weather clothing were racing down the corridor towards the main entrance, and she joined them, sweating, her heart thumping, knowing that she had to escape or die.

The way was blocked. The fire in the kitchen had taken quickly, and whether it was the flour or the gas, something had brought down part of the roof. People were clambering over twisted struts and girders to get up to the bitter cold air. The smell of gas was strong. Then came another explosion, louder than the first and closer. The blast knocked several people over, and cries of fear and pain filled the air.

Lyra struggled up, and with Pantalaimon calling, "This way! This way!" among the other dæmon-cries and flutterings, she hauled herself over the rubble. The air she was breathing was frozen, and she hoped that the children had managed to find their outdoor clothing; it would be a fine thing to escape from the Station only to die of cold.

There really was a blaze now. When she got out on to the roof under the night sky she could see flames licking at the edges of a great hole in the side of the building. There was a throng of children and adults by the main entrance, but this time the adults were more agitated and the children more fearful: much more fearful.

"Roger! Roger!" Lyra called, and Pantalaimon, keen-eyed as an owl, hooted that he'd seen him.

A moment later they found each other.

"Tell 'em all to come with me!" Lyra shouted into his ear.

"They won't – they're all panicky –"

"Tell 'em what they do to the kids that vanish! They cut their dæmons off with a big knife! Tell 'em what you saw this afternoon – all them dæmons we let out! Tell 'em that's going to happen to them too unless they get away!"

Roger gaped, horrified, but then collected his wits and ran to the nearest group of hesitating children. Lyra did the same, and as the message passed along, some children cried out and clutched their dæmons in fear.

"Come with me!" Lyra shouted. "There's a rescue a-coming! We got to get out the compound! Come on, run!"

The children heard her and followed, streaming across the enclosure towards the avenue of lights, their boots pattering and creaking in the hard-packed snow.

Behind them adults were shouting, and there was a rumble and crash as another part of the building fell in. Sparks gushed into the air, and flames billowed out with a sound like tearing cloth; but cutting through this came another sound, dreadfully close and violent. Lyra had never heard it before, but she knew it at once: it was the howl of the Tartar guards' wolf-dæmons. She felt weak from head to foot, and many children turned in fear and stumbled to a stop, for there running at a low swift tireless lope came the first of the Tartar guards, rifle at the ready, with the mighty leaping greyness of his dæmon beside him.

Then came another, and another. They were all in padded mail, and they had no eyes – or at least you couldn't see any eyes behind the snow-slits of their helmets. The only eyes you could see were the round black ends of the rifle-barrels and the blazing yellow eyes of the wolf-dæmons above the slaver dripping from their jaws.

Lyra faltered. She hadn't dreamed of how frightening those wolves were. And now that she knew how casually people at Bolvangar broke the great taboo, she shrank from the thought of those dripping teeth...

The Tartars ran to stand in a line across the entrance to the avenue of lights, their dæmons beside them as disciplined and drilled as they were. In another minute there'd be a second line, because more were coming, and more behind them. Lyra thought with despair: children can't fight soldiers. It wasn't like the battles in the Oxford Claybeds, hurling lumps of mud at the brick-burners' children.

Or perhaps it was! She remembered hurling a handful of clay in the broad face of a brick-burner boy bearing down on her. He'd stopped to claw the stuff out of his eyes, and then the townies leapt on him.

She'd been standing in the mud. She was standing in the snow.

Just as she'd done that afternoon, but in deadly earnest now, she scooped a handful together and hurled it at the nearest soldier.

"Get 'em in the eyes!" she yelled, and threw another.

Other children joined in, and then someone's dæmon had the notion of flying as a swift beside the snowball and nudging it directly at the eye-slits of the target – and then they all joined in, and in a few moments the Tartars were stumbling about spitting and cursing and trying to brush the packed snow out of the narrow gap in front of their eyes.

"Come on!" Lyra screamed, and flung herself at the gate into the avenue of lights.

The children streamed after her, every one, dodging the snapping jaws of the wolves and racing as hard as they could down the avenue towards the beckoning open dark beyond.

A harsh scream came from behind as an officer shouted an order, and then a score of rifle bolts worked at once, and then there was another scream and a tense silence, with only the fleeing children's pounding feet and gasping breath to be heard.

They were taking aim. They wouldn't miss.

But before they could fire, a choking gasp came from one of the Tartars, and a cry of surprise from another.

Lyra stopped and turned to see a man lying on the snow, with a grey-feathered arrow in his back. He was writhing and twitching and coughing out blood, and the other soldiers were looking around to left and right for whoever had fired it, but the archer was nowhere to be seen.

And then an arrow came flying straight down from the sky, and struck another man behind the head. He fell at once. A shout from the officer, and everyone looked up at the dark sky.

"Witches!" said Pantalaimon.

And so they were: ragged elegant black shapes sweeping past high above, with a hiss and swish of air through the needles of the cloud-pine branches they flew on. As Lyra watched, one swooped low and loosed an arrow: another man fell.

And then all the Tartars turned their rifles up and blazed into the dark, firing at nothing, at shadows, at clouds, and more and more arrows rained down on them.

But the officer in charge, seeing the children almost away, ordered a squad to race after them. Some children screamed. And then more screamed, and they weren't moving forward any more, they were turning back in confusion, terrified by the monstrous shape hurtling towards them from the dark beyond the avenue of lights.

"Iorek Byrnison!" cried Lyra, her chest nearly bursting with joy.

The armoured bear at the charge seemed to be conscious of no weight except what gave him momentum. He bounded past Lyra almost in a blur and crashed into the Tartars, scattering soldiers, dæmons, rifles to all sides. Then he stopped and whirled round, with a lithe athletic power, and struck two massive blows, one to each side, at the guards closest to him.

A wolf-dæmon leapt at him: he slashed at her in mid-air, and bright fire spilled out of her as she fell to the snow, where she hissed and howled before vanishing. Her human died at once.

The Tartar officer, faced with this double attack, didn't hesitate. A long high scream of orders, and the force divided itself into two: one to keep off the witches, the bigger part to overcome the bear. His troops were magnificently brave. They dropped to one knee in groups of four and fired their rifles as if they were on the practice range, not budging an inch as Iorek's mighty bulk hurtled towards them. A moment later they were dead.

Iorek struck again, twisting to one side, slashing, snarling, crushing, while bullets flew about him like wasps or flies, doing no harm at all. Lyra urged the children on and out into the darkness beyond the lights. They must get away, because dangerous as the Tartars were, far more dangerous were the adults of Bolvangar.

So she called and beckoned and pushed to get the children moving. As the lights behind them threw long shadows on the snow, Lyra found her heart moving out towards the deep dark of the Arctic night and the clean coldness, leaping forward to love it as Pantalaimon was doing, a hare now delighting in his own propulsion.

"Where we going?" someone said.

"There's nothing out here but snow!"

"There's a rescue party coming," Lyra told them. "There's fifty gyptians or more. I bet there's some relations of yours, too. All the gyptian families that lost a kid, they all sent someone."

"I en't a gyptian," a boy said.

"Don't matter. They'll take you anyway."

"Where?" someone said querulously.

"Home," said Lyra. "That's what I come here for, to rescue you, and I brung the gyptians here to take you home again. We just got to go on a bit further and then we'll find 'em. The bear was with 'em, so they can't be far off."

"D'you see that bear!" one boy was saying. "When he slashed open that dæmon – the man died as if someone whipped his heart out, just like that!"

"I never knew dæmons could be killed," someone else said.

They were all talking now; the excitement and relief had loosened everyone's tongue. As long as they kept moving, it didn't matter if they talked.

"Is that true," said a girl, "about what they do back there?"

"Yeah," Lyra said. "I never thought I'd ever see anyone without their dæmon. But on the way here, we found this boy on his own without any dæmon. He kept asking for her, where she was, would she ever find him. He was called Tony Makarios."

"I know him!" said someone, and others joined in: "Yeah, they took him away about a week back…"

"Well, they cut his dæmon away," said Lyra, knowing how it would affect them. "And a little bit after we found him, he died. And all the dæmons they cut away, they kept them in cages in a square building back there."

"It's true," said Roger. "And Lyra let 'em out during the fire drill."

"Yeah, I seen 'em!" said Billy Costa. "I didn't know what they was at first, but I seen 'em fly away with that goose."

"But why do they do it?" demanded one boy. "Why do they cut people's dæmons away? That's torture! Why do they do it?"

"Dust," suggested someone doubtfully.

But the boy laughed in scorn. "Dust!" he said. "There en't no such thing! They just made that up! I don't believe in it."

"Here," said someone else, "look what's happening to the zeppelin!"

They all looked back. Beyond the dazzle of lights, where the fight was still continuing, the great length of the airship was not floating freely at the mooring mast any longer; the free end was drooping downwards, and beyond it was rising a globe of –

"Lee Scoresby's balloon!" Lyra cried, and clapped her mittened hands with delight.

The other children were baffled. Lyra herded them onwards, wondering how the aëronaut had got his balloon that far. It was clear what he was doing, and what a good idea, to fill his balloon with the gas out of theirs, to escape by the same means that crippled their pursuit!

"Come on, keep moving, else you'll freeze," she said, for some of the children were shivering and moaning from the cold, and their dæmons were crying too in high thin voices.

Pantalaimon found this irritating, and as a wolverine he snapped at one girl's squirrel-dæmon who was just lying across her shoulder whimpering faintly.

"Get in her coat! Make yourself big and warm her up!" he snarled, and the girl's dæmon, frightened, crept inside her coal-silk anorak at once.

The trouble was that coal-silk wasn't as warm as proper fur, no matter how much it was padded out with hollow coal-silk fibres. Some of the children looked like walking puffballs, they were so bulky, but their gear had been made in factories and laboratories far away from the cold, and it couldn't really cope. Lyra's furs looked ragged and they stank, but they kept the warmth in.

"If we don't find the gyptians soon they en't going to last," she whispered to Pantalaimon.

"Keep 'em moving, then," he whispered back. "If they lie down they're finished. You know what Farder Coram said…"

Farder Coram had told her many tales of his own journeys in the North, and so had Mrs Coulter – always supposing that hers were true. But they were both quite clear about one point, which was that you must keep going.

"How far we gotta go?" said a little boy.

"She's just making us walk out here to kill us," said a girl.

"Rather be out here than back there," someone said.

"I wouldn't! It's warm back in the Station. There's food and hot drinks and everything."

"But it's all on fire!"

"What we going to do out here? I bet we starve to death…"

Lyra's mind was full of dark questions that flew around like witches, swift and untouchable, and somewhere, just beyond where she could reach, there was a glory and a thrill which she didn't understand at all.

But it gave her a surge of strength, and she hauled one girl up out of a snowdrift, and shoved at a boy who was dawdling, and called to them all: "Keep going! Follow the bear's tracks! He come up with the gyptians, so the track'll lead us to where they are! Just keep walking!"

Big flakes of snow were beginning to fall. Soon it would have covered Iorek Byrnison's tracks altogether. Now that they were out of sight of the lights of Bolvangar, and the blaze of the fire was only a faint glow, the only light came from the faint radiance of the snow-covered ground. Thick clouds obscured the sky, so there was neither moon nor Northern Lights; but by peering closely, the children could make out the deep trail Iorek Byrnison had ploughed in the snow. Lyra encouraged, bullied, hit, half-carried, swore at, pushed, dragged, lifted tenderly, wherever it was needed, and Pantalaimon (by the state of each child's dæmon) told her what was needed in each case.

I'll get 'em there, she kept saying to herself. I come here to get 'em and I'll bloody get 'em.

Roger was following her example, and Billy Costa was leading the way, being sharper-eyed than most. Soon the snow was falling so thickly that they had to cling on to one another to keep from getting lost, and Lyra thought, perhaps if we all lie close and keep warm like that... Dig holes in the snow...

She was hearing things. There was the snarl of an engine somewhere, not the heavy thump of a zeppelin but something higher like the drone of a hornet. It drifted in and out of hearing.

And howling... Dogs? Sledge dogs? That too was distant and hard to be sure of, blanketed by millions of snowflakes and blown this way and that by little puffing gusts of wind. It might have been the gyptians' sledge dogs, or it might have been wild spirits of the tundra, or even those freed dæmons crying for their lost children.

She was seeing things… There weren't any lights in the snow, were there? They must be ghosts as well… Unless they'd come round in a circle, and were stumbling back into Bolvangar.

But these were little yellow lantern-beams, not the white glare of anbaric lights. And they were moving, and the howling was nearer, and before she knew for certain whether she'd fallen asleep, Lyra was wandering among familiar figures, and men in furs were holding her up: John Faa's mighty arm lifted her clear of the ground, and Farder Coram was laughing with pleasure; and as far through the blizzard as she could see, gyptians were lifting children into sledges, covering them with furs, giving them seal-meat to chew. And Tony Costa was there, hugging Billy and then punching him softly only to hug him again and shake him for joy. And Roger…

"Roger's coming with us," she said to Farder Coram. "It was him I meant to get in the first place. We'll go back to Jordan in the end. What's that noise –"

It was that snarl again, that engine, like a crazed spy-fly ten thousand times the size.

Suddenly there came a blow that sent her sprawling, and Pantalaimon couldn't defend her, because the golden monkey –

Mrs Coulter –

The golden monkey was wrestling, biting, scratching at Pantalaimon, who was flickering through so many changes of form it was hard to see him, and fighting back: stinging, lashing, tearing. Mrs Coulter, meanwhile, her face in its furs a frozen glare of intense feeling, was dragging Lyra to the back of a motorized sledge, and Lyra struggled as hard as her dæmon. The snow was so thick that they seemed to be isolated in a little blizzard of their own, and the anbaric headlights of the sledge only showed up the thick swirling flakes a few inches ahead.

"Help!" Lyra cried, to the gyptians who were just *there* in the blinding snow and who could see nothing. "Help me! Farder Coram! Lord Faa! Oh God, help!"

Mrs Coulter shrieked a high command in the language of the northern Tartars. The snow swirled open, and there they were, a squad of them, armed with rifles, and the wolf-dæmons snarled beside them. The chief saw Mrs Coulter struggling, and picked up Lyra with one hand as if she were a doll and threw her into the sledge, where she lay stunned and dazed.

A rifle banged, and then another, as the gyptians realized what was happening. But firing at targets you can't see is dangerous when you can't see your own side either. The Tartars, in a tight group now around the sledge, were able to blaze at will into the snow, but the gyptians dared not shoot back for fear of hitting Lyra.

Oh, the bitterness she felt! The tiredness!

Still dazed, with her head ringing, she hauled herself up to find Pantalaimon desperately fighting the monkey still, with wolverine-jaws fastened tight in a golden arm, changing no more but grimly hanging on. And who was that?

Not Roger?

Yes, Roger, battering at Mrs Coulter with fists and feet, hurtling his head against hers, only to be struck down by a Tartar who swiped at him like someone brushing away a fly. It was all a phantasmagoria now: white, black, a swift green flutter across her vision, ragged shadows, racing light –

A great swirl lifted curtains of snow aside, and into the cleared area leapt Iorek Byrnison, with a clang and screech of iron on iron. A moment later and those great jaws snapped left, right, a paw ripped open a mailed chest, white teeth, black iron, red wet fur –

Then something was pulling her *up* powerfully, *up*, and she seized Roger too, tearing him out of the hands of Mrs Coulter and clinging tight, each child's dæmon a shrill bird fluttering in amazement as a greater fluttering swept all around them, and then Lyra saw in the air beside her a witch, one of those elegant ragged black shadows from the high air, but close enough to touch; and there was a bow in the witch's bare hands, and she exerted her bare pale arms (in this freezing air!) to pull the string and then loose an arrow into the eye-slit of a mailed and louring Tartar hood only three feet away –

And the arrow sped in and halfway out at the back, and the man's wolf-dæmon vanished in mid-leap even before he hit the ground.

Up! Into mid-air Lyra and Roger were caught and swept, and found themselves clinging with weakening fingers to a cloud-pine branch, where the young witch was sitting tense with balanced grace, and then she leant down and to the left and something huge was looming and there was the ground.

They tumbled into the snow beside the basket of Lee Scoresby's balloon.

"Skip inside," called the Texan, "and bring your friend, by all means. Have ye seen that bear?"

Lyra saw that three witches were holding a rope looped around a rock, anchoring the great buoyancy of the gas-bag to the earth.

"Get in!" she cried to Roger, and scrambled over the leather-bound rim of the basket to fall in a snowy heap inside. A moment later Roger fell on top of her, and then a mighty noise halfway between a roar and a growl made the very ground shake.

"C'mon, Iorek! On board, old feller!" yelled Lee Scoresby, and over the side came the bear in a hideous creak of wicker and bending wood.

Then a swirl of lighter air lifted the mist and snow aside for a moment, and in the sudden clearance Lyra saw everything that was happening around them. She saw a party of gyptian raiders under John Faa harrying the Tartar rearguard and sweeping them back towards the blazing ruins of Bolvangar; she saw the other gyptians helping child after child safe aboard their sledges, tucking them warmly down under the furs; she saw Farder Coram casting around anxiously, leaning on his stick, his autumn-coloured dæmon leaping through the snow and looking this way and that.

"Farder Coram!" Lyra cried. "Over here!"

The old man heard, and turned to look in amazement at the balloon straining against the rope and the witches holding it down, at Lyra waving frantically from the basket.

"Lyra!" he cried. "You're safe, gal? You're safe?"

"As safe as I ever was!" she shouted back. "Goodbye, Farder Coram! Goodbye! Take all the kids back home!"

"We'll do that, sure as I live! Go well, my child – go well – go well, my dear –"

And at the same moment the aëronaut lowered his arm in a signal, and the witches let go of the rope.

The balloon lifted immediately and surged upwards into the snow-thick air at a rate Lyra could scarcely believe. After a moment the ground disappeared in the mist, and up they went, faster and faster, so that she thought no rocket could have left the earth more swiftly. She lay holding on to Roger on the floor of the basket, pressed down by the acceleration.

Lee Scoresby was cheering and laughing and uttering wild Texan yells of delight; Iorek Byrnison was calmly unfastening his armour, hooking a deft claw into all the linkages and undoing them with a twist before packing the separate pieces in a pile. Somewhere outside, the flap and swish of air through cloud-pine needles and witch-garments told that the witches were keeping them company into the upper airs.

Little by little Lyra recovered her breath, her balance and her heartbeat. She sat up and looked around.

The basket was much bigger than she'd thought. Ranged around the edges were racks of philosophical instruments, and there were piles of furs, and bottled air, and a variety of other things too small or confusing to make out in the thick mist they were ascending through.

"Is this a cloud?" she said.

"Sure is. Wrap your friend in some furs before he turns into an icicle. It's cold here but it's gonna get colder."

"How did you find us?"

"Witches. There's one witch-lady who wants to talk to you. When we get clear of the cloud we'll get our bearings and then we can sit and have a yarn."

"Iorek," said Lyra, "thank you for coming."

The bear grunted, and settled down to lick the blood off his fur. His weight meant that the basket was tilted to one side, but that didn't matter. Roger was wary, but Iorek Byrnison took no more notice of him than of a flake of snow. Lyra contented herself with clinging to the rim of the basket, just under her chin when she was standing, and peering wide-eyed into the swirling cloud.

Only a few seconds later the balloon passed out of the cloud altogether and, still rising rapidly, soared on into the heavens.

What a sight!

Directly above them the balloon swelled out in a huge curve. Above and ahead of them the Aurora was blazing, with more brilliance and grandeur than she had ever seen. It was all around, or nearly, and they were nearly part of it. Great swathes of incandescence trembled and parted like angels' wings beating; cascades of luminescent glory tumbled down invisible crags to lie in swirling pools or hang like vast waterfalls.

So Lyra gasped at that, and then she looked below, and saw a sight almost more wondrous.

As far as the eye could see, to the very horizon in all directions, a tumbled sea of white extended without a break. Soft peaks and vaporous chasms rose or opened here and there, but mostly it looked like a solid mass of ice.

And rising through it in ones and twos and larger groups as well came small black shadows, those ragged figures of such elegance, witches on their branches of cloud-pine.

They flew swiftly, without any effort, up and towards the balloon, leaning to one side or another to steer. And one of them, the archer who'd saved Lyra from Mrs Coulter, flew directly alongside the basket, and Lyra saw her clearly for the first time.

She was young – younger than Mrs Coulter; and fair, with bright green eyes; and clad like all the witches in strips of black silk, but wearing no furs, no hood or mittens. She seemed to feel no cold at all. Around her brow was a simple chain of little red flowers. She sat her cloud-pine branch as if it were a steed, and seemed to rein it in a yard from Lyra's wondering gaze.

"Lyra?"

"Yes! And are you Serafina Pekkala?"

"I am."

Lyra could see why Farder Coram loved her, and why it was breaking his heart, though she had known neither of those things a moment before. He was growing old; he was an old broken man; and she would be young for generations.

"Have you got the symbol-reader?" said the witch, in a voice so like the high wild singing of the Aurora itself that Lyra could hardly hear the sense for the sweet sound of it.

"Yes. I got it in my pocket, safe."

Great wing-beats told of another arrival, and then he was gliding beside her: the grey goose-dæmon. He spoke briefly and then wheeled away to glide in a wide circle around the balloon as it continued to rise.

"The gyptians have laid waste to Bolvangar," said Serafina Pekkala. "They have killed twenty-two guards and nine of the staff, and they've set light to every part of the buildings that still stood. They are going to destroy it completely."

"What about Mrs Coulter?"

"No sign of her."

She cried out in a wild yell, and other witches circled and flew in towards the balloon.

"Mr Scoresby," she said. "The rope, if you please."

"Ma'am, I'm very grateful. We're still rising. I guess we'll go on up a while yet. How many of you will it take to pull us north?"

"We are strong," was all she said.

Lee Scoresby was attaching a coil of stout rope to the leather-covered iron ring that gathered the ropes running over the gas-bag, and from which the basket itself was suspended. When it was securely fixed, he threw the free end out, and at once six witches darted towards it, caught hold, and began to pull, urging the cloud-pine branches towards the Polar Star.

As the balloon began to move in that direction, Pantalaimon came to perch on the edge of the basket as a tern. Roger's dæmon came out to look, but crept back again soon, for Roger was fast asleep, as was Iorek Byrnison. Only Lee Scoresby was awake, calmly chewing a thin cigar and watching his instruments.

"So, Lyra," said Serafina Pekkala. "Do you know why you're going to Lord Asriel?"

Lyra was astonished. "To take him the alethiometer, of course!" she said.

She had never considered the question; it was obvious. Then she recalled her first motive, from so long ago that she'd almost forgotten it.

"Or… To help him escape. That's it. We're going to help him get away."

But as she said that, it sounded absurd. Escape from Svalbard? Impossible!

"Try, anyway," she added stoutly. "Why?"

"I think there are things I need to tell you," said Serafina Pekkala.

"About Dust?"

It was the first thing Lyra wanted to know.

"Yes, among other things. But you are tired now, and it will be a long flight. We'll talk when you wake up."

Lyra yawned. It was a jaw-cracking, lung-bursting yawn that lasted almost a minute, or felt like it, and for all that Lyra struggled, she couldn't resist the onrush of sleep. Serafina Pekkala reached a hand over the rim of the basket and touched her eyes, and as Lyra sank to the floor, Pantalaimon fluttered down, changed to an ermine, and crawled to his sleeping-place by her neck.

The witch settled her branch into a steady speed beside the basket as they moved north towards Svalbard.

Part Three

Svalbard

18
Fog and Ice

Lee Scoresby arranged some furs over Lyra. She curled up close to Roger and they lay together asleep as the balloon swept on towards the Pole. The aëronaut checked his instruments from time to time, chewed on the cigar he would never light with the inflammable hydrogen so close, and huddled deeper into his own furs.

"This little girl's pretty important, huh?" he said after several minutes.

"More than she will know," Serafina Pekkala said.

"Does that mean there's gonna be much in the way of armed pursuit? You understand, I'm speaking as a practical man with a living to earn. I can't afford to get busted up or shot to pieces without some kind of compensation agreed in advance. I ain't trying to lower the tone of this expedition, believe me, ma'am. But John Faa and the gyptians paid me a fee that's enough to cover my time and skill and the normal wear and tear on the balloon, and that's all. It didn't include acts-of-war insurance. And let me tell you, ma'am, when we land Iorek Byrnison on Svalbard, that will count as an act of war."

He spat a piece of smoke-leaf delicately overboard.

"So I'd like to know what we can expect in the way of mayhem and ructions," he finished.

"There may be fighting," said Serafina Pekkala. "But you have fought before."

"Sure, when I'm paid. But the fact is, I thought this was a straightforward transportation contract, and I charged according. And I'm a-wondering now, after that little dust-up down there, I'm a-wondering how far my transportation responsibility extends. Whether I'm bound to risk my life and my equipment in a war among the bears, for example. Or whether this little child has enemies on Svalbard as hot-tempered as the ones back at Bolvangar. I merely mention all this by way of making conversation."

"Mr Scoresby," said the witch, "I wish I could answer your question. All I can say is that all of us, humans, witches, bears, are engaged in a war already, although not all of us know it. Whether you find danger on Svalbard or whether you fly off unharmed, you are a recruit, under arms, a soldier."

"Well, that seems kinda precipitate. Seems to me a man should have a choice whether to take up arms or not."

"We have no more choice in that than in whether or not to be born."

"Oh, I like choice, though," he said. "I like choosing the jobs I take and the places I go and the food I eat and the companions I sit and yarn with. Don't you wish for a choice once in a while?"

Serafina Pekkala considered, and then said, "Perhaps we don't mean the same thing by *choice*, Mr Scoresby. Witches own nothing, so we're not interested in preserving value or making profits, and as for the choice between one thing and another, when you live for many hundreds of years you know that every opportunity will come again. We have different needs. You have to repair your balloon and keep it in good condition, and that takes time and trouble, I see that; but for us to fly, all we have to do is tear off a branch of cloud-pine; any will do, and there are plenty more. We don't feel cold, so we need no warm clothes. We have no means of exchange apart from mutual aid. If a witch needs something, another witch will give it to her. If there is a war to be fought, we don't consider cost one of the factors in deciding whether or not it is right to fight. Nor do we have any notion of honour, as bears do, for instance. An insult to a bear is a deadly thing. To us … inconceivable. How could you insult a witch? What would it matter if you did?"

"Well, I'm kinda with you on that. Sticks and stones, I'll break yer bones, but names ain't worth a quarrel. But ma'am, you see my dilemma, I hope. I'm a simple aëronaut, and I'd like to end my days in comfort. Buy a little farm, a few head of cattle, some horses… Nothing grand, you notice. No palace or slaves or heaps of gold. Just the evening wind over the sage, and a ceegar, and a glass of bourbon whiskey. Now the trouble is, that costs money. So I do my flying in exchange for cash, and after every job I send some gold back to the Wells Fargo Bank, and when I've got enough, ma'am, I'm gonna sell this balloon and book me a passage on a steamer to Port Galveston, and I'll never leave the ground again."

"There's another difference between us, Mr Scoresby. A witch would no sooner give up flying than give up breathing. To fly is to be perfectly ourselves."

"I see that, ma'am, and I envy you; but I ain't got your sources of satisfaction. Flying is just a job to me, and I'm just a technician. I might as well be adjusting valves in a gas-engine or wiring up anbaric circuits. But I chose it, you see. It was my own free choice. Which is why I find this notion of a war I ain't been told nothing about, kinda troubling."

"Iorek Byrnison's quarrel with his king is part of it too," said the witch. "This child is destined to play a part in that."

"You speak of destiny," he said, "as if it was fixed. And I ain't sure I like that any more than a war I'm enlisted in without knowing about it. Where's my free will, if you please? And this child seems to me to have more free will than anyone I ever met. Are you telling me that she's just some kind of clockwork toy wound up and set going on a course she can't change?"

"We are all subject to the fates. But we must all act as if we are not," said the witch, "or die of despair. There is a curious prophecy about this child: she is destined to bring about the end of destiny. But she must do so without knowing what she is doing, as if it were her nature and not her destiny to do it. If she's told what she must do, it will all fail; death will sweep through all the worlds; it will be the triumph of despair, for ever. The universes will all become nothing more than interlocking machines, blind and empty of thought, feeling, life…"

They looked down at Lyra, whose sleeping face (what little they could see inside her hood) wore a stubborn little frown.

"I guess part of her knows that," said the aëronaut. "Looks prepared for it, anyways. How about the little boy? You know she came all this way to save him from those fiends back there? They were playmates, back in Oxford or somewhere. Did you know that?"

"Yes, I did know that. Lyra is carrying something of immense value, and it seems that the fates are using her as a messenger to take it to her father. So she came all this way to find her friend, not knowing that her friend was brought to the North by the fates, in order that she might follow and bring something to her father."

"That's how you read it, huh?"

For the first time the witch seemed unsure.

"That is how it seems… But we can't read the darkness, Mr Scoresby. It is more than possible that I might be wrong."

"And what brought *you* into all this, if I can ask?"

"Whatever they were doing at Bolvangar, we felt it was wrong with all our hearts. Lyra is their enemy; so we are her friends. We don't see more clearly than that. But also there is my clan's friendship for the gyptian people, which goes back to the time when Farder Coram saved my life. We are doing this at their bidding. And they have ties of obligation with Lord Asriel."

"I see. So you're towing the balloon to Svalbard for the gyptians' sake. And does that friendship extend to towing us back again? Or will I have to wait for a kindly wind, and depend on the indulgence of the bears in the meantime? Once again, ma'am, I'm asking merely in a spirit of friendly enquiry."

"If we can help you back to Trollesund, Mr Scoresby, we shall do so. But we don't know what we shall meet on Svalbard. The bears' new king has made many changes; the old ways are out of favour; it might be a difficult landing. And I don't know how Lyra will find her way to her father. Nor do I know what Iorek Byrnison has it in mind to do, except that his fate is involved with hers."

"I don't know either, ma'am. I think he's attached himself to the little girl as a kind of protector. She helped him get his armour back, you see. Who knows what bears feel? But if a bear ever loved a human being, he loves her. As for landing on Svalbard, it's never been easy. Still, if I can call on you for a tug in the right direction, I'll feel kinda easier in my mind; and if there's anything I can do for you in return, you only have to say. But just so as I know, would you mind telling me whose side I'm on in this invisible war?"

"We are both on Lyra's side."

"Oh, no doubt about that."

They flew on. Because of the clouds below there was no way of telling how fast they were going. Normally, of course, a balloon remained still with respect to the wind, floating at whatever speed the air itself was moving; but now, pulled by the witches, the balloon was moving through the air instead of with it, and resisting the movement, too, because the unwieldy gas-bag had none of the streamlined smoothness of a zeppelin. As a result, the basket swung this way and that, rocking and bumping much more than on a normal flight.

Lee Scoresby wasn't concerned for his comfort so much as for his instruments, and he spent some time making sure they were securely lashed to the main struts. According to the altimeter, they were nearly ten thousand feet up. The temperature was minus twenty degrees. He had been colder than this, but not much, and he didn't want to get any colder now; so he unrolled the canvas sheet he used as an emergency bivouac, and spread it in front of the sleeping children to keep off the wind, before lying down back to back with his old comrade in arms, Iorek Byrnison, and falling asleep.

When Lyra woke up, the moon was high in the sky, and everything in sight was silver-plated, from the rolling surface of the clouds below to the frost-spears and icicles on the rigging of the balloon.

Roger was sleeping, and so were Lee Scoresby and the bear. Beside the basket, however, the witch-queen was flying steadily.

"How far are we from Svalbard?" Lyra said.

"If we meet no winds, we shall be over Svalbard in twelve hours or so."

"Where are we going to land?"

"It depends on the weather. We'll try to avoid the cliffs, though. There are creatures living there who prey on anything that moves. If we can, we'll set you down in the interior, away from Iofur Raknison's palace."

"What's going to happen when I find Lord Asriel? Will he want to come back to Oxford, or what? I don't know if I ought to tell him I know he's my father, neither. He might want to pretend he's still my uncle. I don't hardly know him at all."

"He won't want to go back to Oxford, Lyra. It seems that there is something to be done in another world, and Lord Asriel is the only one who can bridge the gulf between that world and this. But he needs something to help him."

"The alethiometer!" Lyra said. "The Master of Jordan gave it to me and I thought there was something he wanted to say about Lord Asriel, except he never had the chance. I knew he didn't *really* want to poison him. Is he going to read it and see how to make the bridge? I bet I could help him. I can probably read it as good as anyone now."

"I don't know," said Serafina Pekkala. "How he'll do it, and what his task will be, we can't tell. There are powers who speak to us, and there are powers above them; and there are secrets even from the most high."

"The alethiometer would tell me! I could read it now…"

But it was too cold; she would never have managed to hold it. She bundled herself up and pulled the hood tight against the chill of the wind, leaving only a slit to look through. Far ahead, and a little below, the long rope extended from the suspension-ring of the balloon, pulled by six or seven witches sitting on their cloud-pine branches. The stars shone as bright and cold and hard as diamonds.

"Why en't you cold, Serafina Pekkala?"

"We feel cold, but we don't mind it, because we will not come to harm. And if we wrapped up against the cold, we wouldn't feel other things, like the bright tingle of the stars, or the music of the Aurora, or best of all the silky feeling of moonlight on our skin. It's worth being cold for that."

"Could I feel them?"

"No. You would die if you took your furs off. Stay wrapped up."

"How long do witches live, Serafina Pekkala? Farder Coram says hundreds of years. But you don't look old at all."

"I am three hundred years or more. Our oldest witch-mother is nearly a thousand. One day, Yambe-Akka will come for her. One day she'll come for me. She is the goddess of the dead. She comes to you smiling and kindly, and you know it is time to die."

"Are there men witches? Or only women?"

"There are men who serve us, like the Consul at Trollesund. And there are men we take for lovers or husbands. You are so young, Lyra, too young to understand this, but I shall tell you anyway and you'll understand it later: men pass in front of our eyes like butterflies, creatures of a brief season. We love them; they are brave, proud, beautiful, clever; and they die almost at once. They die so soon that our hearts are continually racked with pain. We bear their children, who are witches if they are female, human if not; and then in the blink of an eye they are gone, felled, slain, lost. Our sons, too. When a little boy is growing, he thinks he is immortal. His mother knows he isn't. Each time becomes more painful, until finally your heart is broken. Perhaps that is when Yambe-Akka comes for you. She is older than the tundra. Perhaps, for her, witches' lives are as brief as men's are to us."

"Did you love Farder Coram?"

"Yes. Does he know that?"

"I don't know, but I know he loves you."

"When he rescued me he was young and strong and full of pride and beauty. I loved him at once. I would have changed my nature, I would have forsaken the star-tingle and the music of the Aurora; I would never have flown again – I would have given all that up in a moment, without a thought, to be a gyptian boat-wife and cook for him and share his bed and bear his children. But you cannot change what you are, only what you do. I am a witch. He is a human. I stayed with him for long enough to bear him a child…"

"He never said! Was it a girl? A witch?"

"No. A boy, and he died in the great epidemic of forty years ago, the sickness that came out of the East. Poor little child; he flickered into life and out of it like a mayfly. And it tore pieces out of my heart, as it always does. It broke Coram's. And then the call came for me to return to my own people, because Yambe-Akka had taken my mother, and I was clan-queen. So I left, as I had to."

"Did you never see Farder Coram again?"

"Never. I heard of his deeds; I heard how he was wounded by the Skraelings, with a poisoned arrow, and I sent herbs and spells to help him recover, but I wasn't strong enough to see him. I heard how broken he was after that, and how his wisdom grew, how much he studied and read, and I was proud of him and his goodness. But I stayed away, for they were dangerous times for my clan, and witch-wars were threatening, and besides, I thought he would forget me and find a human wife…"

"He never would," said Lyra stoutly. "You oughter go and see him. He still loves you, I know he does."

"But he would be ashamed of his own age, and I wouldn't want to make him feel that."

"Perhaps he would. But you ought to send a message to him, at least. That's what I think."

Serafina Pekkala said nothing for a long time. Pantalaimon became a tern and flew to her branch for a second, to acknowledge that perhaps they had been insolent.

Then Lyra said, "Why do people have dæmons, Serafina Pekkala?"

"Everyone asks that, and no one knows the answer. As long as there have been human beings, there have been dæmons. It's what makes us different from animals."

"Yeah! We're different from them all right... Like bears. They're strange, en't they, bears? You think they're like a person, and then suddenly they do something so strange or ferocious you think you'll never understand them... But you know what Iorek said to me, he said that his armour for him was like what a dæmon is for a person. It's his soul, he said. But that's where they're different again, because he *made* this armour hisself. They took his first armour away when they sent him into exile, and he found some sky-iron and made some new armour, like making a new soul. We can't make our dæmons. Then the people at Trollesund, they got him drunk on spirits and stole it away, and I found out where it was and he got it back... But what I wonder is, why's he coming to Svalbard? They'll fight him. They might kill him... I love Iorek. I love him so much I wish he wasn't coming."

"Has he told you who he is?"

"Only his name. And it was the Consul at Trollesund who told us that."

"He is high-born. He is a prince. In fact, if he had not committed a great crime, he would be the king of the bears by now."

"He told me their king was called Iofur Raknison."

"Iofur Raknison became king when Iorek Byrnison was exiled. Iofur is a prince, of course, or he wouldn't be allowed to rule; but he is clever in a human way; he makes alliances and treaties; he lives not as bears do, in ice-forts, but in a new-built palace; he talks of exchanging ambassadors with human nations and developing the fire-mines with the help of human engineers... He is very skilful and subtle. Some say that he provoked Iorek into the deed for which he was exiled, and others say that even if he didn't, he encourages them to think he did, because it adds to his reputation for craft and subtlety."

"What *did* Iorek do? See, one reason I love Iorek, it's because of my father doing what *he* did and being punished. Seems to me they're like each other. Iorek told me he'd killed another bear, but he never said how it came about."

"The fight was over a she-bear. The male whom Iorek killed would not display the usual signals of surrender when it was clear that Iorek was stronger. For all their pride, bears never fail to recognize superior force in another bear and surrender to it, but for some reason this bear didn't do it. Some say that Iofur Raknison worked on his mind, or gave him confusing herbs to eat. At any rate, the young bear persisted, and Iorek Byrnison allowed his temper to master him. The case was not hard to judge; he should have wounded, not killed."

"So otherwise he'd be king," Lyra said. "And I heard something about Iofur Raknison from the Palmerian Professor at Jordan, 'cause he'd been to the North and met him. He said … I wish I could remember what it was … I think he'd tricked his way on to the throne or something… But you know, Iorek said to me once that bears couldn't be tricked, and showed me that I couldn't trick him. It sounds as if they was *both* tricked, him and the other bear. Maybe only bears can trick bears, maybe people can't. Except… The people at Trollesund, they tricked him, didn't they? When they got him drunk and stole his armour?"

"When bears act like people, perhaps they can be tricked," said Serafina Pekkala. "When bears act like bears, perhaps they can't. No bear would normally drink spirits. Iorek Byrnison drank to forget the shame of exile, and it was only that which let the Trollesund people trick him."

"Ah, yes," said Lyra, nodding. She was satisfied with that idea.

She admired Iorek almost without limit, and she was glad to find confirmation of his nobility. "That's clever of you," she said. "I wouldn't have known that if you hadn't told me. I think you're probably cleverer than Mrs Coulter."

They flew on. Lyra chewed some of the seal-meat she found in her pocket.

"Serafina Pekkala," she said after some time, "what's Dust? 'Cause it seems to me that all this trouble's about Dust, only no one's told me what it is."

"I don't know," Serafina Pekkala told her. "Witches have never worried about Dust. All I can tell you is that where there are priests, there is fear of Dust. Mrs Coulter is not a priest, of course, but she is a powerful agent of the Magisterium, and it was she who set up the Oblation Board and persuaded the Church to pay for Bolvangar, because of her interest in Dust. We can't understand her feelings about it. But there are many things we have never understood. We see the Tartars making holes in their skulls, and we can only wonder at the strangeness of it. So Dust may be strange, and we wonder at it, but we don't fret and tear things apart to examine it. Leave that to the Church."

"The Church?" said Lyra. Something had come back to her: she remembered talking with Pantalaimon, in the Fens, about what it might be that was moving the needle of the alethiometer, and they had thought of the photo-mill on the high altar at Gabriel College, and how elementary particles pushed the little vanes around. The Intercessor there was clear about the link between elementary particles and religion. "Could be," she said, nodding. "Most Church things, they keep secret, after all. But most Church things are old, and Dust en't old, as far as I know. I wonder if Lord Asriel might tell me…"

She yawned again.

"I better lie down," she said to Serafina Pekkala, "else I'll probably freeze. I been cold down on the ground, but I never been this cold. I think I might die if I get any colder."

"Then lie down and wrap yourself in the furs."

"Yeah, I will. If I was going to die, I'd rather die up here than down there, any day. I thought when they put us under that blade thing, I thought that was it... We both did. Oh, that was cruel. But we'll lie down now. Wake us up when we get there," she said, and got down on the pile of furs, clumsy and aching in every part of her with the profound intensity of the cold, and lay as close as she could to the sleeping Roger.

And so the four travellers sailed on, sleeping in the ice-encrusted balloon, towards the rocks and glaciers, the fire-mines and the ice-forts of Svalbard.

Serafina Pekkala called to the aëronaut, and he woke at once, groggy with cold, but aware from the movement of the basket that something was wrong. It was swinging wildly as strong winds buffeted the gas-bag, and the witches pulling the rope were barely managing to hold it. If they let go, the balloon would be swept off course at once, and to judge by his glance at the compass, would be swept towards Nova Zembla at nearly a hundred miles an hour.

"Where are we?" Lyra heard him call. She was half-waking herself, uneasy because of the motion, and so cold that every part of her body was numb.

She couldn't hear the witch's reply, but through her half-closed hood she saw, in the light of an anbaric lantern, Lee Scoresby hold on to a strut and pull at a rope leading up into the gas-bag itself. He gave a sharp tug as if against some obstruction, and looked up into the buffeting dark before looping the rope around a cleat on the suspension-ring.

"I'm letting out some gas," he shouted to Serafina Pekkala.

"We'll go down. We're way too high."

The witch called something in return, but again Lyra couldn't hear it. Roger was waking too; the creaking of the basket was enough to wake the deepest sleeper, never mind the rocking and bumping. Roger's dæmon and Pantalaimon clung together like marmosets, and Lyra concentrated on lying still and not leaping up in fear.

" 'S all right," Roger said, sounding much more cheerful than she was. "Soon's we get down we can make a fire and get warm. I got some matches in me pocket. I pinched 'em out of the kitchen at Bolvangar."

The balloon was certainly descending, because they were enveloped a second later in the thick freezing cloud. Scraps and wisps of it flew through the basket, and then everything was obscured, all at once. It was like the thickest fog Lyra had ever known. After a moment or two there came another cry from Serafina Pekkala, and the aëronaut unlooped the rope from the cleat and let go. It sprang upwards through his hands, and even over the creak and the buffeting and the howl of the wind through the rigging, Lyra heard or felt a mighty thump from somewhere far above.

Lee Scoresby saw her wide eyes.

"That's the gas-valve," he shouted. "It works on a spring to hold the gas in. When I pull it down, some gas escapes outa the top, and we lose buoyancy and go down."

"Are we nearly —"

She didn't finish, because something hideous happened. A creature half the size of a man, with leathery wings and hooked claws, was crawling over the side of the basket towards Lee Scoresby. It had a flat head, with bulging eyes and a wide frog-mouth, and from it came wafts of abominable stink. Lyra had no time to scream, even, before Iorek Byrnison reached up and cuffed it away. It fell out of the basket and vanished with a shriek.

"Cliff-ghast," said Iorek briefly.

The next moment Serafina Pekkala appeared, and clung to the side of the basket, speaking urgently.

"The cliff-ghasts are attacking. We'll bring the balloon to the ground, and then we must defend ourselves. They're –"

But Lyra didn't hear the rest of what was said, because there was a rending, ripping sound, and everything tilted sideways. Then a terrific blow hurled the three humans against the side of the balloon where Iorek Byrnison's armour was stacked. Iorek put out a great paw to hold them in, because the basket was jolting so violently. Serafina Pekkala had vanished. The noise was appalling: over every other sound there came the shrieking of the cliff-ghasts, and Lyra saw them hurtling past, and smelt their foul stench.

Then there came another jerk, so sudden that it threw them all to the floor again, and the basket began to sink with frightening speed, spinning all the while. It felt as if they had torn loose from the balloon, and were dropping unchecked by anything; and then came another series of jerks and crashes, the basket being tossed rapidly from side to side as if they were bouncing between rock walls.

The last thing Lyra saw was Lee Scoresby firing his long-barrelled pistol directly in the face of a cliff-ghast; and then she shut her eyes tight, and clung to Iorek Byrnison's fur with passionate fear. Howls, shrieks, the lash and whistle of the wind, the creak of the basket like a tormented animal, all filled the wild air with hideous noise.

Then came the biggest jolt of all, and she found herself hurled out altogether. Her grip was torn loose, and all the breath was knocked out of her lungs as she landed in such a tangle that she couldn't tell which way was up; and her face in the tight-pulled hood was full of powder, dry, cold, crystals –

It was snow; she had landed in a snow-drift. She was so battered that she could hardly think. She lay quite still for several seconds before feebly spitting out the snow in her mouth, and then she blew just as feebly until there was a little space to breathe in.

Nothing seemed to be *hurting* in particular; she just felt utterly breathless. Cautiously she tried to move hands, feet, arms, legs, and to raise her head.

She could see very little, because her hood was still filled with snow. With an effort, as if her hands weighed a ton each, she brushed it off and peered out. She saw a world of grey, of pale greys and dark greys and blacks, where fog-drifts wandered like wraiths.

The only sounds she could hear were the distant cries of the cliff-ghasts, high above, and the crash of waves on rocks, some way off.

"Iorek!" she cried. Her voice was faint and shaky, and she tried again, but no one answered. "Roger!" she called, with the same result.

She might have been alone in the world, but of course she never was, and Pantalaimon crept out of her anorak as a mouse to keep her company.

"I've checked the alethiometer," he said, "and it's all right. Nothing's broken."

"We're lost, Pan!" she said. "Did you see those cliff-ghasts? And Mr Scoresby shooting 'em? God help us if they come down here…"

"We better try and find the basket," he said, "maybe."

"We better not call out," she said. "I did just now, but maybe I better not in case they hear us. I wish I knew where we were."

"We might not like it if we did," he pointed out. "We might be at the bottom of a cliff with no way up, and the cliff-ghasts at the top to see us when the fog clears."

She felt around, once she had rested a few more minutes, and found that she had landed in a gap between two ice-covered rocks. Freezing fog covered everything; to one side there was the crash of waves about fifty yards off, by the sound of it, and from high above there still came the shrieking of the cliff-ghasts, though that seemed to be abating a little. She could see no more than two or three yards in the murk, and even Pantalaimon's owl-eyes were helpless.

She made her way painfully, slipping and sliding on the rough rocks, away from the waves and up the beach a little, and found nothing but rocks and snow, and no sign of the balloon or any of the occupants.

"They *can't* have all just vanished," she whispered.

Pantalaimon prowled cat-formed a little further afield, and came across four heavy sand-bags broken open, with the scattered sand already freezing hard.

"Ballast," Lyra said. "He must've slung 'em off to fly up again…"

She swallowed hard to subdue the lump in her throat, or the fear in her breast, or both.

"Oh, God, I'm frightened," she said. "I hope they're safe."

He came to her arms and then, mouse-formed, crept into her hood where he couldn't be seen. She heard a noise, something scraping on rock, and turned to see what it was.

"Iorek!"

But she choked the word back unfinished, for it wasn't Iorek Byrnison at all. It was a strange bear, clad in polished armour with the dew on it frozen into frost, and with a plume in his helmet.

He stood still, about six feet away, and she thought she really was finished.

The bear opened his mouth and roared. An echo came back

from the cliffs and stirred more shrieking from far above. Out of the fog came another bear, and another. Lyra stood still, clenching her little human fists.

The bears didn't move until the first one said, "Your name?"

"Lyra."

"Where have you come from?"

"The sky."

"In a balloon?"

"Yes."

"Come with us. You are a prisoner. Move, now. Quickly."

Weary and scared, Lyra began to stumble over the harsh and slippery rocks, following the bear, wondering how she could talk her way out of this.

19
Captivity

The bears took Lyra up a gully in the cliffs, where the fog lay even more thickly than on the shore. The cries of the cliff-ghasts and the crash of the waves grew fainter as they climbed, and presently the only sound was the ceaseless crying of seabirds. They clambered in silence over rocks and snowdrifts, and although Lyra peered wide-eyed into the enfolding greyness, and strained her ears for the sound of her friends, she might have been the only human on Svalbard; and Iorek might have been dead.

The bear-sergeant said nothing to her until they were on level ground. There they stopped. From the sound of the waves, Lyra judged them to have reached the top of the cliffs, and she dared not run away in case she fell over the edge.

"Look up," said the bear, as a waft of breeze moved aside the heavy curtain of the fog.

There was little daylight in any case, but Lyra did look, and found herself standing in front of a vast building of stone. It was as tall at least as the highest part of Jordan College, but much more massive, and carved all over with representations of warfare, showing bears victorious and Skraelings surrendering, showing Tartars chained and slaving in the fire-mines, showing zeppelins flying from all parts of the world bearing gifts and tributes to the king of the bears, Iofur Raknison.

At least, that was what the bear-sergeant told her the carvings showed. She had to take his word for it, because every projection and ledge on the deeply sculpted façade was occupied by gannets and skuas, which cawed and shrieked and wheeled constantly around overhead, and whose droppings had coated every part of the building with thick smears of dirty white.

The bears seemed not to see the mess, however, and they led the way in through the huge arch, over the icy ground that was filthy with the spatter of the birds. There was a courtyard, and high steps, and gateways, and at every point bears in armour challenged the incomers and were given a password. Their armour was polished and gleaming, and they all wore plumes in their helmets. Lyra couldn't help comparing every bear she saw with Iorek Byrnison, and always to his advantage; he was more powerful, more graceful, and his armour was real armour, rust-coloured, blood-stained, dented with combat, not elegant, enamelled and decorative like most of what she saw around her now.

As they went further in, the temperature rose, and so did something else. The smell in Iofur's palace was repulsive: rancid seal-fat, dung, blood, refuse of every sort. Lyra pushed back her hood to be cooler, but she couldn't help wrinkling her nose. She hoped bears couldn't read human expressions. There were iron brackets every few yards, holding blubber-lamps, and in their flaring shadows it wasn't always easy to see where she was treading, either.

Finally they stopped outside a heavy door of iron. A guard-bear pulled back a massive bolt, and the sergeant suddenly swung his head at Lyra, knocking her head over heels through the doorway. Before she could scramble up, she heard the door being bolted behind her.

It was profoundly dark, but Pantalaimon became a firefly, and shed a tiny glow around them. They were in a narrow cell where the walls dripped with damp, and there was one stone bench for furniture. In the furthest corner there was a heap of rags she took for bedding, and that was all she could see.

Lyra sat down, with Pantalaimon on her shoulder, and felt in her clothes for the alethiometer.

"It's certainly had a lot of banging about, Pan," she whispered. "I hope it still works."

Pantalaimon flew down to her wrist and sat there glowing, while Lyra composed her mind. With a part of her, she found it remarkable that she could sit here in terrible danger and yet sink into the calm she needed to read the alethiometer; and yet it was so much a part of her now that the most complicated questions sorted themselves out into their constituent symbols as naturally as her muscles moved her limbs: she hardly had to think about them.

She turned the hands and thought the question: "Where is Iorek?"

The answer came at once: "A day's journey away, carried there by the balloon after your crash; but hurrying this way."

"And Roger?"

"With Iorek."

"What will Iorek do?"

"He intends to break into the palace and rescue you, in the face of all the difficulties."

She put the alethiometer away, even more anxious than before.

"They won't let him, will they?" she said. "There's too many of 'em. I wish I was a witch, Pan, then you could go off and find him and take messages and all, and we could make a proper plan…"

Then she had the fright of her life.

A man's voice spoke in the darkness a few feet away, and said, "Who are you?"

She leapt up with a cry of alarm. Pantalaimon became a bat at once, shrieking, and flew around her head as she backed against the wall.

"Eh? Eh?" said the man again. "Who is that? Speak up! Speak up!"

"Be a firefly again, Pan," she said shakily. "But don't go too close."

The little wavering point of light danced through the air and fluttered around the head of the speaker. And it hadn't been a heap of rags after all: it was a grey-bearded man chained to the wall, whose eyes glittered in Pantalaimon's luminance, and whose tattered hair hung over his shoulders. His dæmon, a weary-looking serpent, lay in his lap, flicking out her tongue occasionally as Pantalaimon flew near.

"What's your name?" she said.

"Jotham Santelia," he replied. "I am the Regius Professor of Cosmology at the University of Gloucester. Who are you?"

"Lyra Belacqua. What have they locked you up for?"

"Malice and jealousy… Where do you come from? Eh?"

"From Jordan College," she said.

"What? Oxford?"

"Yes."

"Is that scoundrel Trelawney still there? Eh?"

"The Palmerian Professor? Yes," she said.

"Is he, by God! Eh? They should have forced his resignation long ago. Duplicitous plagiarist! Coxcomb!"

Lyra made a neutral sound.

"Has he published his paper on gamma-ray photons yet?" the Professor said, thrusting his face up towards Lyra's.

She moved back.

"I don't know," she said and then, making it up out of pure habit, "no," she went on. "I remember now. He said he still needed to check some figures. And … he said he was going to write about Dust as well. That's it."

"Scoundrel! Thief! Blackguard! Rogue!" shouted the old man, and he shook so violently that Lyra was afraid he'd have a fit. His dæmon slithered lethargically off his lap as the Professor beat his fists against his shanks. Drops of saliva flew out of his mouth.

"Yeah," said Lyra, "I always thought he was a thief. And a rogue and all that."

If it was unlikely for a scruffy little girl to turn up in his cell knowing the very man who figured in his obsessions, the Regius Professor didn't notice. He *was* mad, and no wonder, poor old man; but he might have some scraps of information that Lyra could use.

She sat carefully near him, not near enough for him to touch, but near enough for Pantalaimon's tiny light to show him clearly.

"One thing Professor Trelawney used to boast about," she said, "was how well he knew the king of the bears –"

"Boast! Eh? Eh? I should say he boasts! He's nothing but a popinjay! And a pirate! Not a scrap of original research to his name! Everything filched from better men!"

"Yeah, that's right," said Lyra earnestly. "And when he does do something of his own, he gets it wrong."

"Yes! Yes! Absolutely! No talent, no imagination, a fraud from top to bottom!"

"I mean, for example," said Lyra, "I bet you know more about the bears than he does, for a start."

"Bears," said the old man, "ha! I could write a treatise on them! That's why they shut me away, you know."

"Why's that?"

"I know too much about them, and they daren't kill me. They daren't do it, much as they'd like to. I know, you see. I have friends. Yes! Powerful friends."

"Yeah," said Lyra. "And I bet you'd be a wonderful teacher," she went on. "Being as you got so much knowledge and experience."

Even in the depths of his madness a little common sense still flickered, and he looked at her sharply, almost as if he suspected her of sarcasm. But she had been dealing with suspicious and cranky scholars all her life, and she gazed back with such bland admiration that he was soothed.

"Teacher," he said, "teacher… Yes, I could teach. Give me the right pupil, and I will light a fire in his mind!"

"Because your knowledge ought not to just vanish," Lyra said encouragingly. "It ought to be passed on so people remember you."

"Yes," he said, nodding seriously. "That's very perceptive of you, child. What is your name?"

"Lyra," she told him again. "Could you teach me about the bears?"

"The bears…" he said doubtfully.

"I'd really like to know about cosmology and Dust and all, but I'm not clever enough for that. You need really clever students for that. But I could learn about the bears. You could teach me about them all right. And we could sort of practise on that and work up to Dust, maybe."

He nodded again.

"Yes," he said, "yes, I believe you're right. There is a correspondence between the microcosm and the macrocosm! The stars are alive, child. Did you know that? Everything out there is alive, and there are grand purposes abroad! The universe is full of *intentions*, you know. Everything happens for a purpose. Your purpose is to remind me of that. Good, good – in my despair I had forgotten. Good! Excellent, my child!"

"So, have you seen the king? Iofur Raknison?"

"Yes. Oh, yes. I came here at his invitation, you know. He intended to set up a university. He was going to make me Vice-Chancellor. That would be one in the eye for the Royal Arctic Society, eh! Eh? And that scoundrel Trelawney! Ha!"

"What happened?"

"I was betrayed by lesser men. Trelawney among them, of course. He was here, you know. On Svalbard. Spread lies and calumny about my qualifications. Calumny! Slander! Who was it discovered the final proof of the Barnard-Stokes hypothesis, eh? Eh? Yes, Santelia, that's who. Trelawney couldn't take it. Lied through his teeth. Iofur Raknison had me thrown in here. I'll be out one day, you'll see. I'll be Vice-Chancellor, oh yes. Let Trelawney come to me then begging for mercy! Let the Publications Committee of the Royal Arctic Society spurn my contributions then! Ha! I'll expose them all!"

"I expect Iorek Byrnison will believe you, when he comes back," Lyra said.

"Iorek Byrnison? No good waiting for that. *He'll* never come back."

"He's on his way now."

"Then they'll kill him. He's not a bear, you see. He's an outcast. Like me. Degraded, you see. Not entitled to any of the privileges of a bear."

"Supposing Iorek Byrnison did come back, though," Lyra said. "Supposing he challenged Iofur Raknison to a fight…"

"Oh, they wouldn't allow it," said the Professor decisively. "Iofur would never lower himself to acknowledge Iorek Byrnison's right to fight him. Hasn't *got* a right. Iorek might as well be a seal now, or a walrus, not a bear. Or worse: Tartar or

Skraeling. They wouldn't fight him honourably like a bear; they'd kill him with fire-hurlers before he got near. Not a hope. No mercy."

"Oh," said Lyra, with a heavy despair in her breast. "And what about the bears' other prisoners? Do you know where they keep them?"

"Other prisoners?"

"Like … Lord Asriel."

Suddenly the Professor's manner changed altogether. He cringed and shrank back against the wall, and shook his head warningly.

"Sssh! Quiet! They'll hear you!" he whispered.

"Why mustn't we mention Lord Asriel?"

"Forbidden! Very dangerous! Iofur Raknison will not allow him to be mentioned!"

"Why?" Lyra said, coming closer and whispering herself so as not to alarm him.

"Keeping Lord Asriel prisoner is a special charge laid on Iofur by the Oblation Board," the old man whispered back. "Mrs Coulter herself came here to see Iofur and offered him all kinds of rewards to keep Lord Asriel out of the way. I know about it, you see, because at the time I was in Iofur's favour myself. I met Mrs Coulter! Yes. Had a long conversation with her. Iofur was besotted with her. Couldn't stop talking about her. Would do anything for her. If she wants Lord Asriel kept a hundred miles away, that's what will happen. Anything for Mrs Coulter, anything. He's going to name his capital city after her, did you know that?"

"So he wouldn't let anyone go and see Lord Asriel?"

"No! Never! But he's afraid of Lord Asriel too, you know. Iofur's playing a difficult game. But he's clever. He's done what they both want. He's kept Lord Asriel isolated, to please Mrs

Coulter; and he's let Lord Asriel have all the equipment he wants, to please *him*. Can't last, this equilibrium. Unstable. Pleasing both sides. Eh? The wave function of this situation is going to collapse quite soon. I have it on good authority."

"Really?" said Lyra, her mind elsewhere, furiously thinking about what he'd just said.

"Yes. My dæmon's tongue can taste probability, you know."

"Yeah. Mine too. When do they feed us, Professor?"

"Feed us?"

"They must put some food in sometime, else we'd starve. And there's bones on the floor. I expect they're seal bones, aren't they?"

"Seal ... I don't know. It might be."

Lyra got up and felt her way to the door. There was no handle, naturally, and no keyhole, and it fitted so closely at top and bottom that no light showed. She pressed her ear to it, but heard nothing. Behind her the old man was muttering to himself. She heard his chain rattle as he turned over wearily and lay the other way, and presently he began to snore.

She felt her way back to the bench. Pantalaimon, tired of putting out light, had become a bat, which was all very well for him; he fluttered around squeaking quietly while Lyra sat and chewed a fingernail.

Quite suddenly, with no warning at all, she remembered what it was that she'd heard the Palmerian Professor saying in the Retiring Room all that time ago. Something had been nagging at her ever since Iorek Byrnison had first mentioned Iofur's name, and now it came back: what Iofur Raknison wanted more than anything else, Professor Trelawney had said, was a dæmon.

Of course, she hadn't understood what he meant; he'd spoken of *panserbjørne* instead of using the English word, so she didn't know he was talking about bears, and she had no idea that Iofur

Raknison wasn't a man. And a man would have had a dæmon anyway, so it hadn't made sense.

But now it was plain. Everything she'd heard about the bear-king added up: the mighty Iofur Raknison wanted nothing more than to be a human being, with a dæmon of his own.

And as she thought that, a plan came to her: a way of making Iofur Raknison do what he would normally never have done; a way of restoring Iorek Byrnison to his rightful throne; a way, finally, of getting to the place where they had put Lord Asriel, and taking him the alethiometer.

The idea hovered and shimmered delicately, like a soap bubble, and she dared not even look at it directly in case it burst. But she was familiar with the way of ideas, and she let it shimmer, looking away, thinking about something else.

She was nearly asleep when the bolts clattered and the door opened. Light spilled in, and she was on her feet at once, with Pantalaimon hidden swiftly in her pocket.

As soon as the bear-guard bent his head to lift the haunch of seal-meat and throw it in, she was at his side, saying:

"Take me to Iofur Raknison. You'll be in trouble if you don't. It's very urgent."

He dropped the meat from his jaws and looked up. It wasn't easy to read bears' expressions, but he looked angry.

"It's about Iorek Byrnison," she said quickly. "I know something about him, and the king needs to know."

"Tell me what it is, and I'll pass the message on," said the bear.

"That wouldn't be right, not for someone else to know before the king does," she said. "I'm sorry, I don't mean to be rude, but you see, it's the rule that the king has to know things first."

Perhaps he was slow-witted. At any rate, he paused, and then threw the meat into the cell before saying, "Very well. You come with me."

He led her out into the open air, for which she was grateful. The fog had lifted and there were stars glittering above the high-walled courtyard. The guard conferred with another bear, who came to speak to her.

"You cannot see Iofur Raknison when you please," he said. "You have to wait till he wants to see you."

"But this is urgent, what I've got to tell him," she said. "It's about Iorek Byrnison. I'm sure His Majesty would want to know it, but all the same I can't tell it to anyone else, don't you see? It wouldn't be polite. He'd be ever so cross if he knew we hadn't been polite."

That seemed to carry some weight, or else to mystify the bear sufficiently to make him pause. Lyra was sure her interpretation of things was right: Iofur Raknison was introducing so many new ways that none of the bears was certain yet how to behave, and she could exploit this uncertainty in order to get to Iofur.

So that bear retreated to consult the bear above him, and before long Lyra was ushered inside the Palace again, but into the State quarters this time. It was no cleaner here, and in fact the air was even harder to breathe than in the cell, because all the natural stinks had been overlaid by a heavy layer of cloying perfume. She was made to wait in the corridor, then in an ante-room, then outside a large door, while bears discussed and argued and scurried back and forth, and she had time to look around at the preposterous decoration: the walls were rich with gilt plasterwork, some of which was already peeling off or crumbling with damp, and the florid carpets were trodden with filth.

Finally the large door was opened from the inside. A blaze of light from half a dozen chandeliers, a crimson carpet, and more of that thick perfume hanging in the air; and the faces of a dozen or more bears, all gazing at her, none in armour but each with some kind of decoration: a golden necklace, a head-dress of purple feathers, a crimson sash. Curiously, the room was also occupied by birds; terns and skuas perched on the plaster cornice, and swooped low to snatch at bits of fish that had fallen out of one another's nests in the chandeliers.

And on a dais at the far end of the room, a mighty throne reared up high. It was made of granite for strength and massiveness, but like so many other things in Iofur's palace, it was decorated with over-elaborate swags and festoons of gilt that looked like tinsel on a mountainside.

Sitting on the throne was the biggest bear she had ever seen. Iofur Raknison was even taller and bulkier than Iorek, and his face was much more mobile and expressive, with a kind of humanness in it which she had never seen in Iorek's. When Iofur looked at her she seemed to see a man looking out of his eyes, the sort of man she had met at Mrs Coulter's, a subtle politician used to power. He was wearing a heavy gold chain around his neck, with a gaudy jewel hanging from it, and his claws – a good six inches long – were each covered in gold leaf. The effect was one of enormous strength and energy and craft; he was quite big enough to carry the absurd over-decoration; on him it didn't look preposterous, it looked barbaric and magnificent.

She quailed. Suddenly her idea seemed too feeble for words.

But she moved a little closer, because she had to, and then she saw that Iofur was holding something on his knee, as a human might let a cat sit there – or a dæmon.

It was a big stuffed doll, a manikin with a vacant stupid human face. It was dressed as Mrs Coulter would dress, and it had a sort of rough resemblance to her. He was pretending he had a dæmon. Then she knew she was safe.

She moved up close to the throne and bowed very low, with

Pantalaimon keeping quiet and still in her pocket.

"Our greetings to you, great King," she said quietly. "Or I mean *my* greetings, not his."

"Not whose?" he said, and his voice was lighter than she had thought it would be, but full of expressive tones and subtleties. When he spoke, he waved a paw in front of his mouth to dislodge the flies that clustered there.

"Iorek Byrnison's, Your Majesty," she said. "I've got something very important and secret to tell you, and I think I ought to tell you in private, really."

"Something about Iorek Byrnison?"

She came close to him, stepping carefully over the bird-spattered floor, and brushed away the flies buzzing at her face.

"Something about dæmons," she said, so that only he could hear.

His expression changed. She couldn't read what it was saying, but there was no doubt that he was powerfully interested. Suddenly he lumbered forward off the throne, making her skip aside, and roared an order to the other bears. They all bowed their heads and backed out towards the door. The birds, which had risen in a flurry at his roar, squawked and swooped around overhead before settling again on their nests.

When the throne room was empty but for Iofur Raknison and Lyra, he turned to her eagerly.

"Well?" he said. "Tell me who you are. What is this about dæmons?"

"I *am* a dæmon, Your Majesty," she said.

He stopped still.

"Whose?" he said.

"Iorek Byrnison's," was her answer.

It was the most dangerous thing she had ever said. She could see quite clearly that only his astonishment prevented him from killing her on the spot. She went on at once:

"Please, Your Majesty, let me tell you all about it first before you harm me. I've come here at my own risk, as you can see, and there's nothing I've got that could hurt you. In fact I want to help you, that's why I've come. Iorek Byrnison was the first bear to get a dæmon, but it should have been you. I would much rather be your dæmon than his, that's why I came."

"How?" he said, breathlessly. "How has a bear got a dæmon? And why him? And how are you so far from him?"

The flies left his mouth like tiny words.

"That's easy. I can go far from him because I'm like a witch's dæmon. You know how they can go hundreds of miles from their humans? It's like that. And as for how he got me, it was at Bolvangar. You've heard of Bolvangar, because Mrs Coulter must have told you about it, but she probably didn't tell you everything they were doing there."

"Cutting…" he said.

"Yes, cutting, that's part of it, intercision. But they're doing all kinds of other things too, like making artificial dæmons. And experimenting on animals. When Iorek Byrnison heard about it he offered himself for an experiment to see if they could make a dæmon for him, and they did. It was me. My name is Lyra. Just like when people have dæmons, they're animal-formed, so when a bear has a dæmon, it'll be human. And I'm his dæmon. I can see into his mind and know exactly what he's doing and where he is and –"

"Where is he now?"

"On Svalbard. He's coming this way as fast as he can."

"Why? What does he want? He must be mad! We'll tear him to pieces!"

"He wants me. He's coming to get me back. But I don't want to be his dæmon, Iofur Raknison, I want to be yours. Because once they saw how powerful a bear was with a dæmon, the people at Bolvangar decided not to do that experiment ever again. Iorek Byrnison was going to be the only bear who ever had a dæmon. And with me helping him, he could lead all the bears against you. That's what he's come to Svalbard for."

The bear-king roared his anger. He roared so loudly that the crystal in the chandeliers tinkled, and every bird in the great room shrieked, and Lyra's ears rang.

But she was equal to it.

"That's why I love you best," she said to Iofur Raknison, "because you're passionate and strong as well as clever. And I just had to leave him and come and tell you, because I don't want him ruling the bears. It ought to be you. And there *is* a way of taking me away from him and making me your dæmon, but you wouldn't know what it was unless I told you, and you might do the usual thing about fighting bears like him that've been outcast; I mean, not fight him properly, but kill him with fire-hurlers or something. And if you did that, I'd just go out like a light and die with him."

"But you – how can –"

"I *can* become your dæmon," she said, "but only if you defeat Iorek Byrnison in single combat. Then his strength will flow into you, and my mind will flow into yours, and we'll be like one person, thinking each other's thoughts; and you can send me miles away to spy for you, or keep me here by your side, whichever you like. And I'd help you lead the bears to capture Bolvangar, if you like, and make them create more dæmons for your favourite bears; or if you'd rather be the only bear with a dæmon, we could destroy Bolvangar for ever. We could do anything, Iofur Raknison, you and me together!"

All the time she was holding Pantalaimon in her pocket with a trembling hand, and he was keeping as still as he could, in the smallest mouse-form he had ever assumed.

Iofur Raknison was pacing up and down with an air of explosive excitement.

"Single combat?" he was saying. "Me? I must fight Iorek Byrnison? Impossible! He is outcast! How can that be? How can I fight him? Is that the only way?"

"It's the only way," said Lyra, wishing it were not, because Iofur Raknison seemed bigger and more fierce every minute. Dearly as she loved Iorek, and strong as her faith was in him, she couldn't really believe that he would ever beat this giant among giant bears. But it was the only hope they had. Being mown down from a distance by fire-hurlers was no hope at all.

Suddenly Iofur Raknison turned.

"Prove it!" he said. "Prove that you are a dæmon!"

"All right," she said. "I can do that, easy. I can find out anything that you know and no one else does, something that only a dæmon would be able to find out."

"Then tell me what was the first creature I killed."

"I'll have to go into a room by myself to do this," she said. "When I'm your dæmon you'll be able to see how I do it, but until then it's got to be private."

"There is an ante-room behind this one. Go into that, and come out when you know the answer."

Lyra opened the door and found herself in a room lit by one torch, and empty but for a cabinet of mahogany containing some tarnished silver ornaments. She took out the alethiometer and asked: "Where is Iorek now?"

"Four hours away, and hurrying ever faster."

"How can I tell him what I've done?"

"You must trust him."

She thought anxiously of how tired he would be. But then she reflected that she was not doing what the alethiometer had just told her to do: she wasn't trusting him.

She put that thought aside and asked the question Iofur Raknison wanted. What was the first creature he had killed?

The answer came: Iofur's own father.

She asked further, and learned that Iofur had been alone on the ice as a young bear, on his first hunting expedition, and had come across a solitary bear. They had argued and fought, and Iofur had killed him. When he learned later that it was his own father (for bears were brought up by their mothers, and seldom saw their fathers) he concealed the truth of what he had done. No one knew about it but Iofur himself.

She put the alethiometer away, and wondered how to tell him about it.

"Flatter him!" whispered Pantalaimon. "That's all he wants."

So Lyra opened the door and found Iofur Raknison waiting for her, with an expression of triumph, slyness, apprehension, and greed.

"Well?"

She knelt down in front of him and bowed her head to touch his left forepaw, the stronger, for bears were left-handed.

"I beg your pardon, Iofur Raknison!" she said. "I didn't know you were so strong and great!"

"What's this? Answer my question!"

"The first creature you killed was your own father. I think you're a new god, Iofur Raknison. That's what you must be. Only a god would have the strength to do that."

"You know! You can see!"

"Yes, because I *am* a dæmon, like I said."

"Tell me one thing more. What did the Lady Coulter promise me when she was here?"

Once again Lyra went into the empty room and consulted the alethiometer before returning with the answer.

"She promised you that she'd get the Magisterium in Geneva to agree that you could be baptised as a Christian, even though you hadn't got a dæmon then. Well, I'm afraid that she hasn't done that, Iofur Raknison, and quite honestly I don't think they'd ever agree to that if you didn't have a dæmon. I think she knew that, and she wasn't telling you the truth. But in any case when you've got me as your dæmon you *could* be baptised if you wanted to, because no one could argue then. You could demand it and they wouldn't be able to turn you down."

"Yes... True. That's what she said. True, every word. And she has deceived me? I trusted her, and she deceived me?"

"Yes, she did. But she doesn't matter any more. Excuse me, Iofur Raknison. I hope you won't mind me telling you, but Iorek Byrnison's only four hours away now, and maybe you better tell your guard bears not to attack him as they normally would. If you're going to fight him for me he'll have to be allowed to come to the Palace."

"Yes..."

"And maybe when he comes I better pretend I still belong to him, and say I got lost or something. He won't know. I'll pretend. Are you going to tell the other bears about me being Iorek's dæmon and then belonging to you when you beat him?"

"I don't know... What should I do?"

"I don't think you better mention it yet. Once we're together, you and me, we can think what's best to do and decide then. What you need to do now is explain to all the other bears why you're going to let Iorek fight you like a proper bear, even though he's an outcast. Because they won't understand, and we got to find a reason for that. I mean, they'll do what you tell them anyway, but if they see the reason for it, they'll admire you even more."

"Yes. What should we tell them?"

"Tell them… Tell them that to make your kingdom completely secure, you've called Iorek Byrnison here yourself to fight him, and the winner will rule over the bears for ever. See, if you make it look like *your* idea that he's coming, and not his, they'll be really impressed. They'll think you're able to call him here from far away. They'll think you can do anything."

"Yes…"

The great bear was helpless. Lyra found her power over him almost intoxicating, and if Pantalaimon hadn't nipped her hand sharply to remind her of the danger they were all in, she might have lost all her sense of proportion.

But she came to herself and stepped modestly back to watch and wait as the bears, under Iofur's excited direction, prepared the combat-ground for Iorek Byrnison; and meanwhile Iorek, knowing nothing about it, was hurrying ever closer towards what she wished she could tell him was a fight for his life.

20

À Outrance

Fights between bears were common, and the subject of much ritual. For a bear to kill another was rare, though, and when that happened it was usually by accident, or when one bear mistook the signals from another, as in the case of Iorek Byrnison. Cases of straightforward murder, like Iofur's killing of his own father, were rarer still.

But occasionally there came circumstances in which the only way of settling a dispute was a fight to the death. And for that, a whole ceremonial was prescribed.

As soon as Iofur announced that Iorek Byrnison was on his way, and a combat would take place, the combat-ground was swept and smoothed, and armourers came up from the fire-mines to check Iofur's armour. Every rivet was examined, every link tested, and the plates were burnished with the finest sand. Just as much attention was paid to his claws. The gold leaf was rubbed off, and each separate six-inch hook was sharpened and filed to a deadly point. Lyra watched with a growing sickness in the pit of her stomach, for Iorek Byrnison wouldn't be having this attention; he had been marching over the ice for nearly twenty-four hours already without rest or food; he might have been injured in the crash. And she had let him in for this fight without his knowledge. At one point, after Iofur Raknison had tested the sharpness of his claws on a fresh-killed walrus, slicing its skin open like paper, and the power of his crashing blows on the walrus's skull (two blows, and it was cracked like an egg), Lyra had to make an excuse to Iofur and go away by herself to weep with fear.

Even Pantalaimon, who could normally cheer her up, had little to say that was hopeful. All she could do was consult the alethiometer: he is an hour away, it told her, and again, she must trust him; and (this was harder to read) she even thought it was rebuking her for asking the same question twice.

By this time, word had spread among the bears, and every part of the combat ground was crowded. Bears of high rank had the best places, and there was a special enclosure for the she-bears, including of course Iofur's wives. Lyra was profoundly curious about she-bears, because she knew so little about them, but this was no time to wander about asking questions. Instead she stayed close to Iofur Raknison and watched the courtiers around him assert their rank over the common bears from outside, and tried to guess the meaning of the various plumes and badges and tokens they all seemed to wear. Some of the highest-ranking, she saw, carried little manikins like Iofur's rag-doll dæmon, trying to curry favour, perhaps, by imitating the fashion he'd begun. She was sardonically pleased to notice that when they saw that Iofur had discarded his, they didn't know what to do with theirs. Should they throw them away? Were they out of favour now? How should they behave?

Because that was the prevailing mood in his court, she was beginning to see. They weren't sure what they were. They weren't like Iorek Byrnison, pure and certain and absolute; there was a constant pall of uncertainty hanging over them, as they watched one another and watched Iofur.

343

And they watched her, with open curiosity. She remained modestly close to Iofur and said nothing, lowering her eyes whenever a bear looked at her.

The fog had lifted by this time, and the air was clear; and as chance would have it, the brief lifting of darkness towards noon coincided with the time Lyra thought Iorek was going to arrive. As she stood shivering on a little rise of dense-packed snow at the edge of the combat-ground, she looked up towards the faint lightness in the sky, and longed with all her heart to see a flight of ragged elegant black shapes descending to bear her away; or to see the Aurora's hidden city, where she would be able to walk safely along those broad boulevards in the sunlight; or to see Ma Costa's broad arms, to smell the friendly smells of flesh and cooking that enfolded you in her presence…

She found herself crying, with tears which froze almost as soon as they formed, and which she had to brush away painfully. She was so frightened. Bears, who didn't cry, couldn't understand what was happening to her; it was some human process, meaningless. And of course Pantalaimon couldn't comfort her as he normally would, though she kept her hand in her pocket firmly around his warm little mouse-form, and he nuzzled at her fingers.

Beside her, the smiths were making the final adjustments to Iofur Raknison's armour. He reared like a great metal tower, shining in polished steel, the smooth plates inlaid with wires of gold; his helmet enclosed the upper part of his head in a glistening carapace of silver-grey, with deep eye-slits; and the underside of his body was protected by a close-fitting sark of chain-mail. It was when she saw this that Lyra realized that she had betrayed Iorek Byrnison, for Iorek had nothing like it. His armour protected only his back and sides. She looked at Iofur

Raknison, so sleek and powerful, and felt a deep sickness in her, like guilt and fear combined.

She said, "Excuse me, Your Majesty, if you remember what I said to you before…"

Her shaking voice felt thin and weak in the air. Iofur Raknison turned his mighty head, distracted from the target three bears were holding up in front for him to slash at with his perfect claws.

"Yes? Yes?"

"Remember, I said I'd better go and speak to Iorek Byrnison first, and pretend –"

But before she could even finish her sentence, there was a roar from the bears on the watch-tower. The others all knew what it meant and took it up with a triumphant excitement. They had seen Iorek.

"Please?" Lyra said urgently. "I'll fool him, you'll see."

"Yes. Yes. Go now. Go and *encourage* him!"

Iofur Raknison was hardly able to speak for rage and excitement.

Lyra left his side and walked across the combat-ground, bare and clear as it was, leaving her little footprints in the snow, and the bears on the far side parted to let her through. As their great bodies lumbered aside, the horizon opened, gloomy in the pallor of the light. Where was Iorek Byrnison? She could see nothing; but then, the watch-tower was high, and they could see what was still hidden from her. All she could do was walk forward in the snow.

He saw her before she saw him. There was a bounding and a heavy clank of metal, and in a flurry of snow Iorek Byrnison stood beside her.

"Oh, Iorek! I've done a terrible thing! My dear, you're going to have to fight Iofur Raknison, and you en't ready – you're tired and hungry, and your armour's –"

"What terrible thing?"

"I told him you was coming, because I read it on the symbol-reader; and he's desperate to be like a person and have a dæmon, just desperate. So I tricked him into thinking that I was your dæmon, and I was going to desert you and be his instead, but he had to fight you to make it happen. Because otherwise, Iorek, dear, they'd never let you fight, they were going to just burn you up before you got close –"

"You tricked Iofur Raknison?"

"Yes. I made him agree that he'd fight you instead of just killing you straight off like an outcast, and the winner would be king of the bears. I had to do that, because –"

"Belacqua? No. You are Lyra Silvertongue," he said. "To fight him is all I want. Come, little dæmon."

She looked at Iorek Byrnison in his battered armour, lean and ferocious, and felt as if her heart would burst with pride.

They walked together towards the massive hulk of Iofur's palace, where the combat-ground lay flat and open at the foot of the walls. Bears clustered at the battlements, white faces filled every window, and their heavy forms stood like a dense wall of misty white ahead, marked with the black dots of eyes and noses. The nearest ones moved aside, making two lines for Iorek Byrnison and his dæmon to walk between. Every bear's eyes were fixed on them.

Iorek halted across the combat-ground from Iofur Raknison. The king came down from the rise of trodden snow, and the two bears faced each other several yards apart.

Lyra was so close to Iorek that she could feel a trembling in him like a great dynamo, generating mighty anbaric forces. She touched him briefly on the neck at the edge of his helmet and said, "Fight well, Iorek, my dear. You're the real king, and he en't. He's nothing."

Then she stood back.

"Bears!" Iorek Byrnison roared. An echo rang back from the palace walls, and startled birds out of their nests. He went on, "The terms of this combat are these. If Iofur Raknison kills me, then he will be king for ever, safe from challenge or dispute. If I kill Iofur Raknison, I shall be your king. My first order to you all will be to tear down that palace, that perfumed house of mockery and tinsel, and hurl the gold and marble into the sea. Iron is bear-metal. Gold is not. Iofur Raknison has polluted Svalbard. I have come to cleanse it. Iofur Raknison, I challenge you."

Then Iofur bounded forward a step or two, as if he could hardly hold himself back.

"Bears!" he roared in his turn. "Iorek Byrnison has come back at my invitation. I drew him here. It is for me to make the terms of this combat, and they are these: if I kill Iorek Byrnison, his flesh shall be torn apart and scattered to the cliff-ghasts. His head shall be displayed above my palace. His memory shall be obliterated. It shall be a capital crime to speak his name…"

He continued, and then each bear spoke again. It was a formula, a ritual faithfully followed. Lyra looked at the two of them, so utterly different: Iofur so glossy and powerful, immense in his strength and health, splendidly armoured, proud and kinglike; and Iorek smaller, though she had never thought he would look small, and poorly equipped, his armour rusty and dented. But his armour was his soul. He had made it and it fitted him. They were one. Iofur was not content with his armour; he wanted another soul as well. He was restless while Iorek was still.

And she was aware that all the other bears were making the comparison too. But Iorek and Iofur were more than just two bears. There were two kinds of beardom opposed here, two futures, two destinies. Iofur had begun to take them in one direction, and Iorek would take them in another, and in the same moment, one future would close for ever as the other began to unfold.

As their ritual combat moved towards the second phase, the two bears began to prowl restlessly on the snow, edging forward, swinging their heads. There was not a flicker of movement from the spectators, but all eyes followed them.

Finally the warriors were still and silent, watching each other face to face across the width of the combat-ground.

Then with a roar and a blur of snow both bears moved at the same moment. Like two great masses of rock balanced on adjoining peaks and shaken loose by an earthquake, that bound down the mountainsides gathering speed, leaping over crevasses and knocking trees into splinters, until they crash into each other so hard that both are smashed to powder and flying chips of stone: that was how the two bears came together. The crash as they met resounded in the still air and echoed back from the Palace wall. But they weren't destroyed, as rock would have been. They both fell aside, and the first to rise was Iorek. He twisted up in a lithe spring and grappled with Iofur, whose armour had been damaged by the collision and who couldn't easily raise his head. Iorek made at once for the vulnerable gap at his neck. He raked the white fur, and then hooked his claws beneath the edge of Iofur's helmet and wrenched it forward.

Sensing the danger, Iofur snarled and shook himself as Lyra had seen Iorek shake himself at the water's edge, sending sheets of water flying high into the air. And Iorek fell away, dislodged, and with a screech of twisting metal Iofur stood up tall, straightening the steel of his back-plates by sheer strength. Then like an avalanche he hurled himself down on Iorek, who was still trying to rise.

Lyra felt her own breath knocked out of her by the force of that crashing fall. Certainly the very ground shook beneath her.

How could Iorek survive that? He was struggling to twist himself and gain a purchase on the ground, but his feet were uppermost, and Iofur had fixed his teeth somewhere near Iorek's throat. Drops of hot blood were flying through the air: one landed on Lyra's fur, and she pressed her hand to it like a token of love.

Then Iorek's rear claws dug into the links of Iofur's chain-mail sark and ripped downwards. The whole front came away, and Iofur lurched sideways to look at the damage, leaving Iorek to scramble upright again.

For a moment the two bears stood apart, getting their breath back. Iofur was hampered now by that chain-mail, because from a protection it had changed all at once into a hindrance: it was still fastened at the bottom, and trailed around his rear legs. However, Iorek was worse off. He was bleeding freely from a wound at his neck, and panting heavily.

But he leapt at Iofur before the king could disentangle himself from the clinging chain-mail, and knocked him head over heels, following up with a lunge at the bare part of Iofur's neck, where the edge of the helmet was bent. Iofur threw him off, and then the two bears were at each other again, throwing up fountains of snow that sprayed in all directions and sometimes made it hard to see who had the advantage.

Lyra watched, hardly daring to breathe, and squeezing her hands together so tight it hurt. She thought she saw Iofur tearing at a wound in Iorek's belly, but that couldn't be right, because a moment later, after another convulsive explosion of snow, both bears were standing upright like boxers, and Iorek was slashing with mighty claws at Iofur's face, with Iofur hitting back just as savagely.

Lyra trembled at the weight of those blows. As if a giant were swinging a sledgehammer, and that hammer were armed with five steel spikes...

Iron clanged on iron, teeth crashed on teeth, breath roared harshly, feet thundered on the hard-packed ground. The snow around was splashed with red and trodden down for yards into a crimson mud.

Iofur's armour was in a pitiful state by this time, the plates torn and distorted, the gold inlay torn out or smeared thickly with blood, and his helmet gone altogether. Iorek's was in much better condition, for all its ugliness: dented, but intact, standing up far better to the great sledgehammer-blows of the bear-king, and turning aside those brutal six-inch claws.

But against that, Iofur was bigger and stronger than Iorek, and Iorek was weary and hungry, and had lost more blood. He was wounded in the belly, on both arms, and at the neck, whereas Iofur was bleeding only from his lower jaw. Lyra longed to help her dear friend, but what could she do?

And it was going badly for Iorek now. He was limping; every time he put his left forepaw on the ground, they could see that it hardly bore his weight. He never used it to strike with, and the blows from his right hand were feebler, too, almost little pats compared with the mighty crushing buffets he'd delivered only a few minutes before.

Iofur had noticed. He began to taunt Iorek, calling him broken-hand, whimpering cub, rust-eaten, soon-to-die, and other names, all the while swinging blows at him from right and left which Iorek could no longer parry. Iorek had to move backwards, a step at a time, and to crouch low under the rain of blows from the jeering bear-king.

Lyra was in tears. Her dear, her brave one, her fearless defender, was going to die, and she would not do him the treachery of looking away, for if he looked at her he must see her shining eyes and their love and belief, not a face hidden in cowardice or a shoulder fearfully turned away.

So she looked, but her tears kept her from seeing what was really happening, and perhaps it would not have been visible to her anyway. It certainly was not seen by Iofur.

Because Iorek was moving backwards only to find clean dry footing and a firm rock to leap up from, and the useless left arm was really fresh and strong. You could not trick a bear, but, as Lyra had showed him, Iofur did not want to be a bear, he wanted to be a man; and Iorek was tricking him.

At last he found what he wanted: a firm rock deep-anchored in the permafrost. He backed against it, tensing his legs and choosing his moment.

It came when Iofur reared high above, bellowing his triumph, and turning his head tauntingly towards Iorek's apparently weak left side.

That was when Iorek moved. Like a wave that has been building its strength over a thousand miles of ocean, and which makes little stir in the deep water, but which when it reaches the shallows rears itself up high into the sky, terrifying the shore-dwellers, before crashing down on the land with irresistible power – so Iorek Byrnison rose up against Iofur, exploding upwards from his firm footing on the dry rock and slashing with a ferocious left hand at the exposed jaw of Iofur Raknison.

It was a horrifying blow. It tore the lower part of his jaw clean off, so that it flew through the air scattering blood-drops in the snow many yards away.

Iofur's red tongue lolled down dripping over his open throat. The bear-king was suddenly voiceless, biteless, helpless. Iorek needed nothing more. He lunged, and then his teeth were in Iofur's throat, and he shook and shook this way, that way, lifting the huge body off the ground and battering it down as if Iofur were no more than a seal at the water's edge.

Then he ripped upwards, and Iofur Raknison's life came away in his teeth.

There was one ritual yet to perform. Iorek sliced open the dead king's unprotected chest, peeling the fur back to expose the narrow white and red ribs like the timbers of an upturned boat. Into the ribcage Iorek reached, and he plucked out Iofur's heart, red and steaming, and ate it there in front of Iofur's subjects.

Then there was acclamation, pandemonium, a crush of bears surging forward to pay homage to Iofur's conqueror.

Iorek Byrnison's voice rose above the clamour.

"Bears! Who is your king?"

And the cry came back, in a roar like that of all the shingle in the world in an ocean-battering storm:

"Iorek Byrnison!"

The bears knew what they must do. Every single badge and sash and coronet was thrown off at once and trampled contemptuously underfoot, to be forgotten in a moment. They were Iorek's bears now, and true bears, not uncertain semi-humans, conscious only of a torturing inferiority. They swarmed to the Palace and began to hurl great blocks of marble from the topmost towers, rocking the battlemented walls in their mighty fists until the stones came loose and then hurling them over the cliffs to crash on the jetty hundreds of feet below.

Iorek ignored them and unhooked his armour to attend to his wounds, but before he could begin, Lyra was beside him, stamping her foot on the frozen scarlet snow and shouting to the bears to stop smashing the Palace, because there were prisoners inside. They didn't hear, but Iorek did, and when he roared they stopped at once.

"Human prisoners?" Iorek said.

"Yes – Iofur Raknison put them in the dungeons – they ought

to come out first and get shelter somewhere, else they'll be killed with all the falling rocks –"

Iorek gave swift orders, and some bears hurried into the Palace to release the prisoners. Lyra turned to Iorek.

"Let me help you – I want to make sure you en't too badly hurt, Iorek dear – oh, I wish there was some bandages or something! That's an awful cut on your belly –"

A bear laid a mouthful of some stiff green stuff, thickly frosted, on the ground at Iorek's feet.

"Bloodmoss," said Iorek. "Press it in the wounds for me, Lyra. Fold the flesh over it and then hold some snow there till it freezes."

He wouldn't let any bears attend to him, despite their eagerness. Besides, Lyra's hands were deft, and she was desperate to help; so the little child bent over the great bear-king, packing in the bloodmoss and freezing the raw flesh till it stopped bleeding. When she had finished, her mittens were sodden with Iorek's blood, but his wounds were staunched.

And by that time the prisoners – a dozen or so men, shivering and blinking and huddling together – had come out. There was no point in talking to the Professor, Lyra decided, because the poor man was mad; and she would have liked to know who the other men were, but there were many other urgent things to do. And she didn't want to distract Iorek, who was giving rapid orders and sending bears scurrying this way and that, but she was anxious about Roger, and about Lee Scoresby and the witches, and she was hungry and tired... She thought the best thing she could do just then was to keep out of the way.

So she curled up in a quiet corner of the combat-ground with Pantalaimon as a wolverine to keep her warm, and piled snow over herself as a bear would do, and went to sleep.

* * *

Something nudged her foot, and a strange bear voice said, "Lyra Silvertongue, the king wants you."

She woke up nearly dead with cold, and couldn't open her eyes, for they had frozen shut; but Pantalaimon licked them to melt the ice on her eyelashes, and soon she was able to see the young bear speaking to her in the moonlight.

She tried to stand, but fell over twice.

The bear said, "Ride on me," and crouched to offer his broad back, and half-clinging, half-falling, she managed to stay on while he took her to a steep hollow, where many bears were assembled.

And among them was a small figure who ran towards her, and whose dæmon leapt up to greet Pantalaimon.

"Roger!" she said.

"Iorek Byrnison made me stay out there in the snow while he came to fetch you away – we fell out the balloon, Lyra! After you fell out we got carried miles and miles, and then Mr Scoresby let some more gas out and we crashed into a mountain, and we fell down such a slope like you never seen! And I don't know where Mr Scoresby is now, nor the witches. There was just me and Iorek Byrnison. He come straight back this way to look for you. And they told me about his fight…"

Lyra looked around. Under the direction of an older bear, the human prisoners were building a shelter out of driftwood and scraps of canvas. They seemed pleased to have some work to do. One of them was striking a flint to light a fire.

"There is food," said the young bear who had woken Lyra.

A fresh seal lay on the snow. The bear sliced it open with a claw and showed Lyra where to find the kidneys. She ate one raw: it was warm and soft and delicious beyond imagining.

"Eat the blubber too," said the bear, and tore off a piece for her. It tasted of cream flavoured with hazelnuts. Roger hesitated, but followed her example. They ate greedily, and within a very few minutes Lyra was fully awake and beginning to be warm.

Wiping her mouth, she looked around, but Iorek was not in sight.

"Iorek Byrnison is speaking with his counsellors," said the young bear. "He wants to see you when you have eaten. Follow me."

He led them over a rise in the snow to a spot where bears were beginning to build a wall of ice-blocks. Iorek sat at the centre of a group of older bears, and he rose to greet her.

"Lyra Silvertongue," he said. "Come and hear what I am being told."

He didn't explain her presence to the other bears, or perhaps they had learned about her already; but they made room for her and treated her with immense courtesy, as if she were a queen. She felt proud beyond measure to sit beside her friend Iorek Byrnison under the Aurora as it flickered gracefully in the polar sky, and join the conversation of the bears.

It turned out that Iofur Raknison's dominance over them had been like a spell. Some of them put it down to the influence of Mrs Coulter, who had visited him before Iorek's exile, though Iorek had not known about it, and given Iofur various presents.

"She gave him a drug," said one bear, "which he fed secretly to Hjalmur Hjalmurson, and made him forget himself."

Hjalmur Hjalmurson, Lyra gathered, was the bear whom Iorek had killed, and whose death had brought about his exile. So Mrs Coulter was behind that! And there was more.

"There are human laws that prevent certain things that she was planning to do, but human laws don't apply on Svalbard. She wanted to set up another station here like Bolvangar, only worse, and Iofur was going to allow her to do it, against all the custom of the bears; because humans have visited, or been imprisoned, but never lived and worked here. Little by little she was going to increase her power over Iofur Raknison, and his over us, until we were her creatures running back and forth at her bidding, and our only duty to guard the abomination she was going to create…"

That was an old bear speaking. His name was Søren Eisarson, and he was a counsellor, one who had suffered under Iofur Raknison.

"What is she doing now, Lyra?" said Iorek Byrnison. "Once she hears of Iofur's death, what will her plans be?"

Lyra took out the alethiometer. There was not much light to see it by, and Iorek commanded that a torch be brought.

"What happened to Mr Scoresby?" Lyra said while they were waiting. "And the witches?"

"The witches were attacked by another witch-clan. I don't know if the others were allied to the child-cutters, but they were patrolling our skies in vast numbers, and they attacked in the storm. I didn't see what happened to Serafina Pekkala. As for Lee Scoresby, the balloon soared up again after I fell out with the boy, taking him with it. But your symbol-reader will tell you what their fate is."

A bear pulled up a sledge on which a cauldron of charcoal was smouldering, and thrust a resinous branch into the heart of it. The branch caught at once, and in its glare Lyra turned the hands of the alethiometer and asked about Lee Scoresby.

It turned out that he was still aloft, borne by the winds towards Nova Zembla, and that he had been unharmed by the cliff-ghasts and had fought off the other witch-clan.

Lyra told Iorek, and he nodded, satisfied.

"If he is in the air, he will be safe," he said. "What of Mrs Coulter?"

The answer was complicated, with the needle swinging from symbol to symbol in a sequence that made Lyra puzzle for a long time. The bears were curious, but restrained by their respect for Iorek Byrnison, and his for Lyra, and she put them out of her mind and sank again into the alethiometric trance.

The play of symbols, once she had discovered the pattern of it, was dismaying.

"It says she's… She's heard about us flying this way, and she's got a transport zeppelin that's armed with machine-guns – I think that's it – and they're a-flying to Svalbard right now. She don't know yet about Iofur Raknison being beaten, of course, but she will soon because… Oh yes, because some witches will tell her, and they'll learn it from the cliff-ghasts. So I reckon there are spies in the air all around, Iorek. She was a-coming to … to pretend to help Iofur Raknison, but really she was going to take over power from him, with a regiment of Tartars that's a-coming by sea, and they'll be here in a couple of days.

"And as soon as she can she's a-going to where Lord Asriel is kept prisoner, and she's going to have him killed. Because… It's coming clear now: something I never understood before, Iorek! It's why she wants to kill Lord Asriel: it's because she knows what he's going to do, and she fears it, and she wants to do it herself and gain control before he does… It must be the city in the sky, it must be! She's trying to get to it first! And now it's telling me something else…"

She bent over the instrument, concentrating furiously as the needle darted this way and that. It moved almost too fast to follow: Roger, looking over her shoulder, couldn't even see it stop, and was conscious only of a swift flickering dialogue between Lyra's fingers turning the hands and the needle answering, as bewilderingly unlike language as the Aurora was.

"Yes," she said finally, putting the instrument down in her lap and blinking and sighing as she woke out of her profound concentration. "Yes, I see what it says. She's after me again. She wants something I've got, because Lord Asriel wants it too. They need it for this… For this experiment, whatever it is…"

She stopped there, to take a deep breath. Something was troubling her, and she didn't know what it was. She was sure that this *something* that was so important was the alethiometer itself, because after all, Mrs Coulter *had* wanted it, and what else could it be? And yet it wasn't, because the alethiometer had a different way of referring to itself, and this wasn't it.

"I suppose it's the alethiometer," she said unhappily. "It's what I thought all along. I've got to take it to Lord Asriel before she gets it. If *she* gets it, we'll all die."

As she said that, she felt so tired, so bone-deep weary and sad that to die would have been a relief. But the example of Iorek kept her from admitting it. She put the alethiometer away and sat up straight.

"How far away is she?" said Iorek.

"Just a few hours. I suppose I ought to take the alethiometer to Lord Asriel as soon as I can."

"I will go with you," said Iorek.

She didn't argue. While Iorek gave commands and organized an armed squad to accompany them on the final part of their journey north, Lyra sat still, conserving her energy. She felt that something had gone out of her during that last reading. She closed her eyes and slept, and presently they woke her and set off.

21

Lord Asriel's Welcome

Lyra rode a strong young bear, and Roger rode another, while Iorek paced tirelessly ahead and a squad armed with a fire-hurler followed, guarding the rear.

The way was long and hard. The interior of Svalbard was mountainous, with jumbled peaks and sharp ridges deeply cut by ravines and steep-sided valleys, and the cold was intense. Lyra thought back to the smooth-running sledges of the gyptians on the way to Bolvangar; how swift and comfortable that progress now seemed to have been! The air here was more penetratingly chill than any she had experienced before; or it might have been that the bear she was riding wasn't as light-footed as Iorek; or it might have been that she was tired to her very soul. At all events, it was desperately hard going.

She knew little of where they were bound, or how far it was. All she knew was what the older bear Søren Eisarson had told her while they were preparing the fire-hurler. He had been involved in negotiating with Lord Asriel about the terms of his imprisonment, and he remembered it well.

At first, he'd said, the Svalbard bears regarded Lord Asriel as being no different from any of the other politicians, kings, or trouble-makers who had been exiled to their bleak island. The prisoners were important, or they would have been killed outright by their own people; they might be valuable to the bears one day, if their political fortunes changed and they returned to rule in their own countries; so it might pay the bears not to treat them with cruelty or disrespect.

So Lord Asriel had found conditions on Svalbard no better and no worse than hundreds of other exiles had done. But certain things had made his jailers more wary of him than of other prisoners they'd had. There was the air of mystery and spiritual peril surrounding anything that had to do with Dust; there was the clear panic on the part of those who'd brought him there; and there were Mrs Coulter's private communications with Iofur Raknison.

Besides, the bears had never met anything quite like Lord Asriel's own haughty and imperious nature. He dominated even Iofur Raknison, arguing forcefully and eloquently, and persuaded the bear-king to let him choose his own dwelling-place.

The first one he was allotted was too low down, he said. He needed a high spot, above the smoke and stir of the fire-mines and the smithies. He gave the bears a design of the accommodation he wanted, and told them where it should be; and he bribed them with gold, and he flattered and bullied Iofur Raknison, and with a bemused willingness the bears set to work. Before long a house had arisen on a headland facing north: a wide and solid place with fireplaces that burned great blocks of coal mined and hauled by bears, and with large windows of real glass. There he dwelt, a prisoner acting like a king.

And then he set about assembling the materials for a laboratory.

With furious concentration he sent for books, instruments, chemicals, all manner of tools and equipment. And somehow it had come, from this source or that; some openly, some smuggled in by the visitors he insisted he was entitled to have. By land, sea and air, Lord Asriel assembled his materials, and within six months of his committal, he had all the equipment he wanted.

And so he worked, thinking and planning and calculating, waiting for the one thing he needed to complete the task that so terrified the Oblation Board. It was drawing closer every minute.

Lyra's first glimpse of her father's prison came when Iorek Byrnison stopped at the foot of a ridge for the children to move and stretch themselves, because they had been getting dangerously cold and stiff.

"Look up there," he said.

A wide broken slope of tumbled rocks and ice, where a track had been laboriously cleared, led up to a crag outlined against the sky. There was no Aurora, but the stars were brilliant. The crag stood black and gaunt, but at its summit was a spacious building from which light spilled lavishly in all directions: not the smoky inconstant gleam of blubber-lamps, nor the harsh white of anbaric spotlights, but the warm creamy glow of naphtha.

The windows from which the light emerged also showed Lord Asriel's formidable power. Glass was expensive, and large sheets of it were prodigal of heat in these fierce latitudes; so to see them here was evidence of wealth and influence far greater than Iofur Raknison's vulgar palace.

They mounted their bears for the last time, and Iorek led the way up the slope towards the house. There was a courtyard that lay deep under snow, surrounded by a low wall, and as Iorek pushed open the gate they heard a bell ring somewhere in the building.

Lyra got down. She could hardly stand. She helped Roger down too and, supporting each other, the children stumbled through the thigh-deep snow towards the steps up to the door.

Oh, the warmth there would be inside that house! Oh, the peaceful rest!

She reached for the handle of the bell, but before she could reach it, the door opened. There was a small dimly-lit vestibule to keep the warm air in, and standing under the lamp was a figure she recognized: Lord Asriel's manservant Thorold, with his pinscher-dæmon Anfang.

Lyra wearily pushed back her hood.

"Who…" Thorold began, and then saw who it was, and went on, "Not Lyra? Little Lyra? Am I dreaming?"

He reached behind him to open the inner door.

A hall, with a coal fire blazing in a stone grate; warm naphtha light glowing on carpets, leather chairs, polished wood… It was like nothing Lyra had seen since leaving Jordan College, and it brought a choking gasp to her throat.

Lord Asriel's snow-leopard dæmon growled.

Lyra's father stood there, his powerful dark-eyed face at first fierce, triumphant, and eager; and then the colour faded from it; his eyes widened, in horror, as he recognized his daughter.

"No! No!"

He staggered back and clutched at the mantelpiece. Lyra couldn't move.

"Get out!" Lord Asriel cried. "Turn round, get out, go! *I did not send for you!*"

She couldn't speak. She opened her mouth twice, three times, and then managed to say:

"No, no, I came because –"

He seemed appalled; he kept shaking his head, he held up his hands as if to ward her off; she couldn't believe his distress.

She moved a step closer to reassure him, and Roger came to stand with her, anxious. Their dæmons fluttered out into the warmth, and after a moment Lord Asriel passed a hand across his brow and recovered slightly. The colour began to return to his cheeks as he looked down at the two children.

"Lyra," he said. "That is Lyra?"

"Yes, Uncle Asriel," she said, thinking that this wasn't the time to go into their true relationship. "I came to bring you the alethiometer from the Master of Jordan."

"Yes, of course you did," he said. "Who is this?"

"It's Roger Parslow," she said. "He's the Kitchen boy from Jordan College. But –"

"How did you get here?"

"I was just going to say, there's Iorek Byrnison outside, he's brought us here. He came with me all the way from Trollesund, and we tricked Iofur –"

"Who's Iorek Byrnison?"

"An armoured bear. He brought us here."

"Thorold," he called, "run a hot bath for these children, and prepare them some food. Then they will need to sleep. Their clothes are filthy; find them something to wear. Do it now, while I talk to this bear."

Lyra felt her head swim. Perhaps it was the heat, or perhaps it was relief. She watched the servant bow and leave the hall, and Lord Asriel go into the vestibule and close the door behind, and then she half-fell into the nearest chair.

Only a moment later, it seemed, Thorold was speaking to her.

"Follow me, miss," he was saying, and she hauled herself up and went with Roger to a warm bathroom, where soft towels hung on a heated rail, and where a tub of water steamed in the naphtha light.

"You go first," said Lyra. "I'll sit outside and we'll talk."

So Roger, wincing and gasping at the heat, got in and washed. They had swum naked together often enough, frolicking in the Isis or the Cherwell with other children, but this was different.

363

"I'm afraid of your uncle," said Roger through the open door. "I mean your father."

"Better keep calling him my uncle. I'm afraid of him too, sometimes."

"When we first come in he never saw me at all. He only saw you. And he was horrified, till he saw me. Then he calmed down all at once."

"He was just shocked," said Lyra. "Anyone would be, to see someone they didn't expect. He last saw me after that time in the Retiring Room. It's bound to be a shock."

"No," said Roger, "it's more than that. He was looking at me like a wolf, or summing."

"You're imagining it."

"I en't. I'm more scared of him than I was of Mrs Coulter, and that's the truth."

He splashed himself. Lyra took out the alethiometer.

"D'you want me to ask the symbol-reader about it?" Lyra said.

"Well, I dunno. There's things I'd rather not know. Seems to me everything I heard of since the Gobblers come to Oxford, everything's been bad. There en't been nothing good more than about five minutes ahead. Like I can see now, this bath's nice, and there's a nice warm towel there, about five minutes away. And once I'm dry maybe I'll think of summing nice to eat, but no further ahead than that. And when I've eaten maybe I'll look forward to a kip in a comfortable bed. But after that, I dunno, Lyra. There's been terrible things we seen, en't there? And more a-coming, more'n likely. So I think I'd rather not know what's in the future. I'll stick to the present."

"Yeah," said Lyra wearily. "There's times I feel like that too."

So although she held the alethiometer in her hands for a little longer, it was only for comfort; she didn't turn the wheels, and the swinging of the needle passed her by. Pantalaimon watched it in silence.

After they'd both washed, and eaten some bread and cheese and drunk some wine and hot water, the servant Thorold said, "The boy is to go to bed. I'll show him where to go. His Lordship asks if you'd join him in the Library, Miss Lyra."

Lyra found Lord Asriel in a room whose wide windows overlooked the frozen sea far below. There was a coal fire under a wide chimneypiece, and a naphtha lamp turned down low, so there was little in the way of distracting reflections between the occupants of the room and the bleak starlit panorama outside. Lord Asriel, reclining in a large armchair on one side of the fire, beckoned her to come and sit in the other chair facing him.

"Your friend Iorek Byrnison is resting outside," he said. "He prefers the cold."

"Did he tell you about his fight with Iofur Raknison?"

"Not in detail. But I understand that he is now the king of Svalbard. Is that true?"

"Of course it's true. Iorek never lies."

"He seems to have appointed himself your guardian."

"No. John Faa told him to look after me, and he's doing it because of that. He's following John Faa's orders."

"How does John Faa come into this?"

"I'll tell you if you tell me something," she said. "You're my father, en't you?"

"Yes. So what?"

"So you should have told me before, that's what. You shouldn't hide things like that from people, because they feel stupid when they find out, and that's cruel. What difference would it make if I knew I was your daughter? You could have said it years ago. You could've told me and asked me to keep it secret, and I would, no matter how young I was, I'd have done that if you asked me. I'd have been so proud nothing would've torn it out of me, if you asked me to keep it secret. But you never. You let other people know, but you never told me."

"Who did tell you?"

"John Faa."

"Did he tell you about your mother?"

"Yes."

"Then there's not much left for me to tell. I don't think I want to be interrogated and condemned by an insolent child. I want to hear what you've seen and done on the way here."

"I brought you the bloody alethiometer, didn't I?" Lyra burst out. She was very near to tears. "I looked after it all the way from Jordan, I hid it and I treasured it, all through what's happened to us, and I learned about using it, and I carried it all this bloody way when I could've just given up and been safe, and you en't even said thank you, nor showed any sign that you're glad to see me. I don't know why I ever done it. But I did, and I kept on going, even in Iofur Raknison's stinking palace with all them bears around me I kept on going, all on me own, and I tricked him into fighting with Iorek so's I could come on here for your sake… And when you *did* see me you like to fainted, as if I was some horrible thing you never wanted to see again. You en't human, Lord Asriel. You en't my *father*. My *father* wouldn't treat me like that. Fathers are supposed to love their daughters, en't they? You don't love me, and I don't love you, and that's a fact. I love Farder Coram, and I love Iorek Byrnison; I love an armoured bear more'n I love my father. And I bet Iorek Byrnison loves me more'n you do."

"You told me yourself he's only following John Faa's orders. If you're going to be sentimental I shan't waste time talking to you."

"Take your bloody alethiometer, then, and I'm going back with Iorek."

"Where?"

"Back to the palace. He can fight with Mrs Coulter and the Oblation Board, when they turn up. If he loses then I'll die too, I don't care. If he wins we'll send for Lee Scoresby and I'll sail away in his balloon and –"

"Who's Lee Scoresby?"

"An aëronaut. He brought us here and then we crashed. Here you are, here's the alethiometer. It's all in good order."

He made no move to take it, and she laid it on the brass fender around the hearth.

"And I suppose I ought to tell you that Mrs Coulter's on her way to Svalbard, and as soon as she hears what's happened to Iofur Raknison, she'll be on her way here. In a zeppelin, with a whole lot of soldiers, and they're a-going to kill us all, by order of the Magisterium."

"They'll never reach us," he said calmly.

He was so quiet and relaxed that some of her ferocity dwindled.

"You don't know," she said uncertainly.

"Yes I do."

"Have you got another alethiometer, then?"

"I don't need an alethiometer for that. Now I want to hear about your journey here, Lyra. Start from the beginning. Tell me everything."

So she did. She began with her hiding in the Retiring Room, and went on to the Gobblers' taking Roger, and her time with Mrs Coulter, and everything else that had happened.

It was a long tale, and when she finished it she said, "So there's one thing I want to know, and I reckon I've got the right to know it, like I had the right to know who I really was. And if you didn't tell me that, you've got to tell me this, in recompense. So: what's Dust? And why's everyone so afraid of it?"

He looked at her as if trying to guess whether she would understand what he was about to say. He had never looked at her seriously before, she thought; until now he had always been like an adult indulging a child in a pretty trick. But he seemed to think she was ready.

"Dust is what makes the alethiometer work," he said.

"Ah … I thought it might! But what else? How did they find out about it?"

"In one way the Church has always been aware of it. They've been preaching about Dust for centuries, only they didn't call it by that name.

"But some years ago a Muscovite called Boris Mikhailovitch Rusakov discovered a new kind of elementary particle. You've heard of electrons, photons, neutrinos and the rest? They're called elementary particles because you can't break them down any further: there's nothing inside them but themselves. Well, this new kind of particle was elementary all right, but it was very hard to measure because it didn't react in any of the usual ways. The hardest thing for Rusakov to understand was why the new particle seemed to cluster where human beings were, as if it were attracted to us. And especially to adults. Children too, but not nearly so much until their dæmons have taken a fixed form. During the years of puberty they begin to attract Dust more strongly, and it settles on them as it settles on adults.

"Now all discoveries of this sort, because they have a bearing on the doctrines of the Church, have to be announced through the Magisterium in Geneva. And this discovery of Rusakov's was so unlikely and strange that the Inspector from the Consistorial Court of Discipline suspected Rusakov of diabolic possession. He performed an exorcism in the laboratory, he interrogated Rusakov under the rules of the Inquisition, but finally they had to accept the fact that Rusakov wasn't lying or deceiving them: Dust really existed.

"That left them with the problem of deciding what it was. And given the Church's nature, there was only one thing they could have chosen. The Magisterium decided that Dust was the physical evidence for original sin. Do you know what original sin is?"

She twisted her lips. It was like being back at Jordan, being quizzed on something she'd been half-taught. "Sort of," she said.

"No, you don't. Go to the shelf beside the desk and bring me the Bible."

Lyra did so, and handed the big black book to her father.

"You do remember the story of Adam and Eve?"

"Course," she said. "She wasn't supposed to eat the fruit and the serpent tempted her, and she did."

"And what happened then?"

"Umm… They were thrown out. God threw them out of the garden."

"God had told them not to eat the fruit, because they would die. Remember, they were naked in the garden, they were like children, their dæmons took on any form they desired. But this is what happened."

He turned to Chapter Three of Genesis, and read:

"And the woman said unto the serpent, We may eat of the fruit of the trees of the garden:

"But of the fruit of the tree which is in the midst of the garden, God hath said, Ye shall not eat of it, neither shall ye touch it, lest ye die.

"And the serpent said unto the woman, Ye shall not surely die:

"For God doth know that in the day ye eat thereof, then your eyes shall be opened, and your dæmons shall assume their true

forms, and ye shall be as gods, knowing good and evil.

"And when the woman saw that the tree was good for food, and that it was pleasant to the eyes, and a tree to be desired to reveal the true form of one's dæmon, she took of the fruit thereof, and did eat, and gave also unto her husband with her; and he did eat.

"And the eyes of them both were opened, and they saw the true form of their dæmons, and spoke with them.

"But when the man and the woman knew their own dæmons, they knew that a great change had come upon them, for until that moment it had seemed that they were at one with all the creatures of the earth and the air, and there was no difference between them:

"And they saw the difference, and they knew good and evil; and they were ashamed, and they sewed fig leaves together to cover their nakedness…"

He closed the book.

"And that was how sin came into the world," he said, "sin and shame and death. It came the moment their dæmons became fixed."

"But…" Lyra struggled to find the words she wanted: "but it en't *true*, is it? Not true like chemistry or engineering, not that kind of true? There wasn't *really* an Adam and Eve? The Cassington Scholar told me it was just a kind of fairy-tale."

"The Cassington Scholarship is traditionally given to a free-thinker; it's his function to challenge the faith of the Scholars. Naturally he'd say that. But think of Adam and Eve like an imaginary number, like the square root of minus one: you can never see any concrete proof that it exists, but if you include it in your equations, you can calculate all manner of things that couldn't be imagined without it.

"Anyway, it's what the Church has taught for thousands of years. And when Rusakov discovered Dust, at last there was a physical proof that something happened when innocence changed into experience.

"Incidentally, the Bible gave us the name Dust as well. At first they were called Rusakov Particles, but soon someone pointed out a curious verse toward the end of the Third Chapter of Genesis, where God's cursing Adam for eating the fruit."

He opened the Bible again and pointed it out to Lyra. She read:

> *"In the sweat of thy face shalt thou eat bread, till thou return unto the ground; for out of it wast thou taken: for dust thou art, and unto dust shalt thou return…"*

Lord Asriel said, "Church scholars have always puzzled over the translation of that verse. Some say it should read not 'unto dust shalt thou return' but 'thou shalt be subject to dust', and others say the whole verse is a kind of pun on the words 'ground' and 'dust', and it really means that God's admitting his own nature to be partly sinful. No one agrees. No one can, because the text is corrupt. But it was too good a word to waste, and that's why the particles became known as Dust."

"And what about the Gobblers?" Lyra said.

"The General Oblation Board… Your mother's gang. Clever of her to spot the chance of setting up her own power base, but she's a clever woman, as I dare say you've noticed. It suits the Magisterium to allow all kinds of different agencies to flourish. They can play them off against one another; if one succeeds, they can pretend to have been supporting it all along, and if it fails, they can pretend it was a renegade outfit which had never been properly licensed.

"You see, your mother's always been ambitious for power. At first she tried to get it in the normal way, through marriage, but that didn't work, as I think you've heard. So she had to turn to the Church. Naturally she couldn't take the route a man could have taken – priesthood and so on – it had to be unorthodox; she had to set up her own order, her own channels of influence, and work through that. It was a good move to specialize in Dust. Everyone was frightened of it; no one knew what to do; and when she offered to direct an investigation, the Magisterium was so relieved that they backed her with money and resources of all kinds."

"But they were *cutting* –" Lyra couldn't bring herself to say it; the words choked in her mouth. "You know what they were doing! Why did the Church let them do anything like that?"

"There was a precedent. Something like it had happened before. Do you know what the word *castration* means? It means removing the sexual organs of a boy so that he never develops the characteristics of a man. A *castrato* keeps his high treble voice all his life, which is why the Church allowed it: so useful in Church music. Some *castrati* became great singers, wonderful artists. Many just became fat spoiled half-men. Some died from the effects of the operation. But the Church wouldn't flinch at the idea of a little *cut*, you see. There was a precedent. And this would be so much more *hygienic* than the old methods, when they didn't have anaesthetics or sterile bandages or proper nursing care. It would be gentle by comparison."

"It isn't!" Lyra said fiercely. "It isn't!"

"No. Of course not. That's why they had to hide away in the far North, in darkness and obscurity. And why the Church was glad to have someone like your mother in charge. Who could doubt someone so charming, so well-connected, so sweet and reasonable? But because it was an obscure and unofficial kind of operation, she was someone the Magisterium could deny if they needed to, as well."

"But whose idea was it to do that *cutting* in the first place?"

"It was hers. She guessed that the two things that happen at adolescence might be connected: the change in one's dæmon and the fact that Dust began to settle. Perhaps if the dæmon were separated from the body, we might never be subject to Dust – to original sin. The question was whether it was possible to separate dæmon and body without killing the person. But she's travelled in many places, and seen all kinds of things. She's travelled in Africa, for instance. The Africans have a way of making a slave called a *zombi*. It has no will of its own; it will work day and night without ever running away or complaining. It looks like a corpse…"

"It's a person without their dæmon!"

"Exactly. So she found out that it was possible to separate them."

"And … Tony Costa told me about the horrible phantoms they have in the Northern forests. I suppose they might be the same kind of thing."

"That's right. Anyway, the General Oblation Board grew out of ideas like that, and out of the Church's obsession with original sin."

Lord Asriel's dæmon twitched her ears, and he laid his hand on her beautiful head.

"There was something else that happened when they made the cut," he went on. "And they didn't see it. The energy that links body and dæmon is immensely powerful. When the cut is made, all that energy dissipates in a fraction of a second. They didn't notice, because they mistook it for shock, or disgust, or moral outrage, and they trained themselves to feel numb towards it. So they missed what it could do, and they never thought of harnessing it…"

Lyra couldn't sit still. She got up and walked to the window, and stared over the wide bleak darkness with unseeing eyes. They were too cruel. No matter how important it was to find out about original sin, it was too cruel to do what they'd done to Tony Makarios and all the others. Nothing justified that.

"And what were *you* doing?" she said. "Did you do any of that cutting?"

"I'm interested in something quite different. I don't think the Oblation Board goes far enough. I want to go to the source of Dust itself."

"The source? Where's it come from, then?"

"From the other universe we can see through the Aurora."

Lyra turned around again. Her father was lying back in his chair, lazy and powerful, his eyes as fierce as his dæmon's. She didn't love him, she couldn't trust him, but she had to admire him, and the extravagant luxury he'd assembled in this desolate wasteland, and the power of his ambition.

"What is that other universe?" she said.

"One of uncountable billions of parallel worlds. The witches have known about them for centuries, but the first theologians to prove their existence mathematically were excommunicated fifty or more years ago. However, it's true; there's no possible way of denying it.

"But no one thought it would ever be possible to cross from one universe to another. That would violate fundamental laws, we thought. Well, we were wrong; we learned to see the world up there. If light can cross, so can we. And we had to *learn* to see it, Lyra, just as you learned to use the alethiometer.

"Now that world, and every other universe, came about as a result of possibility. Take the example of tossing a coin: it can come down heads or tails, and we don't know before it lands which way it's going to fall. If it comes down heads, that means that the possibility of its coming down tails has collapsed. Until that moment the two possibilities were equal.

"But on another world, it does come down tails. And when that happens, the two worlds split apart. I'm using the example of tossing a coin to make it clearer. In fact, these possibility-collapses happen at the level of elementary particles, but they happen in just the same way: one moment several things are possible, the next moment only one happens, and the rest don't exist. Except that other worlds have sprung into being, on which they *did* happen.

"And I'm going to that world beyond the Aurora," he said, "because I think that's where all the Dust in this universe comes from. You saw those slides I showed the Scholars in the Retiring Room. You saw Dust pouring into this world from the Aurora. You've seen that city yourself. If light can cross the barrier between the universes, if Dust can, if we can see that city, then we can build a bridge and cross. It needs a phenomenal burst of energy. But I can do it. Somewhere out there is the origin of all the Dust, all the death, the sin, the misery, the destructiveness in the world. Human beings can't see anything without wanting to destroy it, Lyra. *That's* original sin. And I'm going to destroy it. Death is going to die."

"Is that why they put you here?"

"Yes. They are terrified. And with good reason."

He stood up, and so did his dæmon, proud and beautiful and deadly. Lyra sat still. She was afraid of her father, and she admired him profoundly, and she thought he was stark mad; but who was she to judge?

"Go to bed," he said. "Thorold will show you where to sleep."

He turned to go.

"You've left the alethiometer," she said.

"Ah, yes; I don't actually need that now," he said. "It would be no use to me without the books, anyway. D'you know, I think the

Master of Jordan was giving it to *you*. Did he actually ask you to bring it to me?"

"Well, yes!" she said. But then she thought again, and realized that in fact the Master never had asked her to do that; she had assumed it all the time, because why else would he have given it to her? "No," she said. "I don't know. I thought –"

"Well, I don't want it. It's yours, Lyra."

"But –"

"Good night, child."

Speechless, too bewildered by this to voice any of the dozen urgent questions that pressed at her mind, she took up the alethiometer and wrapped it in its black velvet. Then she sat by the fire and watched him leave the room.

22

Betrayal

She woke to find a stranger shaking her arm, and then as Pantalaimon sprang awake and growled, she recognized Thorold. He was holding a naphtha lamp, and his hand was trembling.

"Miss – miss – get up quickly. I don't know what to do. He's left no orders. I think he's mad, miss."

"What? What's happening?"

"Lord Asriel, miss. He's been almost in a delirium since you went to bed. I've never seen him so wild. He packed a lot of instruments and batteries in a sledge and he harnessed up the dogs and left. But he's got the boy, miss!"

"Roger? He's taken Roger?"

"He told me to wake him and dress him, and I didn't think to argue – I never have – the boy kept on asking for you, miss – but Lord Asriel wanted him alone – you know when you first came to the door, miss? And he saw you and couldn't believe his eyes, and wanted you gone?"

Lyra's head was in such a whirl of weariness and fear that she could hardly think but, "Yes? Yes?" she said.

"It was because he needed a child to finish his experiment, miss! And Lord Asriel has a way special to himself of bringing about what he wants, he just has to call for something and –"

Now Lyra's head was full of a roar, as if she were trying to stifle some knowledge from her own consciousness.

She had got out of bed, and was reaching for her clothes, and then she suddenly collapsed, and a fierce cry of despair enveloped her. She was uttering it, but it was bigger than she was; it felt as if the despair were uttering her. For she remembered his words: *the energy that links body and dæmon is immensely powerful*; and to bridge the gap between worlds needed *a phenomenal burst of energy…*

She had just realized what she'd done.

She had struggled all this way to bring something to Lord Asriel, thinking she knew what he wanted; and it wasn't the alethiometer at all. What he wanted was a child.

She had brought him Roger.

That was why he'd cried out, "I did not send for you!" when he saw her; he had sent for a child, and the fates had brought him his own daughter. Or so he'd thought, until she'd stepped aside and shown him Roger.

Oh, the bitter anguish! She had thought she was *saving* Roger, and all the time she'd been diligently working to betray him…

Lyra shook and sobbed in a frenzy of emotion. It couldn't be true.

Thorold tried to comfort her, but he didn't know the reason for her extremity of grief, and could only pat her shoulder nervously.

"Iorek –" she sobbed, pushing the servant aside. "Where's Iorek Byrnison? The bear? Is he still outside?"

The old man shrugged helplessly.

"Help me!" she said, trembling all over with weakness and fear. "Help me dress. I got to go. *Now!* Do it *quick!*"

He put the lamp down and did as she told him. When she commanded, in that imperious way, she was very like her father, for all that her face was wet with tears and her lips trembling. While Pantalaimon paced the floor lashing his tail, his fur almost sparking, Thorold hastened to bring her stiff, reeking furs and help her into them. As soon as all the buttons were done up and all the flaps secured, she made for the door, and felt the cold strike her throat like a sword and freeze the tears at once on her cheeks.

"Iorek!" she called. "Iorek Byrnison! Come, because I need you!"

There was a shake of snow, a clank of metal, and the bear was there. He had been sleeping calmly under the falling snow. In the light spilling from the lamp Thorold was holding at the window, Lyra saw the long faceless head, the dark eye holes, the gleam of white fur below red-black metal, and wanted to embrace him and seek some comfort from his iron helmet, his ice-tipped fur.

"Well?" he said.

"We got to catch Lord Asriel. He's taken Roger and he's a-going to – I daren't think – oh, Iorek, I beg you, go quick, my dear!"

"Come then," he said, and she leapt on his back.

There was no need to ask which way to go: the tracks of the sledge led straight out from the courtyard and over the plain, and Iorek leapt forward to follow them. His motion was now so much a part of Lyra's being that to sit balanced was entirely automatic. He ran over the thick snowy mantle on the rocky ground faster than he'd ever done, and the armour-plates shifted under her in a regular swinging rhythm.

Behind them, the other bears paced easily, pulling the fire-hurler with them. The way was clear, for the moon was high and the light it cast over the snowbound world was as bright as it had been in the balloon: a world of bright silver and profound black. The tracks of Lord Asriel's sledge ran straight towards a range of jagged hills, strange stark pointed shapes jutting up into a sky as black as the alethiometer's velvet cloth. There was no sign of the sledge itself – or was there a feather-touch of movement on the flank of the highest peak? Lyra peered ahead, straining her eyes, and Pantalaimon flew as high as he could and looked with an owl's clear vision.

"Yes," he said, on her wrist a moment later; "it's Lord Asriel, and he's lashing his dogs on furiously, and there's a child in the back…"

Lyra felt Iorek Byrnison change pace. Something had caught his attention. He was slowing and lifting his head to cast left and right.

"What is it?" Lyra said.

He didn't say. He was listening intently, but she could hear nothing. Then she did hear something: a mysterious, vastly distant rustling and crackling. It was a sound she had heard before: the sound of the Aurora. Out of nowhere a veil of radiance had fallen to hang shimmering in the northern sky. All those unseen billions and trillions of charged particles and possibly, she thought, of Dust, conjured a radiating glow out of the upper atmosphere. This was going to be a display more brilliant and extraordinary than any Lyra had yet seen, as if the Aurora knew the drama that was taking place below, and wanted to light it with the most awe-inspiring effects.

But none of the bears were looking up: their attention was all on the earth. It wasn't the Aurora, after all, that had caught Iorek's attention. He was standing stock still now, and Lyra slipped off his back, knowing that his senses needed to cast around freely. Something was troubling him.

Lyra looked around, back across the vast open plain leading to Lord Asriel's house, back towards the tumbled mountains they'd crossed earlier, and saw nothing. The Aurora grew more intense.

The first veils trembled and raced to one side, and jagged curtains folded and unfolded above, increasing in size and brilliance every minute; arcs and loops swirled across from horizon to horizon, and touched the very zenith with bows of radiance. She could hear more clearly than ever the immense singing hiss and swish of vast intangible forces.

"Witches!" came a cry in a bear-voice, and Lyra turned in joy and relief.

But a heavy muzzle knocked her forward, and with no breath left to gasp she could only pant and shudder, for there in the place where she had been standing was the plume of a green-feathered arrow. The head and the shaft were buried in the snow.

Impossible! she thought weakly, but it was true, for another arrow clattered off the armour of Iorek, standing above her. These were not Serafina Pekkala's witches; they were from another clan. They circled above, a dozen of them or more, swooping down to shoot and soaring up again, and Lyra swore with every word she knew.

Iorek Byrnison gave swift orders. It was clear that the bears were practised at witch-fighting, for they had moved at once into a defensive formation, and the witches moved just as smoothly into attack. They could only shoot accurately from close range, and in order not to waste arrows they would swoop down, fire at the lowest part of their dive, and turn upwards at once. But when they reached the lowest point, and their hands were busy with bow and arrow, they were vulnerable, and the bears would explode upwards with raking paws to drag them down. More than one fell, and was quickly dispatched.

Lyra crouched low beside a rock, watching for a witch-dive. A few shot at her, but the arrows fell wide; and then Lyra, looking up at the sky, saw the greater part of the witch-flight peel off and turn back.

If she was relieved by that, her relief didn't last more than a few moments. Because from the direction in which they'd flown, she saw many others coming to join them; and in mid-air with them there was a group of gleaming lights; and across the broad expanse of the Svalbard plain, under the radiance of the Aurora, she heard a sound she dreaded. It was the harsh throb of a gas-engine. The zeppelin, with Mrs Coulter and her troops on board, was catching up.

Iorek growled an order and the bears moved at once into another formation. In the lurid flicker from the sky Lyra watched as they swiftly unloaded their fire-hurler. The advance-guard of the witch-flight had seen them too, and began to swoop downwards and rain arrows on them, but for the most part the bears trusted to their armour and worked swiftly to erect the apparatus: a long arm extending upwards at an angle, a cup or bowl a yard across; and a great iron tank wreathed in smoke and steam.

As she watched, a bright flame gushed out, and a team of bears swung into practised action. Two of them hauled the long arm of the fire-thrower down, another scooped shovelfuls of fire into the bowl, and at an order they released it, to hurl the flaming sulphur high into the dark sky.

The witches were swooping so thickly above them that three fell in flames at the first shot alone, but it was soon clear that the real target was the zeppelin. The pilot either had never seen a fire-hurler before, or was underestimating its power, for he flew straight on towards the bears without climbing or turning a fraction to either side.

Then it became clear that they had a powerful weapon in the zeppelin too: a machine-rifle mounted on the nose of the gondola. Lyra saw sparks flying up from some of the bears' armour, and saw them huddle over under its protection, before she heard the rattle of the bullets. She cried out in fear.

"They're safe," said Iorek Byrnison. "Can't pierce armour with little bullets."

The fire-thrower worked again: this time a mass of blazing sulphur hurtled directly upwards to strike the gondola and burst in a cascade of flaming fragments on all sides. The zeppelin banked to the left, and roared away in a wide arc before making again for the group of bears working swiftly beside the apparatus. As it neared, the arm of the fire-thrower creaked downwards; the machine-rifle coughed and spat, and two bears fell, to a low growl from Iorek Byrnison; and when the aircraft was nearly overhead, a bear shouted an order, and the spring-loaded arm shot upwards again.

This time the sulphur hurtled against the envelope of the zeppelin's gas-bag. The rigid frame held a skin of oiled silk in place to contain the hydrogen, and although this was tough enough to withstand minor scratches, a hundredweight of blazing rock was too much for it. The silk ripped straight through, and sulphur and hydrogen leapt to meet each other in a catastrophe of flame.

At once the silk became transparent; the entire skeleton of the zeppelin was visible, dark against an inferno of orange and red and yellow, hanging in the air for what seemed like an impossibly long time before drifting to the ground almost reluctantly. Little figures black against the snow and the fire came tottering or running from it, and witches flew down to help drag them away from the flames. Within a minute of the zeppelin's hitting the ground it was a mass of twisted metal, a pall of smoke, and a few scraps of fluttering fire.

But the soldiers on board, and the others too (though Lyra was too far away by now to spot Mrs Coulter, she knew she was there) wasted no time. With the help of the witches they dragged the machine-gun out and set it up, and began to fight in earnest on the ground.

"On," said Iorek. "They will hold out for a long time."

He roared, and a group of bears peeled away from the main group and attacked the Tartars' right flank. Lyra could feel his desire to be there among them, but all the time her nerves were screaming: On! On! and her mind was filled with pictures of Roger and Lord Asriel; and Iorek Byrnison knew, and turned up the mountain and away from the fight, leaving his bears to hold back the Tartars.

On they climbed. Lyra strained her eyes to look ahead, but not even Pantalaimon's owl-eyes could see any movement on the flank of the mountain they were climbing. Lord Asriel's sledge-tracks were clear, however, and Iorek followed them swiftly, loping through the snow and kicking it high behind them as he ran. Whatever happened behind now was simply that: behind. Lyra had left it. She felt she was leaving the world altogether, so remote and intent she was, so high they were climbing, so strange and uncanny was the light that bathed them.

"Iorek," she said, "will you find Lee Scoresby?"

"Alive or dead, I will find him."

"And if you see Serafina Pekkala…"

"I will tell her what you did."

"Thank you, Iorek," she said.

They spoke no more for some time. Lyra felt herself moving into a kind of trance beyond sleep and waking: a state of conscious dreaming, almost, in which she was dreaming that she was being carried by bears to a city in the stars.

She was going to say something about it to Iorek Byrnison, when he slowed down and came to a halt.

"The tracks go on," said Iorek Byrnison. "But I cannot."

Lyra jumped down and stood beside him to look. He was

standing at the edge of a chasm. Whether it was a crevasse in the ice or a fissure in the rock was hard to say, and made little difference in any case; all that mattered was that it plunged downwards into unfathomable gloom.

And the tracks of Lord Asriel's sledge ran to the brink … and on, across a bridge of compacted snow.

This bridge had clearly felt the strain of the sledge's weight, for a crack ran across it close to the other edge of the chasm, and the surface on the near side of the crack had settled down a foot or so. It might support the weight of a child: it would certainly not stand under the weight of an armoured bear.

And Lord Asriel's tracks ran on beyond the bridge and further up the mountain. If she went on, it would have to be by herself.

Lyra turned to Iorek Byrnison.

"I got to go across," she said. "Thank you for all you done. I don't know what's going to happen when I get to him. We might all die, whether I get to him or not. But if I come back I'll come and see you to thank you properly, King Iorek Byrnison."

She laid a hand on his head. He let it lie there and nodded gently.

"Goodbye, Lyra Silvertongue," he said.

Her heart thumping painfully with love, she turned away and set her foot on the bridge. The snow creaked under her, and Pantalaimon flew up and over the bridge, to settle in the snow on the far side and encourage her onwards. Step after step she took, and wondered with every step whether it would be better to run swiftly and leap for the other side, or go slowly as she was doing and tread as lightly as possible. Halfway across there came another loud creak from the snow; a piece fell off near her feet and tumbled into the abyss, and the bridge settled down another few inches against the crack.

She stood perfectly still. Pantalaimon was crouched leopard-formed ready to leap down and reach for her.

The bridge held. She took another step, then another, and then she felt something settling down below her feet and leapt for the far side with all her strength. She landed belly-down in the snow as the entire length of the bridge fell into the crevasse with a soft *whoosh* behind her.

Pantalaimon's claws were in her furs, holding tight.

After a minute she opened her eyes and crawled up away from the edge. There was no way back. She stood and raised her hand to the watching bear. Iorek Byrnison stood on his hind legs to acknowledge her, and then turned and made off down the mountain in a swift run to help his subjects in the battle with Mrs Coulter and the soldiers from the zeppelin.

Lyra was alone.

23
The Bridge to the Stars

Once Iorek Byrnison was out of sight, Lyra felt a great weakness coming over her, and she turned blindly and felt for Pantalaimon.

"Oh, Pan, dear, I can't go on! I'm so frightened – and so tired – all this way, and I'm scared to death! I wish it was someone else instead of me, I do honestly!"

Her dæmon nuzzled at her neck in his cat-form, warm and comforting.

"I just don't know what we got to do," Lyra sobbed. "It's too much for us, Pan, we can't…"

She clung to him blindly, rocking back and forth and letting the sobs cry out wildly over the bare snow.

"And even if – if Mrs Coulter got to Roger first there'd be no saving him, because she'd take him back to Bolvangar, or worse, and they'd kill me out of vengeance… Why *do* they do these things to children, Pan? Do they all hate children so much, that they want to tear them apart like this? Why *do* they do it?"

But Pantalaimon had no answer; all he could do was hug her close. Little by little, as the storm of fear subsided, she came to a sense of herself again. She was Lyra, cold and frightened by all means, but herself.

"I wish..." she said, and stopped. There was nothing that could be gained by wishing for it. A final deep shaky breath, and she was ready to go on.

The moon had set by now, and the sky to the south was profoundly dark, though the billions of stars lay on it like diamonds on velvet. They were outshone, though, by the Aurora, outshone a hundred times. Never had Lyra seen it so brilliant and dramatic; with every twitch and shiver, new miracles of light danced across the sky. And behind the ever-changing gauze of light that other world, that sunlit city, was clear and solid.

The higher they climbed, the more the bleak land spread out below them. To the north lay the frozen sea, compacted here and there into ridges where two sheets of ice had pressed together, but otherwise flat and white and endless, reaching to the Pole itself and far beyond, featureless, lifeless, colourless, and bleak beyond Lyra's imagination. To the east and west were more mountains, great jagged peaks thrusting sharply upwards, their scarps piled high with snow and raked by the wind into blade-like edges as sharp as scimitars. To the south lay the way they had come, and Lyra looked most longingly back, to see if she could spy her dear friend Iorek Byrnison and his troops; but nothing stirred on the wide plain. She was not even sure if she could see the burned wreckage of the zeppelin, or the crimson-stained snow around the corpses of the warriors.

Pantalaimon flew high, and swooped back to her wrist in his owl-form.

"They're just beyond the peak!" he said. "Lord Asriel's laid out all his instruments, and Roger can't move away –"

And as he said that, the Aurora flickered and dimmed, like an anbaric bulb at the end of its life, and then *went out* altogether. In the gloom, though, Lyra sensed the presence of the Dust, for the air seemed to be full of dark intentions, like the forms of thoughts not yet born.

In the enfolding dark she heard a child's cry:

"Lyra! Lyra!"

"I'm a-coming!" she cried back, and stumbled upwards, clambering, sprawling, struggling, at the end of her strength; but hauling herself on and further on through the ghostly-gleaming snow.

"Lyra! Lyra!"

"I'm nearly there," she gasped. "Nearly there, Roger!"

Pantalaimon was changing rapidly, in his agitation: lion, ermine, eagle, wildcat, hare, salamander, owl, leopard, every form he'd ever taken, a kaleidoscope of forms among the Dust –

"*Lyra!*"

Then she reached the summit, and saw what was happening.

Fifty yards away in the starlight Lord Asriel was twisting together two wires that led to his upturned sledge, on which stood a row of batteries and jars and pieces of apparatus, already frosted with crystals of cold. He was dressed in heavy furs, his face illuminated by the flame of a naphtha lamp. Crouching like the Sphinx beside him was his dæmon, her beautiful spotted coat glossy with power, her tail moving lazily in the snow.

In her mouth she held Roger's dæmon.

The little creature was struggling, flapping, fighting, one moment a bird, the next a dog, then a cat, a rat, a bird again, and calling every moment to Roger himself, who was a few yards off, straining, trying to pull away against the heart-deep tug, and crying out with the pain and the cold. He was calling his dæmon's name, and calling Lyra; he ran to Lord Asriel and plucked his arm, and Lord Asriel brushed him aside. He tried again, crying and pleading, begging, sobbing, and Lord Asriel took no notice except to knock him to the ground.

They were on the edge of a cliff. Beyond them was nothing but a huge illimitable dark. They were a thousand feet or more above the frozen sea.

All this Lyra saw by starlight alone; but then, as Lord Asriel connected his wires, the Aurora blazed all of a sudden into brilliant life. Like the long finger of blinding power that plays between two terminals, except that this was a thousand miles high and ten thousand miles long: dipping, soaring, undulating, glowing, a cataract of glory.

He was *controlling* it...

Or leading power down from it; for there was a wire running off a huge reel on the sledge, a wire that ran directly upwards to the sky. Down from the dark swooped a raven, and Lyra knew it for a witch-dæmon. A witch was helping Lord Asriel, and she had flown that wire into the heights.

And the Aurora was blazing again.

He was nearly ready.

He turned to Roger and beckoned, and Roger helplessly came, shaking his head, begging, crying, but helplessly going forward.

"No! Run!" Lyra cried, and hurled herself down the slope at him.

Pantalaimon leapt at the snow leopard and snatched Roger's dæmon from her jaws. In a moment the snow leopard had leapt after him, and Pantalaimon let the other dæmon go, and both young dæmons, changing flick-flick-flick, turned and battled with the great spotted beast.

She slashed left-right with needle-filled paws, and her snarling roar drowned even Lyra's cries. Both children were fighting her, too; or fighting the forms in the turbid air, those dark intentions, that came thick and crowding down the streams of Dust –

And the Aurora swayed above, its continual surging flicker picking out now this building, now that lake, now that row of palm trees, so close you'd think that you could step from this world to that.

Lyra leapt up and seized Roger's hand.

She pulled hard, and then they tore away from Lord Asriel and ran, hand in hand, but Roger cried and twisted, because the leopard had his dæmon again; and Lyra knew that heart-convulsing pain and tried to stop –

But they couldn't stop.

The cliff was sliding away beneath them.

An entire shelf of snow, sliding inexorably down –

The frozen sea, a thousand feet below –

"LYRA!"

Heart–beats –

Tight–clutching hands –

And high above, the greatest wonder.

The vault of heaven, star-studded, profound, was suddenly pierced as if by a spear.

A jet of light, a jet of pure energy released like an arrow from a great bow, shot upwards. The sheets of light and colour that were the Aurora tore apart; a great rending, grinding, crunching, tearing sound reached from one end of the universe to the other; there was dry land in the sky –

Sunlight!

Sunlight shining on the fur of a golden monkey…

For the fall of the snow-shelf had halted; perhaps an unseen ledge had broken its fall; and Lyra could see, over the trampled snow of the summit, the golden monkey spring out of the air to the side of the leopard, and she saw the two dæmons bristle, wary and powerful. The monkey's tail was erect, the snow leopard's swept powerfully from side to side. Then the monkey reached out a tentative paw, the leopard lowered her head with a graceful sensual acknowledgement, they touched –

And when Lyra looked up from them, Mrs Coulter herself stood there, clasped in Lord Asriel's arms. Light played around them like sparks and beams of intense anbaric power. Lyra, helpless, could only imagine what had happened: somehow Mrs Coulter must have crossed that chasm, and followed her up here…

Her own parents, together!

And embracing so passionately: an undreamt-of thing.

Her eyes were wide. Roger's body lay dead in her arms, still, quiet, at rest. She heard her parents talking:

Her mother said, "They'll never allow it –"

Her father said, "Allow it? We've gone beyond being *allowed*, as if we were children. I've made it possible for anyone to cross, if they wish."

"They'll forbid it! They'll seal it off and excommunicate anyone who tries!"

"Too many people will want to. They won't be able to prevent them. This will mean the end of the Church, Marisa, the end of the Magisterium, the end of all those centuries of darkness! Look at that light up there: that's the sun of another world! Feel the warmth of it on your skin, now!"

"They are stronger than anyone, Asriel! You don't know –"

"I don't know? I? No one in the world knows better than I how strong the Church is! But it isn't strong enough for this. The Dust will change everything, anyway. There's no stopping it now."

"Is that what you wanted? To choke us and kill us all with sin and darkness?"

"I wanted to break out, Marisa! And I have done. Look, look at the palm trees waving on the shore! Can you feel that wind? A wind from another world! Feel it on your hair, on your face..."

Lord Asriel pushed back Mrs Coulter's hood and turned her head to the sky, running his hands through her hair. Lyra watched breathless, not daring to move a muscle.

The woman clung to Lord Asriel as if she were dizzy, and shook her head, distressed.

"No – no – they're coming, Asriel – they know where I've gone –"

"Then come with me, away and out of this world!"

"I daren't –"

"You? *Dare* not? Your child would come. Your child would dare anything, and shame her mother."

"Then take her and welcome. She's more yours than mine, Asriel."

"Not so. You took her in; you tried to mould her. You wanted her then."

"She was too coarse, too stubborn. I'd left it too late... But where is she now? I followed her footsteps up..."

"You want her, still? Twice you've tried to hold her, and twice she's got away. If I were her I'd run, and keep on running, sooner than give you a third chance."

His hands, still clasping her head, tensed suddenly and drew her towards him in a passionate kiss. Lyra thought it seemed more like cruelty than love, and looked at their dæmons, to see a strange sight: the snow leopard tense, crouching with her claws just pressing in the golden monkey's flesh, and the monkey relaxed, blissful, swooning on the snow.

Mrs Coulter pulled fiercely back from the kiss and said, "No, Asriel – my place is in this world, not that –"

"Come with me!" he said, urgent, powerful. "Come and work with me!"

"We couldn't work together, you and I."

"No? You and I could take the universe to pieces and put it together again, Marisa! We could find the source of Dust and stifle it for ever! And you'd like to be part of that great work; don't lie to me about it. Lie about everything else, lie about the Oblation Board, lie about your lovers – yes, I know about Boreal, and I care nothing – lie about the Church, lie about the child, even, but don't lie about what you truly want…"

And their mouths were fastened together with a powerful greed. Their dæmons were playing fiercely; the snow leopard rolled over on her back, and the monkey raked his claws in the soft fur of her neck, and she growled a deep rumble of pleasure.

"If I don't come, you'll try and destroy me," said Mrs Coulter, breaking away.

"Why should I want to destroy you?" he said, laughing, with the light of the other world shining around his head. "Come with me, work with me, and I'll care whether you live or die. Stay here, and you lose my interest at once. Don't flatter yourself that I'd give you a second's thought. Now stay and work your mischief in this world, or come with me."

Mrs Coulter hesitated; her eyes closed, she seemed to sway as if she were fainting; but she kept her balance and opened her eyes again, with an infinite beautiful sadness in them.

"No," she said. "No."

Their dæmons were apart again. Lord Asriel reached down and curled his strong fingers into the snow leopard's fur. Then he turned his back and walked up and away without another word. The golden monkey leapt into Mrs Coulter's arms, making little sounds of distress, reaching out to the snow leopard as she paced away, and Mrs Coulter's face was a mask of tears. Lyra could see them glinting; they were real.

Then her mother turned, shaking with silent sobs, and moved down the mountain and out of Lyra's sight.

Lyra watched her coldly, and then looked up towards the sky. Such a vault of wonders she had never seen.

The city hanging there so empty and silent looked new-made, waiting to be occupied; or asleep, waiting to be woken. The sun of that world was shining into this, making Lyra's hands golden, melting the ice on Roger's wolfskin hood, making his pale cheeks transparent, glistening in his open sightless eyes.

She felt wrenched apart with unhappiness. And with anger, too; she could have killed her father: if she could have torn out his heart, she would have done so there and then, for what he'd done to Roger. And to her: tricking her – how *dare* he?

She was still holding Roger's body. Pantalaimon was saying something, but her mind was ablaze, and she didn't hear until he pressed his wildcat-claws into the back of her hand to make her. She blinked.

"What? What?"

"Dust!" he said.

"What are you talking about?"

"Dust. He's going to find the source of Dust and destroy it, isn't he?"

"That's what he said."

"And the Oblation Board and the Church and Bolvangar and Mrs Coulter and all, they want to destroy it too, don't they?"

"Yeah… Or stop it affecting people… Why?"

"Because if *they* all think Dust is bad, it must be good."

She didn't speak. A little hiccup of excitement leapt in her chest.

Pantalaimon went on:

"We've heard them all talk about Dust, and they're so afraid of it, and you know what? We believed them, even though we could see that what they were doing was wicked and evil and wrong… We thought Dust must be bad too, because they were grown-up and they said so. But what if it isn't? What if it's –"

She said breathlessly, "Yeah! What if it's really *good*…"

She looked at him and saw his green wildcat-eyes ablaze with her own excitement. She felt dizzy, as if the whole world were turning beneath her.

If Dust were a *good* thing… If it were to be sought and welcomed and cherished…

"We could look for it too, Pan!" she said.

That was what he wanted to hear.

"We could get to it before he does," he went on, "and…"

The enormity of the task silenced them. Lyra looked up at the blazing sky. She was aware of how small they were, she and her dæmon, in comparison with the majesty and vastness of the universe; and of how little they knew, in comparison with the profound mysteries above them.

"We *could*," Pantalaimon insisted. "We came all this way, didn't we? We *could* do it."

"We'd be alone. Iorek Byrnison couldn't follow us and help. Nor could Farder Coram or Serafina Pekkala, or Lee Scoresby or no one."

"Just us, then. Don't matter. We're not alone, anyway; not like…"

She knew he meant *not like Tony Makarios; not like those poor lost dæmons at Bolvangar; we're still one being; both of us are one.*

"And we've got the alethiometer," she said. "Yeah. I reckon we've got to do it, Pan. We'll go up there and we'll search for Dust, and when we've found it we'll know what to do."

Roger's body lay still in her arms. She let him down gently.

"And we'll do it," she said.

She turned away. Behind them lay pain and death and fear; ahead of them lay doubt, and danger, and fathomless mysteries. But they weren't alone.

So Lyra and her dæmon turned away from the world they were born in, and looked towards the sun, and walked into the sky.

NOW READ . . .

BOOK II in Philip Pullman's best-selling,
award-winning trilogy

HIS DARK MATERIALS

THE SUBTLE KNIFE

"Quite outstanding . . . all we can do is to keep
reading in the hope that it will never end"

Scotsman

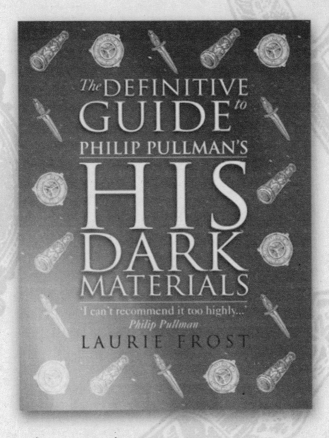

The extraordinary world of
Philip Pullman's bestselling trilogy
is explored in all the detail any
fan or researcher of the
books will ever need.